P9-CPV-674

This Book Comes With a Website

Nolo's award-winning website has a page dedicated just to this book, where you can:

KEEP UP TO DATE – When there are important changes to the information in this book, we'll post updates

READ BLOGS – Get the latest info from Nolo authors' blogs

LISTEN TO PODCASTS – Listen to authors discuss timely issues on topics that interest you

WATCH VIDEOS – Get a quick introduction to a legal topic with our short videos

You'll find the link in the introduction.

And that's not all. Nolo.com contains thousands of articles on everyday legal and business issues, plus a plain-English law dictionary, all written by Nolo experts and available for free. You'll also find more useful **books, software, online services,** and **downloadable forms.**

Get updates and more at
www.nolo.com

4th Edition

The Essential Guide to Federal Employment Laws

Lisa Guerin, J.D. & Amy DelPo, J.D.

SOCIETY FOR HUMAN
RESOURCE MANAGEMENT

FOURTH Edition	APRIL 2013
Cover Design	SUSAN PUTNEY
Book Design	TERRI HEARSH
Proofreading	ROBERT WELLS
Index	THÉRÈSE SHERE
Printing	BANG PRINTING

Guerin, Lisa, 1964-
  The essential guide to federal employment laws / Lisa Guerin, J.D. & attorney Amy DelPo. -- 4th edition.
      p. cm.
  Includes index.
  ISBN 978-1-4133-1813-5 (pbk.) -- ISBN 978-1-4133-1814-2 (epub ebook)
  1. Labor laws and legislation--United States--Popular works. I. DelPo, Amy, 1967- II. Title.
  KF3455.G835 2013
  344.7301--dc23

                                    2012044054

This book covers only United States law, unless it specifically states otherwise.

Please note

We believe accurate, plain-English legal information should help you solve many of your own legal problems. But this text is not a substitute for personalized advice from a knowledgeable lawyer. If you want the help of a trained professional—and we'll always point out situations in which we think that's a good idea—consult an attorney licensed to practice in your state.

Acknowledgments

The authors would like to thank:

Jake Warner, who came up with the idea that turned into this book. His encouragement and advice were invaluable.

Janet Portman, for helping us trim the fat, explain the technicalities, and bring this material down to earth.

Albin Renauer, for his amazing database and his help in organizing the book.

Laura Lawson and **Margaret Clark**, for their thoughtful comments and assistance on the first edition.

Christopher Anzalone, manager of book publishing, and **Allen Smith**, manager for workplace law content, and our other reviewers from the **Society for Human Resource Management**, for their assistance and insightful comments.

Attorney Dan Feinberg of Sigmund, Lewis and Feinberg in Oakland, California, and **Attorney Lee Trucker** of Trucker Huss in San Francisco, California, for their generous assistance.

Ella Hirst, for her unsurpassed research skills and for creating most of the 50-state charts that appear in this book.

Alayna Schroeder, Drew Wheaton, and **Stephen Stine** for updating and streamlining the state material.

Stan Jacobsen, for his research assistance and general good cheer.

Susan Putney, for making the book look good.

About the Author

Lisa Guerin, J.D.

Lisa Guerin is an editor at Nolo specializing in employment law. She is the author or coauthor of several Nolo books, including *The Manager's Legal Handbook, Dealing With Problem Employees, The Essential Guide to Workplace Investigations, Create Your Own Employee Handbook*, and *Smart Policies for Workplace Technologies*. Ms. Guerin has practiced employment law in government, public interest, and private practice where she represented clients at all levels of state and federal courts and in agency proceedings. She is a graduate of Boalt Hall School of Law at the University of California at Berkeley.

Amy DelPo, J.D.

Amy DelPo is an author and consulting editor who specializes in employment and family law issues. She brings years of criminal and civil law experience to her work at Nolo, having litigated cases at all levels of state and federal courts, including the California Supreme Court and the United States Supreme Court. She is the author or coauthor of numerous employment law titles, including *The Performance Appraisal Handbook, Dealing With Problem Employees*, and *Create Your Own Employee Handbook*. She is also the editor of *Parent Savvy*, a book that answers parents' practical, financial, and legal questions. Ms. DelPo currently divides her time between writing on legal issues and chasing after her two busy children, Sophia and Charlie. Ms. DelPo received her law degree with honors from the University of North Carolina at Chapel Hill.

Table of Contents

Appendixes

Overview

Most managers and human resources professionals—particularly those who work for larger companies—have to deal with federal employment laws every day. These laws reach into nearly every stage of the employment relationship, from hiring and first-day paperwork, to providing benefits and time off, to termination and layoffs. Whether you are developing workplace policies, creating forms and notices for your company to use with employees, or handling employee performance and discipline issues, you have to understand your company's legal obligations—and make sure that you don't inadvertently violate the law.

It can be tough to find out exactly what these federal laws require. That's where this book comes in. It explains all of the major federal employment laws: whom they protect, who has to follow them, what they require, and what they prohibit. Each chapter covers a single federal employment law, including the obligations employers have under each law, deadlines, posting requirements, and record-keeping rules. If you need more information, each chapter includes a list of resources. And many of the chapters include charts that provide information on state laws.

Health Care Reform: Still a Work in Progress

Although the Patient Protection and Affordable Care Act (known in various circles as the PPACA, the ACA, Obamacare, or simply health care reform) passed in 2010, it has taken a long and winding road toward implementation. Contrary to what many commentators expected, the Supreme Court upheld the law's individual mandate in the summer of 2012. Just a few months later, however, the Court reopened a case challenging the law's employer mandate and requirement for contraceptive coverage, asking a federal Court of Appeals to decide these issues (which lays the groundwork for further Supreme Court review).

Agencies are still drafting and finalizing the regulations implementing the law, states are still deciding whether and how they will participate, and courts are busy hearing challenges and defenses to the law. Given this state of flux, it's just too early to spell out the precise contours of the law's employer requirements, prohibitions, exceptions, and so on, as we have for the laws in this book. We will post updates and information on the employer provisions of the PPACA at this book's online companion page; see the end of this chapter for more information.

This first chapter gives you the information you need to get the most out of this book. First, we explain how to figure out which laws your company has to follow, including which federal laws apply to your company and when and how state and local laws might come into play. Next, we cover a handful of practical strategies that will help your company comply with these laws, such as consulting with a lawyer, documentation, and training. Finally, we explain what to do if you need more help.

What This Book Doesn't Cover

Some employment situations are *not* covered in this book. If you fall into one of the following categories, the information you need is likely beyond the scope of this book:

- **Government employers.** Although we explain which (if any) federal, state, and local government workers are covered by each law, we don't detail the special rules that may apply to government employees. For example, although federal government workers are protected from certain types of discrimination by Title VII (see Chapter 18), they have to follow a special complaint process that doesn't apply to private companies. We don't cover that process here.
- **Federal contractors.** Private employers who contract to do work for the federal government are subject to additional employment laws. We don't cover those laws here.

Which Laws Your Company Must Follow

Employment law comes from many sources. Each of the federal laws (also called "statutes") covered in this book has been interpreted and refined by court decisions and sometimes by regulations issued by the federal agency responsible for enforcing and administering the law. Many of the topics these laws cover are also addressed by state, and sometimes even local, laws. If more than one law applies, employers generally have to follow whichever law—federal, state, or local—is more beneficial to employees.

You can use this book to figure out which federal laws apply to your company, whether those laws protect particular employees, and whether the situation you're facing is addressed by a federal employment law. "Which Federal Laws Apply," below, will help you get to this information quickly.

This book also provides some information on state laws, in the form of charts briefly describing the laws of the 50 states and the District of Columbia, at the end of some chapters. However, you may have to do some research on your own—or talk to a lawyer—to find out whether a state or local law applies to your situation. This is covered in "Which State and Local Laws Apply," below.

Which Federal Laws Apply

Federal employment law consists of the statutes themselves, any regulations issued by the federal agency responsible for administering the law, and court decisions interpreting the law and regulations. Together, these sources determine what the terms in the law mean, what employers have to do to comply with the law, and how violations of the law will be handled. Each chapter of this book covers a federal employment statute, any regulations interpreting it, and the major court cases decided under the law.

Because the employment laws explained here are federal statutes, they apply throughout the country, regardless of what state the company or worker is in. This means that every federal law in this book has the potential to apply to your company if it operates in the United States. We say "potential" because no law described here applies to every employer and employee, in every situation. Instead, most laws specify which employers need to follow them, which employees are protected by them, and which specific actions they prohibit and require.

To figure out whether a particular federal employment law applies to your company and your situation, you'll need to answer these five questions:
- Does your company have enough employees?
- Is your company otherwise covered by the law?
- Is the employee covered by the law?
- Do all of the law's provisions apply?
- Is this situation covered by the law?

Sources of Federal Employment Law

Statutes started out as bills passed by the U.S. Congress and signed into law by the president. Statutes are collected in a set of books called the U.S. Code. The first page of each chapter of this book includes the location of the statute in the U.S. Code. For example, the Age Discrimination in Employment Act (ADEA) is found at 29 U.S.C. §§ 621-634; this means that it's located in Title 29 of the U.S. Code, at Sections 621 through 634. Each chapter also provides a link to a website where you can view the statute online.

Regulations are rules issued by federal agencies. When Congress passes a law, it usually designates a federal agency to interpret and enforce that law. In employment law, these agencies are often responsible for taking complaints, creating the paperwork (such as posters or notice forms) employers must use to comply with the law, and imposing penalties on employers that don't meet their obligations. Sometimes agencies also issue regulations—rules that typically fill in some of the gaps not addressed by the statute. Regulations are collected in the Code of Federal Regulations (C.F.R.). If regulations have been issued interpreting one of the laws we cover, you'll find a citation for those regulations—and a website where you can access them online—at the beginning of the chapter. Regulations are updated frequently; our citation is to the most recent version, but you should always check to see whether the regulations have been revised.

Court decisions are opinions written by judges deciding the outcome of a lawsuit. Often, judges have to interpret what a law means in order to decide who should win in court. For example, a court might have to decide what constitutes a reasonable accommodation for an employee with a disability or whether an employer's decision to transfer an employee who complained of harassment constitutes illegal retaliation. Decisions by the U.S. Supreme Court are the most influential, because they dictate how federal employment laws will be interpreted throughout the country. Decisions by lower courts, such as the U.S. Courts of Appeal and the U.S. District Courts, are binding only in the states or regions those courts cover.

Different Rules for Unions

If your company is unionized, the first place to look for answers to your employment questions is not the law, but the collective bargaining agreement (CBA) between the union and the company. If the CBA gives workers more rights in certain areas (most commonly, wage and hour issues, time off, discipline, and termination procedures), it supersedes the law.

For example, let's say you want to know how much time an employee can take off for childbirth and parental leave. You look up the Family and Medical Leave Act in this book and see that it requires covered employers to provide up to 12 weeks of unpaid leave. Your company's CBA, however, gives employees up to 16 weeks of paid leave. Even though the CBA is more generous than the law, you must follow its provisions.

Generally, unions are not allowed to bargain away their members' federal rights in a collective bargaining agreement. Therefore, a CBA typically does not provide workers less than what the federal law requires. However, there are some exceptions to this rule. For example, most courts have upheld a common CBA provision that requires workers to make certain workplace claims only through the union grievance procedure, rather than bringing them to court (which they would otherwise have the right to do). And some laws allow unions and management to bend the rules in a CBA; for example, although some state laws require employers to give workers specified meal and rest breaks, these laws may not apply to a workplace governed by a CBA.

Does Your Company Have Enough Employees?

Many employment laws apply only to employers that have at least a minimum number of employees. You'll find these rules under the heading "Regulated Employers" in each chapter. For example, an employer with only 20 employees is not covered by the Family and Medical Leave Act (FMLA); only employers with at least 50 employees must comply with that law.

Laws That Apply by Size or Operations of Employer

Law	Acronym	Involved in interstate commerce	Involved in interstate commerce or have $500,000 or more in annual gross sales	All public companies (publicly traded or required to register with the SEC)	All private employers (1 or more employees)	15 or more employees	20 or more employees	50 or more employees	100 or more employees
Age Discrimination in Employment Act	ADEA						■	■	■
Americans with Disabilities Act of 1990	ADA					■	■	■	■
Consolidated Omnibus Budget Reconciliation Act	COBRA						■	■	■
Employee Polygraph Protection Act	EPPA		■						
Equal Pay Act	EPA		■						
Fair Credit Reporting Act	FCRA				■	■	■	■	■
Fair Labor Standards Act	FLSA		■						
Family and Medical Leave Act	FMLA							■	■
Genetic Information Nondiscrimination Act	GINA					■	■	■	■
Immigration Reform and Control Act of 1986	IRCA				■	■	■	■	■
National Labor Relations Act	NLRA	■							

Laws That Apply by Size or Operations of Employer (continued)

Law	Acronym	Involved in interstate commerce	Involved in interstate commerce or have $500,000 or more in annual gross sales	All public companies (publicly traded or required to register with the SEC)	All private employers (1 or more employees)	15 or more employees	20 or more employees	50 or more employees	100 or more employees
Occupational Safety and Health Act	OSH Act				■	■	■	■	■
Older Workers Benefit Protection Act	OWBPA						■	■	■
Personal Responsibility and Work Opportunity Reconciliation Act	PRWORA				■	■	■	■	■
Pregnancy Discrimination Act	PDA					■	■	■	■
Sarbanes-Oxley Act of 2002	SOX			■					
Section 1981 of the Civil Rights Act of 1866	Section 1981				■	■	■	■	■
Title VII of the Civil Rights Act of 1964	Title VII					■	■	■	■
Uniformed Services Employment and Reemployment Rights Act	USERRA				■	■	■	■	■
Worker Adjustment and Retraining Notification Act	WARN								■

Is Your Company Otherwise Covered?

Some employment laws don't impose a minimum size requirement, but instead apply only to companies that engage in "interstate commerce" (and, in a few cases, meet a minimum volume of business requirement). These rules are included in the chart, "Laws That Apply by Size or Operations of Employer," above.

All but the smallest local companies are engaged in interstate commerce within the meaning of these laws. For example, if your company buys, sells, or handles materials or products that have come from or will go to another state, or if your company's employees communicate across state lines as part of their job duties, your company is most likely engaged in interstate commerce.

For decades, the U.S. Supreme Court has defined "interstate commerce" very broadly, to encompass virtually any activity that does—or could—exceed a state's borders. This expansive definition allows the Court to uphold Congressional legislation: The Constitution gives Congress the right to regulate interstate commerce, so Congress has the most extensive possible reach when interstate commerce is defined in broad strokes.

In recent years, however, the Court has been scaling back this definition to occasionally find that Congress has overstepped its bounds. For example, although the Court ultimately upheld the Affordable Care Act (the health care reform law) on other grounds, a majority of the Court found that Congress exceeded its authority to regulate interstate commerce. This recent holding signals that the definition of interstate commerce remains in flux. If, after reading the relevant chapter in this book, you believe that your company is not covered, you should probably check your conclusion with a lawyer.

Even laws that impose a minimum size requirement don't apply to every employer that is large enough to be covered. Some laws include exceptions for particular types of employers and some apply only to certain types of companies. For example, the Sarbanes-Oxley Act of 2002 applies only to companies that are publicly traded or required to register with the Securities and Exchange Commission. You'll find this information under the heading "Regulated Employers" in each chapter.

Is the Employee Covered?

Some employment laws apply only to employees who have worked for the employer for a certain period of time. Some exclude independent contractors, apply only to employees in certain occupations, or apply to people who don't even work for the employer. For example, the Consolidated Omnibus Budget Reconciliation Act (COBRA) applies not only to employees and former employees, but also to an employee's spouse and dependents, if they are covered by the employer's group health insurance plan. Each chapter explains whom the law protects under the heading "Covered Workers."

Do All of the Provisions Apply?

Some laws have provisions that apply only to certain workers and/or certain employers. For example, the provisions of the Fair Labor Standards Act that require employers to pay overtime and minimum wages don't apply to certain types of employees, including certain computer specialists, seamen, and criminal investigators. Similarly, only employers that have at least four employees are subject to the antidiscrimination provision of the Immigration Reform and Control Act (IRCA), but all employers—regardless of size—have to comply with IRCA's verification provision, which requires employers to verify that their employees are legally authorized to work in the United States.

You can find this additional coverage information within the discussion of each provision of the law, under the headings "Regulated Employers" and/or "Covered Workers."

Is Your Situation Covered?

Each law covers a limited spectrum of employment issues and may not extend to the problem or question you're facing. We've included two charts below to help you figure out which chapters to review. The first, "What Each Law Covers," gives a very brief summary of the law. The second, "Laws That Apply to Common Employment Situations," lets you know which aspects of the employment relationship are covered by each law. Once you decide which laws might apply, you'll need to read the sections called "What's Prohibited" and "What's Required" in the chapters covering those laws to find out whether your particular situation is addressed.

For example, if you have a question about discrimination, you'll see that several laws prohibit discrimination in employment. You'll also see that these laws prohibit different types of discrimination—for instance, the Civil Rights Act of 1866 prohibits only race discrimination, while the Equal Pay Act prohibits only gender-based wage discrimination. To find out precisely what each law requires and prohibits, turn to the appropriate chapters.

What Each Law Covers

Law	Summary
ADEA	**Age Discrimination in Employment Act:** prohibits age discrimination in every aspect of employment
ADA	**Americans with Disabilities Act:** prohibits discrimination against qualified employees with disabilities; requires employers to make reasonable accommodations for employees and applicants with disabilities
COBRA	**Consolidated Omnibus Budget Reconciliation Act:** requires employers to provide continued group health insurance coverage for up to 36 months to employees (and possibly their spouses and dependents) who would otherwise lose coverage
EPPA	**Employee Polygraph Protection Act:** prohibits employers from requiring or asking employees or applicants to take a polygraph test in most circumstances
EPA	**Equal Pay Act:** requires employers to give male and female employees equal pay for doing equal work
FCRA	**Fair Credit Reporting Act:** requires employers to provide notice and get consent before getting a credit report or other types of background or investigative reports on employees or applicants; requires employers to give certain information to employees or applicants before taking negative action based on a report; establishes standards employers must follow to destroy consumer records
FLSA	**Fair Labor Standards Act:** establishes the minimum wage; determines what constitutes work time for purposes of calculating pay; requires overtime pay for certain employees; restricts child labor
FMLA	**Family and Medical Leave Act:** entitles employees to take up to 12 weeks of unpaid leave per year, with continued health benefits, to bond with a new child, to care for a family member with a serious health condition, for their own serious health condition, or for a qualified exigency due to a family member's call to active duty; family members of servicemembers who suffer a serious injury or illness may take up to 26 weeks of leave in a single 12-month period
GINA	**Genetic Information Nondiscrimination Act:** prohibits employers from making employment decisions based on genetic information or requiring employees to provide genetic information; requires employers to keep employees' genetic information confidential
IRCA	**Immigration Reform and Control Act:** prohibits discrimination on the basis of citizenship and national origin in every aspect of employment; requires employers to verify that employees are authorized to work in the United States and keep records to that effect

What Each Law Covers (continued)	
Law	**Summary**
NLRA	**National Labor Relations Act:** regulates the relationship of employers and unions; prohibits employers and unions from engaging in unfair labor practices; protects employees who engage in concerted activities to improve working terms and conditions, whether the workplace is unionized or not
OSH Act	**Occupational Safety and Health Act:** requires employers to comply with workplace safety and health standards
OWBPA	**Older Workers Benefit Protection Act:** prohibits age discrimination in the provision of benefits; explains the criteria to be used in determining whether equal benefits have been provided; requires employers to include particular language in waivers of an employee's right to sue for age discrimination
PRWORA	**Personal Responsibility and Work Opportunity Reconciliation Act:** requires employers to report new hires to a state registry, which uses the information to enforce child support obligations
PDA	**Pregnancy Discrimination Act:** prohibits discrimination on the basis of pregnancy or childbirth in every aspect of employment; requires employers to treat pregnant women who are temporarily unable to work the same way they treat workers who are temporarily disabled for other reasons
SOX	**Sarbanes-Oxley Act of 2002:** prohibits employers from retaliating against employees who complain of shareholder fraud; requires companies to establish procedures allowing employees to submit anonymous complaints about accounting and auditing practices; requires companies to establish procedures for taking, handling, and retaining such complaints
Section 1981	**Section 1981 of the Civil Rights Act of 1866:** prohibits race discrimination in the making or enforcement of contracts, which includes every aspect of the employment relationship
Title VII	**Title VII of the Civil Rights Act of 1964:** prohibits discrimination on the basis of race, color, national origin, religion, and sex in every aspect of employment
USERRA	**Uniformed Services Employment and Reemployment Rights Act:** prohibits discrimination against applicants and employees who serve in the armed services; requires employers to reinstate employees who take up to five years off to serve in the armed services and restore their benefits; prohibits employers from firing reinstated employees, except for cause, for up to one year after they return
WARN	**Worker Adjustment and Retraining Notification Act:** requires employers to give 60-days' notice to employees who will lose their jobs through large layoffs or plant closings, with limited exceptions

Laws That Apply to Common Employment Situations*

Law	Hiring	Background Checks	Testing	First-Day Paperwork	Benefits	Compensation	Hours	Health and Safety	Investigations	Discrimination/Harassment	Leave/Time Off	Unions/Organizing	Whistleblowing	Layoffs	Terminations
ADEA	■	■	■		■	■	■		■	■	■			■	■
ADA	■	■	■		■	■	■	■	■	■	■			■	■
COBRA					■									■	■
EPPA	■		■						■						■
EPA					■	■				■					
FCRA	■	■							■						■
FLSA						■	■	■			■				
FMLA					■			■	■		■			■	■
GINA	■	■	■		■	■	■	■	■	■	■			■	■
IRCA	■	■	■	■	■	■	■		■	■	■			■	■
NLRA					■	■	■				■	■		■	■
OSHA								■	■				■		
OWBPA					■	■				■				■	■
PRWORA				■											
PDA	■	■	■		■	■	■	■	■	■	■			■	■
SOX									■	■			■		■
Sec. 1981	■	■	■		■	■	■		■	■	■			■	■
Title VII	■	■	■		■	■	■		■	■	■			■	■
USERRA	■	■	■		■	■	■		■	■	■			■	■
WARN														■	

* You'll see that most of the antidiscrimination laws appear with nearly every issue. Because these laws prohibit discrimination in every aspect of employment, employers could violate them by undertaking any common employment practice with the intent to discriminate. For example, let's say an employer required only applicants who have served in the military to take a psychological test, based on the hiring manager's belief that such applicants are more likely to be mentally unstable. This would violate USERRA's ban on discrimination against those who have served in the military, even though USERRA doesn't explicitly address the issue of testing.

In addition, some laws make exceptions for certain situations in which employers are not required to comply with the law. You can find this information in the "Exceptions" section of each chapter. For example, although the Worker Adjustment and Retraining Notification Act (WARN) generally requires certain employers to give employees advance notice of a layoff, employers don't have to give notice if the layoff results from a strike or the closing of a temporary facility.

Which State and Local Laws Apply

Even if you follow every applicable federal employment law to the letter, your company could still be violating other legal obligations to its employees. The federal government isn't alone in regulating the employment relationship—state and local governments often adopt their own employment laws as well. If your company and situation are covered by more than one law, you must follow the law that is the most beneficial to the employee in a particular situation.

This book will help you get started in figuring out which state laws might apply. At the end of many chapters, you'll find charts summarizing the laws of the 50 states and the District of Columbia on the same topic. For example, at the end of the chapter on the FLSA, you'll find charts on state minimum wage, overtime, and meal and rest break laws. However, these charts may not provide the details you need. In that case, you should contact your state's labor or fair employment practices department (you can find contact information in Appendix A), consult a resource on the employment laws of your state, or talk to a local employment lawyer.

To find out whether local laws might come into play, you'll have to find out what your city or county requires. Some local governments post their laws (often called "ordinances") or information for local employers on their websites; you can find links to many city and county websites at www. statelocalgov.net. You can also find out what local laws require by talking to a local employment attorney.

State and local laws can be quite similar to federal employment laws: They cover similar topics, apply to only certain employers (often those with a minimum number of employees), and protect only certain types of employees. However, state and local laws very often provide workers with more benefits— and apply to more employers.

Putting It All Together

Here are a couple of examples to illustrate how to figure out which laws your company has to follow.

EXAMPLE 1: The only manager of a four-employee graphic design company in Berkeley, California, wants to know what the company's obligations are to applicants with disabilities. The federal Americans with Disabilities Act governs this issue, but it applies only to private employers with at least 15 employees. California also has an antidiscrimination law that prohibits disability discrimination, but it applies only to employers with at least five employees. However, the city of Berkeley prohibits all companies that contract with the city from discriminating on the basis of disability. Therefore, if the company wins a bid to redesign the city's website, it will have to comply with this municipal law.

EXAMPLE 2: A national restaurant chain is considering expanding to New Mexico. Its HR director does some research and learns that New Mexico's minimum wage is $7.50 an hour. Because this is higher than the current federal minimum wage ($7.25 an hour), the chain will have to pay its workers at least the higher state amount. But if the chain decides to open in Santa Fe, it will have to pay workers at least $10.29 an hour, because that city has adopted a living wage law that applies to all employers required to have a business license or registration from the city. Santa Fe doesn't require employers to pay any straight wages to tipped employees as long as their tips add up to at least the minimum wage, if the employee receives at least $100 in tips for the month. However, both federal and New Mexico law require employers to pay tipped workers a wage of at least $2.13 an hour, in addition to tips. So, the restaurant will have to pay tipped workers in Santa Fe at least the $2.13 an hour required by federal and state law, and their total pay—including tips—will have to add up to at least the city's minimum wage of $10.29.

As you can see, things can get confusing if your company is covered by two or more laws that impose different requirements or seem to contradict each other. If you find yourself in this position, you may need some help figuring out what to do. This is a good time to consult with an employment lawyer.

Basic Compliance Tools

This book will help you understand which federal employment laws your company must follow and what those laws mean. However, to stay out of legal trouble, your company must do more than simply follow the letter of the law. It will also have to adopt some practical strategies to make sure that it meets its legal obligations. These compliance tools are not strictly "required" by the laws covered in this book, but a company that wants to avoid legal problems should consider them standard operating procedures.

This section briefly explains a handful of basic strategies every company should follow, but it is only an introduction to these important topics. The ins and outs of creating an effective compliance program are well beyond the scope of this book. However, SHRM and Nolo both have plenty of detailed resources that will help you design and implement procedures for compliance; see "If You Need More Information," below.

Lawyers

Even the most conscientious HR professional occasionally needs help from a lawyer. Although you can handle many employment issues on your own, some are particularly tricky and require some legal expertise. As you read this book, you'll see that we sometimes advise you to see a lawyer if you need more information on a difficult topic. And with good reason: Although lawyers don't come cheap, your company can save money by paying a lawyer for advice and information that would be very time-consuming and difficult to research on your own.

There are no hard and fast rules determining when you should consult with a lawyer. You'll have to decide when it's time to get some expert help based on a number of factors, including your own comfort level, how important the issue is, how many employees are affected, whether your company is facing significant legal exposure, and your company's budget. However, a good general rule is to consider consulting a lawyer sooner rather than later in any potentially difficult situation.

You can use a lawyer for a variety of tasks, including:

- **Document drafting or review.** A lawyer can create or troubleshoot documents you use over and over again, such as employment contracts, employee notice forms, waivers, your employee handbook, and other written policies.
- **Advice on employment decisions.** Of course, your company would quickly go out of business if it consulted a lawyer every time an employee was hired or disciplined, but there are times when a lawyer's advice will be very valuable. If, for example, you are considering firing a worker who is on FMLA leave or has recently complained of sexual harassment, a lawyer can help you make sure that you have adequate legal support for your decision.
- **Help understanding your legal obligations.** As noted above, companies must follow whichever law—federal, state, or local—provides the most benefits for workers. A lawyer can help you untangle these obligations and assist you in figuring out your responsibilities when several laws overlap.
- **Representation in legal or administrative proceedings.** If an employee files a complaint with an administrative agency or a lawsuit, your company should consult with a lawyer right away. Good legal advice at the outset can make the difference between winning and losing the case.

Training

Training is a great way to keep your company's legal exposure to a minimum—and give your company an opportunity to deal with potential problems early on, before they have a chance to escalate. Training is a vital component of a company's efforts to combat harassment and discrimination, for example. In this type of training, employees learn about harassment and discrimination and about how to report possible misconduct to the appropriate people. Managers should also be trained to recognize harassment and discrimination and take appropriate action if they learn that harassment or discrimination might be taking place. You can learn more about discrimination and harassment training from the Training Institute of the Equal Employment Opportunity Commission, www.eeotraining.eeoc.gov.

As a legal matter, training can help limit your company's liability if it faces a harassment lawsuit. Companies that take reasonable care to prevent and correct harassment—through adopting an antiharassment policy, training managers in their responsibilities, investigating complaints effectively, and taking swift action if harassment occurs—have a potential legal defense to certain harassment claims.

You can also use training to help your company maintain a safe and healthy workplace (a requirement of the OSH Act). In fact, the OSH Act requires companies in certain industries to provide specific types of training to their employees. Safety training might include information on how to use particular tools or equipment, ergonomics, working with hazardous materials, and reporting possible unsafe conditions. You can learn more about safety training from OSHA's Directorate of Training and Education Training Resources, www.osha.gov/dte.

Policies

Your company's written policies or employee handbook can make or break your efforts to comply with the law and can help limit your company's legal exposure. By clearly communicating what it expects from its employees and managers, a company can nip certain legal problems in the bud—or at least give itself an opportunity to resolve problems when they first arise. If everyone at your company understands, for example, what retaliation is and that the company will not tolerate it, managers will be less likely to retaliate against employees who raise concerns or complaints, and employees will be more likely to report retaliation right away, before their relationship with the company has been damaged beyond repair.

When writing or updating your company's policies, you must choose your words with care: At the most basic level, your company's policies must not contradict what the law requires or allows. For example, if your company's employee handbook says that employees may take only four weeks off per calendar year, strict enforcement of that policy could well violate several federal employment laws, including the Family and Medical Leave Act, the Uniformed Services Employment and Reemployment Rights Act, the Pregnancy Discrimination Act, and the Americans with Disabilities Act. If your company's policies lead employees to believe that they aren't entitled to the rights provided by these laws, the company could face major legal problems.

As you'll learn in later chapters, a company's policies sometimes also determine its legal responsibilities to employees. In some situations, a company may take certain actions only if its policies provide for it, even though the actions are otherwise legally allowed. For example, a company is legally allowed to pay less than the minimum wage to employees who earn tips (known as taking a "tip credit") under the Fair Labor Standards Act, but only if the company clearly informs employees that it will do so. To take full advantage of its legal rights, your company must make sure that its policies meet these standards.

Some policies can also be used as a legal defense to claims of harassment and discrimination. As noted above under "Training," companies that have antiharassment and antidiscrimination policies and take quick action to investigate and resolve complaints may be able to avoid liability for certain harassment and discrimination claims. Every company should have written policies prohibiting harassment and discrimination and outlining the steps the company will take if an employee comes forward with a complaint.

Companies that don't have written policies, or don't review their policies periodically to make sure that they are legally valid and up to date, are placing themselves at legal risk.

Responding to Legal Violations

If you learn of a possible legal violation—for example, hazardous working conditions, discriminatory statements by a supervisor, or a manager's refusal to allow an eligible employee to take FMLA leave—you must take action right away. You may need to investigate the situation first, to find out what happened and who's responsible. Once you know that your company has a problem, however, you should step in quickly to resolve it.

There are many very good reasons for taking action to correct legal violations. Perhaps most important, taking action will show employees that the company cares about their well-being and wants to do the right thing. This will help build the type of loyalty and positive feelings that can provide a strong deterrent to lawsuits. Putting a stop to illegal behavior will also limit an employee's damages, if he or she decides to take legal action against the company. And dealing quickly with troublemakers will send the strong message that your company doesn't tolerate misconduct, which will help prevent similar problems in the future.

Outsourcing

A few of the laws in this book—particularly those that deal with benefit plans, such as COBRA—can be difficult to understand and administer. That's why many companies hire outside service providers to handle their obligations under these laws. Outsourcing these responsibilities is a great way to maximize efficiency: Rather than spending weeks of your time trying to understand what these laws require, you can hire a company that specializes in compliance to take care of everything for you.

But use caution when hiring a third party to discharge your company's obligations. Generally, your company will remain legally liable for any actions taken by an outside provider (although the provider may have to indemnify your company—repay the costs it incurs—if your company is sued for the provider's actions). This is why you must choose service providers very carefully; create a clear, written agreement about what you expect the provider to do for your company; monitor the provider's performance; and periodically review your outside contracts to make sure that your company is getting what it pays for.

Among the factors your company should consider when hiring an outside service provider are:

- **The services to be provided.** Is your company looking to outsource its entire HR function or only the administration of its pension plan or benefits programs?
- **Performance benchmarks.** How will you measure whether the provider is meeting its obligations to your company?
- **Pricing.** What will your company pay, and how will the price be calculated (for example, per employee, per task, or a set monthly or annual rate)?
- **Control.** Does your company want to have some input on the tasks you are outsourcing, or will the provider be solely responsible for those issues?
- **Liability.** Does using an outside provider create additional obligations or legal exposure—as is true, for example, if you outsource certain obligations created by the Fair Credit Reporting Act? If an employee or applicant sues, will the provider indemnify your company?

- **Handling problems.** How will you deal with disagreements or other problems in the company's relationship with the provider, and under what circumstances can either of you end the arrangement?

By carefully considering these issues up front, and getting some legal assistance in drafting and reviewing provider contracts, you can ensure that your company gets the most benefit from outsourcing administrative functions.

Documentation

As you'll see, many of the laws we cover require companies to keep certain documents—for example, payroll records, job applications, or forms signed by employees. In addition to complying with these legal requirements, your company should carefully document in writing all important decisions and required actions relating to its employees. Even if this type of documentation is not specifically required by the law, it's the best way to prove that you complied with the law, if necessary.

For example, the Fair Credit Reporting Act requires covered employers to provide written notice and obtain an applicant's or employee's consent before requesting a consumer report on that person. Because the law doesn't specifically obligate employers to keep copies of these records, an employer is technically free to shred these documents. But what if the employee claims never to have consented to the report? If the employer saved these records, it would have a written consent signed by the employee. If not, it will have no written proof that it complied with the law.

Companies should also carefully document employment decisions. For example, when a manager fires, promotes, disciplines, gives a pay raise to, or transfers an employee, or otherwise changes an employee's status or situation, he or she should fully document the reasons for the action. This will help the company if the employee later complains that the action was taken for illegal reasons (for example, discrimination or retaliation). The manager will have an easier time remembering the details and explaining the basis for the decision. The company will have a contemporaneous record (that is, one made at the time of the decision) of what it did and why. And, ultimately, documents will help the company persuade a government agency, jury, or judge that it acted properly.

If You Need More Information

You may need more information than this book provides. You may have to figure out exactly how your company can comply with apparently conflicting federal, state, and local laws on the same topic. You may need help with the practical aspects of compliance, such as how to conduct an investigation of sexual harassment or develop an appropriate procedure for taking anonymous complaints of shareholder fraud under Sarbanes-Oxley. Or, you may need help developing employment contracts or an employee handbook. This section will direct you to some other resources that might help.

Government Agencies

Your first stop should be the federal or state agency that administers and enforces the law you're interested in. At the end of our discussion of each law, we give you a list of resources available from the federal agency that interprets and enforces the law. But these lists aren't exhaustive—some of these agencies have dozens of fact sheets, guidance memoranda, and special bulletins for employers and small businesses that can help you figure out the law's requirements. These agencies also have staff members available to help answer your questions or point you toward the information you need.

If your question involves state law, you can start your research by contacting the state agency that enforces the law. For questions about employment discrimination, contact your state fair employment practices agency. For other employment-related questions, contact your state labor department. Appendix A includes contact information for the federal agencies that enforce and interpret the laws covered in this book, as well as the fair employment practices agency and labor department of each of the 50 states and the District of Columbia.

SHRM and Nolo Resources

The Society for Human Resource Management and Nolo both provide a number of resources on employment law, policies and procedures, and other issues of special interest to the HR profession. Both organizations have websites with lots of information on HR topics, and both offer written materials on a variety of subjects. If you need help with an HR question or issue, you should be able to find the answers in our products. See Appendix B for a list of resources you might find helpful.

Get Updates and More Online

When the information in this book changes, we'll post updates at this book's online companion page: **www.nolo.com/back-of-book/FEMP.html**
You'll find information there on evolving issues, such as health care reform, and developments in the field, like important Supreme Court cases or new regulations. You'll also find blogs, podcasts, and more.

Age Discrimination in Employment Act (ADEA)

Statute: 29 U.S.C. §§ 621–634

http://uscode.house.gov/download/pls/29C14.txt

Regulations: 29 C.F.R. §§ 1625–1627

www.gpo.gov/fdsys/pkg/CFR-2012-title29-vol4/pdf/CFR-2012-title29-vol4-part1625.pdf

Overview of the ADEA

The Age Discrimination in Employment Act (ADEA) prohibits age discrimination against employees and applicants age 40 or older. Congress passed the ADEA in 1967 to address the difficulties older employees face in the workplace, including mandatory retirement cutoffs and discrimination in the hiring process. The ADEA outlaws age discrimination, but does create a few limited exceptions, recognizing that advanced age may, in some circumstances, affect a worker's ability to perform certain jobs effectively.

Regulated Employers

The ADEA covers:

- private employers with 20 or more employees (defined as an employer that has 20 or more employees on each working day in each of 20 or more calendar weeks in the current or preceding calendar year)
- state and local governments (but state employees may not sue their employer for ADEA violations; see "Covered Workers," below)
- employment agencies, and
- labor organizations.

The ADEA covers multinational employers with operations in the United States or its territories, unless the employer is covered by a treaty or other binding international agreement—for example, a treaty permitting the company to prefer its own citizens for specific jobs.

The ADEA covers employers with operations in other countries if the employer is incorporated in the United States, based in the United States, or controlled by a U.S. company. However, an employer is exempt from the ADEA's requirements if complying with the ADEA would violate a law of the country in which it operates.

One section of the ADEA (29 U.S.C. § 633a) requires most federal agencies not to discriminate on the basis of age against employees or applicants who are at least 40 years old.

Definitions

Bona fide employee benefit plan A benefit plan that has been accurately described, in writing, to all employees and that actually provides the benefits promised.

Bona fide executive A top-level employee who exercises substantial executive authority over a significant number of employees and a large volume of business. Examples include the head of a large regional operation of a national employer or the head of a major corporate division.

Bona fide occupational qualification (BFOQ) A limited exception to the ADEA that allows employers to discriminate on the basis of age if the nature of the job requires them to do so.

Bona fide seniority system A seniority system that uses length of service with the employer as the primary criterion for deciding who will receive available employment opportunities and perquisites. For the system to qualify as "bona fide," its essential terms and conditions must be communicated to employees and applied uniformly to all workers, regardless of age.

Firefighter An employee whose primary duties are to perform work directly connected with controlling and extinguishing fires or maintaining and using firefighting apparatus and equipment, including an employee engaged in any of these activities who is transferred to a supervisory or administrative position.

High policy-making position A top-level position that carries significant responsibility, held by someone who plays a substantial role in the development and effective implementation of corporate policy. This definition may include employees who do not supervise other workers, such as a company's chief research scientist or head economist.

Law enforcement officer An employee whose primary duties are the investigation, apprehension, or detention of those suspected or convicted of violating criminal laws, including an employee engaged in this activity who is transferred to a supervisory or administrative position. Prison guards and other employees assigned to guard incarcerated prisoners are law enforcement officers.

Legal Developments

- **Final regulations issued on disparate impact cases and defense.** In 2005, the Supreme Court ruled that an employee can bring a disparate impact case under the ADEA: a lawsuit alleging that the employer's seemingly neutral policy or practice had a disproportionately negative effect on older workers. (*Smith v. City of Jackson*, 544 U.S. 228.) Several years later, the Court found that an employer defending this type of case bears the burden of proving that the policy or practice creating the disparate impact was in fact based on a "reasonable factor other than age" (RFOA). (*Meacham v. Knolls Atomic Power Laboratory*, 554 U.S. 84 (2008).) In 2012, the EEOC issued final regulations that provide a framework for these cases, including a list of considerations for courts trying to determine whether the employer's RFOA really was reasonable. These regulations are covered in this chapter.

- **Different rules apply in age discrimination mixed motive cases.** In *Gross v. FBL Financial Services, Inc.*, 129 S.Ct. 2343 (2009), the Supreme Court decided that an employee bringing an age discrimination case has to prove not only that age was a motivating factor in the employer's decision, but that it was the "but for" cause of the decision (that is, that the decision would not have been made if not for the employee's age). This standard is different than the one used for other types of discrimination. In Title VII cases, if the employee can show that a protected characteristic (such as race or national origin) was a motivating factor in the employer's decision, the burden of proof then shifts to the employer, who must prove that the same decision would have been made regardless.

Covered Workers

The ADEA covers employees and applicants of regulated employers. However, not all employees and applicants are covered: The ADEA protects only those who are at least 40 years old. Unlike other antidiscrimination laws, the ADEA does not prohibit "reverse discrimination." Those who are younger than 40 have no rights under the law.

Although state government workers are protected by the ADEA, they do not have the right to sue their employers (the states for which they work) in court to enforce those rights; only the EEOC may sue a state to protect state employees from age discrimination.

The ADEA protects foreign nationals working for a covered employer, even if the employee is not authorized to work in the United States. Such an employee still has rights under the ADEA, although his or her available remedies may be limited. For example, although reinstatement is a common remedy for an unlawfully fired employee, a foreign national may not be reinstated to a job in the United States if he or she is not authorized to work in the United States.

The ADEA also protects U.S. citizens working outside the United States for employers that are incorporated in the United States, based in the United States, or controlled by a U.S. employer.

Did You Know ...

- Experts estimate that more than half of the workforce were at least 40 years old—and, therefore, covered by the ADEA—by 2010.
- In 2010 and 2011, almost one-quarter of all of the age discrimination charges filed with the EEOC included an age discrimination claim. More than 23,000 age discrimination charges were filed in each of these years, continuing the significant jump that began with the economic crisis in 2008.
- An AARP survey, conducted in May 2012, found that more than a third of older respondents had experienced, or knew someone who had experienced, age discrimination in the workplace. Almost two-thirds of respondents believed that those who were at least 50 years old faced discrimination at work. And, 16% of the retirees surveyed said they might have to return to work for financial reasons.

What's Prohibited

The ADEA prohibits age discrimination against applicants and employees who are at least 40 years old. The ADEA applies to all aspects of employment, including:

- hiring
- firing
- compensation
- benefits
- job assignments and transfers
- employee classifications
- promotions
- layoffs and recalls
- training and apprenticeship programs
- retirement plans, and
- time off.

The ADEA also prohibits employers from retaliating against employees who complain of age discrimination or otherwise assert their rights under the law. (For more information, see "Retaliation," below.)

Key Facts

- The ADEA protects workers who are at least 40 years old from age discrimination. It does not apply or provide any rights to workers who are younger than 40, and it does not prohibit an employer from favoring older workers, even if some of the younger workers who are not favored have already reached the age of 40.
- There are several explicit exceptions for firefighters, law enforcement officers, and certain types of executives and policy makers. In addition, an employer may discriminate based on age if it can prove that age is a bona fide occupational qualification for the job.
- Although the ADEA prohibits neutral policies and practices that have a disproportionate negative impact on older workers, different rules apply to these "disparate impact" lawsuits under the ADEA than under other civil rights laws, including Title VII of the Civil Rights Act of 1964. (See Chapter 18 for more on Title VII.)

Discrimination

Among the practices that might constitute age discrimination under the ADEA are:

- requiring workers to retire once they reach a certain age
- treating older workers worse than younger workers by, for example, targeting them for layoffs or discipline
- giving younger workers higher pay, more favorable assignments, or more responsibilities than older workers because of age, and
- making decisions based on stereotypes about older people (for example, refusing to include older workers in training programs because of a belief that they are unwilling or unable to learn new things).

The ADEA's prohibitions apply even if the "younger" workers who receive better treatment are older than 40. For instance, an employer who treats a 60-year-old worker more favorably than a 70-year-old worker because of age has violated the ADEA, even though both workers are protected from age discrimination under the law.

The ADEA also prohibits employers from adopting facially neutral policies or practices that have a disproportionately negative effect on older workers. These "disparate impact" claims often come up in layoff cases, if a significant number of the employees who lose their jobs are older than 40.

The ADEA gives employers a defense to disparate impact claims: An employer can escape liability if it can prove that the policy or practice that created the disparate impact was based on a reasonable factor other than age (RFOA). In 2008, the Supreme Court decided that the RFOA is an affirmative defense, which means the employer must prove it at trial. But this left open the question of exactly what qualifies as an RFOA, including which factors are "reasonable" for an employer to consider when making job decisions and how much responsibility an employer has to try to reduce the negative impact on older workers.

In 2012, the EEOC issued final regulations that attempt to answer these questions. Among other things, the regulations define an RFOA as a "non-age" factor that is objectively reasonable when viewed from the position of a prudent employer mindful of its obligations under the ADEA. The employer must show both that the employment practice it used was reasonably designed to achieve a legitimate business purpose, and that the employer applied the factor in a way that reasonably achieves that purpose.

The regulations make clear that a court must consider all of the relevant facts and circumstances in deciding whether an employer has adequately proven an RFOA. Among the things a court can consider when deciding whether an employer's practice or policy counts as an RFOA are:

- the factor's relationship to the employer's stated business purpose
- the extent to which the employer defined the factor accurately and applied it fairly and accurately, including whether managers and supervisors received training as to how to apply the factor in making decisions and avoid discrimination
- whether (and how much) the employer limited supervisors' discretion to evaluate employees subjectively, particularly if the factor is known to be subject to negative stereotypes based on age
- whether the employer assessed the adverse impact of its practice on older employees, and
- how much the practice harmed older workers (in severity and number) and whether the employer took steps to reduce that harm, given the burden involved in taking such steps.

Harassment

Harassment occurs when an employee is forced to endure a hostile, offensive, or intimidating work environment because of his or her age. Harassment might include:

- age-related slurs or offensive remarks
- offensive jokes about a worker's age
- cartoons or pictures that depict older people unfavorably
- threats, intimidation, or hostility, or
- physical violence.

Although harassment has been recognized as a form of discrimination under Title VII (see Chapter 18), there have been very few lawsuits by workers claiming age-based harassment. As a result, the U.S. Supreme Court and most of the federal courts of appeal have not explicitly said that harassment claims can be brought under the ADEA. Most legal scholars believe that age-based harassment is illegal under the ADEA; the EEOC holds this view as well. However, because the language of the ADEA is slightly different from the language of Title VII, some commentators still consider this an open question.

Advertising Prohibitions

The ADEA specifically prohibits employers from printing or publishing any job advertisement or notice that expresses a preference or limitation based on age. Terms such as "college student," "youthful," or "recent college graduate" all run afoul of this rule. Job notices seeking applicants of a particular age are also illegal.

Retaliation

The ADEA prohibits employers from retaliating against employees who complain about age discrimination, file a charge of age discrimination with the EEOC, participate in an investigation of age discrimination, file or testify in a lawsuit alleging age discrimination, or otherwise exercise their rights under the ADEA.

An employer retaliates when it takes a negative job action against an employee for exercising his or her legal rights. It might include firing, demotion, discipline, pay cuts, or less-favorable job assignments.

In a 2008 case, the U.S. Supreme Court found that federal employees are also protected from retaliation for complaining of age discrimination. (*Gomez-Perez v. Potter*, 553 U.S. 474 (2008).)

Exceptions

Employers may use age as a basis for employment decisions in a few limited circumstances. If an employer who relies on one of these exceptions is sued for age discrimination, the employer will bear the burden of proving that its actions fell within the exception.

Bona Fide Seniority System

An employer may use a *bona fide seniority system* as a basis for employment decisions, even if that results in more favorable treatment of younger workers. For example, an employer can adopt a policy of laying off workers who have the least seniority with the company, even if older workers disproportionately lose their jobs as a result.

This exception is rarely used. Because older workers tend to have greater seniority than younger workers, they are unlikely to be disadvantaged by an employer's decision to lay off workers who have little or no seniority. A "reverse" seniority system that benefits workers with less seniority or penalizes workers with more seniority does not qualify as a bona fide seniority system under the ADEA.

Bona Fide Occupational Qualification

An employer may discriminate on the basis of age in filling a particular job if age is a *bona fide occupational qualification (BFOQ)* for the position—that is, if the job, by its very nature, must be filled by an employee of a particular age. In age discrimination cases, the BFOQ defense comes up most often in the context of age limits, when an employer refuses to hire anyone older than a certain age for certain positions.

An employer may use the BFOQ defense only if the age limit or other age-related policy is reasonably necessary to the essence of the employer's business and either of the following is true:

- All or substantially all people who are older than the age limit would be unable to perform the job.
- Some people who are older than the age limit would be unable to perform the job and testing each person individually to determine whether he or she can perform the job would be impossible or highly impractical for the employer.

If the employer's goal in using the BFOQ is public safety, the employer must also show not only that the challenged age limit achieves that goal, but also that there is no acceptable alternative that is less discriminatory.

Bona Fide Employee Benefit Plan

In some cases, an employer may reduce benefits paid to older workers if the employer acts in accordance with a *bona fide employee benefit plan*. This exception is discussed in detail in Chapter 13, which covers the Older Workers Benefit Protection Act.

Firefighters and Law Enforcement Officers

State and local governments may institute a mandatory retirement age of 55 or older for firefighters and law enforcement officers.

Bona Fide Executives and High Policy Makers

Employers may require a high-ranking employee to retire or step down to a lesser position if all of the following conditions are met:

- The employee is at least 65 years old.
- The employee has worked for at least the previous two years as a *bona fide executive* or in a *high policy-making position*.
- The employee is entitled to an immediate, nonforfeitable annual retirement benefit of at least $44,000 from the employer. A benefit is immediate if payments start (or could have started, at the employee's election) within 60 days of the effective date of the employee's retirement. A benefit is nonforfeitable if no plan provisions could cause payments to cease. For example, if the plan requires payments to be suspended if the employee files a lawsuit, that benefit would be forfeitable. In calculating whether a benefit pays at least $44,000 annually, employers may not count Social Security contributions, employee contributions, contributions of former employers, or rollover contributions.

How the ADEA Is Enforced

Individual Complaints

Employees may file a complaint (also called a charge) of age discrimination with the EEOC. The deadlines for filing a charge depend on whether the state where the discrimination charge will be filed also has an antidiscrimination law. In states without antidiscrimination laws, an employee has 180 days from the date of the discriminatory act to complain. In states that have their own laws prohibiting age discrimination, this deadline is extended to 300 days. (You can find a list of states with antidiscrimination laws, and information on what those laws prohibit, at the end of Chapter 18.)

An employee may also file a lawsuit for age discrimination. However, the employee first must file a charge of discrimination with the EEOC and get a "right to sue" letter (see "Agency Enforcement," below). An employee must file the lawsuit within 90 days of receiving a right to sue letter from the EEOC.

Agency Enforcement

The federal agency responsible for investigating ADEA complaints is the EEOC. (See Appendix A for information on how to contact the EEOC.) An employee usually initiates the process by filing a charge (complaint) of age discrimination with the EEOC, although the agency can also act on its own initiative. The EEOC has the power to investigate, negotiate with employers, and bring lawsuits against employers to stop discriminatory practices.

Complying With the ADEA

Reporting Requirements

The ADEA imposes no reporting requirements.

Posting Requirements

All regulated employers must post a notice regarding the ADEA. Employers must post this notice in a prominent location, where it can be easily seen and read by employees and job applicants. The EEOC has created a poster, *Equal Employment Is the Law*, which fulfills this requirement. You can order the poster in English, Spanish, or Chinese from the EEOC's website. (See "Agency Resources," below.)

Record-Keeping Requirements

Employers must make and keep records for three years that contain the following information for each employee:

- name
- address
- date of birth
- occupation
- pay rate, and
- compensation earned each week.

Employers must keep any records relating to the following employment matters for one year after the action occurs:

- job applications, resumes, responses to job advertisements, inquiries about jobs, and any other records relating to the failure to hire any applicant
- promotion, demotion, transfer, selection for training, layoff, recall, or termination
- job orders submitted by the employer to an employment agency or labor organization to recruit applicants for job openings
- test papers completed by applicants for any position
- results of any physical examination considered by the employer in connection with any personnel action, and
- job notices or advertisements relating to job openings, promotions, training programs, or opportunities to work overtime.

Employers must also keep copies of any employment benefit plan and any written seniority system and merit system for one year beyond the date when the plan expires. If such a plan or system is not written, the employer must keep a memorandum fully outlining its terms and the manner in which it has been communicated to employees for the same time period.

Penalties

If a court finds that an employer has violated the ADEA, the employer may be ordered to do any or all of the following:

- pay the employee all wages, benefits, and other forms of compensation lost as a result of the discrimination
- take action to remedy the results of the discrimination by, for example, reinstating or promoting the worker. If the court finds that such action is warranted but impractical (for example, if the employee's position has been eliminated or the work relationship is irrevocably poisoned), the court may require the employer to pay front pay—compensation for future earnings lost—instead.
- pay a penalty (called "liquidated damages"), equal to all of the wages, benefits, and other compensation owed the employee at the time of trial, if the employer knew that its conduct was illegal or showed reckless disregard as to whether its conduct violated the ADEA or
- pay the employee's court costs and attorneys' fees.

Agency Resources

- The order form for the official notice employers must post regarding the ADEA:

  Equal Employment Is the Law
  www.eeoc.gov/employers/poster.cfm

- Information about the EEOC's charge-processing procedures:

  The Charge Handling Process
  www.eeoc.gov/employers/process.cfm

- Basic facts about the ADEA:

  Facts About Age Discrimination
  www.eeoc.gov/facts/age.html

State Laws Relating to Age Discrimination

Most states have antidiscrimination laws, many of which prohibit age discrimination. Some states follow the ADEA's lead by prohibiting discrimination only against older workers. Other states prohibit all age discrimination—including discrimination against younger workers. To find out whether your state has an age discrimination law, consult the chart at the end of Chapter 18.

Americans with Disabilities Act of 1990 (ADA)

Statute: 42 U.S.C. § 1201 and following
http://uscode.house.gov/download/pls/42C126.txt

Regulations: 29 C.F.R. § 1630 and following
www.gpo.gov/fdsys/pkg/CFR-2012-title29-vol4/pdf/CFR-2012-title29-vol4-part1630.pdf

Overview of the ADA

The Americans with Disabilities Act of 1990 (ADA) is a sweeping civil rights law that protects people with *disabilities* in many contexts, including employment, government services, public accommodations, and telecommunications. This discussion is limited to the ADA's employment provisions, which can be found in Title I of the Act.

The ADA's main employment provisions prohibit covered employers from discriminating against *qualified individuals with a disability*. This prohibition applies to all terms, conditions, and privileges of employment, and it protects both applicants and current employees. In addition, the ADA requires employers to provide *reasonable accommodations* to qualified individuals with a disability, to enable them to perform the job.

In 2008, President Bush signed the Americans with Disabilities Act Amendments Act (ADAAA), which makes a number of changes to the ADA. The stated purpose of the ADAAA was to make clear that Congress intended for the term "disability" to be interpreted broadly, in order to provide a national mandate to end discrimination against people with disabilities. Several Supreme Court decisions had limited the scope of the ADA, and the ADAAA explicitly overturns those decisions. This discussion includes the provisions of the ADAAA, which went into effect on January 1, 2009.

Regulated Employers

The following employers must comply with the ADA's employment provisions:
- private employers with 15 or more employees
- employment agencies
- labor organizations
- joint labor/management committees, and
- local governments.

State employers are required to follow the ADA, but their employees may not sue them for money damages for violating the law. However, state employees may sue their employers for injunctive relief—that is, to ask the court to require the state to take some action or refrain from taking some action (for example, to prohibit the state from requiring all applicants for employment to take a physical or to require the state to provide reasonable test-taking accommodations to

Definitions

Direct threat A significant and immediate risk of substantial harm to the health or safety of an employee with a disability or other employees that cannot be reduced or eliminated by a *reasonable accommodation.*

Disability A long-lasting physical or mental impairment that substantially limits a *major life activity*; a history of such an impairment; or being regarded as having such an impairment.

Essential functions The fundamental, not marginal, duties of a job.

Major bodily functions The proper working of bodily processes, functions, or systems, such as the immune system, normal cell growth, and the digestive, bowel, bladder, neurological, brain, respiratory, circulatory, endocrine, and reproductive functions.

Major life activities Activities that are of central importance to daily life, including *major bodily functions.*

Mitigating measures Equipment, supplies, technology, aids, appliances, and other devices or items used to ameliorate the effects of a physical or mental condition, such as medication, medical supplies, prosthetics, hearing aids, mobility devices, assistive technology, oxygen therapy equipment, and learned behavioral or adaptive neurological modifications. Ordinary eyeglasses or contact lenses are not considered mitigating measures.

Qualified individual with a disability A person who has a *disability* and who, with or without a *reasonable accommodation,* can perform the *essential functions* of a job that the person holds or would like to have. The ADA protects only qualified individuals with a disability.

Reasonable accommodation Providing assistance or making changes in the job or workplace that will enable a worker with a disability to do his or her job.

Retaliation A negative employment action taken by an employer (or someone who works for the employer) against an employee for complaining about harassment or discrimination

applicants who must take civil service exams). State employees may also be able to sue their employers under state antidiscrimination laws.

The EEOC can sue state employers on behalf of state employees whose ADA rights have been violated.

The ADA does not cover the federal government, but a similar law—the Rehabilitation Act of 1973 (29 U.S.C. § 701 and following)—does.

The ADA covers multinational employers with operations in the United States or its territories, unless the employer is covered by a treaty or another binding international agreement—for example, a treaty permitting the company to prefer its own citizens for specific jobs.

The ADA covers an employer with operations in other countries if the employer is incorporated in the United States, based in the United States, or controlled by a U.S. company. However, an employer is exempt from the ADA's requirements if complying with the ADA would violate a law of the country in which it operates.

Covered Workers

The ADA covers all qualified individuals with a *disability* who are either current or prospective employees of a covered employer, including part-time and probationary employees. To get the benefits of the ADA's employment provisions, a person must:

- be a current or prospective employee of a covered employer
- be qualified for the position, and
- have a disability within the meaning of the ADA.

The sections below explain these requirements.

Current or Prospective Employee

The ADA's employment provisions protect only current employees of or applicants for jobs with a covered employer. The ADA's employment provisions do not cover independent contractors, vendors, or customers (though they may be covered by some of the ADA's other provisions, such as those mandating access to public accommodations).

The ADA covers foreign nationals working for a covered employer, even if the employee is not authorized to work in the United States. Such an employee still has rights under the ADA, although his or her available remedies may be limited. For example, although reinstatement is a common remedy for an unlawfully fired employee, a foreign national may not be reinstated to a job in the United States if he or she is not authorized to work in the United States.

The ADA also protects U.S. citizens working outside the United States for employers that are:

- incorporated in the United States
- based in the United States, or
- controlled by a U.S. employer.

Qualified for the Position

A person is qualified for a position if both of the following are true:

- The person satisfies the prerequisites for the position (for example, has the right level of education, employment experience, skills, and licenses).
- The person is able to perform the *essential functions* of the position, with or without a reasonable accommodation from the employer.

The term essential functions refers to the fundamental, as opposed to marginal, duties of a job. A job duty is an essential function if any of the following are true:

- The reason the job exists is to perform that function (for example, an essential function of a pilot is to fly the plane).
- Only a few employees can perform the function.
- The function is so highly specialized that the employer hires people into the position specifically because of their expertise in performing that function.

The following types of information are relevant to determining whether a job duty is an essential function:

- written job descriptions prepared before advertising or interviewing for a position
- the employer's opinion
- the amount of time that people who hold that job have to spend performing that duty
- the consequences of giving the job to someone who could not perform that duty
- the terms of a collective bargaining agreement
- the work experience of people who have held the job in the past, and
- the work experience of people who are currently holding the job.

With a Disability

Not all physical or mental impairments are disabilities under the ADA. A worker has a disability as defined by the ADA only if he or she falls into one of these three categories:

- The worker has a physical or mental impairment that substantially limits a *major life activity*, without taking *mitigating measures* into account.
- The worker has a record or history of such an impairment.
- The employer incorrectly regards the worker as having a disability.

For an impairment to be a disability under the ADA, it must be long term. Temporary impairments, such as pregnancy or broken bones, are not covered by the ADA (but they may be covered by other laws).

The EEOC's regulations say specifically that the following are not disabilities: transvestism, transsexualism, pedophilia, gender identity disorders (other than those that result from a physical impairment), other sexual behavior disorders, compulsive gambling, kleptomania, pyromania, psychoactive substance use disorders resulting from current illegal drug use, homosexuality, and bisexuality.

Physical or Mental Impairment

A physical impairment means a disorder, condition, cosmetic disfigurement, or an anatomical loss that negatively affects the body's functioning. A mental impairment is any mental or psychological disorder—for example, mental retardation, organic brain syndrome, emotional or mental illness, or a learning disability.

An impairment is different from a condition or trait. Only impairments can be disabilities; conditions and traits cannot. For example, height and weight, when they are in the normal range, are traits, not impairments. Personality traits, such as poor judgment or a quick temper, are also not impairments (unless they are symptoms of a mental or psychological disorder).

The regulations interpreting the ADA provide a list of impairments that will "as a factual matter, virtually always" be disabilities, because of their effect on major life activities. These impairments include deafness, blindness, intellectual disabilities, missing limbs or mobility impairments requiring the use of a wheelchair, autism, cancer, cerebral palsy, diabetes, epilepsy, HIV infection, muscular dystrophy, major depressive disorder, bipolar disorder, posttraumatic stress disorder, obsessive-compulsive disorder, and schizophrenia.

Legal Developments

- Effective January 1, 2009, these changes from the ADAAA went into effect (each is explained in more detail in this chapter):
  - Major life activities include major bodily functions, like the proper functioning of the immune system and normal cell growth.
  - Impairments can be disabilities even if they are in remission or episodic, as long as they substantially limit a major life activity when they are active.
  - An employee may not make a "regarded as" claim of disability discrimination—a claim that the employer discriminated against the employee not because the employee actually had a disability, but because the employer regarded the employee as having a disability—based on a minor and transitory impairment, defined as one with an expected duration of six months or less.
  - Mitigating measures, other than ordinary prescription glasses and contact lenses, may not be considered in determining whether an employee has a disability.
- **EEOC issues final regulations implementing the ADAAA.** Among other things, these regulations clarify that the ADA should be interpreted in favor of broad coverage, and define "substantially limits a major life activity"—the standard that determines whether someone has a disability—more expansively.
- **Supreme Court recognizes a "ministerial exception" to the ADA.** In 2012, the Supreme Court found that an employee could not bring an ADA lawsuit over a religious employer's decision to fire her from a ministerial role. The employer was a Lutheran school, which refused to reinstate the employee to her teaching position after she took a leave of absence for her disability (narcolepsy), then fired her after she said that she had spoken to a lawyer and intended to assert her rights. The Court threw out the teacher's lawsuit for retaliation and disability discrimination, finding that the school and other religious employers must be free to decide who will preach its beliefs and teach its faith. In the Court's view, allowing employees to sue over these decisions infringes that right by asking a court to tell the religious employer whom it must hire or retain.

Substantial Limitation

An impairment that substantially limits a major life activity is a disability. Prior to the passage of the ADAAA, the EEOC and the courts used to interpret this standard to mean that a person had to be either unable to perform a major life activity or significantly restricted in the condition, manner, or duration of performing that activity to qualify as having a disability. In enacting the ADAAA, however, Congress stated that this definition was too narrow and excluded too many people from the ADA's reach. Congress instructed the EEOC to revise its regulations to redefine "substantially limits" more broadly.

In keeping with this directive, the final regulations interpreting the ADAAA state that the term is "not meant to be a demanding standard." They also clarify that a person can be substantially limited in performing a major life activity even if that person is not prevented, or significantly restricted, from performing that activity. The final regulations indicate that the condition, manner, and duration of the person's performance of the activity should be examined. For example, can the person perform the activity only for a brief period? Must the person expend significant effort to perform the activity? Is it painful or otherwise difficult for the person to perform the activity? Do the side effects of medication or other treatment make it harder for the person to perform the activity?

Conditions that are in remission or are episodic in nature are now covered by the ADA, as long as they would substantially limit a major life activity when they are active. For example, an employee whose cancer is in remission or who suffers from chronic asthma would likely be covered under this clarification in the ADAAA.

Major Life Activities

Major life activities are activities that are of essential importance to daily life, including:
- caring for oneself
- performing manual tasks
- walking
- seeing
- hearing
- speaking
- breathing

- learning, and
- working.

The ADAAA added *major bodily functions* to the list of major life activities. This means that serious conditions which have not yet appeared as outwardly debilitating will be covered as disabilities. For example, many types of cancer wreak havoc on the body's internal functioning (such as proper cell growth or the normal functioning of the immune or other bodily systems) before they substantially limit a person's ability to breath, walk, or work. These conditions will now be covered by the ADA without question.

Did You Know ...

- According to the *2010 Disability Status Report*, more than 10% of the working age population (ages 21 through 64) has a disability. Ambulatory disabilities were the most common, followed by cognitive disabilities. About one-third of working age adults with disabilities were employed, as compared to about three-quarters of the working age population without a disability.
- The same report states that the median annual income of Americans with disabilities who were employed full time for a full year was $35,900, more than $5,000 less than those without disabilities earned. Those with hearing disabilities earned the most, while those with cognitive disabilities earned the least.
- When the EEOC drafted its proposed regulations on the ADAAA in 2009, it pulled together various statistics and studies on the cost of reasonable accommodations. Those studies show significant variations in the reported mean cost of an accommodation, ranging from $462 up to more than $1,400. Where the studies agree, however, is that many (the majority, in some studies) reasonable accommodations are free.

Mitigating Measures

The ADAAA also changed the rules on mitigating measures. Previously, courts (including the Supreme Court) had found that mitigating measures had to be considered when determining whether someone had a disability. For example, an employee who takes medication to control seizures would be found to have a disability only if his or her impairment, as medicated, substantially limited a major life activity. This meant that employees whose disabilities were largely controlled or ameliorated by equipment, medication, or other assistive devices were often found not to have disabilities.

The ADAAA overturned this rule. Now, an employee's condition must be considered without mitigating measures in determining whether an employee has a disability. This change will result in more employees found to have disabilities under the ADA. The only exception to this rule is for ordinary prescription eyeglasses and contact lenses, which may be considered in evaluating an employee's condition.

Illegal Drug Use

An applicant or employee who currently engages in illegal drug use is not a qualified individual with a disability and is, therefore, not entitled to the ADA's protections.

This exception applies only to employees and job applicants who are currently using drugs illegally. The ADA still protects employees and applicants who:

- have successfully completed a drug rehabilitation program and are no longer using drugs illegally
- are currently participating in a drug rehabilitation program and are no longer using drugs illegally, or
- are erroneously believed to use drugs illegally when, in fact, they do not.

What's Prohibited

Discrimination

Covered employers may not discriminate against qualified individuals with a disability in any aspect of employment, including:

- recruitment
- job application procedures
- hiring
- promotion and training

- time off
- job assignments
- benefits
- wages, and
- layoff and termination.

Covered employers also may not discriminate against a person for associating with a person with a disability. For example, a covered employer cannot refuse to hire someone because he or she is married to someone with AIDS. Nor may an employer refuse to hire someone with a developmentally disabled child because the employer fears the person will miss work too often.

Key Facts

- The ADA prohibits discrimination in all aspects of employment against qualified individuals with disabilities and requires employers to make reasonable accommodations to allow those with disabilities to apply for a position or to perform a job.
- Employers may not inquire about a job applicant's disabilities. However, an employer may ask an applicant to describe how he or she would perform the essential functions of a job.
- An employer may refuse to hire a qualified individual with a disability if doing so would pose a *direct threat* to the employee's own health or safety or to the health or safety of other workers.

Tests and Qualification Standards

An employer may not base tests or qualification standards for a job on an employee's uncorrected vision unless such a requirement is job related and consistent with business necessity. This new rule was added by the ADAAA.

Harassment

The ADA prohibits harassment of employees with a disability. Harassment consists of unwelcome comments or offensive conduct that is severe or pervasive enough to alter the conditions of employment. This test is the same as that used under Title VII. (See Chapter 18 for more about harassment.)

Segregation

Employers may not segregate employees with disabilities. For example, if coworkers feel uncomfortable working with a person who has a disability, the employer may not transfer that person or require him or her to work at home.

Medical Examinations

Covered employers may not require job applicants to take a medical examination. However, employers may require a medical examination after making a conditional offer of employment to an applicant if the following are true:

- All entering employees must take the exam regardless of disability.
- The medical exam is the last stage in the applicant-screening process (for example, after the background check).
- The employer keeps the medical exam results in a separate and confidential medical file.

A test for illegal drug use is not a medical exam and is, therefore, not prohibited or governed by the ADA.

An employer may require current employees to take a medical examination only if the employer reasonably believes either of the following:

- The employee is unable to perform the essential functions of the job due to a medical condition.
- The employee poses a *direct threat* to him- or herself or other employees because of a medical condition.

Inquiries About Disabilities

Employers may not ask job applicants questions about whether they have a disability or about the nature or severity of a disability. However, employers can explain what the application process involves and ask applicants whether they will need a reasonable accommodation.

They can also explain what the job entails and ask applicants whether they are capable of performing job-related functions.

Retaliation

Covered employers may not take a negative employment action against a person for asserting his or her rights under the ADA. Negative employment actions might include demotion, discipline, firing, salary reduction, or change in job assignment. To do so constitutes prohibited *retaliation*. (See Chapter 18 for more information on retaliation.)

What's Required

Employers must provide a reasonable accommodation for a qualified individual with a disability who needs the accommodation to apply for a job, perform a job, or access work facilities and benefits. Employers are excused from providing an accommodation only if it would cause the employer undue hardship. (See "Undue Hardship," below.)

Accommodating a worker means providing assistance or making changes in the job or workplace that will enable the worker to do a job despite a disability. For example, an employer might lower the height of a desktop to accommodate a worker in a wheelchair, provide TDD telephone equipment for a worker whose hearing is impaired, or provide a quiet, distraction-free workspace for a worker with Attention Deficit Disorder.

Reasonable accommodations fall into three broad categories:

- changes to the job application process that enable a qualified individual with a disability to apply and be considered for the position
- changes to the work environment, the circumstances in which the job is performed, or the manner in which the job is performed that enable a qualified individual with a disability to perform the job's essential functions, and
- changes that enable an employee with a disability to enjoy the same benefits and privileges that other employees enjoy.

It is the applicant's or employee's responsibility to request the accommodation initially. The employer does not have to anticipate this need. Someone other than the applicant or employee (such as a spouse, friend, or coworker) can request the accommodation on the worker's behalf. Employees or job applicants do not have to make the request in writing, nor do they have to use any particular words—for example, they don't have to mention the ADA or use the words "reasonable accommodation." They simply need to request that some change be made because of a medical condition or impairment.

Once the applicant or employee makes the request, the employer and the worker must talk and work together to see if a reasonable accommodation is possible. The employer does not have to grant the specific accommodation that the employee or applicant requests, as long as the employer works with the person to find an effective accommodation.

If the disability or need for accommodation is not obvious, the employer may ask the employee to submit medical verification of the disability and limitations.

The following accommodations are considered unreasonable, and an employer is not required to make these changes:
- eliminating an essential function of the job
- lowering production or performance standards, or
- providing personal use items, such as a wheelchair, eyeglasses, hearing aid, or prosthetic limb.

An employer need not provide a reasonable accommodation for an employee who qualifies as having a disability only because the employer incorrectly "regards" the employee as disabled. Although such employees are protected from discrimination, they are not entitled to a reasonable accommodation.

Exceptions

There are four major exceptions to employers' responsibilities under the ADA:
- *Undue hardship.* Employers are not required to make an accommodation for a qualified person with a disability if making the accommodation would cause the employer an undue hardship.
- *Direct threat.* Employers may refuse to hire a qualified person with a disability if hiring him or her for the job would pose a direct threat to the applicant's own health or safety or to the health or safety of other workers.
- *Religious institutions.* Churches and other religious institutions may prefer applicants who conform to the tenets of their religion over otherwise qualified applicants with a disability.

- *Food handling.* If a job requires food handling, an employer can refuse to hire someone with an infectious or communicable disease if a reasonable accommodation cannot eliminate the risk of transmitting the disease.

Undue Hardship

An accommodation creates an undue hardship if it would involve significant difficulty or expense for the employer or if it would fundamentally alter the nature or operation of the business. Whether an accommodation creates an undue hardship depends on a number of factors, including:
- the accommodation's cost
- the size and financial resources of the business
- the business structure, and
- the effect the accommodation would have on the business.

An undue hardship can be financial, but it doesn't have to be. For example, suppose a library clerk with a hearing disability requested that a loud bell and speaker be added to the telephone, which would enable him to hear and answer calls. Although the accommodation is probably inexpensive, it would disturb library patrons and destroy the quiet atmosphere of the library. This means that the accommodation probably creates an undue hardship for the library.

Direct Threat

A covered employer may refuse to hire qualified individuals with disabilities—or may transfer or terminate them without violating the ADA—if hiring them for the job would pose a direct threat to their own health or safety or to the health or safety of other workers. To determine whether a direct threat exists, the employer must make an individualized assessment of a person's ability to safely perform the essential functions of the job, taking into account the judgment of a medical professional. The following factors should be considered:
- the duration of the risk
- the nature and severity of the potential harm to the person with the disability and/or other employees
- the likelihood of harm occurring, and
- whether the harm is imminent.

Religious Institutions

Religious institutions may give preference to job applicants of a particular religion. For example, a Jewish temple may hire a qualified Jewish applicant instead of a qualified applicant with a disability who is not Jewish. Religious institutions may also require that the applicant conform to the tenets of the religion. For example, a Catholic college may fire a professor with a disability who renounces his faith, even though he is otherwise able to perform his job.

The Supreme Court has clarified that applicants for, and employees in, ministerial positions may not sue religious employers for discrimination or retaliation under the ADA. The First Amendment's guarantee of religious freedom requires courts to steer clear of religious employer's decisions about who will preach their message and mission. This exception applies only to employees who act as "ministers" of the religious employer's faith. However, the Supreme Court declined to adopt clear rules as to who does and does not qualify as a minister, so it remains unclear how closely courts will scrutinize the employee's actual job responsibilities and duties in applying this exception.

Infectious Diseases

If a job requires food handling, an employer can refuse to hire someone with an infectious or communicable disease that is transmitted through food handling only if a reasonable accommodation cannot eliminate the risk of transmitting the disease.

How the ADA Is Enforced

Individual Complaints

The ADA is enforced under the same procedures as Title VII. (See Chapter 18.)

Agency Enforcement

The ADA is enforced under the same procedures as Title VII. (See Chapter 18.)

Complying With the ADA

Reporting Requirements

The reporting requirements for the ADA are the same as those for Title VII. (See Chapter 18.)

Posting Requirements

Covered employers must post notices informing current and prospective employees about the ADA. This notice is included in the poster, *Equal Employment Is the Law*, available from the EEOC. (See Chapter 18 for more information.)

Record-Keeping Requirements

The record-keeping requirements for the ADA are the same as those for Title VII. (See Chapter 18.)

Penalties

For the most part, failure to comply with the ADA carries the same penalties as failure to comply with Title VII. (See Chapter 18.) However, courts disagree on whether plaintiffs who bring a lawsuit for retaliation under the ADA may recover compensation for emotional distress, pain and suffering and so on, or punitive damages intended to punish the employer for egregious violations of the law. This conflict has not yet been resolved by the U.S. Supreme Court.

In addition to the penalties available under Title VII, a court might order an employer to make a reasonable accommodation for an employee's disability.

Agency Resources

- Basic information on the ADA
  Facts About the Americans with Disabilities Act
  www.eeoc.gov/facts/fs-ada.html

The ADA: Questions and Answers
www.eeoc.gov/facts/adaqa1.html

- Information for employers about their obligations under the ADA

    The ADA: Your Responsibilities as an Employer
    www.eeoc.gov/facts/ada17.html

- A detailed handbook on how to comply with the ADA

    The Americans with Disabilities Act: A Primer for Small Business
    www.eeoc.gov/facts/adahandbook.html

- A guide to reasonable accommodations under the ADA for small businesses

    Small Employers and Reasonable Accommodation
    www.eeoc.gov/facts/accommodation.html

- A guide to the ADA during the job application process

    Job Applicants and the Americans with Disabilities Act
    www.eeoc.gov/facts/jobapplicant.html

- Facts on telecommuting as a reasonable accommodation

    Work At Home/Telework as a Reasonable Accommodation
    www.eeoc.gov/facts/telework.html

- A detailed guide to the ADA for the food service industry

    How to Comply with the Americans with Disabilities Act:
    A Guide for Restaurants and Other Food Service Employers
    www.eeoc.gov/facts/restaurant_guide.html

- Question and answer series on the ADA and specific issues or disabilities

    Questions and Answers About Blindness and Vision Impairments in the
    Workplace and the Americans with Disabilities Act
    www.eeoc.gov/facts/blindness.html

    Questions and Answers About the Association Provision of the Americans with
    Disabilities Act
    www.eeoc.gov/facts/association_ada.html

    Questions and Answers About Cancer in the Workplace and the Americans
    with Disabilities Act (ADA)
    www.eeoc.gov/facts/cancer.html

    Questions and Answers About Diabetes in the Workplace and the Americans
    with Disabilities Act (ADA)

www.eeoc.gov/facts/diabetes.html

Questions and Answers About Epilepsy in the Workplace and the Americans with Disabilities Act (ADA)
www.eeoc.gov/facts/epilepsy.html

Questions & Answers About Persons with Intellectual Disabilities in the Workplace and the Americans with Disabilities Act
www.eeoc.gov/facts/intellectual_disabilities.html

State Laws Relating to Disability Discrimination

At the end of Chapter 18, you'll find a chart of state laws that prohibit employment discrimination, including disability discrimination.

Consolidated Omnibus Budget Reconciliation Act (COBRA)

Statute: 29 U.S.C. §§ 1161–1169
http://uscode.house.gov/download/pls/29C18.txt

Regulations: 26 C.F.R. § 54.4980B-0 and following
www.gpo.gov/fdsys/pkg/CFR-2012-title26-vol17/pdf/CFR-2012-title26-vol17-sec54-4980B-0.pdf

Overview of COBRA

The Consolidated Omnibus Budget Reconciliation Act of 1985 (COBRA) enables employees and their families to continue health care coverage under an employer's *group health plan* even after they experience an event—such as a layoff or termination—that would end their coverage under ordinary circumstances.

Employees and their families must pay the entire cost of COBRA coverage: the full premium at the employer-negotiated group rate, which is often less expensive than an individual policy. (Although the stimulus package paid about two-thirds of the COBRA premium for employees and their families who lost their jobs between September 2008 and May 2010, the subsidy has expired. Because the subsidy was available for a maximum of 15 months, those who lost their jobs at the end of the subsidy window had to start paying their full COBRA premiums at the end of August 2011.)

This continued coverage lasts for 18 to 36 months, depending on the *qualifying event* that entitled the *qualified beneficiary* to coverage.

COBRA requires both the employer and qualified beneficiaries to meet certain notice requirements. Many employers choose to outsource their administrative obligations under COBRA; others take on those responsibilities themselves.

Regulated Employers

COBRA covers private employers with 20 or more employees. (See "Counting Employees," below, for information on how to figure out which workers qualify.)

Separate provisions of COBRA apply to state and local governments. (42 U.S.C. § 300bb-1.) These provisions are administered and enforced by the Department of Health and Human Services. Although COBRA does not cover the federal government, federal employees and their families are covered by similar, but not identical, provisions in the Federal Employees Health Benefits Amendments Act. (5 U.S.C. § 8905a.)

COBRA does not cover *church plans*.

Definitions

Church plan A *group health plan* that is established and maintained by a church or an association or convention of churches that is tax exempt under Internal Revenue Code § 501(a).

Election notice A document the plan administrator must send to qualified beneficiaries after a *qualifying event* has occurred, letting them know how to elect to continue health care coverage under COBRA.

ERISA The Employee Retirement Income Security Act, a federal law that sets minimum standards for establishing, administering, and maintaining certain employee benefit plans, including most group health plans sponsored by employers.

Gross misconduct Employee wrongdoing that is willful, intentional, reckless, or deliberately indifferent to the employer's interests. Neither the statute nor the regulations define this term, but court decisions consistently hold that *gross misconduct* must be something more than mere carelessness or incompetence. Examples of gross misconduct include:
- theft
- embezzlement
- violation of company policy
- lies
- driving a vehicle under the influence of alcohol, or
- off-site assault on a coworker.

Group health plan An employee benefit plan that provides medical care to participants (typically employees, their spouses, and their dependents). Medical care includes inpatient and outpatient hospital care, physician care, surgery and other major medical benefits, prescription drugs, dental care, and vision care. It does not include life insurance, disability benefits, or amounts employers contribute to a *medical savings account*.

Initial/general notice A document the plan administrator must give to employees and their spouses when they become eligible to participate in an employer's *group health plan*. The notice must provide specific information about continuation coverage under the plan.

Definitions (continued)

Medical savings account A tax-exempt account employees can use to pay certain medical expenses. A medical savings account may be funded by employer or employee contributions.

Multiemployer plan A plan to which more than one employer is required to contribute and which is maintained pursuant to at least one collective bargaining agreement between at least one employee organization and more than one employer. Multiemployer plans are allowed to follow slightly different rules for COBRA notices.

Noncompliance period A period of time used to calculate the excise tax an employer has to pay for failing to comply with COBRA. The noncompliance period begins on the first day the employer fails to continue coverage for a *qualified beneficiary* and ends on the earlier of (1) the date the employer corrects the violation, or (2) six months after the last day of the *qualified beneficiary's* coverage period.

Qualified beneficiary An individual who is covered by an employer's *group health plan* on the day before a *qualifying event*. Individuals who are qualified beneficiaries are eligible to receive COBRA benefits.

Qualifying event An event that makes a *qualified beneficiary* eligible for COBRA coverage. For a current employee, a qualifying event is one that would otherwise disqualify the employee from the employer's *group health plan*, such as a resignation or layoff. If the employee's dependents are covered through the employer's *group health plan*, the employee's death or divorce is a qualifying event as well.

Qualifying event notice Notice provided by the employer or by a *qualified beneficiary* to the plan, stating that a *qualifying event* has occurred.

Second qualifying event A qualifying event that occurs after a first *qualifying event* and would have caused the *qualified beneficiary* to lose coverage under the plan had the first *qualifying event* not already done so. A second qualifying event (sometimes referred to as a "subsequent qualifying event") may entitle the *qualified beneficiary* to an extension of COBRA coverage.

Counting Employees

Figuring out whether your company has 20 or more employees for purposes of COBRA is not always a simple matter of counting heads. To determine whether COBRA applies:

- Count both full- and part-time employees. Each part-time employee counts as a fraction of an employee, equal to the fraction of a full-time day that employee works. For example, if a part-time employee works four hours a day, but full-time employees work eight hours a day, then the part-time employee would count as four-eighths—or half—an employee.
- Don't count self-employed people, independent contractors, and corporate directors as employees. These workers may be entitled to COBRA coverage, however (see "Covered Workers," below).

Covered Workers

To be eligible for COBRA's benefits, a person must:

- be a qualified beneficiary, and
- have a relationship with the employer that will be affected by a qualifying event. Those who have such a relationship to the employer include employees, former employees, family members of current and former employees, and others associated, formerly associated, or in a business relationship with the employer (including members of a union who are not currently employees).

Unlike most other employment laws, COBRA provides benefits not only to current and former employees, but also to their spouses and children if they were covered by the employer's group health plan.

Qualified Beneficiary

A qualified beneficiary is a person (typically, an employee, the employee's spouse, or the employee's dependent child) covered by the employer's group health plan on the day before a qualifying event, such as a layoff. Employees and their family members who were not covered by their employer's group health plan prior to the qualifying event are not entitled to COBRA's coverage or notice rights.

Retired employees, their spouses, and their dependent children can also be qualified beneficiaries if the employer files for certain types of bankruptcy. We don't cover these rules here.

If a child is born to a covered employee or placed for adoption with a covered employee while the employee is on COBRA, the child is a qualified beneficiary.

Agents, independent contractors, and directors who are not employees, but who, nonetheless, participate in the group health plan, can also be qualified beneficiaries.

Qualifying Event

There are many events that affect an individual's relationship with an employer, but only a qualifying event makes the individual eligible for COBRA coverage. What constitutes a qualifying event differs for employees, their spouses, and their dependents.

Employees

The following are qualifying events for employees:
- The employee quits or otherwise voluntarily terminates the employment.
- The employer involuntarily terminates the employment for reasons other than *gross misconduct*. For example, the employee is laid off for economic reasons or fired because he or she lacks the necessary skills for the position.
- The employee's work hours are reduced to an amount that would otherwise make the employee ineligible for benefits. For example, if an employer provides health insurance benefits only to employees who work 40 hours a week, and a full-time employee chooses to switch to a 30-hour-a-week schedule, that employee becomes ineligible for health insurance benefits under the employer's rules.

Spouses

The following are qualifying events for spouses of employees:
- The employee experiences any of the events listed under "Employees," above.
- The employee becomes entitled to Medicare.
- The spouse and the employee divorce or legally separate.
- The employee dies.

Dependent Children

The qualifying events for dependent children are the same as those listed under "Spouses," above, with one addition: It is a qualifying event if the child loses dependent status under the plan. For example, if the plan states that children are covered as dependents only until they turn 18, a child's 18th birthday is a qualifying event that triggers the child's right to continuation coverage.

Did You Know ...

- According to the Bureau of Labor Statistics, 70% of all employees in private industry had access to medical care benefits through their employers, and slightly more than half of all private employees actually participated in their employers' plans, as of March 2012.
- Most private industry employees who receive medical care benefits from their employers are required to contribute to the cost of coverage. In 2010, employees contributed an average of 21% of the cost of their own coverage and 32% of the cost of family coverage.
- Employees and their families who opt for COBRA coverage have to foot the whole bill themselves. How much does coverage run? In 2011, a survey by the Kaiser Family Foundation showed that the average total cost of employer-provided health insurance was $5,429 a year for individuals and $15,073 for families.

What's Prohibited

Employers may not refuse COBRA coverage to a qualified beneficiary because that person would not have been insurable on the day before the qualifying event. If the group health plan actually covered the employee, spouse, or dependent on the day before the qualifying event, then that person is entitled to COBRA coverage, regardless of whether the plan would choose to insure him or her at that time in ordinary circumstances. This rule prevents termination of benefits to those who arguably need them the most:

people who have developed serious health conditions that might make it difficult for them to find insurance coverage if their benefits were cut off.

Key Facts

- COBRA enables employees and their families to continue health care coverage under an employer's group health plan even after an event—such as a layoff or termination—that would otherwise end their coverage. Usually, employees and their families must pay for the coverage, but they get to pay at the employer-negotiated group rate, which is usually less expensive than an individual rate.
- Employers must give employees several different notices relating to COBRA eligibility, as well as notices for unavailability or early termination of COBRA coverage. Specific rules govern the content and timing of each notice.
- If a qualified beneficiary elects continuation coverage under COBRA, the group health plan must continue to cover the beneficiary for 18 to 36 months, depending on the type of beneficiary and the qualifying event.

What's Required

Notice Requirements

A plan administrator—who may either be the employer (if it administers the health care plan itself) or a third party hired by the employer to administer the plan—has several notice obligations under COBRA. (Slightly different rules apply to *multiemployer plans*; these rules are not covered in this book.)

Initial or General Notice

A plan administrator must provide an *initial or general notice* to employees when they become eligible to participate in the plan—for example, when they are hired, if their employer allows new hires to immediately be covered by health insurance. Plan administrators must provide this notice in writing to a covered employee and to his or her spouse within 90 days after coverage begins. If the employee and spouse enroll in the plan within the same 90-day period and reside at the same address, the plan administrator can send one notice to both; otherwise, it must send a separate notice to the spouse. The employer need not send separate notices to any dependent children who reside with the employee and/or spouse.

Because employers typically have to provide a summary plan description to new participants during this same time period, a plan administrator may include the general COBRA notice along with the summary plan description, as long as it is given to the employee within the required 90-day period and the spouse is properly notified.

The notice must provide the plan's name; the name, address, and telephone number of a person to contact for information about the plan; a description of the continuation coverage available; and information on how to notify the plan of qualifying events, among other things. For more specific information, consult the Department of Labor (DOL) publications *An Employer's Guide to Group Health Continuation Coverage Under COBRA* and *Model General Notice of COBRA Continuation Coverage Rights*. For information on how to obtain these publications, see "Agency Resources," below.

Qualifying Event Notice

Either the employer or the employee (or qualified beneficiary) is responsible for notifying the plan that a qualifying event has occurred. This is done by sending a *qualifying event notice* to the plan administrator. Who is required to send this notice depends on the type of qualifying event.

The employer has 30 days to notify the plan administrator of the following qualifying events:

- voluntary or involuntary termination of employment
- reduction of hours
- death of the covered employee, or
- the covered employee's eligibility for Medicare.

If the employer administers its own plan, it does not have to send itself a qualifying event notice.

The employee or a qualified beneficiary is responsible for notifying the plan administrator of the following qualifying events:

- divorce
- legal separation
- a child losing dependent status under the plan

- the employee's disability, or
- a *second qualifying event* that occurs after the employee or qualified beneficiary is already eligible for continuation coverage under COBRA.

The plan must include reasonable procedures for employees or qualified beneficiaries to provide notice of these qualifying events. These procedures should be included in the plan's summary plan description, allow enough time after the event for the beneficiary to give notice (at least 60 days), specify the time limits for giving notice, describe how and to whom notice must be given, and describe what information the notice must include. If a plan fails to establish such reasonable procedures, a beneficiary can fulfill his or her obligation to notify the plan of a qualifying event by providing oral or written notice to the person or department that handles employee benefit issues for the employer.

The employee or a qualified beneficiary is required to notify the plan administrator if the Social Security Administration determines that the employee is no longer disabled. This notice must be provided within 30 days.

Election Notice

After a qualifying event, a plan administrator must provide an *election notice* to the qualified beneficiaries, informing them of their right to choose COBRA continuation coverage.

- If the employer has a separate plan administrator, the plan administrator has 14 days after learning of the qualifying event to provide an election notice to the qualified beneficiaries.
- If the employer is the plan administrator, and the qualifying event is one that the employee or another qualified beneficiary must report to the plan, then the employer has 14 days after learning of the qualifying event to provide an election notice to the qualified beneficiaries.
- If the employer is the plan administrator, and the qualifying event is one that the employer must report to the plan, then the employer must provide the election notice no later than 44 days after the qualifying event. Or, if the employer's plan states that COBRA coverage begins with the loss of regular coverage, the employer must provide the election notice no later than 44 days after the beneficiary loses coverage under the employer's plan due to a qualifying event.

The election notice must contain a significant amount of information as specified by the DOL. For details, consult the DOL's publications

An Employer's Guide to Group Health Continuation Coverage Under COBRA and *Model COBRA Continuation Coverage Election Notice.* (See "Agency Resources," below, for more information.)

Other Notices

If a plan denies a request for COBRA coverage or a request for an extension of COBRA coverage, the plan administrator must provide the beneficiary with a notice of unavailability of continuation coverage within 14 days after receiving the request. This notice must explain why the request was denied.

If a plan ends continuation coverage before the maximum period allowed under the circumstances (between 18 and 36 months) has passed, the plan administrator must provide the beneficiary with a notice of early termination of continuation coverage as soon as possible and practicable after the decision to terminate the coverage is made. This notice must include the date coverage will end, the reason for terminating coverage, and any rights the beneficiary may have to elect other coverage.

Coverage Requirements

If a qualified beneficiary chooses to take advantage of COBRA benefits, the group health plan must continue to cover the beneficiary for a period of time. The length of continuation coverage depends on the type of beneficiary and the qualifying event, as shown in the chart below.

Coverage Periods		
Qualifying Event	**Qualified Beneficiary**	**Coverage Period**
Voluntary termination Involuntary termination Reduction of hours	Employee Spouse Dependent child	18 months
Divorce Legal separation Employee's death Employee on Medicare*	Spouse Dependent child	36 months
Loss of dependent child status	Dependent child	36 months
* But see "Medicare," below.		

The law allows the employer to choose to extend COBRA benefits beyond the required statutory coverage period. In addition, the coverage periods described above may be lengthened if certain events occur, as described in "Exceptions," below.

COBRA beneficiaries are entitled to the same coverage they would have received if the qualifying event had not occurred. In other words, the employer or plan may not provide lesser or different benefits to those who receive coverage under COBRA.

The qualified beneficiary is responsible for paying the full premium. The employer may charge a 2% administrative fee, making the total cost to the employee 102% of the coverage costs. (Employers may choose to pay for the coverage, but the law does not require them to do so.)

Each qualified beneficiary has individual election rights. This means that even within the same family, some qualified beneficiaries could choose to elect coverage, while others could choose not to. For example, if an employee goes to work for a new employer that provides coverage for employees only, the employee might choose to enroll in the new plan while his or her spouse and child continue coverage under the former employer's plan, using COBRA.

Exceptions

The coverage periods described in "Coverage Requirements," above, may be lengthened in certain circumstances. Longer coverage may be required in case of any of the following:
- The qualified beneficiary has or develops a disability.
- A second qualifying event occurs.
- A covered employee becomes entitled to Medicare coverage.
- The employer files for bankruptcy.

Disability

If the qualifying event is voluntary or involuntary termination of employment or reduction in hours, COBRA coverage lasts for 18 months. However, if a qualified beneficiary is disabled at the time of the qualifying event or becomes disabled during the first 60 days of COBRA coverage, COBRA coverage can be extended for up to 29 months.

In order to qualify for this exception, the beneficiary must be determined by the Social Security Administration (SSA) to be disabled as defined by Titles II or XVI of the Social Security Act (42 U.S.C. § 401 and following or § 1381 and following, respectively). The SSA uses strict criteria to determine whether a person is disabled and, therefore, eligible for disability benefits. To be eligible, a person must be unable to do the work he or she did before or to adjust to other work because of his or her condition, and the disability must be expected to last at least a year or to result in the person's death. For detailed information on these criteria, go to the SSA's website, www.ssa.gov, and browse the information under the heading "Disability."

If coverage is extended due to a disability, coverage is extended for all qualified beneficiaries who became entitled to COBRA because of the initial qualifying event. For example, if an employee is laid off, and that employee along with his or her spouse and dependent children all choose to continue coverage under COBRA, the entire family would be entitled to a disability extension if the employee became disabled.

The employer may increase the charge for the last 11 months of coverage from 102% of the premium to 150% of the premium.

Second Qualifying Event

If a beneficiary is using the 18-month coverage period and a second qualifying event occurs during that coverage period, the beneficiary can extend the coverage period to 36 months from the date of the first qualifying event. This rule applies only if the second qualifying event is death, divorce, or a child's reaching the age at which he or she is no longer covered by the plan—events that allow for a 36-month continuation period. If, for example, an employee's hours are reduced, then the employee is laid off, there would be no extension of the initial 18-month coverage period.

Medicare

If a former employee becomes entitled to Medicare benefits while he or she is receiving continuation coverage, COBRA coverage may be terminated. (In contrast, current employees cannot have their group health coverage terminated solely because they become entitled to Medicare.) Because Medicare does not cover the employee's family, their COBRA coverage will continue. How long this coverage must continue—18 or 36 months—is currently the subject of some debate, however.

Previously, most plans treated Medicare eligibility as a second qualifying event that extended the initial 18-month coverage period to a total of 36 months for the employee's spouse and children. In February 2004, however, the IRS gave a different interpretation. In the IRS's view, an employee's entitlement to Medicare does not count as a subsequent qualifying event because, if the employee were still employed, the plan could not terminate his or her medical care coverage simply because the employee became eligible for Medicare. (IRS Revenue Ruling 2004-22.) Therefore, according to the IRS, plans do not have to extend coverage for dependents if the employee becomes entitled to Medicare after becoming eligible for COBRA coverage. Because this ruling contradicts previous interpretations of the law, you should consult an attorney for more information on extension of COBRA benefits when a former employee becomes eligible for Medicare.

How COBRA Is Enforced

Individual Complaints

Individuals may bring a civil action in court to enforce COBRA rights. These lawsuits fall under the civil enforcement provisions of the Employee Retirement Income Security Act of 1974 (ERISA).

Agency Enforcement

The Employee Benefits Security Administration (formerly the Pension and Welfare Benefits Administration) of the DOL enforces COBRA's disclosure and notice provisions.

The Internal Revenue Service and the DOL share jurisdiction for enforcement of COBRA's eligibility, coverage, and premium provisions.

The Social Security Administration (SSA) determines whether someone is disabled under the Social Security Act.

Complying With COBRA

Deadlines

- The plan administrator must send the initial or general notice within *90 days* after the employee and qualified beneficiaries begin coverage under the plan.
- The employer must send a qualifying event notice to the plan administrator within *30 days* after the following qualifying events: the employee quits, the employee is fired for reasons other than gross misconduct, the employee becomes entitled to Medicare, or the employee's hours are reduced to a level that would make him or her ineligible for benefits under the employer's group health plan.
- The employee or a qualified beneficiary has at least *60 days* to send a qualifying event notice to the plan administrator after the following qualifying events: divorce, legal separation, a child's losing dependent status under the plan, the employee is found to be disabled by the Social Security Administration, or a second qualifying event occurs after the employee or qualified beneficiary is already eligible for COBRA coverage.
- The employee has *30 days* to notify the plan administrator if the Social Security Administration determines that the employee is no longer disabled.
- The plan administrator has *14 days* after receiving the qualifying event notice to send the employee and qualified beneficiaries an election notice. If the employer is also the plan administrator, the employer also has *14 days* to send the election notice, if the qualifying event is one that the employee or qualified beneficiary must report to the plan administrator.
- The employer has *44 days* after a qualifying event to send the employee and qualified beneficiaries an election notice, if the employer is also the plan administrator and the qualifying event is not one that the employee or qualified beneficiary must report to the plan administrator.
- If a plan denies a request for COBRA coverage or a request for an extension of COBRA coverage, the plan administrator must provide the beneficiary with a notice of unavailability of continuation coverage within *14 days* after receiving the request.

Reporting Requirements

COBRA has no specific reporting requirements.

Posting Requirements

COBRA imposes no posting requirements.

Record-Keeping Requirements

COBRA has no specific record-keeping requirements.

Penalties

A private sector employer that fails to comply with COBRA faces any or all of the following sanctions:

- excise taxes (see "Excise Taxes," below, for more information)
- fines for failing to satisfy COBRA's notice and disclosure rules
- civil liability to individuals who suffered losses because they did not receive the health insurance coverage to which they were entitled, and/or
- attorneys' fees.

Excise Taxes

An employer must pay a $100 excise tax (also called a penalty tax) for every day that it fails to meet the continuation rules during the *noncompliance period*. This excise tax applies separately for each qualified beneficiary for whom the employer fails to provide the required coverage. However, if the affected qualified beneficiaries are in the same family, then the tax is capped at $200 per day for the family.

The noncompliance period begins on the first day of the violation and ends on the earlier of: (1) the date the employer corrects the violation, or (2) six months after the last day of the qualified beneficiary's coverage period.

The employer will not have to pay the excise tax if either of the following applies:

- The failure is not intentional and the employer has a reasonable explanation.

- The employer corrects the violation within 30 days of finding out about the violation.

Agency Resources

- A detailed booklet describing employer rights and obligations under COBRA

  An Employer's Guide to Group Health Continuation Coverage Under COBRA
  www.dol.gov/ebsa/pdf/cobraemployer.pdf

- General Notice Form

  Model General Notice of COBRA Continuation Coverage Rights
  www.dol.gov/ebsa/modelgeneralnotice.doc (English)
  www.dol.gov/ebsa/ModelGeneralNoticeSP.doc (Spanish)

- Election Notice Form

  Model COBRA Continuation Coverage Election Notice
  www.dol.gov/ebsa/pdf/modelelectionnotice.pdf (English)
  www.dol.gov/ebsa/pdf/modelelectionnoticesp.pdf (Spanish)

- Information answering common questions on COBRA

  FAQ For Employees About COBRA Continuation Health Coverage
  www.dol.gov/ebsa/faqs/faq-consumer-cobra.html

State Laws Relating to Health Coverage Continuation

Many states also have laws requiring employers to provide continued health insurance coverage. These laws sometimes go beyond what COBRA requires. For example, some states require employers with fewer than 20 employees to provide continuation coverage, or require employers to continue coverage for vision, dental, or prescription drug benefits.

The chart below provides some basic information on state health insurance continuation laws. To find out more about your state's requirements, contact your state insurance department.

State Health Insurance Continuation Laws

Alabama

Ala. Code § 27-55-3(4)

Special Situations: 18 months for subjects of domestic abuse who have lost coverage they had under abuser's insurance and who do not qualify for COBRA.

Arizona

Ariz. Rev. Stat. §§ 20-1377, 20-1408

Employers affected: All employers who offer group disability insurance.

Length of coverage for dependents: Insurer must either continue coverage for dependents or convert to individual policy upon death of covered employee or divorce. Coverage must be the same unless the insured chooses a lesser plan.

Qualifying event: Death of an employee; change in marital status.

Time employer has to notify employee of continuation rights: No provisions for employer. Insurance policy must include notice of conversion privilege. Clerk of court must provide notice to anyone filing for divorce that dependent spouse entitled to convert health insurance coverage.

Time employee has to apply: 31 days after termination of existing coverage.

Arkansas

Ark. Code Ann. §§ 23-86-114 to 23-86-116

Employers affected: All employers who offer group health insurance.

Eligible employees: Continuously insured for previous 3 months.

Length of coverage for employee: 120 days.

Length of coverage for dependents: 120 days.

Qualifying event: Termination of employment; change in insured's marital status.

Time employee has to apply: 10 days.

California

Cal. Health & Safety Code §§ 1373.6, 1373.621; Cal. Ins. Code §§ 10128.50 to 10128.59

Employers affected: Employers who offer group health insurance and have 2 to 19 employees.

Eligible employees: All covered employees are eligible.

Length of coverage for employee: 36 months.

Length of coverage for dependents: 36 months.

Qualifying event: Termination of employment; reduction in hours; death of employee; change in marital status; loss of dependent status.

Time employer has to notify employee of continuation rights: 15 days.

Time employee has to apply: 60 days.

Special situations: Employee who is at least 60 years old and has worked for employer for previous 5 years may continue benefits for self and spouse beyond COBRA or Cal-COBRA limits (also applies to COBRA employers). Employee who began receiving COBRA coverage on or after 1/1/03 and whose COBRA coverage is for less than 36 months may use Cal-COBRA to bring total coverage up to 36 months.

State Health Insurance Continuation Laws (continued)

Colorado

Colo. Rev. Stat. § 10-16-108

Employers affected: All employers who offer group health insurance.

Eligible employees: Employees continuously insured for previous 6 months.

Length of coverage for employee: 18 months.

Length of coverage for dependents: 18 months.

Qualifying event: Termination of employment; reduction in hours; death of employee; change in marital status.

Time employer has to notify employee of continuation rights: 60 days.

Time employee has to apply: 30 days after termination; 60 days if employer fails to give notice.

Connecticut

Conn. Gen. Stat. Ann. §§ 38a-538, 38a-554; 31-51o

Employers affected: All employers who offer group health insurance.

Eligible employees: Full-time employees or employees who have either worked or expect to work twenty hours a week for at least 26 weeks in a 12-month period.

Length of coverage for employee: 30 months, or until eligible for Social Security benefits.

Length of coverage for dependents: 30 months, or until eligible for Social Security benefits; 36 months in case of employee's death or divorce.

Qualifying event: Layoff; reduction in hours; termination of employment; death of employee; change in marital status.

Time employer has to notify employee of continuation rights: 60 days.

Time employee has to apply: 60 days.

Special situations: When facility closes or relocates, employer must pay for insurance for employee and dependents for 120 days or until employee is eligible for other group coverage, whichever comes first (does not affect employee's right to conventional continuation coverage which begins when 120-day period ends).

Delaware

18 Del.Code Ann. tit. 18, § 3571F

Employers affected: Employers that offer group health insurance and have 1 to 19 employees.

Eligible employees: Employees continuously insured for previous three months.

Length of coverage for employee: 9 months.

Length of coverage for dependents: 9 months.

Qualifying event: Employee's death; termination of employment; divorce or legal separation; employee's eligibility for Medicare; loss of dependent status.

Time employer has to notify employee of continuation rights: Within 30 days of the qualifying event.

Time employee has to apply: 30 days.

State Health Insurance Continuation Laws (continued)

District of Columbia

D.C. Code Ann. §§ 32-731 to 32-732

Employers affected: Employers with fewer than 20 employees.

Eligible employees: All covered employees are eligible.

Length of coverage for employee: Three months or for the period of time during which the employee is eligible for ARRA subsidy.

Length of coverage for dependents: Three months or for the period of time during which the employee is eligible for ARRA subsidy.

Qualifying event: Any reason employee or dependent becomes ineligible for coverage, except employee's termination for gross misconduct.

Time employer has to notify employee of continuation rights: Within 15 days of termination of coverage.

Time employee has to apply: 45 days after termination of coverage.

Florida

Fla. Stat. Ann. § 627.6692

Employers affected: Employers with fewer than 20 employees.

Eligible employees: Full-time (25 or more hours per week) employees covered by employer's health insurance plan.

Length of coverage for employee: 18 months.

Length of coverage for dependents: 18 months.

Qualifying event: Layoff; reduction in

hours; termination of employment; death of employee; change in marital status.

Time employer has to notify employee of continuation rights: Carrier notifies within 14 days of learning of qualifying event (beneficiary has 63 days to notify carrier of qualifying event).

Time employee has to apply: 30 days from receipt of carrier's notice.

Georgia

Ga. Code Ann. §§ 33-24-21.1 to 33-24-21.2

Employers affected: All employers who offer group health insurance.

Eligible employees: Employees continuously insured for previous 6 months.

Length of coverage for employee: 3 months plus any part of the month remaining at termination.

Length of coverage for dependents: 3 months plus any part of the month remaining at termination.

Qualifying event: Termination of employment (except for cause).

Special situations: Employee, spouse, or former spouse, who is 60 years old and who has been covered for previous 6 months may continue coverage until eligible for Medicare. (Applies to companies with more than 20 employees; does not apply when employee quits for reasons other than health.)

Hawaii

Haw. Rev. Stat. §§ 393-11, 393-15

Employers affected: All employers required to offer health insurance (those paying a

State Health Insurance Continuation Laws (continued)

regular employee a monthly wage at least 86.67 times state hourly minimum—about $542).

Length of coverage for employee: If employee is hospitalized or prevented from working by sickness, employer must pay insurance premiums for 3 months or for as long employer continues to pay wages, whichever is longer.

Qualifying event: Employee is hospitalized or prevented by sickness from working.

Illinois

215 Ill. Comp. Stat. §§ 5/367e, 5/367.2, 5/367.2-5

Employers affected: All employers who offer group health insurance.

Eligible employees: Employees continuously insured for previous 3 months.

Length of coverage for employee: 12 months.

Length of coverage for dependents: Upon death or divorce, 2 years' coverage for spouse under 55 and eligible dependents who were on employee's plan; until eligible for Medicare or other group coverage for spouse over 55 and eligible dependents who were on employee's plan. A dependent child who has reached plan age limit or who was not already covered by plan, is also entitled to 2 years' continuation coverage.

Qualifying event: Termination of employment; reduction in hours; death of employee; divorce.

Time employer has to notify employee of continuation rights: 10 days.

Time employee has to apply: 30 days after termination or reduction in hours or receiving notice from employer, whichever is later, but not more than 60 days from termination or reduction in hours.

Iowa

Iowa Code §§ 509B.3, 509B.5

Employers affected: All employers who offer group health insurance.

Eligible employees: Employees continuously insured for previous 3 months.

Length of coverage for employee: Nine months.

Length of coverage for dependents: Nine months.

Qualifying event: Any reason employee or dependent becomes ineligible for coverage.

Time employer has to notify employee of continuation rights: 10 days after termination of coverage.

Time employee has to apply: 10 days after termination of coverage or receiving notice from employer, whichever is later, but no more than 31 days from termination of coverage.

Kansas

Kan. Stat. Ann. § 40-2209(i)

Employers affected: All employers who offer group health insurance.

Eligible employees: Employees continuously insured for previous 3 months.

Length of coverage for employee: 18 months.

Length of coverage for dependents: 18 months.

State Health Insurance Continuation Laws (continued)

Qualifying event: Any reason employee or dependent becomes ineligible for coverage.

Time employer has to notify employee of continuation rights: Reasonable notice.

Kentucky

Ky. Rev. Stat. Ann. § 304.18-110

Employers affected: All employers who offer group health insurance.

Eligible employees: Employees continuously insured for previous 3 months.

Length of coverage for employee: 18 months.

Length of coverage for dependents: 18 months.

Qualifying event: Any reason employee or dependent becomes ineligible for coverage.

Time employer has to notify employee of continuation rights: Employer must notify insurer as soon as employee's coverage ends; insurer then notifies employee.

Time employee has to apply: 31 days from receipt of insurer's notice, but no more than 90 days after termination of group coverage.

Louisiana

La. Rev. Stat. Ann. §§ 22:1045, 22:1046

Employers affected: All employers who offer group health insurance and have fewer than 20 employees.

Eligible employees: Employees continuously insured for previous 3 months.

Length of coverage for employee: 12 months.

Length of coverage for dependents: 12

months.

Qualifying event: Termination of employment; death of insured; divorce.

Time employee has to apply: By the end of the month following the month in which the qualifying event occurred.

Special situations: Surviving spouse who is 50 or older may have coverage until remarriage or eligibility for Medicare or other insurance.

Maine

Me. Rev. Stat. Ann. tit. 24-A, § 2809-A

Employers affected: All employers who offer group health insurance.

Eligible employees: Employees employed for at least 6 months.

Length of coverage for employee: One year.

Length of coverage for dependents: One year.

Qualifying event: Temporary layoff; permanent layoff if employee is eligible for federal premium assistance for laid-off employees who continue coverage; loss of employment because of a work-related injury or disease.

Time employee has to apply: 31 days from termination of coverage.

Maryland

Md. Code Ann., [Ins.] §§ 15-407 to 15-410.

Employers affected: All employers who offer group health insurance.

Eligible employees: Employees continuously insured for previous 3 months.

State Health Insurance Continuation Laws (continued)

Length of coverage for employee: 18 months.

Length of coverage for dependents: 18 months upon death of employee; upon change in marital status, 18 months or until spouse remarries or becomes eligible for other coverage.

Qualifying event: Involuntary termination of employment; death of employee; change in marital status.

Time employer has to notify employee of continuation rights: Must notify insurer within 14 days of receiving employee's continuation request.

Time employee has to apply: 45 days from termination of coverage. Employee begins application process by requesting an election of continuation notification form from employer.

Massachusetts

Mass. Gen. Laws ch. 175, §§ 110G, 110I; ch. 176J, § 9

Employers affected: All employers who offer group health insurance and have fewer than 20 employees.

Eligible employees: All covered employees are eligible.

Length of coverage for employee: 18 months; 29 months if disabled.

Length of coverage for dependents: 18 months upon termination or reduction in hours; 29 months if disabled; 36 months on divorce, death of employee, employee's eligibility for Medicare, or employer's bankruptcy.

Qualifying event: Involuntary layoff; death of insured employee; change in marital status.

Time employer has to notify employee of continuation rights: Carrier must notify beneficiary within 14 days of learning of qualifying event.

Time employee has to apply: 60 days.

Special situations: Termination due to plant closing: 90 days' coverage for employee and dependents, at the same payment terms as before closing.

Minnesota

Minn. Stat. Ann. § 62A.17

Employers affected: All employers who offer group health insurance and have 2 or more employees.

Eligible employees: All covered employees are eligible.

Length of coverage for employee: 18 months; indefinitely if employee becomes totally disabled while employed.

Length of coverage for dependents: 18 months for current spouse or child after termination of employment; divorced or widowed spouse can continue until eligible for Medicare or other group health insurance. Upon divorce or death of employee, dependent children can continue until they no longer qualify as dependents under plan.

Qualifying event: Termination of employment; reduction in hours.

Time employer has to notify employee of continuation rights: Within 14 days of termination of coverage.

State Health Insurance Continuation Laws (continued)

Time employee has to apply: 60 days from termination of coverage or receipt of employer's notice, whichever is later.

Mississippi

Miss. Code Ann. § 83-9-51

Employers affected: All employers who offer group health insurance and have fewer than 20 employees.

Eligible employees: Employees continuously insured for previous 3 months.

Length of coverage for employee: 12 months.

Length of coverage for dependents: 12 months.

Qualifying event: Termination of employment; divorce; employee's death; employee's eligibility for Medicare; loss of dependent status.

Time employer has to notify employee of continuation rights: Insurer must notify former or deceased employee's dependent child or divorced spouse of option to continue insurance within 14 days of their becoming ineligible for coverage on employee's policy.

Time employee has to apply: Employee must apply and submit payment before group coverage ends; dependents or former spouse must elect continuation coverage within 30 days of receiving insurer's notice.

Missouri

Mo. Rev. Stat. § 376.428

Employers affected: All employers who offer group health insurance and are not subject to COBRA.

Eligible employees: All employees.

Length of coverage for employee: 18 months.

Length of coverage for dependents: 18 months if eligible due to termination or reduction in hours; 36 months if eligible due to death or divorce.

Qualifying event: Termination of employment; death of employee; divorce; reduction in hours; employee's eligibility for Medicare; loss of dependent status.

Time employer has to notify employee of continuation rights: Same rules as COBRA.

Time employee has to apply: Same rules as COBRA.

Montana

Mont. Code Ann. §§ 33-22-506 to 33-22-507

Employers affected: All employers who offer group disability insurance.

Eligible employees: All employees.

Length of coverage for employee: One year (with employer's consent).

Qualifying event: Reduction in hours.

Special situations: Insurer may not discontinue benefits to child with disabilities after child exceeds age limit for dependent status.

Nebraska

Neb. Rev. Stat. §§ 44-1640 and following, 44-7406

Employers affected: Employers not subject to federal COBRA laws.

Eligible employees: All covered employees.

Length of coverage for employee: Six months.

State Health Insurance Continuation Laws (continued)

Length of coverage for dependents: One year upon death of insured employee. Subjects of domestic abuse who have lost coverage under abuser's plan and who do not qualify for COBRA may have 18 months' coverage (applies to all employers).

Qualifying event: Involuntary termination of employment (layoff due to labor dispute not considered involuntary).

Time employer has to notify employee of continuation rights: Within 10 days of termination of employment must send notice by certified mail.

Time employee has to apply: 10 days from receipt of employer's notice.

Nevada

Nev. Rev. Stat. Ann. §§ 689B.245 and following, 689B.035

Employers affected: Employers with fewer than 20 employees.

Eligible employees: Employees continuously insured for previous 12 months.

Length of coverage for employee: 18 months.

Length of coverage for dependents: 36 months; insurer cannot terminate coverage sooner because dependent child is too old to qualify as a dependent under the plan if the child is disabled.

Qualifying event: Involuntary termination of employment; involuntary reduction in hours; death of employee; divorce or legal separation; loss of dependent status; employee's eligibility for Medicare.

Time employer has to notify employee of continuation rights: 14 days after receiving

notice of employee's eligibility.

Time employee has to apply: Must notify employer within 60 days of becoming eligible for continuation coverage; must apply within 60 days after receiving employer's notice.

Special situations: While employee is on leave without pay due to disability, 12 months for employee and dependents (applies to all employers).

New Hampshire

N.H. Rev. Stat. Ann. §§ 415:18

Employers affected: All employers who offer group health insurance.

Eligible employees: All insured employees are eligible.

Length of coverage for employee: 18 months; 29 months if disabled at termination or during first 60 days of continuation coverage.

Length of coverage for dependents: 18 months; 29 months if disabled at termination or during first 60 days of continuation coverage; 36 months upon death of employee, divorce or legal separation, loss of dependent status, or employee's eligibility for Medicare.

Qualifying event: Any reason employee or dependent becomes ineligible for coverage.

Time employer has to notify employee of continuation rights: Carrier must notify beneficiary within 30 days of receiving notice of loss of coverage.

Time employee has to apply: Within 45 days of receipt of notice.

Special situations: Layoff or termination

State Health Insurance Continuation Laws (continued)

due to strike: 6 months' coverage with option to extend for an additional 12 months. Surviving, divorced, or legally separated spouse who is 55 or older may continue benefits available until eligible for Medicare or another employer-based group insurance.

New Jersey

N.J. Stat. Ann. §§ 17B:27-51.12, 17B:27A-27

Employers affected: Employers with 2 to 50 employees.

Eligible employees: Employed full time (25 or more hours).

Length of coverage for employee: 18 months; 29 months if disabled at termination or during first 60 days of continuation coverage.

Length of coverage for dependents: 18 months; 36 months upon death of employee, divorce or legal separation, loss of dependent status, or employee's eligibility for Medicare.

Qualifying event: Termination of employment; reduction in hours; change in marital status; death.

Time employer has to notify employee of continuation rights: At time of qualifying event, employer notifies employee.

Time employee has to apply: Within 30 days of qualifying event.

Special benefits: Coverage must be identical to that offered to current employees.

Special situations: Total disability: employee who has been insured for previous 3 months and employee's dependents, entitled to continuation

coverage that includes all benefits offered by group policy (applies to all employers).

New Mexico

N.M. Stat. Ann. § 59A-18-16

Employers affected: All employers who offer group health insurance.

Eligible employees: All insured employees are eligible.

Length of coverage for employee: Six months.

Length of coverage for dependents: May continue group coverage or convert to individual policies upon death of covered employee or divorce or legal separation.

Qualifying event: Termination of employment.

Time employer has to notify employee of continuation rights: Insurer or employer gives written notice at time of termination.

Time employee has to apply: 30 days after receiving notice.

New York

N.Y. Ins. Law §§ 3221(f), 3221(m)

Employers affected: All employers who offer group health insurance.

Eligible employees: All covered employees are eligible.

Length of coverage for employee: 36 months.

Length of coverage for dependents: 36 months.

Qualifying event: Termination of employment; death of employee; divorce or legal separation; loss of dependent status; employee's eligibility for Medicare.

State Health Insurance Continuation Laws (continued)

Time employee has to apply: 60 days after termination or receipt of notice, whichever is later.

North Carolina

N.C. Gen. Stat. §§ 58-53-5 to 58-53-40

Employers affected: All employers who offer group health insurance.

Eligible employees: Employees continuously insured for previous 3 months.

Length of coverage for employee: 18 months.

Length of coverage for dependents: 18 months.

Qualifying event: Termination of employment.

Time employer has to notify employee of continuation rights: Employer has option of notifying employee as part of the exit process.

Time employee has to apply: 60 days.

North Dakota

N.D. Cent. Code §§ 26.1-36-23, 26.1-36-23.1

Employers affected: All employers who offer group health insurance.

Eligible employees: Employees continuously insured for previous 3 months.

Length of coverage for employee: 39 weeks.

Length of coverage for dependents: 39 weeks; 36 months if required by divorce or annulment decree.

Qualifying event: Termination of employment; change in marital status, if divorce or annulment decree requires employee to continue coverage.

Time employee has to apply: Within 10 days of termination or of receiving notice of continuation rights, whichever is later, but no more than 31 days from termination.

Ohio

Ohio Rev. Code Ann. §§ 3923.38, 1751.53

Employers affected: All employers who offer group health insurance.

Eligible employees: Employees continuously insured for previous 3 months who were involuntarily terminated for reasons other than gross misconduct on the part of the employee.

Length of coverage for employee: 12 months.

Length of coverage for dependents: 12 months.

Qualifying event: Involuntary termination of employment.

Time employer has to notify employee of continuation rights: At termination of employment.

Time employee has to apply: Whichever is earlier: 31 days after coverage terminates; 10 days after coverage terminates if employer notified employee of continuation rights prior to termination; 10 days after employer notified employee of continuation rights, if notice was given after coverage terminated.

Oklahoma

Okla. Stat. Ann. tit. 36, § 4509

Employers affected: All employers who offer group health insurance.

State Health Insurance Continuation Laws (continued)

Eligible employees: Employees insured for at least 6 months; (all other employees and their dependents entitled to 30 days' continuation coverage).

Length of coverage for employee: 63 days for basic coverage; 6 months for major medical at the same premium rate prior to termination of coverage (only for losses or conditions that began while group policy in effect).

Length of coverage for dependents: 63 days for basic coverage; 6 months for major medical at the same premium rate prior to termination of coverage (only for losses or conditions that began while group policy in effect).

Qualifying event: Any reason coverage terminates (except employment termination for gross misconduct).

Time employer has to notify employee of continuation rights: Carrier must notify employee in writing within 30 days of receiving notice of termination of employee's coverage.

Time employee has to apply: 31 days after receipt of notice.

Special benefits: Includes maternity care for pregnancy begun while group policy was in effect.

Oregon

Or. Rev. Stat. §§ 743.600 to 743.610

Employers affected: Employers not subject to federal COBRA laws.

Eligible employees: Employees continuously insured for previous 3 months.

Length of coverage for employee: 9 months.

Length of coverage for dependents: 9 months.

Qualifying event: Termination of employment; reduction in hours; employee's eligibility for Medicare; loss of dependent status; termination of membership in group covered by policy; death of employee.

Time employee has to apply: 10 days after termination or after receiving notice of continuation rights, whichever is later.

Special situations: Surviving, divorced, or legally separated spouse who is 55 or older and dependent children entitled to continuation coverage until spouse remarries or is eligible for other coverage; must include dental, vision, or prescription drug benefits, if they were offered in original plan (applies to employers with 20 or more employees).

Pennsylvania

Pa. Stat. 40 P.S. § 764j

Employers affected: Employers that offer group health insurance and have 2 to 19 employees.

Eligible employees: Employees continuously insured for at least 3 months.

Length of coverage for employee: 9 months.

Length of coverage for dependents: 9 months.

Qualifying event: Termination of employment; reduction in hours; death of employee; change in marital status; employer's bankruptcy.

State Health Insurance Continuation Laws (continued)

Time employer has to notify employee of continuation rights: 30 days after qualifying event.

Time employee has to apply: 30 days after receiving notice.

Rhode Island

R.I. Gen. Laws §§ 27-19.1-1, 27-20.4-1 to 27-20-4-2

Employers affected: All employers who offer group health insurance.

Eligible employees: All insured employees are eligible.

Length of coverage for employee: 18 months (but not longer than continuous employment); cannot be required to pay more than one month premium at a time.

Length of coverage for dependents: 18 months (but not longer than continuous employment); cannot be required to pay more than one month premium at a time.

Qualifying event: Involuntary termination of employment; death of employee; change in marital status; permanent reduction in workforce; employer's going out of business.

Time employer has to notify employee of continuation rights: Employers must post a conspicuous notice of employee continuation rights.

Time employee has to apply: 30 days from termination of coverage.

Special situations: If right to receiving continuing health insurance is stated in the divorce judgment, divorced spouse has right to continue coverage as long as employee remains covered or until

divorced spouse remarries or becomes eligible for other group insurance. If covered employee remarries, divorced spouse must be given right to purchase an individual policy from same insurer.

South Carolina

S.C. Code Ann. § 38-71-770

Employers affected: All employers who offer group health insurance.

Eligible employees: Employees continuously insured for previous 6 months.

Length of coverage for employee: Six months (in addition to part of month remaining at termination).

Length of coverage for dependents: Six months (in addition to part of month remaining at termination).

Qualifying event: Any reason employee or dependent becomes ineligible for coverage.

Time employer has to notify employee of continuation rights: At time of termination must clearly and meaningfully advise employee of continuation rights.

South Dakota

S.D. Codified Laws Ann. §§ 58-18-7.5, 58-18-7.12; 58-18C-1

Employers affected: All employers who offer group health insurance.

Eligible employees: All covered employees.

Length of coverage for employee: 18 months; 29 months if disabled at termination or during first 60 days of continuation coverage.

Length of coverage for dependents: 18 months; 29 months if disabled at

State Health Insurance Continuation Laws (continued)

termination or during first 60 days of continuation coverage; 36 months upon death of employee, divorce or legal separation, loss of dependent status, or employee's eligibility for Medicare.

Qualifying event: Termination of employment; death of employee; divorce or legal separation; loss of dependent status; employee's eligibility for Medicare.

Special situations: When employer goes out of business: 12 months' continuation coverage available to all employees. Employer must notify employees within 10 days of termination of benefits; employees must apply within 60 days of receipt of employer's notice or within 90 days of termination of benefits if no notice given.

Tennessee

Tenn. Code Ann. § 56-7-2312

Employers affected: All employers who offer group health insurance.

Eligible employees: Employees continuously insured for previous 3 months.

Length of coverage for employee: Three months (in addition to part of month remaining at termination).

Length of coverage for dependents: 3 months (in addition to part of month remaining at termination); 15 months upon death of employee or divorce (in addition to part of month remaining at termination).

Qualifying event: Termination of employment; death of employee; change in marital status.

Special situations: Employee or dependent who is pregnant at time of termination

entitled to continuation benefits for 6 months following the end of pregnancy.

Texas

Tex. Ins. Code Ann. §§ 1251.252 to 1251.255; 1251.301 to 1251.310

Employers affected: All employers who offer group health insurance.

Eligible employees: Employees continuously insured for previous 3 months.

Length of coverage for employee: Nine months; for employees eligible for COBRA, 6 months after COBRA coverage ends.

Length of coverage for dependents: 9 months; for employees eligible for COBRA, 6 months after COBRA coverage ends. Three years for dependents with coverage due to the death or retirement of employee or severance of the family relationship.

Qualifying event: Termination of employment (except for cause); employee leaves for health reasons; severance of family relationship; retirement or death of employee.

Time employee has to apply: 60 days from termination of coverage or receiving notice of continuation rights from employer or insurer, whichever is later. Must give notice within 15 days of severance of family relationship. Within 60 days of death or retirement of family member or severance of family relationship, dependent must give notice of intent to continue coverage.

Special situations: Layoff due to a labor dispute: employee entitled to continuation benefits for duration of dispute, but no longer than 6 months.

State Health Insurance Continuation Laws (continued)

Utah

Utah Code Ann. § 31A-22-722

Employers affected: All employers who offer group health insurance.

Eligible employees: Employees continuously insured for previous 3 months.

Length of coverage for employee: 12 months.

Length of coverage for dependents: 12 months.

Qualifying event: Termination of employment; retirement; death; divorce; reduction in hours; sabbatical; disability; loss of dependent status.

Time employer has to notify employee of continuation rights: In writing within 30 days of termination of coverage.

Time employee has to apply: Within 60 days of qualifying event.

Vermont

Vt. Stat. Ann. tit. 8, §§ 4090a to 4090c

Employers affected: All employers who offer group health insurance and have fewer than 20 employees.

Eligible employees: All covered employees are eligible.

Length of coverage for employee: 18 months.

Length of coverage for dependents: 18 months.

Qualifying event: Termination of employment; reduction in hours; death of employee; change of marital status; loss of dependent status.

Time employer has to notify employee of continuation rights: Within 30 days of qualifying event.

Time employee has to apply: Within 60 days of receiving notice following the occurrence of a qualifying event.

Virginia

Va. Code Ann. §§ 38.2-3541 to 38.2-3452; 38.2-3416

Employers affected: All employers who offer group health insurance.

Eligible employees: Employees continuously insured for previous 3 months.

Length of coverage for employee: 12 months.

Length of coverage for dependents: 12 months.

Qualifying event: Any reason employee or dependent becomes ineligible for coverage; for 9-month coverage provision: involuntary termination of employment.

Time employer has to notify employee of continuation rights: 14 days from termination of coverage.

Time employee has to apply: Within 31 days of receiving notice of eligibility, but no more than 60 days following termination.

Special situations: Employee may convert to an individual policy instead of applying for continuation coverage (must apply within 31 days of termination of coverage).

Washington

Wash. Rev. Code Ann. § 48.21.075

Employers affected: All employers who offer disability insurance.

State Health Insurance Continuation Laws (continued)

Eligible employees: Insured employees on strike.

Length of coverage for employee: Six months if employee goes on strike.

Length of coverage for dependents: Six months if employee goes on strike.

Qualifying event: If employee goes on strike.

West Virginia

W.Va. Code §§ 33-16-2, 33-16-3(e)

Employers affected: Employers providing insurance for between 2 and 20 employees.

Eligible employees: All employees are eligible.

Length of coverage for employee: 18 months in case of involuntary layoff.

Qualifying event: Involuntary layoff.

Time employer has to notify employee of continuation rights: Carrier must notify beneficiaries within 15 days of receiving notice from beneficiary of intent to apply.

Time employee has to apply: 20 days to send notice of intention to apply; 30 days to apply after receiving election and premium notice.

Wisconsin

Wis. Stat. Ann. § 632.897

Employers affected: All employers who offer group health insurance.

Eligible employees: Employees continuously insured for previous 3 months.

Length of coverage for employee: 18 months (or longer at insurer's option).

Length of coverage for dependents: 18 months (or longer at insurer's option).

Qualifying event: Any reason employee or dependent becomes ineligible for coverage (except employment termination due to misconduct).

Time employer has to notify employee of continuation rights: 5 days from termination of coverage.

Time employee has to apply: 30 days after receiving employer's notice.

Wyoming

Wyo. Stat. § 26-19-113

Employers affected: Employers not subject to federal COBRA laws.

Eligible employees: Employees continuously insured for previous 3 months.

Length of coverage for employee: 12 months.

Length of coverage for dependents: 12 months.

Time employee has to apply: 31 days from termination of coverage.

Employee Polygraph Protection Act (EEPA)

Statute: 29 U.S.C. §§ 2001–2009
http://uscode.house.gov/download/pls/29C22.txt

Regulations: 29 C.F.R. § 801
www.gpo.gov/fdsys/pkg/CFR-2012-title29-vol3/pdf/CFR-2012-title29-vol3-part801.pdf

Overview of the EPPA

The Employee Polygraph Protection Act (EPPA) prohibits most private employers from requiring job applicants or current employees to take lie detector tests, except in very limited circumstances. In the few situations when an employer is legally allowed to use a *polygraph* test, the EPPA places strict limits on how the employer can use the results of the test.

The EPPA contains provisions on:

- **Polygraph use.** Employers generally may not ask or require workers to take a polygraph test, with a few narrow exceptions.
- **Test results.** Employers may use the results of a polygraph test against an employee only if additional evidence supports the decision.
- **Employees' rights.** Employees are entitled to certain information and protections before, during, and after a polygraph test.
- **Polygraph examiners.** Those who administer the test must meet certain job qualifications and render their conclusions in a prescribed format.
- **Retaliation.** Employers may not take any *adverse employment action* against employees who exercise their rights under the law.

Regulated Employers

Private employers are subject to the EPPA if they are covered by the Fair Labor Standards Act (FLSA). (For information on FLSA coverage, see Chapter 7.) The EPPA does not apply to governmental employers, whether federal, state, or local.

Foreign employers are subject to the EPPA for any actions they take within the United States relating to the administration of lie detector tests. For example, if a foreign corporation has an office in the United States and prepares paperwork in that office relating to polygraph testing, the EPPA applies to that employer, even if the polygraph tests will be conducted in a foreign country.

The EPPA also applies to any person acting in an employer's interest in relation to an employee or applicant. For example, employment placement agencies, job recruiting firms, and vocational trade schools may be subject to the EPPA for job applicants whom they refer to prospective employers. However, these referring organizations will be liable for violations of the EPPA only if they had reason to know that the prospective employer would require applicants to take a polygraph test or otherwise violate the EPPA.

Definitions

Access The opportunity to cause, or help cause, a specific economic loss or loss of a controlled substance. An employee need not have regular contact with property to have access to it. If the employee is able to get at the property (by working in its vicinity or knowing the combination to a safe where it is kept, for example), the employee has access, even if the employee's job does not require contact with or use of the property.

Adverse employment action Firing, disciplining, discriminating against, or refusing to hire or promote an applicant or current employee.

Counterintelligence Information gathered and activities conducted to protect against espionage and other clandestine intelligence activities, sabotage, terrorism, or assassinations conducted by or on behalf of foreign governments, foreign or domestic organizations, or people.

Currency, negotiable securities, and precious commodities Assets that are typically handled by, protected for, and transported between commercial and financial institutions. Also includes cash assets handled by casinos, racetracks, lotteries, and other businesses in which cash constitutes the inventory or stock in trade; and gold, silver, or diamonds.

Direct access Contact with or responsibility for a controlled substance, as part of an employee's job responsibilities. An employee whose job requires dispensing, obtaining, manufacturing, storing, testing, distributing, packaging, transporting, taking inventory of, providing security for, or prescribing controlled substances has direct access, as long as the employee's job duties include either physical contact with the substances or the opportunity to get possession of such substances.

Economic loss or injury Financial harm to an employer's business, including loss due to theft, embezzlement, misappropriation of trade secrets, or sabotage of an employer's property; use of an employer's business to commit a crime, such as money laundering or check kiting; or theft or harm to property belonging to a third party, if the employer is responsible for protecting that property. Examples of losses that do not fall within this definition are theft of a client's property (unless the employer is responsible for that property), threatened or potential

Definitions (continued)

harm, losses caused by legal or unintentional conduct (for example, damages caused by a workplace accident), or theft of another employee's property.

Facilities, materials, or operations having a significant impact on the national security of the United States or the health or safety of any state or political subdivision thereof Facilities, operations, or materials that are targets of acts of sabotage, espionage, terrorism, or other destructive or illegal acts, where the consequences of such destructive acts could significantly affect the general public's safety or health or national security. Examples include government office buildings, prisons, nuclear or electric power facilities, the public water supply, shipment or storage of toxic waste, public transportation, public schools, military posts or laboratories, factories or plants used to produce, store, or process products related to the national defense, factories that produce hazardous chemicals, public and private energy supplies and reserves, the Federal Reserve System, and hospitals.

Lie detector Any mechanical or electrical device that is used, or the results of which are used, for the purpose of rendering a diagnostic opinion about whether a person is telling the truth. Polygraphs, deceptographs, voice stress analyzers, and psychological stress evaluators all constitute lie detectors under the EPPA. However, medical tests to determine whether an employee has taken drugs or alcohol, written or oral honesty tests, and handwriting tests are not considered lie detector tests and are not subject to the EPPA's restrictions.

Ongoing investigation An existing investigation into a specific incident of economic loss the employer has suffered.

Polygraph An instrument that (1) records continuously, visually, permanently, and simultaneously any changes in cardiovascular, respiratory, and electro-dermal patterns and (2) is used, or the results of which are used, for the purpose of rendering an opinion about whether a person is honest or dishonest.

Primary business purpose For purposes of the security services exception (see the "Exceptions" sections under "Polygraph Use," below), an employer's primary business purpose is providing security services if at least 50% of its annual dollar volume of business derives from that activity.

Definitions (continued)

Proprietary information Business assets such as trade secrets, manufacturing processes, research and development data, and cost or pricing data.

Reasonable suspicion A demonstrable factual basis for believing that a particular employee was involved in, or responsible for, an economic loss or injury to the employer's business. In deciding whether an employer had a reasonable suspicion for testing a particular employee, courts will consider all of the circumstances, including reliable information from coworkers, an employee's demeanor or conduct, or inconsistencies between facts or statements that come up during the investigation. Generally, an employee's opportunity to cause the loss will not be enough, on its own, to create reasonable suspicion.

Did You Know ...

- Polygraphs work by using sensors to measure things like pulse, breathing rate, blood pressure, and perspiration while the examinee is asked questions. Significant changes (typically, increases) in any of these vital signs while the employee is responding to a particular question are thought to indicate that the examinee is lying.
- Most Fortune 1000 companies use some form of psychological or personality testing in the hiring process. Some experts believe that use of these types of tests increased after the EPPA essentially prohibited the use of polygraph tests in hiring.

Covered Workers

The EPPA covers all job applicants and employees who work for a regulated private employer. It does not cover federal, state, or local government employees.

The EPPA also protects former employees from discrimination. For example, if an employee decides to quit rather than take a polygraph test, an employer may not threaten or take negative action against that person (by attempting to prevent him or her from getting another job, for example).

What's Prohibited

Employers are prohibited from requiring applicants or employees to take lie detector tests, except in very limited circumstances. Those employers who are legally allowed to conduct polygraph tests may not rely on the results to take an adverse employment action against an employee unless they have additional evidence of the employee's guilt.

What's Required

Employers who are legally allowed to administer polygraph tests must carefully observe the tested employee's rights throughout the process by, among other things, providing a written statement of the nature of and reasons for the test. Employers must use polygraph examiners who meet certain qualifications and requirements as spelled out in the law.

Employers are also required to post a notice in the workplace (prepared by the Department of Labor) describing the EPPA's provisions. (See "Agency Resources," below.)

Exceptions

There are several exceptions to the EPPA's prohibition on private employers' use of lie detector tests. These exceptions are discussed in "Major Provisions of the EPPA," below.

Major Provisions of the EPPA

Polygraph Use

In general, the EPPA prohibits private employers from requiring any applicant or current employee to take a lie detector test. The law also prohibits private employers from firing, disciplining, discriminating against, or refusing to hire or promote any applicant or current employee for refusing to take a lie detector test.

However, the law lists several circumstances in which certain private employers may require employees or applicants to take polygraph tests. (See "Exceptions: Private Employers," below.) In addition, the law allows certain public employers to administer lie detector tests to employees of private employers. (See "Exceptions: Public Employers Testing Private Employees," below.)

Key Facts: Polygraph Use

- Generally, employers cannot require or ask an employee or applicant to take a lie detector test, nor can they discipline, fire, or refuse to hire an employee for refusing to take one.
- Public officials may require the employees of certain private employers to submit to lie detector tests, in limited circumstances.
- Private companies that deal with controlled substances or provide security services are allowed to require certain applicants and employees to take a polygraph test, in specified circumstances.
- A private company may require an employee to take a polygraph test as part of an ongoing investigation of an economic loss or injury, but only if a number of conditions are met.

Regulated Employers

All regulated employers are subject to these provisions unless they fall within one of the law's exceptions.

Covered Workers

All covered workers are subject to these provisions.

What's Prohibited

Unless they fall within one of the exceptions outlined below, employers may not, directly or indirectly, require, suggest, request, or cause any applicant or employee to take or submit to a lie detector test.

What's Required

An employer who falls within one of the law's exceptions (see "Exceptions: Public Employers Testing Private Employees" and "Exceptions: Private Employers," below) and wishes to request or administer a test still has to meet the law's other requirements, as explained below.

Exceptions: Public Employers Testing Private Employees

There are two circumstances in which federal, state, or local authorities can require private employees to take lie detector tests. In these circumstances, the private employers for whom these employees work cannot be held liable for the testing under the EPPA.

Law Enforcement Exception

If a private employer reports a theft or another economic loss to law enforcement authorities, and those authorities deem it necessary in the normal course of investigating the incident to administer a polygraph test to a suspected employee, that testing is not prohibited by the EPPA. The employer may cooperate with law enforcement officials in the investigation—for example, by allowing the police to test a suspect on the employer's premises or letting the employee leave work early to take a polygraph test at the police station. However, if an employer participates actively in the testing, by administering the test itself or by reimbursing police for the costs of testing, the employer will be subject to the EPPA—and the employer will have violated the law unless one of the private employer exceptions (see "Exceptions: Private Employers," below) applies.

Federal Government Counterintelligence Exception

If a private employer does work for the federal government, the government may, in the performance of its *counterintelligence* functions, require its employees to take lie detector tests. This exception allows the government to require lie detector tests of:

- any expert or consultant under contract to, or any employee of any contractor of, the Department of Defense
- any expert or consultant under contract to, or any employee of any contractor of, the Department of Energy in connection with its atomic energy defense activities
- anyone assigned or detailed to, any expert or consultant under contract to, any employee of a contractor of, or any person assigned to, a space where sensitive cryptologic information is produced, processed, or stored for the National Security Agency, Defense Intelligence Agency, National Imagery and Mapping Agency, or the Central Intelligence Agency
- any expert or consultant under contract to, or any employee of any contractor of, any department, agency, or program of the federal government, if that person's duties involve access to information that has been classified as top secret or designated as being within a special access program, and
- any employee of any contractor to the Federal Bureau of Investigation, if that employee actually performs any work under the contract.

Exceptions: Private Employers

There are three exceptions available to private employers. These exceptions apply only to polygraph tests. Private employers are always prohibited from administering lie detector tests other than polygraph tests, even if one of the exceptions applies.

Controlled Substances Exception

Employers who are authorized by the Drug Enforcement Administration (DEA) to manufacture, distribute, or dispense specified controlled substances (those listed in Schedule I, II, III, or IV of the Controlled Substances Act (21 U.S.C. § 812)) may require polygraph testing only of:

- job applicants who would, if hired, have *direct access* to the manufacture, storage, distribution, or sale of a controlled substance, and
- current employees in connection with an *ongoing investigation* of criminal or other misconduct involving actual or potential loss or injury to the manufacture, distribution, or dispensing of a controlled substance, but only if the employee had access to the person or property that is the subject of the investigation.

This exception applies only to employers who have DEA authorization to deal in these controlled substances. It does not apply to other employers, even if their employees may come in contact with controlled substances as a normal part of their jobs, as might be true of truck drivers or warehouse employees.

The term "job applicants," as used in this exception, might include current employees who apply for transfer or promotion to a different position. For example, if an employee who currently works in a position with no direct access to controlled substances applies for a position that provides such access, that employee can be required to take a polygraph test as a job applicant under the rule.

Security Services Exception

Certain private employers that provide security services may require job applicants to take a polygraph test. This exception applies only if:

- the employer's *primary business purpose* is providing armored car personnel; personnel who design, install, and maintain security alarm systems; or other uniformed or plainclothes security personnel
- the employer's function includes protecting (1) *facilities, materials, or operations having a significant impact on the national security of the United States or the health or safety of any state or political subdivision thereof*; or (2) *currency, negotiable securities, precious commodities, or proprietary information*, and
- the applicant tested would be employed to protect the facilities, materials, operations, or assets listed above. An applicant for a position that would allow the opportunity to cause or participate in a security breach is covered by this requirement.

The term "job applicants," as used in this exception, might include current employees who apply for transfer or promotion to a different position. For example, if an employee who currently provides security for an appliance store applies for a position guarding a nuclear facility, that employee can be required to take a polygraph test under the rule applicable to job applicants.

Ongoing Investigation Exception

A private employer may ask an employee to submit to a polygraph test if all of the following conditions are met:

- The test is administered in connection with an ongoing investigation of *economic loss or injury* to the employer's business.
- The employee had access to the property that is the subject of the investigation.
- The employer has a *reasonable suspicion* that the employee was involved in the incident or activity under investigation.
- The employer gives the employee a written statement, at least two working days before the test, that:
  - describes the specific incident or activity under investigation and the basis for testing the employee
  - identifies the specific economic loss or injury to the employer's business
  - states that the employee had access to the property that is the subject of the investigation
  - describes the basis for the employer's reasonable suspicion of the employee, and
  - is signed by someone authorized to legally bind the employer, such as an officer or director of the company.

This statement must be signed by the employee and must indicate the time and date when the employee received the statement.

An employer may not request polygraph testing to determine whether any economic losses have been incurred; testing is allowed only in response to a specific, identifiable incident of loss. Nor may employers request polygraph testing to investigate a continuing loss. For example, regular inventory shortages that occur all the time in a warehouse would not be a sufficiently specific incident to allow testing.

Test Results

Unless one of the exceptions listed under "Polygraph Use," above, applies, employers may not:

- use, accept, refer to, or inquire about the results of any lie detector test taken by an applicant or a current employee, or
- take any adverse employment action against an employee or applicant on the basis of the results of a lie detector test or the employee's or applicant's refusal to take a lie detector test.

Key Facts: Test Results

- An employer may not use or ask about the results of a polygraph test unless one of the exceptions listed under "Polygraph Use," above, applies.
- Even if one of the exceptions applies, an employer may not decide to fire, refuse to hire, or discipline an employee based solely on the polygraph test results. The employer must have additional evidence supporting its decision; the type of evidence necessary depends on the exception that applies.

If one of the exceptions applies, employers may use the results of a polygraph test—or an employee's refusal to take a properly supported polygraph test—as one basis for taking an adverse employment action against the employee. However, the employer must administer the test properly, by following the requirements described in "Employees' Rights" and "Polygraph Examiners," below.

And the employer may not rely solely on the results of the polygraph test or the employee's refusal to take it. An employer must have additional reasons for the decision; what's required depends on the exception that applies.

Ongoing Investigation Exception

An employer may not use the results of a polygraph test administered under the ongoing investigation exception or the employee's refusal to take such a test as the basis for an adverse employment action against an employee without additional supporting evidence. Such evidence might include:

- evidence showing that the employee had access to the property that is the subject of the investigation, and
- evidence creating a reasonable suspicion that the employee was involved in the incident or activity under investigation.

Admissions or statements made by the employee before, during, or after the polygraph test may also create sufficient additional supporting evidence to act on the results of the test.

Controlled Substances and Security Services Exceptions

An employer may not use the results of a polygraph test administered under the controlled substances or security services exceptions, or the employee's refusal to take such a test, as the sole basis for an adverse employment action against an employee. An employer must have another reason for the decision, supported by evidence. Such a reason might include:

- traditional factors on which employers rely to make job decisions, such as job performance or prior employment experience, or
- admissions or statements made by the employee before, during, or after a polygraph test.

Employees' Rights

Employers may rely on the results of a polygraph test only if they meet a long list of requirements designed to protect an employee's rights before, during, and after a polygraph test. Some of these requirements (for example, those about the manner in which the test is conducted) rely on the cooperation of the polygraph examiner. In these cases, the employer is responsible for ensuring that the examiner does not violate the employee's rights.

Key Facts: Employees' Rights

- Before a polygraph test, the employee who will be tested is entitled to written information about the test and a written notice detailing the employee's rights. The employee is also entitled to see every question that will be asked.
- During a polygraph test, the employee has the right to end the test at any time. In addition, the employee cannot be asked any questions that were not revealed in advance, any questions that are unnecessarily intrusive or degrading, or questions about religious beliefs, sexual activities, or certain other matters.
- If an employer plans to take action based on the results of the polygraph test, it must first interview the employee further and provide certain written information about the test questions and results.
- An employer may disclose the results of the test only to the employee; a court, mediator, agency, or other fact finder pursuant to a court order; or a law enforcement agency, if the employee admitted committing a crime.

Pretest Rights

The pretest phase of a polygraph test refers to the period of questioning and other methods of preparing an employee to take the test. During this phase, the employee must receive:

- written notice, in a language the employee understands, of the date, time, and location of the test, and the employee's right to consult with an attorney or an employee representative before each phase of the test. The notice must be signed by the employee and must indicate the date and time the employee received it. The employee must receive this notice two working days before the test.
- written and oral notice of the nature and characteristics of the polygraph instrument and examination, including an explanation of how the polygraph instrument works and the procedure to be used during the examination
- the opportunity to review, in writing, all questions the examiner will ask during the test
- written notice, in a language the employee understands, indicating:
  - whether the testing area contains a two-way mirror, camera, or another device to observe the employee
  - whether any other device (such as a tape recorder or another monitoring instrument) will be used during the test
  - that the employee has a right to record the test, if the employer is told of the recording
  - that the employee may stop the test at any time
  - that the employee has the right, and will be given the opportunity, to review all questions to be asked during the test
  - that the employee may not be asked questions in a manner that is degrading or needlessly intrusive
  - that the employee may not be asked any questions about religious beliefs or opinions, beliefs regarding racial matters, political beliefs or affiliations, matters of sexual behavior, or beliefs, affiliations, opinions, or lawful activities relating to unions or labor organizations
  - that the test may not be conducted if a physician provides sufficient written evidence that the employee suffers from a medical or psychological condition or is undergoing treatment that might cause abnormal responses during the test

- that the test cannot be required as a condition of employment
- that the employer may not take an adverse employment action against the employee based on the results of the test, or the employee's refusal to take the test, without additional evidence to support the action
- if the test is given under the ongoing investigation exception, that the additional evidence required to support the adverse employment action may include evidence that the employee had access to the property and evidence supporting the employer's reasonable suspicion that the employee was involved in the incident
- that any statements the employee makes before, during, or after the test may provide additional evidence to support an adverse employment action
- that any admission of criminal conduct may be transmitted to an appropriate government law enforcement agency
- that information gained from the test may be disclosed by the examiner or the employer only to: the employee; any person whom the employee specifically authorizes, in writing, to receive the results; the employer; a court, governmental agency, arbitrator, or mediator, pursuant to court order; an official of the U.S. Department of Labor, if the employee authorizes such disclosure in writing; or an appropriate governmental law enforcement agency, if the information is an admission of criminal conduct
- a description of the employee's legal rights if the employer violates the law
- that the employee has the right to consult with legal counsel or another representative during every phase of the test, although that person may be excluded from the room when the test is actually conducted, and
- that the employee may not give up his or her rights under the EPPA, voluntarily or involuntarily, by contract or otherwise, except as part of a written settlement agreement.

The employer must give the employee this notice and read the notice to the employee. The Department of Labor has prepared a standard form that the employer can use to fulfill this requirement. (See "Agency Resources," below, for more information.)

Rights During the Test

During the polygraph test, the employee has the right:

- to end the test at any time
- not to be asked questions in a manner designed to degrade or needlessly intrude on the employee
- not to be asked any question about (1) religious beliefs or affiliations, (2) beliefs or opinions regarding racial matters, (3) political beliefs or affiliations, (4) any matter relating to sexual behavior, or (5) beliefs, affiliations, opinions, or lawful activities regarding unions or labor organizations
- not to be tested if a physician provides sufficient written evidence that the employee is suffering from a medical or psychological condition or is undergoing treatment that might cause abnormal responses to the test
- to be asked only questions that were presented to the employee for review, in writing, before the test, and
- to a test of no less than 90 minutes in length (unless the employee ends the test before it is complete).

Rights After the Test

Before taking any adverse employment action based on the results of a test, the employer must:

- interview the employee further, based on the results of the test, and
- give the employee (1) a written copy of any opinion or conclusion rendered as a result of the test, and (2) a copy of the questions asked during the test and the corresponding charted responses (copies of the charts of the entire examination, showing the employee's physiological responses to each question).

Disclosure of Test Results

Although the employee who takes the test can disclose the results as he or she sees fit, the EPPA strictly limits the circumstances in which an employer or polygraph examiner may reveal test results.

An examiner may disclose results only to:

- the employee or any other person whom the employee authorizes, in writing, to receive the results

- the employer that requested the test, or
- any court, governmental agency, arbitrator, or mediator, pursuant to a court order requiring such disclosure.

An employer may disclose polygraph results only to:

- the employee or any other person whom the employee authorizes, in writing, to receive the results
- any court, governmental agency, arbitrator, or mediator, pursuant to a court order requiring such disclosure, or
- a governmental law enforcement agency, if the disclosed information is an admission of criminal conduct.

Polygraph Examiners

Even if an employer is entitled to request or conduct a polygraph test pursuant to one of the exceptions listed under "Polygraph Use," above, that test will violate the EPPA unless the employer uses a polygraph examiner who meets certain qualifications and requirements. The examiner must:

- have a valid, current license, if required in the state where the polygraph will be conducted (over half the states require licenses)
- maintain a minimum $50,000 bond or an equivalent amount of professional liability coverage
- administer no more than five polygraph tests in any single day on which a test or tests subject to the EPPA is conducted (not including any tests terminated voluntarily by the employee), and
- administer no polygraph examination that is less than 90 minutes long (unless the test is terminated voluntarily by the employee).

In addition, if the examiner renders any opinion or conclusion regarding the employee's truthfulness or deception, the report must:

- be in writing
- be based solely on an analysis of polygraph test charts
- not contain information other than admissions, information, case facts, and interpretation of the charts relevant to the purpose and stated objectives of the test, and
- not include any recommendation about the employment of the employee.

The examiner must also retain all opinions, reports, charts, written questions, lists, and other records relating to the test (including written notices signed by the employee and electronic recordings of the test) for at least three years after the test is conducted.

Key Facts: Polygraph Examiners

- If one of the exceptions to the EPPA allows an employer to require or request a polygraph test, the employer must use a polygraph examiner who meets certain requirements. The examiner must be licensed, if the state where he or she does business requires it.
- If the examiner gives an opinion about whether the employee was telling the truth, the examiner must include specified information to support that opinion in the report.
- Examiners are legally required to retain certain records of polygraph tests for up to three years.

Retaliation

An employer may not take, or threaten to take, an adverse employment action against an employee or job applicant for exercising rights granted the by EPPA (by, for example, filing an administrative complaint or testifying in a lawsuit).

Key Facts: Retaliation

- An employer may not fire, discipline, refuse to hire, or otherwise take adverse action against an employee or applicant for exercising his or her EPPA rights.
- An employer may not take adverse employment action against an employee who asserts his or her EPPA rights, including the right not to take or be asked to take a polygraph test.

How the EPPA Is Enforced

Individual Complaints

An employee who wishes to file a complaint under the EPPA has two options. The employee may make a complaint to the Wage and Hour Division of the Department of Labor (DOL). (See Appendix A for contact information.) Or, the employee may bypass the DOL and file a lawsuit in state court or in federal district court. The employee must file this lawsuit within three years of the date the employer violated the EPPA.

Agency Enforcement

If an employee files a complaint with the DOL, the agency may choose to investigate the employer—particularly if the employer conducts a lot of polygraph tests, which raises the possibility that many employees' rights have been violated.

DOL investigations are similar to audits. An investigator may contact the employer ahead of time or may simply show up at the workplace. The investigator will examine the employer's records and interview employees who may have information about the complaint. Once the investigation is complete, the investigator will meet with the employer to try to resolve any problems the investigation uncovered. The investigator will tell the employer whether it violated the law and how it can correct those violations—for example, by reinstating an employee who was fired illegally for refusing to take a polygraph test or by immediately ceasing to require all applicants to take a polygraph test.

If the employer refuses to comply, the secretary of labor can file a lawsuit in federal district court on behalf of the employees whose rights were violated.

The secretary may also impose civil penalties of up to $10,000 against the employer—these penalties are assessed in an administrative hearing process, not a lawsuit. However, if the employer objects to the penalties, it has the right to appeal to federal district court.

Complying With the EPPA

Deadlines

If one of the exceptions to the EPPA applies and the employer is entitled to administer a polygraph test, the employee is entitled to receive written notice of the test, including the detailed information listed under "Employee Rights," above, *two working days* before the test. The employer or the polygraph examiner may provide this notice.

Reporting Requirements

The EPPA imposes no reporting requirements.

Posting Requirements

Employers are required to post a notice (prepared by the DOL) in the workplace describing the EPPA's provisions. Employers must post this notice in a prominent spot in every business location, where it can be easily seen and read by employees and job applicants. See "Agency Resources," below, for information on downloading this poster.

Record-Keeping Requirements

Employers must keep the following records for at least three years from the date the polygraph test is conducted (or from the date the employer asks the employee to take the test, if no test is ever conducted):

- a copy of the employer's written notice to the polygraph examiner identifying the person(s) to be tested
- copies of all opinions, reports, or other records that the polygraph examiner gives to the employer
- if the test is administered under the ongoing investigation exception, a copy of the statement to the employee setting forth the specific incident under investigation and the basis for testing that particular employee, and

- if the test is administered to a current employee under the controlled substances exception, records specifically identifying the loss or injury under investigation and the nature of the employee's access to the person or property investigated.

The employer must make these records available to the secretary of labor or an investigator from the DOL within 72 hours after they are requested.

Penalties

Employers who violate the EPPA may be required to:
- take action to remedy the violation, such as hiring, promoting, or reinstating a worker who was wrongfully asked or required to take a polygraph test, or who was improperly subjected to an adverse employment action in violation of the law
- pay the worker for any benefits or wages lost because of the employer's violation, and
- pay the worker's attorneys' fees and court costs.

The language of the EPPA does not specifically allow for compensatory damages (money awarded to the plaintiff for emotional distress, pain and suffering, and other injuries that cannot be remedied with back pay). However, a couple of courts have awarded compensatory damages to successful plaintiffs. These courts have also indicated that punitive damages (a money award intended to punish the employer for particularly egregious misconduct) might be available under the law. These issues are still undecided because there are so few reported lawsuits interpreting the EPPA.

As the result of an audit by the DOL, the secretary of labor may impose civil penalties of up to $10,000 against an employer that violates the EPPA. These penalties are assessed in an administrative hearing process, not a lawsuit. If the employer objects to the penalties, it has the right to appeal to federal district court.

Agency Resources

- The DOL's poster on the EPPA (in English or Spanish)

  Notice: Employee Polygraph Protection Act
  www.dol.gov/whd/regs/compliance/posters/eppa.htm

- A fact sheet on the EPPA's provisions

  - *Fact Sheet #36: The Employee Polygraph Protection Act of 1988*
  - www.dol.gov/whd/regs/compliance/whdfs36.htm

- A fact sheet explaining DOL audits

  Fact Sheet #44: Visits to Employers
  www.dol.gov/whd/regs/compliance/whdfs44.htm

- A list of the addresses and telephone numbers of local offices of the Wage and Hour Division

  District Office Locations
  www.dol.gov/whd/america2.htm

State Laws Relating to Polygraph Tests

Many states also have laws that prohibit or restrict employers from using lie detector tests in connection with hiring or employment. Some of these laws go further than the EPPA and prohibit employers from even suggesting such a test. The chart below summarizes state polygraph testing laws. If you need more information, contact your state department of labor (Appendix A provides contact information).

State Employee Polygraph Examination Laws

Alaska

Alaska Stat. § 23.10.037

Employers covered: All

What's prohibited: Employer may not suggest, request, or require that employee or applicant take a lie detector test.

California

Cal. Lab. Code § 432.2

Employers covered: All

What's prohibited: Employer may not demand or require that employee or applicant take a lie detector test.

What's allowed: Employer may request a test, if applicant is advised in writing of legal right to refuse to take it.

Connecticut

Conn. Gen. Stat. Ann. § 31-51g

Employers covered: All, including employment agencies

What's prohibited: Employer may not request or require that employee or applicant take a lie detector test.

Delaware

Del. Code Ann. tit. 19, § 704

Employers covered: All

What's prohibited: Employer may not suggest, request, or require that employee or applicant take a lie detector test in order to obtain or continue employment.

District of Columbia

D.C. Code Ann. §§ 32-901 to 32-903

Employers covered: All

What's prohibited: Employer may not administer, have administered, use, or accept the results of any polygraph examination.

Hawaii

Haw. Rev. Stat. § 378-26.5

Employers covered: All

What's prohibited: Employer may not require employee or applicant to take lie detector test.

What's allowed: Employer may request test if current or prospective employee is told, orally and in writing, that refusing to take test will not result in being fired or hurt chances of getting job.

Idaho

Idaho Code § 44-903

Employers covered: All

What's prohibited: Employer may not require an employee or applicant to take a lie detector test.

Illinois

225 Ill. Comp. Stat. § 430/14.1

Employers covered: All

What's prohibited: Unless directly related to employment, examination may not include questions about:
- political, religious, or labor-related beliefs, affiliations, or lawful activities
- beliefs or opinions on racial matters, or
- sexual preferences or activity.

Iowa

Iowa Code § 730.4

State Employee Polygraph Examination Laws (continued)

Employers covered: All

What's prohibited: Employer may not request, require, administer, or attempt or threaten to administer a lie detector test; may not request or require that employee or applicant sign waiver of any action prohibited by this law.

Maine

Me. Rev. Stat. Ann. tit. 32, § 7166

Employers covered: All

What's prohibited: Employer may not request, require, suggest, or administer a lie detector test.

What's allowed: Employee may voluntarily request a test if these conditions are met:
- results cannot be used against employee
- employer must give employee a copy of the law when employee requests test, and
- test must be recorded or employee's witness must be present during the test, or both.

Maryland

Md. Code Ann. [Lab. & Empl.] § 3-702

Employers covered: All

What's prohibited: Employer may not require or demand that employee or applicant take a lie detector test.

What's required: All employment applications must include specified notice that no person can be required to take a lie detector test as a condition of obtaining or continuing employment and must include space for applicant to sign and acknowledge notice.

Massachusetts

Mass. Gen. Laws ch. 149, § 19B

Employers covered: All

What's prohibited: Employer may not request, require, or administer a lie detector test.

What's required: All employment applications must include specified notice that it is unlawful to require a lie detector test as a condition of obtaining or continuing employment.

Michigan

Mich. Comp. Laws §§ 37.203, 338.1719

Employers covered: All

What's prohibited: Employer may not request, require, administer, or attempt or threaten to administer a lie detector test; may not request or require that employee or applicant sign waiver of any action prohibited by this law.

What's allowed: Employee may voluntarily request a test if these conditions are met:
- before taking test employee is given copy of the law
- employee is given copies of test results and reports
- no questions asked about sexual practices; marital relationship; or political, religious, or labor or union affiliations, unless questions are relevant to areas under examination, and
- examiner informs employee:
  - of all questions that will be asked
  - of right to accept, refuse, or stop test at any time
  - that employee is not required to

State Employee Polygraph Examination Laws (continued)

answer questions or give information, and

- that information volunteered could be used against employee or made available to employer, unless otherwise agreed to in writing.

Minnesota

Minn. Stat. Ann. §§ 181.75, 181.76

Employers covered: All

What's prohibited: Employer may not directly or indirectly solicit or require an applicant or employee to take a lie detector test.

What's allowed: Employee may request a test, but only if employer informs employee that test is voluntary. Results of voluntary test may be given only to those authorized by employee.

Montana

Mont. Code Ann. § 39-2-304

What's prohibited: Employer may not require an employee or applicant to take a lie detector test.

Nebraska

Neb. Rev. Stat. § 81-1932

Employers covered: All

What's prohibited: Employer may not require an employee or applicant to take a lie detector test.

What's allowed: Employer may request that test be taken, but only if these conditions are met:

- No questions are asked about sexual practices; marital relationship; or

political, religious, or labor or union affiliations.

- An examinee is given written and oral notice that test is voluntary and may be discontinued at any time.
- An examinee signs a form stating that test is being taken voluntarily.
- Prospective employees are asked only job-related questions and are not singled out for testing in a discriminatory manner.
- An employee is requested to take test only in connection with a specific investigation.
- Results of a test are not the sole reason for terminating employment.
- All questions and responses are kept on file by the employer for at least one year.

Nevada

Nev. Rev. Stat. Ann. §§ 613.480 to 613.510

Employers covered: All

Exceptions: Manufacturers or distributors of controlled substances; providers or designers of security systems and other security personnel; ongoing investigation.

What's prohibited: Employer may not directly or indirectly require, request, suggest, or cause a lie detector test to be taken; may not use, accept, refer to, or ask about the results of any test. May not take adverse employment action solely on the basis of test results or a refusal to take test.

What's allowed: Nevada law allows testing in the same limited circumstances as the federal EPPA, with similar rules and restrictions on when and how the test is given.

State Employee Polygraph Examination Laws (continued)

New Jersey

N.J. Stat. Ann. § 2C:40A-1

Employers covered: All

Exceptions: Employers that deal with controlled, dangerous substances

What's prohibited: Employer may not influence, request, or require applicant or employee to take a lie detector test.

What's allowed: Employers who are allowed to test must observe these rules:

- The job must require direct access to controlled substance.
- The test is limited to preceding 5 years.
- Questions must be work related or pertain to improper handling, use, or illegal sale of legally distributed controlled dangerous substances.
- The test taker has right to legal counsel.
- The written copy of test results must be given to test taker upon request.
- Test information may not be released to any other employer or person.
- An employee or prospective employee must be informed of right to present results of a second independently administered test prior to any personnel decision being made.

New York

N.Y. Lab. Law §§ 733 to 739

Employers covered: All

What's prohibited: Employer may not require, request, suggest, permit, or use results of a lie detector test.

Oregon

Or. Rev. Stat. Ann. §§ 659.840, 659A.300

Employers covered: All

What's prohibited: Employer may not require an employee or applicant to take a lie detector test.

Pennsylvania

18 Pa. Cons. Stat. Ann. § 7321

Employers covered: All

Exceptions: Employers with positions that have access to narcotics or dangerous drugs.

What's prohibited: Employer may not require an employee or applicant to take a lie detector test.

Rhode Island

R.I. Gen. Laws §§ 28-6.1-1 to 28-6.1-4

Employers covered: All

What's prohibited: Employer may not request, require, subject, nor directly or indirectly cause an employee or applicant to take a lie detector test.

Tennessee

Tenn. Code Ann. §§ 62-27-123, 62-27-128

Employers covered: All

What's prohibited: Employer may not take any personnel action based solely upon the results of a polygraph examination. No questions may be asked about:

- religious, political, or labor-related beliefs, affiliations, or lawful activities
- beliefs or opinions about racial matters
- sexual preferences or activities
- disabilities covered by the Americans with Disabilities Act, or
- activities that occurred more than five years before the examination, except

State Employee Polygraph Examination Laws (continued)

for felony convictions and violations of the state drug control act.

(Exception: Examination is part of an investigation of illegal activity in one of the above subject areas.)

What's required: Prospective examinee must be told if examiner is a law enforcement or court official and informed that any illegal activity disclosed may be used against examinee. Must receive and sign a written notice of rights including:

- right to refuse to take the test or to answer any question
- right to terminate examination at any time
- right to request an audio recording of examination and pretest interview, and
- right to request examination results within 30 days of taking it.

Vermont

Vt. Stat. Ann. tit. 21, §§ 494 to 494e

Employers covered: All

Exceptions: Employers whose primary business is sale of precious metals, gems, or jewelry; whose business includes manufacture or sale of regulated drugs and applicant's position requires contact with drugs; employers authorized by federal law to require a test.

What's prohibited: Employer may not request, require, administer, or attempt or threaten to administer a lie detector test. May not request or require that employee or applicant sign waiver of any action prohibited by state law. May not discriminate against employee who files a complaint of violation of laws.

When testing is allowed, no questions may be asked about:

- political, religious, or labor union affiliations
- sexual practices, social habits, or marital relationship (unless clearly related to job performance), or
- any matters unrelated to job performance.

What's required: Prior to taking test examinee must receive a copy of state laws and a copy of all questions to be asked. Must be told that any information disclosed could be used against examinee or made available to employer, unless there is a signed written agreement to the contrary. Examinee must be informed of rights including:

- right to accept or refuse to take examination
- right to refuse to answer any questions or give any information
- right to stop examination at any time, and
- right to a copy of examination results and of any reports given to employer.

Virginia

Va. Code Ann. § 40.1-51.4:3

Employers covered: All

What's prohibited: Employer may not require an applicant to answer questions about sexual activities in a polygraph test, unless the sexual activity resulted in a conviction for violation of state law.

What's required: Any record of examination results must be destroyed or maintained on a confidential basis, open

State Employee Polygraph Examination Laws (continued)

to inspection only upon agreement of the employee.

Washington

Wash. Rev. Code Ann. § 49.44.120

Employers covered: All

Exceptions: Applicant or employee who manufactures, distributes, or dispenses controlled substances, or who works in a sensitive position directly involving national security.

What's prohibited: Employer may not require, directly or indirectly, that an employee or applicant take a lie detector test.

West Virginia

W.Va. Code §§ 21-5-5a to 21-5-5d

Employers covered: All

Exceptions: Employees or applicants with direct access to controlled substances.

What's prohibited: Employer may not require or request, directly or indirectly, that an employee or applicant take a lie

detector test; may not knowingly use the results of a lie detector test.

Wisconsin

Wis. Stat. Ann. § 111.37

Employers covered: All

Exceptions: Manufacturers or distributors of controlled substances; providers or designers of security systems and other security personnel; ongoing investigation.

What's prohibited: Employer may not directly or indirectly require, request, suggest, or cause an applicant or employee to take a lie detector test; may not use, accept, refer to, or inquire about the results of a test. May not take adverse employment action solely on the basis of test results or a refusal to take test. May not discriminate or retaliate against employee who files a complaint of violation of laws.

What's allowed: Wisconsin law allows testing in the same limited circumstances as the federal EPPA, with similar rules and restrictions on when and how the test is given.

Equal Pay Act (EPA)

Statute: 29 U.S.C. § 206(d)
http://uscode.house.gov/download/pls/29C8.txt

Regulations: 29 C.F.R. §§ 516, 1620, and 1621
www.gpo.gov/fdsys/pkg/CFR-2012-title29-vol3/pdf/CFR-2012-title29-vol3-part516.pdf

www.gpo.gov/fdsys/pkg/CFR-2012-title29-vol4/pdf/CFR-2012-title29-vol4-part1620.pdf

www.gpo.gov/fdsys/pkg/CFR-2012-title29-vol4/pdf/CFR-2012-title29-vol4-part1621.pdf

Overview of the EPA

The Equal Pay Act (EPA) requires employers to give men and women equal pay for equal work. Congress passed the EPA to combat "the ancient but outmoded belief that a man, because of his role in society, should be paid more than a woman." (*Corning Glass Works v. Brennan*, 417 U.S. 188, 195 (1974).) Despite its gender-specific origins, however, the EPA protects both men and women from wage discrimination based on sex.

Regulated Employers

Most government and private employers must comply with the EPA. The EPA also applies to unions.

Government Employers

All state and local governments must comply with the EPA.

Most, but not all, federal government agencies and departments must comply, including:

- military departments that employ civilians (only the civilian employees are covered by the law; see "Covered Workers," below)
- all executive agencies
- the United States Postal Service and Postal Rate Commission
- the Library of Congress
- any unit of the judicial or legislative branch that has positions in the *competitive service* (only employees in these positions are covered by the law; see "Covered Workers," below), and
- *nonappropriated fund instrumentalities.*

Private Employers

Not every private employer is subject to the EPA, although most are. Generally, a business is covered if it has $500,000 or more in annual gross sales. Businesses that generate lower sales will still be covered if they are involved in interstate commerce. Practically speaking, this means that most businesses are covered: Any employer whose workers produce or buy goods that have come from or will be sent to another state, transport goods or services interstate, and/or sell products or services that have come from or will go to another state engages in interstate commerce.

Definitions

Competitive service Jobs in the executive branch of the federal government that are subject to the federal civil service laws. Jobs at certain agencies, including the Federal Bureau of Investigation and the Central Intelligence Agency, are not part of the competitive service.

Effort The amount of physical or mental exertion a job generally requires. In determining how much effort a job requires, courts will take into account aspects of the job that are particularly stressful or tiring, as well as job factors that alleviate fatigue. Two jobs may require equal effort even if they require different types of effort.

Establishment A distinct physical place of business (such as a factory or an office) rather than an employer's entire business or enterprise. Separate workplaces can constitute a single establishment if their operations are connected and personnel and pay decisions are made centrally.

Nonappropriated fund instrumentalities Federal organizations that are under the jurisdiction of the armed forces and whose activities are conducted for the support, pleasure, recreation, or improvement of members of the armed forces. Employees of these organizations are paid with nonappropriated funds (funds that are not appropriated by Congress, but are generated by military and civilian personnel of the Department of Defense).

Responsibility The level of accountability a job carries. In assessing responsibility, courts consider how important a particular task is to the employer, as well as how much time a worker spends on that task. Examples of job tasks that require significant responsibility include supervising other workers, generating substantial revenues, or approving financial transactions.

Skill The abilities or aptitudes required to perform a job. Skill includes experience, training, education, and ability. In determining whether two jobs require equal skill, courts look only at the skills actually required to do the job, not any additional skills the employees may happen to possess.

Willful violation An employer commits a willful violation of the EPA if it violates the law knowingly or with reckless disregard as to whether its conduct was illegal.

Working conditions The environment in which a job must be performed. Working conditions include physical surroundings, such as temperature, ventilation, and location, as well as hazards, like exposure to toxic chemicals or dangerous terrain.

Unions

The EPA prohibits unions from causing, or trying to cause, employers to violate the law's provisions. If, for example, a union seeks a collective bargaining agreement that sets higher pay scales for men than for women doing equal work, the union has violated the EPA.

Did You Know ...

- The Bureau of Labor Statistics (BLS) has reported that women who worked full time in 2010 earned about 81 cents for every dollar earned by men who worked full time. This is an improvement of more than 20 cents since the Equal Pay Act was signed in 1963.
- According to the BLS, women in these professions earned the highest pay in 2010, calculated as a weekly median: physicians and surgeons ($1,618), pharmacists ($1,605), chief executives ($1,598), lawyers ($1,461), computer software engineers ($1,445), and computer and information systems managers ($1,415).
- When the EPA was passed, a number of states had labor laws that distinguished between men and women—for example, laws that prohibited women from working overtime, required employers to give women (but not men) breaks during the workday, and allowed employers to refuse to hire women for jobs that required heavy lifting. Some opponents of the EPA argued that these protective laws made it more expensive for employers to hire women, and so justified paying them a lower wage.

Covered Workers

The EPA protects all employees who work for a regulated employer, as defined above, except:

- Uniformed service members are not covered, even if they are employed by a federal agency that also has civilian employees.
- Federal employees of the judicial or legislative branch of government are not covered unless they are in the competitive service.

What's Prohibited

Employers are prohibited from paying workers of one sex more than workers of the opposite sex to do equal work.

Key Facts

- Most employers are covered by the Equal Pay Act. Unlike most antidiscrimination statutes, the EPA's application depends on the type and volume of business your company does, not the number of employees it has.
- The EPA requires companies to compensate men and women who do equal work at the same pay rate.
- Jobs must be quite similar to qualify as "equal work." They must require substantially equal skill, effort, and responsibility, and they must be performed under similar working conditions.

What's Required

Employers must give equal pay to men and women for doing equal work. However, the equal pay requirement applies only to those working in substantially similar jobs, as defined by the EPA. And the EPA requires only that workers performing equal work be paid at the same pay rate, not that workers receive the same total amount of pay.

Equal Work

Male and female employees are entitled to equal pay even if their jobs are not absolutely identical. The equal pay requirement applies when the jobs are substantially equal—that is, the jobs require substantially equal *skill*, *effort*, and *responsibility*, and are performed under similar *working conditions* within the same *establishment*.

Two jobs may constitute equal work even if they require different types of skill, effort, or responsibility. For example, if two employees work as salespeople in a retail establishment and each has some additional responsibilities—one to keep the financial books and the other to supervise temporary sales help—a court might find that their jobs require equal responsibility, even though each has a different type of responsibility.

Generally, however, courts will find that two jobs constitute equal work only where they are quite similar. Although operating a jack hammer might require as much effort and skill as drafting detailed architectural designs, no court would find that these two jobs are equal work requiring equal pay.

Job titles do not determine whether two jobs are substantially equal. Courts will look at the actual tasks a worker has to perform rather than the job description or designation. For example, an employer may not pay a male "administrative assistant" more than a female "secretary" if both do essentially the same tasks.

Equal Pay and Benefits

The EPA requires more than equal wages. If employees do equal work, they are also entitled to equal fringe benefits, such as insurance coverage, pensions, and use of a company car. And the EPA applies to other forms of compensation, such as vacation time, profit sharing, and bonuses.

However, the EPA requires only that employers pay workers at the same rate, not that they pay workers the same total amount. If an employer pays on commission or by the piece, for example, the employer must use the same formula—such as 10% of the company's gross profit per sale or $1 per unit produced—to calculate pay for men and women. If one worker earns more than another because of higher productivity (making more sales or turning out more units), that does not violate the EPA.

Financial incentives for good performance work the same way. An employer may not offer men the opportunity to earn a bonus for high sales volume or productivity while denying the same opportunity to women. However, if a bonus is offered on the same terms to all employees and the only workers who meet the criteria for the bonus are men, an employer may legally pay the bonus to those men only.

Exceptions

There are four exceptions to the EPA. An employer may pay workers of one sex at a higher rate than workers of the opposite sex for doing equal work only if the difference is based on one of these factors:

- **Seniority.** An employer may pay more to workers who have been with the company longer, even if this results in workers of one sex getting paid more to do the same job.
- **Merit.** An employer may pay higher rates (by giving larger bonuses or performance-based raises, for example) to workers whose performance is better, regardless of gender.
- **Quantity or quality of production.** An employer may pay a higher rate for better quality work or pay workers based on their productivity (by the piece or on commission, for example), as long as both men and women have the opportunity to earn this higher rate.
- **Any factor other than sex.** This catchall exception is intended to encompass any legitimate reason why an employer might pay one worker more than another to do the same job, as long as that discrepancy isn't based on the workers' genders. It would not violate the EPA for an employer to pay a shift premium to all workers on the night shift, for example.

How the EPA Is Enforced

Individual Complaints

An employee who wants to file a complaint against an employer for violating the EPA can file a charge (also called a complaint) of discrimination at the Equal Employment Opportunity Commission (EEOC). (See Appendix A for contact information.)

However, an employee does not have to file a charge at the EEOC. Instead, the employee may bypass the agency and go straight to state or federal court to file a lawsuit.

The employee must file a lawsuit within two years after the employer violated the EPA. This time limit is extended to three years if the employer committed a willful violation of the law. These time limits can be extended if the employee did not know about the violation because the employer lied about or concealed it.

Agency Enforcement

The federal agency responsible for investigating EPA complaints is the EEOC. An employee usually initiates the investigation process by filing a charge (complaint) of wage discrimination with the EEOC, although the agency can also act on its own initiative. The EEOC has the power to investigate, negotiate with employers, and bring lawsuits against employers to stop discriminatory practices.

Complying With the EPA

Reporting Requirements

There are no reporting requirements under the EPA.

Posting Requirements

All regulated employers must post a notice regarding the EPA. Employers must post this notice in a prominent location, where it can be easily seen and read by employees and job applicants. The EEOC has created a poster, *Equal Employment Is the Law*, which fulfills this requirement. You can order the poster in English, Spanish, or Chinese from the EEOC's website. (See "Agency Resources," below.)

Record-Keeping Requirements

The EPA requires employers to keep two types of records: basic wage and hour records, as required by the Fair Labor Standards Act (see Chapter 7), and records relating specifically to differences in pay between men and women. Employers must keep these records for at least two years.

Wage and Hour Records

The EPA is part of the Fair Labor Standards Act (FLSA). Employers subject to the EPA must comply with the FLSA's record-keeping requirements. (For a detailed description of these requirements, see Chapter 7.)

Records of Pay Differences

In addition to general wage and hour records, employers subject to the EPA must also keep all records that:

- describe or explain the basis for any difference in wages between men and women, and
- may help show whether that differential is based on a factor other than sex.

Such records include documents regarding:

- payment of wages
- wage rates
- job evaluations
- job descriptions
- merit systems
- seniority systems
- collective bargaining agreements, and
- pay practices.

Penalties

If a court finds that an employer has violated the EPA, the employer may be ordered to do any or all of the following:

- pay back wages, equal to the difference between what the employee actually earned and what employees of the opposite sex earned for doing equal work; an employee can collect up to two years' worth of back pay, or three years' worth if the employer committed a willful violation of the EPA
- pay an additional penalty (called "liquidated damages") equal to the entire back pay award, unless the employer can demonstrate that it acted in good faith and had reasonable grounds to believe that its conduct did not violate the EPA
- pay the employee's costs of suit and attorneys' fees, and

• change its pay policies to avoid further violations of the law. In making these changes, an employer may not reduce any employee's pay rate. Rather, the employer must raise the pay of employees who were underpaid.

Agency Resources

• A fact sheet and other EEOC resources on equal pay
  Facts About Equal Pay and Compensation Discrimination
  www.eeoc.gov/eeoc/publications/fs-epa.cfm

• The EEOC's compliance manual on wage discrimination
  Compensation Discrimination
  www.eeoc.gov/policy/docs/compensation.html

• A list of the addresses and phone numbers of EEOC offices throughout the United States
  EEOC Field Offices
  www.eeoc.gov/field/index.cfm

State Laws Relating to Equal Pay

Some states have their own equal pay laws. To find out whether your state has such a law, contact your state department of labor. You can find a list of state labor departments in Appendix A.

Fair Credit Reporting Act (FCRA)

> **Statute:** 15 U.S.C. § 1681 and following
> http://uscode.house.gov/download/pls/15C41.txt
>
> **Regulations:** 16 C.F.R. § 600.1 and following
> www.gpo.gov/fdsys/pkg/CFR-2012-title16-vol1/pdf/CFR-2012-title16-vol1-chapI-subchapF.pdf
>
> 16 C.F.R. § 660 (the Furnisher Rule)
> www.gpo.gov/fdsys/pkg/CFR-2012-title16-vol1/pdf/CFR-2012-title16-vol1-part660.pdf
>
> 16 C.F.R. § 681 (the Address Discrepancy Rule)
> www.gpo.gov/fdsys/pkg/CFR-2012-title16-vol1/pdf/CFR-2012-title16-vol1-part681.pdf
>
> 16 C.F.R. § 682 (the Disposal Rule)
> www.gpo.gov/fdsys/pkg/CFR-2012-title16-vol1/pdf/CFR-2012-title16-vol1-part682.pdf

Overview of the FCRA

The Fair Credit Reporting Act (FCRA) has two goals:

- to protect the privacy of consumer credit information by restricting access to those who have both a legitimate need for the information and the consent of the person whose records are sought, and
- to ensure the accuracy of that information by giving people the right to see their credit reports (and other records, in some circumstances), the right to know whether someone has decided not to give them credit, employment, housing, or other benefits based on that information, and the right to dispute information that is incorrect or incomplete.

To those ends, the FCRA imposes a number of legal obligations on *consumer reporting agencies*—such as credit bureaus—and on those who use credit information and other information gathered by third parties to make important decisions. For example, a bank might consider someone's credit report in deciding whether to extend a loan; a landlord might hire an agency to call the former landlords of prospective tenants and ask whether the tenants have paid rent on time, damaged rental property, or been evicted; or an employer might hire a company to run detailed background checks on applicants for high-level positions. This chapter covers only the employment aspects of the FCRA.

The FCRA places limits and obligations on employers who investigate prospective and current employees and independent contractors. In the context of employment, the FCRA has five main provisions:

- **Notice, authorization, and certification procedures.** Before seeking a consumer report or an investigative consumer report for employment purposes, employers must notify the employee, applicant, or contractor, in writing, that they want a report. In addition, they must obtain written authorization from that person before actually requesting the report. They must then verify to the consumer reporting agency that they have given notice and received authorization.
- **Address-checking procedures.** If an employer receives a notice of address discrepancy from a consumer reporting agency from which it has requested a report, the employer must take steps to make sure that the

report it receives actually relates to the person about whom it requested the report.

- **Adverse action procedures.** Employers who take an adverse action based on a consumer report or an investigative consumer report must provide the subject of the report with specific types of information about both the report and the consumer reporting agency that provided it.
- **Disposal rules.** Employers that gather or use consumer reports or information must limit access to that information. They must also follow specified methods of destroying the information to prevent identity theft and other unauthorized uses of that information.
- **Furnisher rules.** Certain employers who provide information on current or former employees to credit reporting agencies must take steps to ensure the information is accurate and complete. If an employee disputes that information, the employer must investigate, inform the employee of its findings, and correct any inaccurate information.

Regulated Employers

The FCRA covers all employers, including:
- the federal government
- state governments
- local and municipal governments, and
- private employers, regardless of size.

Covered Workers

The FCRA applies to anyone about whom the employer gathers information in a way covered by the FCRA. This means that any time an employer seeks a consumer report or an investigative consumer report for employment purposes, the employer must comply with the FCRA.

Definitions

Accuracy When information a *furnisher* provides to a *consumer reporting agency* about someone identifies the correct person and correctly reflects the terms of the relationship and the person's performance and other conduct with respect to the relationship.

Adverse action Any decision made by an employer for *employment purposes* that negatively affects an employee or applicant. Examples include refusing to hire, refusing to promote, and firing.

Consumer report In the context of employment, written or oral information that (1) will be used for *employment purposes*, (2) comes from a *consumer reporting agency*, and (3) relates to a person's:

- creditworthiness
- credit standing
- credit capacity
- general reputation
- personal characteristics, or
- lifestyle.

Examples of consumer reports include criminal background checks, educational history checks, and license checks.

Consumer reporting agency A person or an entity that regularly provides *consumer reports* to third parties. Examples of consumer reporting agencies include credit bureaus, private investigators, records search firms, law firms, and background-checking services. Employers are not consumer reporting agencies. A state entity that is required to keep certain information as a matter of public record—for example, a court clerk—is not a consumer reporting agency, and any information it provides is not a *consumer report*.

Employment purposes To use information to decide whether to hire, promote, reassign, or terminate someone. Although the term refers to employment, it extends to applicants and independent contractors as well as employees.

Definitions (continued)

Furnisher An entity that provides information relating to consumers to a *consumer reporting agency* for inclusion in a *consumer report*. A furnisher does not include:

- an entity that provides information to a consumer reporting agency for the sole purpose of obtaining a consumer report (for example, an employer that provides an applicant's identifying information in order to pull the applicant's credit report)
- a consumer reporting agency
- the person that is the subject of the information, or
- a neighbor or friend, an associate, or another person who is acquainted with or has knowledge of the subject of the report, and who provides information about the person's character, general reputation, personal characteristics, or mode of living in response to a specific request from a consumer reporting agency.

Integrity When information a *furnisher* provides to a *consumer reporting agency* about someone is substantiated by the furnisher's records when it is provided, and is provided in a form and manner designed to minimize the likelihood that the information may be incorrectly reflected in a consumer report.

Investigative consumer report A *consumer report* based at least in part on personal interviews that go beyond simply verifying facts that the person has provided to the employer. To qualify as an investigative consumer report, the information must have been gathered by a *consumer reporting agency*. For example, if a consumer reporting agency phones a college to verify the degree an applicant earned, a written record of that phone call would not be an investigative consumer report. If, however, the agency phoned the applicant's professors to get their opinions about the applicant, a written record of those phone calls would be an investigative consumer report.

Notice of address discrepancy A notice sent by a consumer reporting agency to someone who requested a consumer report, stating that there is a substantial difference between the address provided to request the report and the address in the agency's file for the consumer.

Legal Developments

- **Welcome the Consumer Financial Protection Bureau (CFPB)!** The Federal Trade Commission (FTC) was long the federal agency responsible for enforcing the FCRA. However, that enforcement responsibility moved to the newly created CFPB in 2010. So far, the CFPB has done little in the credit reporting area, other than to update the official consent and disclosure forms to include the name of the new enforcement agency.
- **Some states restrict employer use of credit reports.** In response to the economic downturn that began in 2008, some states passed laws restricting an employer's right to use credit reports in making hiring decisions. To date, at least seven states (California, Connecticut, Hawaii, Illinois, Maryland, Oregon, and Washington) have enacted legislation prohibiting employers from pulling credit reports on applicants at all or limiting how and when employers may use them in making hiring and other job decisions. State laws—like these—that are more restrictive than the FCRA trump the federal law.
- **Employers may be furnishers, too.** Most employer responsibilities under the FCRA are as users of consumer reports. But employers may also contribute to consumer reports if they furnish information to credit reporting agencies regarding current or former employees (for example, by providing payroll or other information about employees to an outside agency to which the employer has outsourced its unemployment processing or reference checking). Under rules that went into effect in 2010, employers that act as furnishers must take steps to ensure the accuracy and integrity of the information they provide. If a current or former employee disputes the information, the employer must investigate the dispute and correct any inaccurate information provided.

Did You Know ...

- When the FCRA was passed in 1970, there were no federal restrictions on access to consumer credit information, and there was no way for a person to challenge the information in his or her credit report.
- Before the FCRA was amended in 2003, the Federal Trade Commission (FTC), the agency then responsible for interpreting and enforcing the law, took the position that it applied to investigations of workplace misconduct. The FTC announced this interpretation in the "Vail letter," an opinion letter providing guidance on the law's application in response to a question from an attorney. After human resources professionals, including the Society for Human Resource Management (SHRM), pointed out the problems this interpretation created for employers, the law was amended to create an exception for these investigations.
- In a 2010 survey conducted by SHRM, 13% of the respondents stated that their companies run credit checks on all applicants; 47% stated that they run credit checks on select job candidates; and the remaining 40% said that their companies never check applicants' credit reports.

Major Provisions of the FCRA

Notice, Authorization, and Certification Procedures

Employers must follow the procedures described in this section before obtaining a consumer report or an investigative consumer report on an applicant or employee.

Regulated Employers

All regulated employers are subject to these provisions.

Covered Workers

All covered workers are subject to these provisions.

Key Facts: Notice Procedures

- Employers may request a consumer report or an investigative consumer report on an applicant or employee only for employment purposes.
- Before requesting a consumer report on someone, an employer must notify that person properly, obtain his or her authorization, and then verify to the consumer reporting agency that notice was given and authorization received.
- Before obtaining an investigative consumer report, an employer must make additional disclosures to the person about whom the report will be obtained.
- Certain exceptions to these requirements exist for employers in the trucking industry and employers hiring third parties to investigate alleged employee misconduct.

What's Prohibited

Employers may request a consumer report or an investigative consumer report only for employment purposes. For example, an employer that is fighting a union cannot request reports on pro-union employees if the purpose of getting the reports is to gain information to hamper the organizing effort.

Employers cannot request a consumer report or an investigative consumer report without notifying the subject of the report and receiving his or her authorization. (For more on this, see "What's Required," below.)

What's Required

Employers must do all of the following to obtain a consumer report or an investigative consumer report on a current or prospective employee or contractor:

- Notify the subject of the report, in writing, that they want to obtain a report. The employer cannot include any other information on this document: It must consist only of this notice.
- Obtain the person's written authorization before asking a consumer reporting agency for a report.
- Verify to the consumer reporting agency that they have notified the subject of the report and obtained written authorization.

Special Rules for Investigative Consumer Reports

In addition to following the rules described above, an employer that wants an investigative consumer report must give the following information to the subject of the report, in writing, after requesting the report:

- a statement that the requested report is an investigative consumer report
- a statement briefly identifying the type(s) of information the report will contain—such as information about the individual's character, general reputation, personal characteristics, or way of life, and
- a statement that the individual has the right to submit a written request for complete and accurate information about the nature and scope of the investigation.

Special Rules for Medical Information

When an employer seeks medical information as part of a consumer report on an applicant, employee, or independent contractor, these additional rules apply:

- The information must be relevant to the employment.
- The employer must get specific written consent from the applicant, employee, or independent contractor that describes in "clear and conspicuous language" how the information will be used.

Exceptions

Investigations of Alleged Workplace Misconduct

When an employer uses an outside party (such as an investigative agency or a law firm) to investigate an employee's suspected misconduct, violation of a law or regulation, or violation of a written employment policy, the investigation is excluded from the definition of "consumer report" under the FCRA. This means that the employer need not provide notice and obtain authorization before conducting such an investigation. To fall within this exception, the investigation must be employment related, and its results must not be disclosed to anyone except the employer and certain governmental entities.

This exclusion is significant because the FTC had previously interpreted the requirements of the FCRA to include third-party investigations into alleged workplace misconduct as investigative consumer reports that triggered FCRA protections. Requiring employers to inform—and get the consent of—the employee under investigation before proceeding created a number of problems. For example, what if an employer was legally obligated to investigate a sexual harassment claim, but the employee accused of harassment refused to consent to the investigation? The FCRA was amended, in part, in response to these concerns.

The amendments do, however, require disclosure after an investigation that results in an adverse employment action. (For more on this, see "Adverse Action Procedures," below.)

The Trucking Industry

Unlike other employers, which must notify individuals in writing and receive written authorization, the trucking industry can meet the notice and authorization requirements by oral, written, or electronic means. This exception applies only to applicants and only if none of the interactions between the applicant and employer prior to obtaining the report have been in person—if all communications have taken place by phone or email, for example. If there is any in-person contact between the employer and the applicant, the exception doesn't apply. For example, if the applicant stops by the employer's office to pick up a job application, the employer must follow the standard written notice and authorization rules.

Address-Checking Procedures

An employer that receives a notice of address discrepancy from a consumer reporting agency after requesting a consumer report must take steps to verify the identity of the subject of the report.

Regulated Employers

All regulated employers are subject to these provisions.

Covered Workers

All covered workers are subject to these provisions.

Key Facts: Address-Checking Procedures

- Once an employer receives a notice of address discrepancy, it must follow reasonable procedures to determine that the report is actually about the person on whom the employer requested the report.
- An employer can do this by checking its own records, verifying the information with the employee or applicant, or verifying the information through third-party sources.
- The employer must report the employee or applicant's correct address back to the agency if it has a reasonable belief that the report relates to the person about whom the employer requested the report; the employer establishes a continuing relationship with the person; and the employer regularly provides information to the agency in the ordinary course of business.

What's Required

If an employer asks a consumer reporting agency for a consumer report on someone, it might receive a notice of address discrepancy from the agency. This notice means that the address the employer supplied for the person about whom it requested the report is substantially different from the address in the agency's file.

Once an employer receives a notice of address discrepancy, it must follow reasonable procedures and policies sufficient to allow it to form a reasonable belief that the employee or applicant about whom it requested the report is the same person described in the report. There are no legally required procedures, but examples of procedures that might be reasonable include:

- comparing the information provided by the agency to information in its own records, such as change of address notifications or employment applications
- checking the information provided by the agency with a third party source, and
- verifying the information provided by the agency directly with the employee or applicant.

The employer might also have to provide the employee or applicant's correct address to the agency, but only if the following apply:

- The employer reasonably believes that the report it received from the agency related to the person about whom the employer requested the report.
- The employer establishes a continuing relationship with the person about whom it requested the report (for example, by hiring him or her).
- The employer regularly furnishes information to the agency in the ordinary course of business.

If all of these criteria are met, the employer must provide the address it has reasonably confirmed as accurate as part of the information it regularly furnishes to the agency, in the reporting period in which it establishes a continuing relationship with the employee or applicant.

Adverse Action Procedures

If an employer takes adverse action against an individual as a result of information the employer learns in a report, the employer must take some additional steps.

Key Facts: Adverse Action

- Before taking adverse action against someone based on a consumer report, an employer must provide the person with a copy of the report and a copy of the FTC's document summarizing a consumer's rights under the FCRA.
- After taking adverse employment action against someone based on a consumer report, an employer must provide the person with an "adverse action notice" that contains certain disclosures about the consumer reporting agency and the individual's rights.
- Certain exceptions to these requirements exist for employers in the trucking industry, national security investigations, and third-party investigations of alleged employee misconduct.

Regulated Employers

All regulated employers are subject to these provisions.

Covered Workers

All covered workers are subject to these provisions.

What's Required

If an employer takes adverse action against someone based on information in a consumer report or an investigative consumer report, the employer must make certain disclosures to that person both before and after the adverse action.

Before Taking Adverse Action

Prior to taking adverse action, the employer must give the subject of the report two documents:

- a copy of the report, and
- a copy of a document from the Federal Trade Commission (FTC) called *A Summary of Your Rights Under the Fair Credit Reporting Act*. (To learn how to obtain this document from the FTC, see "Agency Resources," below.)

After Taking Adverse Action

After taking adverse action against someone, the employer must give that person an adverse action notice. This notice can be oral, written, or electronic and must contain the following information:

- the name, address, and phone number of the consumer reporting agency that supplied the report
- a statement that the consumer reporting agency did not make the decision to take the adverse action and cannot give the individual the specific reasons for the adverse action
- a statement that the individual has a right to dispute the accuracy or completeness of the information in the report, and
- a statement that the individual has a right to request a free copy of the report from the consumer reporting agency.

Exceptions

Investigations of Alleged Workplace Misconduct

The FCRA imposes more limited obligations on employers who take adverse action against an employee based on an investigation into the employee's alleged misconduct, violation of law or regulation, or violation of a workplace rule. In these circumstances, the employer must provide the employee with a summary of the investigation report. The summary should cover the "nature and substance" of the investigation that led to the adverse action, but need not disclose the sources of the information (for example, the names of witnesses who provided information).

National Security Investigations

If a federal agency or department requests a consumer report or an investigative consumer report for employment purposes, it does not have to comply with the adverse action procedures if the head of the department or agency states the following in writing:
- The report is part of a national security investigation.
- The agency or department has jurisdiction over the investigation.
- Negative consequences—including danger to life or physical safety, destruction of evidence, or flight from prosecution—will result if the agency or department complies with the standard adverse action procedures.

The Trucking Industry

Because it is difficult to correspond with applicants who are on the road, trucking companies are allowed to take adverse action without prior notice as long as they give the applicant the required information within three days of the action.

Proper Disposal of Consumer Information

The FCRA also requires any person or business that has consumer information to dispose of it properly. To enforce this provision, the FTC created new regulations on the proper destruction of consumer information, including both paper and electronic reports and information identifiable as derived from those reports. These regulations are known as the "Disposal Rule."

Key Facts: The Disposal Rule

- Under the Disposal Rule, all businesses must properly destroy consumer reports and information derived from them in both paper and electronic formats.
- Businesses must use reasonable and appropriate methods to avoid unauthorized access to or use of such consumer information—for example, by shredding paper and erasing disks or computer files.
- Any business that fails to follow these rules can be held liable for resulting damages (for example, unauthorized credit card charges).

Regulated Employers

All regulated employers are subject to these provisions.

Covered Workers

All covered workers are subject to these provisions.

What's Required

The Disposal Rule requires all businesses to safeguard and eventually destroy consumer reports and any information derived from those reports—for example, a manager's handwritten notes based on a background check of a potential employee.

To comply with these rules, businesses should store consumer reports and other documents that include consumer information securely—for example, in a locked cabinet or under a closely guarded password if stored on computers or electronically. Businesses should also limit access to trusted people who have a legitimate need for the information.

When an employer no longer has a legitimate business reason to keep consumer reports and information, it must dispose of them properly, using a level of document destruction that is reasonable in the context of the business. For example, a small business with only a few employees might shred paper documents and erase or render unreadable computer files, discs, CDs, and the like, whereas a major corporation with a large human resources department might want to contract with a disposal service. If an employer does contract with a disposal service, however, it must exercise due diligence to make sure that the service's disposal methods comply with the Disposal Rule.

The Disposal Rule does not impose time limits for destroying consumer information. When determining when to destroy consumer information, employers must remember that they may need these reports long after they've rejected or accepted an applicant—for example, to refute an employment discrimination claim.

Rules for Employers Who Provide Information

Employers don't just use consumer reports; they may contribute to these reports as well. When an employer provides information on its employees to outside agencies to which it has outsourced functions such as checking references or processing claims for unemployment, the employer may qualify as a furnisher. For example, an employer that outsources its background checks may also regularly provide information to the outside firm on its own current and former employees. The employer's information may then become part of the firm's consumer reports about those employees. In this situation, the employer is considered a "furnisher" of information, which means it must establish procedures to ensure the accuracy and integrity of the information it provides. If an employee disputes the information provided, the employer must investigate and take steps to correct inaccuracies.

Key Facts: Employers Who Furnish Information

- Employers who provide information on current or former employees to outside consumer reporting agencies must take steps to ensure the accuracy and integrity of the information. Such steps include reasonable written policies and procedures appropriate to the nature, size, complexity, and scope of the employer's activities.
- An employer who furnishes information must conduct a reasonable investigation of disputes raised by the current or former employee who is the subject of the information. If the investigation reveals a problem with the information the employer provided, the employer must notify the employee and the consumer reporting agency to which it furnished the information.

Regulated Employers

All regulated employers are subject to these provisions

Covered Workers

All covered workers are subject to these provisions

What's Required

Employers who furnish information about current or former employees to consumer reporting agencies to which the employer has outsourced certain personnel functions must implement reasonable written policies and procedures to ensure the *accuracy* and *integrity* of that information. These policies and procedures must be appropriate to the nature, size, complexity, and scope of the employer's activities. The rules suggest that employers should identify potential problem areas, evaluate current procedures for supplying information, and modify procedures as necessary. Some of the topics an employer's policies might address are standard formats and procedures for compiling and providing information, record-keeping requirements, internal controls for making sure information is accurate, training, and oversight of outside service providers.

If a current or former employee disputes the information an employer has provided, the employer must conduct a reasonable investigation. The regulations deal primarily with creditors and the information they provide regarding debt, payments, credit accounts, and so on. However, the rules state that a furnisher must investigate disputes over the person's "performance or other conduct concerning an account or other relationship with the furnisher," as well as disputes regarding information provided that bears on the person's "creditworthiness, credit standing, credit capacity, character, general reputation, personal characteristics, or mode of living," both of which encompass the type of information an employer might supply to a third-party consumer reporting agency.

To raise a dispute, the employee must provide the employer with identifying information, the specific information the employee is disputing, why the employee disputes the information, and all supporting documentation or other information necessary to substantiate the dispute (such as a copy of the consumer report that includes the disputed information). The employer must conduct its investigation and report the findings to the employee within

30 days. If the employer determines that the information it furnished was inaccurate, it must promptly notify every agency to which the information was sent and provide the correct information.

Exceptions

The employer does not have to investigate a dispute if any of the following are true:

- The dispute relates only to identifying information, such as the employee's name, birth date, Social Security number, address, or phone number.
- The dispute relates only to the identity of past or present employers.
- The dispute relates to information provided by a different furnisher or information derived from public records.
- The dispute relates to inquiries or requests for a consumer report.
- The employee did not provide sufficient information for the employer to investigate.
- The dispute is substantially the same as one previously submitted by, or on behalf of, the employee.

How the FCRA Is Enforced

Individual Complaints

Individuals who think that an employer has violated the FCRA can sue the employer in federal district court within two years of the violation. If the employer gives false information to the individual about its obligations or actions under the FCRA, then the individual can bring the lawsuit within two years after discovering the false information.

Individuals may also file a complaint with the Consumer Financial Protection Bureau (CFPB).

Agency Enforcement

The CFPB enforces the FCRA and can, on its own initiative, investigate and bring a civil action against anyone it suspects of violating the FCRA. (For information on how to contact the CFPB, see Appendix A.)

The states and several other federal agencies and departments also have the power to enforce this law. (See "Complying With the FCRA," below, for more information.)

Complying With the FCRA

Reporting Requirements

The FCRA imposes no reporting requirements, other than the obligation, in some instances, to report an employee or applicant's correct address to a consumer reporting agency, as explained in "Address-Checking Procedures," above.

Posting Requirements

The FCRA imposes no posting requirements.

Record-Keeping Requirements

The FCRA does not require any particular record keeping. The FCRA does, however, require proper safeguarding and destruction of consumer information. (See "Proper Disposal of Consumer Information," above.)

Penalties

The penalties for violating the FCRA depend on who is bringing the lawsuit—an individual, a consumer reporting agency, the CFPB, another federal agency, or a state.

Liability to Individuals

If an individual sues an employer over violations of the FCRA, the penalties the employer might face depend on whether the employer's actions were willful or negligent. A willful action occurs when the employer knowingly and intentionally violates the law. A negligent action occurs when the employer doesn't know that it is violating the law, but should know.

Willful Actions. If an employer is found guilty of willfully failing to comply with any of the FCRA's provisions, it must:

- pay the actual damages the person suffered—at least $100 but not more than $1,000
- pay any punitive damages that the court might order, and
- pay the attorneys' fees and court costs of the person bringing the action.

Negligent Actions. If an employer is found guilty of negligently failing to comply with the FCRA, the employer will have to pay the individual actual damages, the costs of the action, and attorneys' fees.

Liability to Consumer Reporting Agencies

An employer that misleads a consumer reporting agency must pay the agency either its actual damages or $1,000, whichever is greater.

Liability to the Consumer Financial Protection Bureau

If the CFPB investigates an employer and finds that it has repeatedly and knowingly violated the FCRA, the employer must pay a penalty of not more than $2,500 per violation.

Liability to Others

Other federal agencies (including the Federal Deposit Insurance Corporation and the National Credit Union Administration) and state governments may also investigate and penalize wrongdoers. Those penalties are beyond the scope of this chapter.

Agency Resources

- A guide for employers on how to follow the FCRA when doing background checks on employees

  Using Consumer Reports: What Employers Need to Know
  http://business.ftc.gov/documents/bus08-using-consumer-reports-what-employers-need-know

- The document that employers must give to individuals as part of the disclosure before taking an adverse employment action based on a consumer report

    A Summary of Your Rights Under the Fair Credit Reporting Act
    www.ftc.gov/bcp/edu/pubs/consumer/credit/cre35.pdf

- Information about businesses' responsibilities under the FTC's Consumer Report Disposal Rule

    Disposing of Consumer Report Information? New Rule Tells How
    http://business.ftc.gov/documents/alt152-disposing-consumer-report-information-new-rule-tells-how

- The FTC's main Web page about the FCRA; includes links and recent highlights

    www.ftc.gov/os/statutes/fcrajump.shtm

- Compliance information on the identity theft rule

    Fighting Fraud With the Red Flags Rule
    www.ftc.gov/redflagsrule

State Laws Relating to Credit Reporting

Some states have their own fair credit reporting laws. To find out about the laws of your state, contact the state agency that handles consumer issues (often called the consumer protection agency or department of consumer affairs).

Fair Labor Standards Act (FLSA)

Statute: 29 U.S.C. §§ 201–219
http://uscode.house.gov/download/pls/29C8.txt

Regulations: 29 C.F.R. § 500 and following
www.gpo.gov/fdsys/pkg/CFR-2012-title29-vol3/pdf/CFR-2012-title29-vol3-subtitleB-chapV.pdf

Overview of the FLSA

The Fair Labor Standards Act (FLSA) regulates wages and hours, how much workers must be paid, how many hours they can be required to work, and the special rules that apply to younger workers. The law includes provisions on:

- minimum wages
- hours worked
- overtime, and
- child labor.

Regulated Employers

The FLSA applies to most employers, including:

- the federal government
- state and local governments
- companies with annual gross sales of at least $500,000
- businesses that engage in interstate commerce or the production of goods for interstate commerce—that is, businesses whose employees:
  - handle, sell, produce, or otherwise work on goods or materials that have come from, or will go to, another state; or
  - use the mail, telephone, or other equipment to communicate across state lines
- hospitals and businesses that are primarily engaged in institutional care of the sick, aged, or mentally ill, and
- preschools, elementary schools, secondary schools, and schools for mentally or physically disabled or gifted children.

Covered Workers

The FLSA applies to all employees of regulated employers, set forth above. In addition, the FLSA applies to any employee who is engaged in interstate commerce or the production of goods for interstate commerce. Even if an employer is not covered by the FLSA, some of its employees may be protected under this test. However, many workers (see "Exempt Employees," below) are not entitled to minimum wage or overtime under the FLSA, although they are covered by the law.

Definitions

Agriculture All aspects of farming, including soil cultivation and tilling; dairy work; production, cultivation, growth, and harvest of agricultural or horticultural products; raising livestock, bees, poultry, or fur-bearing animals; and any incidental practices on a farm, including forestry, lumbering, preparation for market, and delivery to storage, market, or carrier.

Exempt employee An employee who is not covered by the FLSA's minimum wage and/or overtime compensation provisions.

Independent contractor Someone who performs services for another person or business under contract, not as an employee. In determining whether a worker is an independent contractor rather than an employee, courts consider whether the worker has the right to control how to do the job, whether the worker has an opportunity for profit or loss depending on the worker's skill, whether the worker has invested in equipment or material or hired helpers, whether the worker's job requires special skills, the permanence of the work relationship, and whether the worker's job constitutes an essential part of the employer's business.

Outside salespeople Employees who customarily and regularly work away from the employer's business selling, or taking orders to sell, goods, services, or the use of facilities.

Primary duty The major, main, principal, or most important duty an employee performs.

Willful violation A violation of the FLSA committed by an employer that knew its conduct was illegal or showed reckless disregard as to whether its conduct violated the law.

Legal Developments

- **Final clean-up regulations clarify tip credits and more.** In 2011, the Department of Labor issued its final "clean-up" regulations, tweaking a number of rules to bring them in line with laws passed and court cases decided since the regulations were last reviewed. Among the most important changes are clearer guidelines on when and how employers may take a tip credit (discussed below), modifications to some of the categories of exempt employees, and exclusion of stock options from an employee's regular rate of pay (used to calculate overtime).

- **Proposed regulations address domestic service workers.** In response to huge growth in the home health care industry, the Department of Labor has proposed regulations to expand the reach of the FLSA to some of these workers. Domestic service workers who provide companionship are currently exempt from the law. The proposed regulations clarify that this exemption is not intended to exclude aides who provide more than minimal help with personal care, perform any medical tasks, or do chores for other family members. The exemption would also apply only to those who are employed directly by the family, not employees who come from an outside agency.

- **Minimum wage increases for the first time in ten years.** As part of a law governing spending on the war in Iraq, Congress passed a three-step increase to the minimum wage in May 2007. In July 2007, the minimum wage went from $5.15 an hour (the rate since 1997) to $5.85 an hour. It went up again, to $6.55 an hour on July 24, 2008, and on July 24, 2009, it increased to the current rate of $7.25.

Exempt Employees

The minimum wage and overtime requirements of the FLSA do not apply to every worker whom the law covers. Some workers, called *exempt employees*, are not entitled to minimum wage or overtime, although they are still protected by the rest of the FLSA's provisions.

Employers of exempt workers remain covered by the FLSA as far as the rest of their workforce is concerned; they have to pay minimum wage and overtime to their nonexempt employees (those who do not fall within one of the exceptions listed below). They also have to follow the FLSA's record-keeping and child labor requirements.

The following workers are exempt from the FLSA's minimum wage and overtime rules:

- executive, administrative, and professional employees who are paid on a salary basis (see "Salaried Executive, Administrative, and Professional Employees," below)
- independent contractors
- volunteer workers
- outside salespeople
- certain computer specialists—systems analysts, programmers, and software engineers who earn at least $27.63 an hour or $455 a week
- employees of seasonal amusement or recreational businesses, like ski resorts or county fairs
- employees of organized camps or religious and nonprofit educational conference centers that operate fewer than seven months a year
- employees of certain small newspapers and newspaper deliverers
- workers engaged in fishing operations
- seamen on international vessels
- employees who work on small farms
- certain switchboard operators, and
- casual domestic babysitters and persons who provide companionship to those who are unable to care for themselves. The Department of Labor has introduced proposed regulations that would limit this exemption only to those who are employed directly by the family (not by a third-party agency, for example) and whose duties are limited to companionship, such as spending time together watching television, engaging in hobbies, or taking walks. Although the exemption would still apply to companions who spend a limited amount of time helping with personal care (such as dressing and bathing), these activities may not take up more than 20% of the companion's time. And, someone who performs medical tasks or does chores that benefit other members of the household (such as laundry, preparing meals, or cleaning) would not be covered by the exemption.

In addition, certain workers are exempt from the FLSA's overtime provisions only. (For details, see "Overtime," below.)

Salaried Executive, Administrative, and Professional Employees

Probably the most commonly used and most confusing exemptions to the FLSA's overtime and minimum wage requirements are for "white collar workers"—executive, administrative, and professional employees who are paid on a salary basis. To fall within one of these exemptions, an employee must meet two tests: a salary test and a job duties test.

Salary Test. To qualify as exempt administrative, executive, or professional employees, workers must earn at least $455 per week ($23,660 per year) and be paid on a salary basis. Workers are paid on a salary basis if they receive their full salary for any week in which they perform any work, regardless of how many hours they work or the quality or amount of work they do.

An employer may not dock an exempt worker's pay for absences of less than a full week unless the worker takes at least a full day off for one of the following reasons:

- to handle personal affairs
- to take unpaid family or medical leave under the Family and Medical Leave Act (see Chapter 8)
- for disability or illness, if the employer has a plan (such as disability insurance or sick leave) that compensates employees for this time off
- to serve on a jury, as a witness, or on temporary military leave, if the employer deducts only the amount the employee receives as jury or witness fees or as military pay
- because the employee did not work a full first or last week of work
- as a penalty imposed in good faith for infractions of safety rules of major significance (rules that prevent serious danger in the workplace or to other workers), or
- to serve an unpaid disciplinary suspension imposed in good faith for infractions of workplace conduct rules, but only if the employer has a written policy regarding such suspensions that applies to all employees.

If an employer improperly docks a worker's pay (that is, the employer docks the worker's pay for reasons that don't fall within one of the exceptions listed above), the employer might have to pay overtime to all workers who (1) are in the job classification for which the improper deductions were made, and (2) report to the same manager who made the deductions. However, an employer falls within the law's "safe harbor" provision—and will not face these consequences—if either of the following is true:

- any improper deductions were isolated or inadvertent, and the employer reimburses the employees for the money improperly withheld, or
- the employer has a clearly communicated policy prohibiting improper deductions (including a complaint procedure), reimburses employees for the money improperly withheld, and makes a good-faith effort to comply with the law in the future.

Job Duties Test. An employee must perform certain job duties to qualify as an administrator, executive, or professional.

Administrative employees. An administrative employee's primary duty must be performing office or other nonmanual work directly related to the management of general business operations of the employer or the employer's customers. This work must include the exercise of discretion and independent judgment regarding matters of significance.

Executive employees. An executive employee must meet all of the following requirements:

- The employee's primary duty must be managing the company or a recognized department or subdivision of the company.
- The employee must customarily and regularly supervise at least two full-time employees (or their equivalent).
- The employee must have the authority to hire and fire, or the employee's recommendations as to hiring, firing, promotions, or any other change in employee status must be given particular weight.

Professional employees. There are two types of professional employees: learned professionals and creative professionals.

Learned professionals must meet all of these requirements:

- The employee's primary duty is performing work that requires advanced knowledge, is predominantly intellectual in nature, and requires the consistent exercise of discretion and judgment.
- The advanced knowledge is in a field of science or learning.
- The advanced knowledge is customarily acquired through a prolonged course of instruction.

Creative professionals must have the primary duty of performing work that requires invention, imagination, originality, or talent in a recognized artistic or creative field.

Did You Know ...

- The FLSA was enacted as part of President Franklin D. Roosevelt's New Deal. One purpose of the law was to create an incentive for employers to spread their work among more employees, which lawmakers thought would help the country recover from the Great Depression.
- The original minimum wage when the FLSA was enacted was 25 cents an hour.
- Under the National Industrial Recovery Act, which preceded the FLSA, businesses that voluntarily agreed to abolish child labor, pay a minimum wage, and limit work hours were allowed to display a "Blue Eagle" poster with the motto, "We Do Our Part."

Major Provisions of the FLSA

Minimum Wage

The FLSA sets the minimum wage for all covered employees. It includes special rules for employees who receive tips, younger workers, and workers who can be paid less than the minimum wage pursuant to certificates issued by the DOL.

Key Facts: Minimum Wage

- The federal minimum wage is $7.25. Some states impose a higher minimum wage.
- You can pay a lower minimum wage to certain workers, including teenagers, apprentices, and messengers, in some circumstances.
- In many states, you can pay tipped employees less than the minimum wage—as little as $2.13 an hour, as long as the tips they actually earn bring their hourly wage up to at least the minimum wage.

Regulated Employers

All regulated employers are subject to these provisions with regard to covered workers.

Covered Workers

All covered, nonexempt workers are subject to these provisions.

What's Required

Basic Minimum Wage Requirement

Employers must pay covered employees at least the minimum wage, $7.25 per hour. Employers are not required to pay employees by the hour, however. Employers may pay a salary, commission, or piece rate, for example, as long as the total amount paid divided by the total number of hours worked is equal to the minimum wage.

Each state is free to impose a higher minimum wage requirement, and some have done so. Some local governments have also passed minimum wage laws. The employer must pay whichever amount is higher, the federal, state, or local minimum wage. (See "State Laws Relating to Wages and Hours," below, for information on your state's law.)

Youth Minimum Wage

Employers may pay workers under the age of 20 a lower minimum wage for a few months. Employers must pay youth workers at least $4.25 an hour for the first 90 calendar days of their employment. Once the worker reaches the age of 20, the employer must pay that worker the regular minimum wage ($7.25), even if the worker has not yet worked 90 days for the employer. Employers may not displace other employees or reduce their hours, wages, or benefits in order to hire workers who qualify for this lower wage.

Some states do not recognize or allow a separate minimum wage for younger workers. Employers doing business in such states must pay younger workers the same minimum wage as they pay everyone else.

Subminimum Wage Certificates

Employers may apply to the DOL for a certificate allowing them to pay certain workers a subminimum wage. The DOL can issue such a certificate only if necessary to prevent the curtailment of employment opportunities for these workers. Employers can apply for a certificate for the following employees:

- **messengers:** those employed primarily in delivering letters and messages for a company whose principal business is providing these delivery services
- **apprentices:** employees who are at least 16 years old and are employed to learn a skilled trade
- **full-time students:** students who are employed in retail, a service industry, or agriculture, or who work for the institution in which they are enrolled
- **student learners:** students who are receiving instruction in an accredited school and working part-time in a vocational training program
- **learners:** employees being trained for certain occupations for which skill, dexterity, and judgment must be learned, and who produce little or nothing of value when initially employed, and
- **disabled employees:** workers whose earning or productive capacity is impaired by a physical or mental disability. (For more on disability, see Chapter 2.)

Tipped Employees

If an employee makes at least $30 per month in tips, the employer may pay that employee only $2.13 an hour. However, if the employee's wage plus the tips the employee actually earns do not add up to the minimum wage in any pay period, the employer must make up the difference. Employers that wish to pay tipped employees a lower minimum wage must give employees notice that the employer will take a tip credit, which includes:

- the hourly cash wage the employer will pay the employee
- the amount of tips that the employer will take as a tip credit (that is, the amount the employer will count toward the employee's wages, to meet the minimum wage requirement)
- that the employee is entitled to retain all tips received except any amount the employee is required to contribute to a valid tip pooling arrangement, and
- that the tip credit won't apply to any employee who has not been informed of these requirements.

This notice can be made orally, but the better practice is to put it in writing.

Whether or not an employer takes a tip credit, all tips an employee earns belong to that employee, except for any amount the employee is required to "tip out" (contribute to a legitimate tip pool). Employers aren't entitled to any part of the tip pool. Only employees who regularly and customarily receive tips can participate in the tip pool. Employees who don't typically receive tips, such as cooks and dishwashers, may not participate in the pool.

Some states do not allow employers to pay tipped employees a lower minimum wage. Employers doing business in such states must pay tipped employees the same minimum wage as they pay everyone else. Other states require employers to pay tipped employees more than $2.13 an hour, but less than the regular minimum wage. (See "State Laws Relating to Wages and Hours," below, for information on each state's laws regarding tips.)

Deductions

The FLSA allows employers to withhold money from a worker's paycheck to satisfy a debt the worker owes the employer or to cover the cost of certain employment expenses (such as uniforms or tools). However, the employer may not deduct so much that the employee's earnings for the pay period drop below the minimum wage.

The FLSA makes an exception for deductions for room and board. An employer may deduct the reasonable cost of meals and housing provided to a worker, even if these deductions cause the worker's pay to fall below minimum wage. However, the employer can make such deductions only if all of the following requirements are met:
- The employer customarily pays the expenses.
- The items are provided for the benefit of the employee.
- The employee is told, in advance, about the deductions.
- The employee voluntarily agrees to accept less than the minimum wage in exchange for the food and lodging provided.

Some states do not allow employers to charge employees for certain expenses.

Hours Worked

For purposes of the minimum wage and overtime rules, the FLSA requires employers to pay employees for any of their time that benefits the employer and that the employer controls. The rules for several common situations are set forth below, in "What's Required."

Key Facts: Hours Worked

- Although the FLSA doesn't require meal and/or rest breaks, many state laws do; some states also require employers to pay employees for this time.
- Whether an employee is entitled to pay for time spent on call depends on a number of factors, including where the employee must spend this time, how often the employee has to respond to calls, and what restrictions the employer places on the employee's use of this time.
- Employers don't have to pay for time an employee spends commuting to work but must pay for travel during the workday (for example, time spent traveling from one work site to another).

Regulated Employers

All regulated employers are subject to these provisions with regard to covered workers.

Covered Workers

All covered, nonexempt workers are subject to these provisions.

What's Required

Employers must pay employees for time that the employer controls. Conversely, employees are not entitled to be paid for time that they can spend as they wish. The FLSA does not provide much guidance on what constitutes work time, but the DOL and the courts have addressed some of the most common questions.

On-Call Time

Employers must pay employees for all of the time they spend on site waiting for work, even if they do not spend that time actually working. If employees are on call elsewhere, an employer must pay for those hours over which the employees have little or no control and which they cannot spend as they wish. The more restrictions an employer places on an employee on call, the more likely that employee is entitled to be paid. Courts will consider a number of factors to determine whether on-call time should be paid, including:

- **How many calls an employee gets while on call.** The more calls an employee has to respond to, the more likely he or she is entitled to pay, particularly if any of the calls require the employee to report to work or give advice or guidance over the phone.
- **How long an employee has to respond after a call.** If an employer requires employees to report in immediately after being paged, for example, such employees have a better argument that they should be paid for their time.
- **Where the employee can go while on call.** Employees who must stay within a limited distance from work are more likely to be entitled to compensation.
- **What the employee may do while on call.** If an employer sets a lot of rules for on-call workers, such as a ban on alcohol or a requirement that they respond quickly and in person to calls (which can be difficult if the employee is out running or taking the kids to school), the employer may have to pay for this time.

Meals and Breaks

Employers are not required to pay employees for time spent on a meal or rest break during the workday, as long as the employee is relieved of all work duties during the break. If the employee has to do some work while on break, that time must be paid.

Many states require employers to provide workers with specified breaks for meals or rest during the workday, and some states require that this time be paid. (For more information on state meal and rest break laws, see "State Laws Relating to Wages and Hours," below.)

Sleeping Breaks

Employers must pay employees for any time during which they are allowed to sleep during a shift. However, if an employee has to be on duty for more than 24 hours at a time, the employer and employee may agree that eight of those hours will be for meals and sleep periods and will not be paid. If the employee has to actually work during that period, or is unable to get at least five hours of sleep because of work conditions, the eight hours must be paid.

Travel and Commuting

Commuting time—the time it takes a worker to get from home to the workplace—does not count as work time. However, an employer must pay employees for travel time if travel is part of the job—for example, if employees are required to go out on service or sales calls or have to drive from one work site to another during the workday.

Changing Clothes

Time employees spend putting on protective clothing or safety gear—such as hard hats, sanitary outer clothing, work boots, and so on—counts as work time, as does the time it takes an employee to walk from the changing area to the work area.

Overtime

Certain employees are entitled to overtime pay (time and a half) for each additional hour worked if they work more than 40 hours a week.

Key Facts: Overtime

- Employees who earn less than $455 per week ($23,660 per year) are entitled to overtime, regardless of their job duties.
- Nonexempt employees must be paid overtime if they work more than 40 hours in a week; a few states require employers to pay overtime to employees who work more than eight hours in one day.
- Compensatory time is generally illegal for private employers; however, employers can rearrange an employee's hours during the workweek or pay period to allow additional time off rather than paying overtime.

Regulated Employers

All regulated employers are subject to these provisions with regard to covered workers (see below).

Covered Workers

All covered, nonexempt workers are entitled to these protections, with the following exceptions:

- rail, air, and motor carrier employees
- employees who buy poultry, eggs, cream, or milk in their unprocessed state
- those who sell cars, trucks, farm implements, trailers, boats, or aircraft
- mechanics or parts persons who service cars, trucks, or farm implements
- announcers, news editors, and chief engineers of certain broadcasting stations
- local delivery drivers or drivers' helpers who are compensated on a trip rate plan
- agricultural workers
- taxi drivers
- movie theater employees, and
- domestic service workers who live in the employer's home. Under proposed regulations released by the Department of Labor, this exemption would apply only to workers who are employed directly by the family with whom they live, not to those employed by third-party agencies. The proposed regulations would also impose record-keeping requirements on employers of these workers.

What's Required

Employers must pay an overtime premium to covered employees who work more than a certain number of hours during a work period. The FLSA uses 40 hours per week as the standard: Any employee who works more than 40 hours in a week is entitled to an overtime premium for the extra hours worked. Some states have a daily overtime standard. (For information on your state's law, see "State Laws Relating to Wages and Hours," below).

The overtime premium is 50% of the employee's hourly wage. An employee who works overtime must be paid his or her usual hourly wage plus the 50% overtime premium, called time and a half, for every overtime hour worked.

Compensatory Time

Private employers may not give employees straight compensatory time (one hour off for every overtime hour worked) instead of overtime. Private employers that wish to provide time off rather than overtime pay have only two options. They may adjust an employee's hours within a workweek so that the employee does not earn overtime (for example, by allowing an employee who has worked four ten-hour days to take the rest of the week off). However, this won't be legal in states that have a daily overtime standard.

The other option is to provide the employee an hour and a half of time off for each overtime hour worked, as long as the time off is taken during the same period as the extra hours are worked.

Some state and local government employees are entitled to compensatory time; check with your state's department of labor for more information. (For contact information, see Appendix A.)

Child Labor

The FLSA regulates the employment of workers under the age of 18 by limiting the types of work they are legally allowed to do and the hours during which they can work.

Key Facts: Child Labor

- Employers may hire teenagers who are at least 16 to do any type of work that has not been deemed "hazardous" by the secretary of labor.
- Workers who are 14 or 15 may be hired to do certain types of work, but they can only work limited hours, particularly during the school year.
- The child labor laws don't apply to certain younger workers, including newspaper deliverers, child actors, and children who work for their parents.

Regulated Employers

All regulated employers are subject to these provisions.

Covered Workers

All covered workers are subject to these provisions.

What's Prohibited

The FLSA limits the types of jobs younger workers can do. These restrictions differ depending on whether the work is hazardous and whether the work is agricultural.

Hazardous Work

The secretary of labor has the authority to designate certain occupations as hazardous for minors. These occupations include:

- mining
- driving or being an outside helper on a motor vehicle (those who are at least 17 may do certain jobs that require incidental or occasional driving, provided that the teens are properly licensed, have no moving violations, and meet a number of other requirements)
- working with explosives
- logging and sawmilling
- working with radioactive substances
- working with power-driven woodworking or paper products machines
- working with power-driven hoisting equipment
- working with power-driven metal-forming, punching, and shearing machines
- slaughtering and meat packing
- manufacturing tile and brick
- working with power-driven bakery machines
- working with power-driven circular saws, band saws, or guillotine shears
- wrecking, demolition, and shipbreaking operations
- excavation operations, and
- roofing and other activities that take place on a roof, such as installing satellite dishes or working on gutters and downspouts.

Agricultural Work

Employers who own or operate a farm or another agricultural business must follow these rules:

- Children aged 16 and older may be hired to do any type of work, for unlimited hours.
- Children aged 14 or 15 may be hired to do any nonhazardous work, outside of school hours.
- Children aged 12 or 13 may be hired to do any nonhazardous work outside of school hours, but only if the child's parents work on the same farm or have consented in writing to the arrangement.
- Children aged ten or 11 may be hired to harvest crops by hand for no more than eight weeks per calendar year, but only if the DOL has granted the employer a waiver.
- Children of any age may be hired by their own parents or by a person standing in the place of their parents to do any type of agricultural work, if the parents own or operate the business.

Nonagricultural Work

Employers seeking younger workers for nonagricultural work must follow these rules:

- Children aged 16 and 17 may be hired to do any nonhazardous work, for unlimited hours.
- Children aged 14 and 15 may be hired to do certain retail, food service, and service station jobs; the regulations specify which types of jobs are acceptable. However, they may not work more than three hours per school day, 18 hours per school week, eight hours on a nonschool day, and 40 hours in a nonschool week. Also, they cannot begin work before 7 a.m. or end after 7 p.m. (except during the summer, when they can work until 9 p.m.).

Exceptions

Certain employees are not covered by the child labor laws. Such workers include:

- child actors or performers
- newspaper carriers

- children younger than 16 who are employed by their parents in an occupation other than mining, manufacturing, or another hazardous job, and
- children younger than 16 who are engaged in certain training and apprenticeship programs.

How the FLSA Is Enforced

Individual Complaints

An employee who wishes to file a complaint regarding the FLSA's minimum wage and overtime requirements has two choices. The employee may make a complaint to the Wage and Hour Division of the DOL. (See "Agency Enforcement," below.) An employee does not have to complain to a government agency, however. The employee may choose instead to file a lawsuit in state court or in federal district court. The employee must file this lawsuit within two years of the date the employer violated the law, or within three years if the employer committed a *willful violation.*

Only the DOL may enforce the FLSA's restrictions on child labor. This means that individual employees do not have the right to file a lawsuit alleging child labor violations.

Agency Enforcement

If an employee files a complaint with the DOL, the agency may choose to investigate the employer. Although the agency can also conduct random audits, it is much more likely to investigate following a complaint.

A DOL investigator may contact the employer ahead of time or may simply show up at the workplace. The investigator will examine the employer's records and interview employees who may have information about the complaint. Once the investigation is complete, the investigator will meet with the employer to try to resolve any problems the investigation uncovered. The investigator will tell the employer whether it has violated the law, and how it can correct those violations—for example, by paying overdue wages to its workers.

If the employer refuses to comply, the secretary of labor can file a lawsuit in federal district court on behalf of the employees whose rights were violated. However, if the secretary of labor files a lawsuit on behalf of one or more employees, the employee no longer has the right to sue the company on his or her own. The secretary may also impose civil penalties against the employer; these penalties are assessed in an administrative hearing process, not a lawsuit, and they are paid to the government, not to the employee.

Complying With the FLSA

Reporting Requirements

The FLSA has no general reporting requirements. However, employers who apply for a subminimum wage certificate (see "Minimum Wage," above) or a waiver from the child labor laws (see "Child Labor," above) may have to provide certain information to the DOL.

Posting Requirements

All employers subject to the FLSA are required to post a notice (created by the DOL) describing the law's provisions. A copy of the notice must be posted conspicuously in every establishment, where every employee can readily see it. This notice is available free from the DOL. (See "Agency Resources," below.)

Employers who hire disabled workers at a subminimum wage pursuant to a certificate issued by the DOL (see "Minimum Wage," above) must post an official DOL notice about this program. This notice is available from the DOL free of charge. (See "Agency Resources," below.)

Record-Keeping Requirements

Employers must keep specified wage and hour records for each worker. You do not have to create or keep the records in any particular format, and you do not have to require your workers to punch a time clock or fill in time cards.

The following records must be kept for three years:

- payroll records showing each employee's name, address, occupation, sex, birth date (if the worker is under the age of 19), hour and day when the workweek begins, total wages paid each pay period, and the date of the payment for each pay period

- plans, trusts, collective bargaining agreements, and individual employment contracts
- all certificates or notices required by the FLSA, and
- records showing the total dollar volume of the business and the total volume of goods purchased or received.

For employees who are entitled to overtime and/or the minimum wage, employers must keep these additional records for each employee for three years:

- total hours worked each day and week
- total daily or weekly earnings
- regular hourly pay rate in any week when the employee works overtime
- total overtime pay for each week, and
- any deductions from or additions to pay for each pay period.

For exempt employees, employers must keep records sufficient to calculate the employee's total compensation per pay period, including fringe benefits. These records, which must be kept for two years, include:

- time cards or other records showing workers' daily stop and start times
- records showing the amount of work accomplished by individual employees on a daily, weekly, or pay period basis, if those amounts affect the employees' wages (for example, if they are paid on commission or by the piece)
- wage rate tables or other documents that show the rates used to compute piecework pay, straight time earnings wages, salary, or overtime pay
- order, shipping, and billing records, and
- records of additions to, or deductions from, wages paid, including records used by the employer to determine the original cost, operating cost, maintenance cost, depreciation, and interest charges, if these amounts are used to determine additions to or deductions from wages.

The regulations require employers to keep different types of records or additional records for certain types of employees, such as local delivery workers, seamen, and tipped employees. For more information on these requirements, see 29 C.F.R. § 516, which sets forth the FLSA's record-keeping requirements in detail.

Penalties

If a court finds that an employer has violated the FLSA, it may order the employer to:

- Pay retroactive wages (called back pay), equal to the difference between what the employee actually earned and what the employee should have earned if the employer had followed the law, plus interest. An employee can collect up to two years' worth of back pay, or three years' worth if the employer committed a willful violation of the statute.
- Pay an additional penalty (known as "liquidated damages"), equal to the entire back pay award, if the employer willfully violated the statute.

For violations of the child labor laws, employers may face penalties of up to $50,000, depending on the type of violation.

Agency Resources

- A guide to the FLSA's requirements
  Elaws—Fair Labor Standards Act Advisor
  www.dol.gov/elaws/flsa.htm

- The rules on employing minors in nonagricultural jobs
  Child Labor Bulletin 101
  www.dol.gov/whd/regs/compliance/childlabor101_text.htm

- A fact sheet on calculating overtime pay
  Overtime Pay Requirements of the FLSA
  www.dol.gov/whd/regs/compliance/whdfs23.pdf

- A fact sheet on what types of activities count as work
  Hours Worked Under the Fair Labor Standards Act (FLSA)
  www.dol.gov/whd/regs/compliance/whdfs22.pdf

- A fact sheet on employees exempt from overtime and minimum wage laws
  Exemption For Executive, Administrative, Professional, Computer & Outside Sales Employees Under the Fair Labor Standards Act (FLSA)
  www.dol.gov/whd/regs/compliance/fairpay/fs17a_overview.pdf

- A guide to the FLSA's record-keeping rules
  Recordkeeping Requirements under the Fair Labor Standards Act (FLSA)
  www.dol.gov/whd/regs/compliance/whdfs21.pdf

- Poster on the FLSA that employers are required to display
  Employee Rights Under the Fair Labor Standards Act
  www.dol.gov/whd/regs/compliance/posters/minwagebw.pdf

- Poster employers must display if they employ disabled workers at
  subminimum wage
  Employee Rights for Workers with Disabilities Paid at Special Minimum Wages
  www.dol.gov/regs/compliance/posters/disabc.pdf

- A list of the addresses and telephone numbers of local offices of the Wage
  and Hour Division
  Wage and Hour Division (WHD): WHD Local Offices
  www.dol.gov/whd/america2.htm

State Laws Relating to Wages and Hours

Most states have their own wage and hour laws, and some of them are almost
as extensive as the FLSA. Here, you'll find the state rules on minimum wage,
overtime, and meal and rest breaks. However, to find out whether your state
has rules on hours worked, child labor, exempt versus nonexempt employees,
or other wage and hour issues, contact your state labor department.

State Minimum Wage Laws for Tipped and Regular Employees

The chart below gives the basic state minimum wage laws. Depending on the occupation, the size of the employer's business, or the conditions of employment, the minimum wage may vary from the one listed here. Minimum wage rates in a number of states change from year to year; to be sure of your state's current minimum, contact your state department of labor or check its website, where most states have posted the minimum wage requirements. (See Appendix A for contact information.) Also, some local governments have enacted ordinances that set a higher minimum wage—contact your city or county government for more information. "Maximum Tip Credit" is the highest amount of tips that an employer can subtract from the employee's hourly wage. The employee's total wages minus the tip credit cannot be less than the state minimum wage. If an employee's tips exceed the maximum tip credit, the employee gets to keep the extra amount.

"Minimum Cash Wage" is the lowest hourly wage that an employer can pay a tipped employee.

State and Statute	Notes	Basic Minimum Hourly Rate (*=tied to federal rate)	Maximum Tip Credit	Minimum Cash Wage for Tipped Employee	Minimum Tips to Qualify as a Tipped Employee (monthly unless noted otherwise)
United States 29 U.S.C. § 206 29 U.S.C. § 203	This is the current federal minimum wage	$7.25	$5.12	$2.13	More than $30
Alabama	No minimum wage law				
Alaska Alaska Stat. § 23.10.065		$7.75	No tip credit	$7.75	N/A
Arizona Ariz. Rev. Stat. § 23-363	Adjusts annually for inflation, posted at www.ica.state. az.us/Labor/Labor_ MinWag_main. aspx; does not apply to small businesses (those with gross revenue of less than $500,000 that are exempt from federal minimum wage laws)	$7.80	$3.00	$4.80	Averaged total of actual tips and cash minimum must equal minimum wage for each pay period

State Minimum Wage Laws for Tipped and Regular Employees (continued)

State and Statute	Notes	Basic Minimum Hourly Rate (*=tied to federal rate)	Maximum Tip Credit	Minimum Cash Wage for Tipped Employee	Minimum Tips to Qualify as a Tipped Employee (monthly unless noted otherwise)
Arkansas Ark. Code Ann. §§ 11-4-210 and 11-4-212	Applies to employers with 4 or more employees	$6.25	$3.63	$2.63	Not specified
California Cal. Lab. Code § 1182.12		$8.00	No tip credit	$8.00	N/A
Colorado Colo. Const. Art. 18, § 15; 7 Colo. Code Regs. § 1103-1	Adjusted annually for inflation, posted at www. coworkforce.com	$7.78	$3.02	$4.76	More than $30
Connecticut Conn. Gen. Stat. Ann. §§ 31-58(j), 31-60; Conn. Admin. Code § 31-61-E2		$8.25 or FLSA + ½%	31% in hotel and restaurant industries; 11% bartenders; 35¢ others	$5.69 in hotel and restaurant industries; $7.34 bartenders; $7.90 others	$10 per week (full-time employees); $2 per day (part-time employees)
Delaware Del. Code Ann. tit. 19, § 902(a)		$7.15 or FLSA rate if higher	$5.02	$2.23	More than $30
District of Columbia D.C. Code Ann. § 32-1003		$7 or FLSA + $1.00 ($8.25) if DC rate is below the federal rate	$5.48	$2.77	Not specified
Florida Fla. Const., Art. X § 24; Fla. Stat. Ann. § 448.110	Adjusted annually, posted at www. floridajobs.org	$7.79	$3.02	$4.77	More than $30

State Minimum Wage Laws for Tipped and Regular Employees (continued)

State and Statute	Notes	Basic Minimum Hourly Rate (*=tied to federal rate)	Maximum Tip Credit	Minimum Cash Wage for Tipped Employee	Minimum Tips to Qualify as a Tipped Employee (monthly unless noted otherwise)
Georgia *Ga. Code Ann. § 34-4-3*	Applies to employers with 6 or more employees and more than $40,000 per year in sales	$5.15	Minimum wage does not apply to tipped employees	N/A	N/A
Hawaii *Haw. Rev. Stat. §§ 387-1 to 387-2*		$7.25	25¢	$7.00	More than $20; employee's cash wage plus tips must be at least 50¢ higher than the minimum wage
Idaho *Idaho Code § 44-1502*		$7.25	$3.90	$3.35	More than $30
Illinois *820 Ill. Comp. Stat. § 105/4; Ill. Admin. Code tit. 56, § 210.110*	Applies to employers with 4 or more employees	$8.25	40%	$4.95	At least $20
Indiana *Ind. Code Ann. § 22-2-2-4*	Applies to employers with 2 or more employees	$7.25*	$5.12	$2.13	Not specified
Iowa *Iowa Code § 91D.1*	In first 90 calendar days of employment, minimum wage is $6.35	$7.25	40%	$4.35	At least $30

State Minimum Wage Laws for Tipped and Regular Employees (continued)

State and Statute	Notes	Basic Minimum Hourly Rate (*=tied to federal rate)	Maximum Tip Credit	Minimum Cash Wage for Tipped Employee	Minimum Tips to Qualify as a Tipped Employee (monthly unless noted otherwise)
Kansas *Kan. Stat. Ann. § 44-1203*	Applies to employers not covered by the FLSA	$7.25	40%	$2.13	More than $20
Kentucky *Ky. Rev. Stat. Ann. § 337.275*		$7.25*	$5.12	$2.13	More than $30
Louisiana	No minimum wage law				
Maine *Me. Rev. Stat. Ann. tit. 26, §§ 663(8), 664*		$7.50*	50%	$3.75	More than $30
Maryland *Md. Code Ann., [Lab. & Empl.] §§ 3-413, 3-419*		$7.25*	50%	$3.63	More than $30
Massachusetts *Mass. Gen. Laws ch. 151, § 1; Mass. Regs. Code tit. 455, § 2.02*		$8.00 or 10¢ above FLSA rate if it is higher	$5.37	$2.63	More than $20
Michigan *Mich. Comp. Laws §§ 408.382 to 408.387a*	Applies to employers with 2 or more employees; excludes all employers subject to the FLSA, unless state minimum wage is higher than federal	$7.40	$4.75	$2.65	Not specified

State Minimum Wage Laws for Tipped and Regular Employees (continued)

State and Statute	Notes	Basic Minimum Hourly Rate (*=tied to federal rate)	Maximum Tip Credit	Minimum Cash Wage for Tipped Employee	Minimum Tips to Qualify as a Tipped Employee (monthly unless noted otherwise)
Minnesota *Minn. Stat. Ann. § 177.24*	$5.25 for small employer (business with annual receipts of less than $625,000)	$6.15	No tip credit	$6.15	N/A
Mississippi	No minimum wage law				
Missouri *Mo. Rev. Stat. §§ 290.502, 290.512*	Doesn't apply to retail or service business with gross annual sales of less than $500,000	$7.35	Up to 50%	$3.675	Not specified
Montana *Mont. Code Ann. §§ 39-3-404, 39-3-409; Mont. Admin. R. 24.16.1508 & following*	$4.00 for businesses with gross annual sales of $110,000 or less; adjusted annually. http://erd.dli.mt.gov/labor-standards/wage-and-hourwage-payment-act/102-montanas-wage-and-hour-labor-law-reference-guide.html	$7.80	No tip credit	$7.80	N/A
Nebraska *Neb. Rev. Stat. § 48-1203*	Applies to employers with 4 or more employees	$7.25	$5.12	$2.13	Not specified

State Minimum Wage Laws for Tipped and Regular Employees (continued)

State and Statute	Notes	Basic Minimum Hourly Rate (*=tied to federal rate)	Maximum Tip Credit	Minimum Cash Wage for Tipped Employee	Minimum Tips to Qualify as a Tipped Employee (monthly unless noted otherwise)
Nevada *Nev. Rev. Stat. Ann. § 608.160; Nev. Admin. Code ch. 608 § 110; Nev. Const. Art. 15 § 16*	Adjusted annually, posted at www.laborcommissioner.com	$7.25 if employer provides health benefits; $8.25 if no health benefits provided	No tip credit	$7.25 if employer provides health benefits; $8.25 if no health benefits provided	N/A
New Hampshire *N.H. Rev. Stat. Ann. § 279:21*		$7.25	55%	45%	More than $30
New Jersey *N.J. Stat. Ann. § 34:11-56a4*		$7.25*	$5.12*	$2.13	Not specified
New Mexico *N.M. Stat. Ann. § 50-4-22*		$7.50	$5.37	$2.13	More than $30
New York *N.Y. Lab. Law § 652; N.Y. Comp. Codes R. & Regs. tit. 12, §§ 137-1.4, 138-2.1*		$7.25*	Depends on occupation	Depends on occupation	Depends on occupation
North Carolina *N.C. Gen. Stat. §§ 95-25.2(14), 95-25.3*		$7.25	$5.12	$2.13	More than $20

State Minimum Wage Laws for Tipped and Regular Employees (continued)

State and Statute	Notes	Basic Minimum Hourly Rate (*=tied to federal rate)	Maximum Tip Credit	Minimum Cash Wage for Tipped Employee	Minimum Tips to Qualify as a Tipped Employee (monthly unless noted otherwise)
North Dakota N.D. Cent. Code § 34-06-22; N.D. Admin. Code R. 46-02-07-01 to -03		$7.25	33% of minimum wage	67% of minimum wage	More than $30
Ohio Ohio Rev. Code Ann. § 4111.02; Ohio Const. art. II § 34a	Same as federal minimum wage for employers with gross income under $271,000; adjusted annually, posted at www.com.ohio.gov/laws	$7.85	50%	50% of minimum wage	More than $30
Oklahoma Okla. Stat. Ann. tit. 40, §§ 197.2, 197.4, 197.16	Applies to employers with 10 or more full-time employees OR gross annual sales over $100,000 not otherwise subject to FLSA	$7.25	50% of minimum wage for tips, food, and lodging combined	50% of minimum wage	Not specified
Oregon Or. Rev. Stat. §§ 653.025, 653.035(3)	Adjusted annually; posted at www.boli.state.or.us	$8.95	No tip credit	$8.95	N/A
Pennsylvania 43 Pa. Cons. Stat. Ann. §§ 333.103 and 333.104; 34 Pa. Code §§ 231.1 and 231.103		$7.25*	$4.42	$2.83	More than $30

State Minimum Wage Laws for Tipped and Regular Employees (continued)

State and Statute	Notes	Basic Minimum Hourly Rate (*=tied to federal rate)	Maximum Tip Credit	Minimum Cash Wage for Tipped Employee	Minimum Tips to Qualify as a Tipped Employee (monthly unless noted otherwise)
Rhode Island R.I. Gen. Laws §§ 28-12-3 & 28-12-5		$7.75	$4.86	$2.89	Not specified
South Carolina	No minimum wage law				
South Dakota S.D. Codified Laws Ann. §§ 60-11-3 to -3.1		$7.25	$5.12	$2.13	More than $35
Tennessee	No minimum wage law				
Texas Tex. Lab. Code Ann. §§ 62.051 & 62.052		$7.25	$5.12	$2.13	More than $20
Utah Utah Code Ann. § 34-40-102; Utah Admin. R. 610-1		$7.25	$5.12	$2.13	More than $30
Vermont Vt. Stat. Ann. tit. 21, § 384(a); Vt. Code R. 24 090 003	Applies to employers with 2 or more employees; adjusted annually, posted at www.vtlmi.info	$8.60	$4.43	$4.17 for employees of hotels, motels, restaurants, and tourist places; no tip credit otherwise	More than $120
Virginia Va. Code Ann. §§ 40.1-28.9 and 28.10	Applies to employees not covered by FLSA	$7.25	Tips actually received	Minimum wage less tips actually received	Not specified

State Minimum Wage Laws for Tipped and Regular Employees (continued)

State and Statute	Notes	Basic Minimum Hourly Rate (*=tied to federal rate)	Maximum Tip Credit	Minimum Cash Wage for Tipped Employee	Minimum Tips to Qualify as a Tipped Employee (monthly unless noted otherwise)
Washington *Wash. Rev. Code Ann. § 49.46.020; Wash. Admin. Code § 296-126-022*	Adjusted annually; posted at www.lni. wa.gov	$9.19	No tip credit	$9.19	N/A
West Virginia *W.Va. Code §§ 21-5C-1, 21-5C-2, 21-5C-4*	Applies to employers with 6 or more employees at one location who are not covered by the FLSA	$7.25	20% of minimum wage	80% of minimum wage	Not specified
Wisconsin *Wis. Admin. Code DWD § 272.03*		$7.25	$4.92	$2.33	Not specified
Wyoming *Wyo. Stat. § 27-4-202*		$5.15	$3.02	$2.13	More than $30

State Overtime Laws

This chart covers private-sector employment only. The overtime rules summarized are not applicable to all employers or all employees. Occupations that generally are not subject to overtime laws include health care and attendant care, emergency medical personnel, seasonal workers, agricultural labor, camp counselors, nonprofits exempt under the FLSA, salespeople working on a commission, transit drivers, babysitters, and other household workers, and many others. For more information, contact your state's department of labor and be sure to check its website, where most states have posted their overtime rules. (See Appendix A for contact details.)

Alabama

No state overtime rules that differ from FLSA.

Alaska

Alaska Stat. § 23.10.060 and following

Time and a half after x hours per DAY: 8

Time and a half after x hours per WEEK: 40

Employment overtime laws apply to: Employers of 4 or more employees; commerce or manufacturing businesses.

Notes: Voluntary flexible work hour plan of 10-hour day, 40-hour week, with premium pay after 10 hours is permitted.

Arizona

No overtime limits for private sector employers.

Arkansas

Ark. Code Ann. §§ 11-4-211, 11-4-203

Time and a half after x hours per WEEK: 40

Employment overtime laws apply to: Employers of 4 or more employees.

Notes: Employees in retail and service establishments who spend up to 40% of their time on nonexempt work must be paid at least twice the state's minimum wage ($572 per week).

California

Cal. Lab. Code §§ 500–511; Cal. Code Regs. tit. 8, §§ 11010 and following

Time and a half after x hours per DAY: Eight; after 12 hours, double time.

Time and a half after x hours per WEEK: 40; on 7th day, time and a half for the first 8 hours; after 8 hours, double time.

Notes: Alternative four-day, 10-hour-day workweek is permitted, if established prior to 7/1/99.

Colorado

7 Colo. Code Regs. § 1103-1(4)

Time and a half after x hours per DAY: 12

Time and a half after x hours per WEEK: 40

Employment overtime laws apply to: Employees in retail and service, commercial support service, food and beverage, health and medical industries.

Connecticut

Conn. Gen. Stat. Ann. §§ 31-76b and 31-76c; Conn. Admin. Code § 31-62-E1

Time and a half after x hours per DAY: 8 hours or the employee's normal working hours or regular working hours, whatever the case may be.

State Overtime Laws (continued)

Time and a half after x hours per WEEK: 40; premium pay on weekends, holidays, or 6th or 7th consecutive day.

Notes: In restaurants and hotels, time-and-a-half pay required for the 7th consecutive day of work or for hours that exceed 40 per week.

Delaware

No state overtime rules that differ from FLSA.

District of Columbia

D.C. Code Ann. § 32-1003(c); D.C. Mun. Regs. tit. 7, § 906

Time and a half after x hours per WEEK: 40

Employment overtime laws apply to: Retail or service establishments.

Notes: Employees must be paid one hour minimum wage for each day a split shift is worked, but not if the employee lives on the premises.

Florida

No state overtime rules that differ from FLSA.

Georgia

No state overtime rules that differ from FLSA.

Hawaii

Haw. Rev. Stat. §§ 387-1; 387-3

Time and a half after x hours per WEEK: 40. Dairy, sugarcane, and seasonal agricultural work: 48 hours per week.

Notes: No employer shall employ any employee in split shifts unless all of the shifts within a period of twenty-four hours fall within a period of fourteen consecutive hours, except in case of extraordinary emergency.

Idaho

No state overtime rules that differ from FLSA.

Illinois

820 Ill. Comp. Stat. §§ 105/3(d), 105/4a

Time and a half after x hours per WEEK: 40

Employment overtime laws apply to: Employers of 4 or more employees.

Indiana

Ind. Code Ann. § 22-2-2-4(j)

Time and a half after x hours per DAY: 8

Time and a half after x hours per WEEK: 40, & sixth and seventh day of the workweek.

Notes: Collective bargaining agreements ratified by the NLRB may have different overtime provisions. Domestic service work is not excluded from overtime laws.

Iowa

No state overtime rules that differ from FLSA.

Kansas

Kan. Stat. Ann. § 44-1204

Time and a half after x hours per WEEK: 46

Kentucky

Ky. Rev. Stat. Ann. §§ 337.050, 337.285; 803 Ky. Admin. Regs. § 1:060

Time and a half after x hours per WEEK: 40

Notes: 7th day, time and a half.

State Overtime Laws (continued)

Louisiana

No state overtime rules that differ from FLSA.

Maine

Me. Rev. Stat. Ann. tit. 26, § 664(3)

Time and a half after x hours per WEEK: 40

Maryland

Md. Code Ann., [Lab. & Empl.] § 3-420

Time and a half after x hours per WEEK: 40; 48 hours for bowling alleys and residential employees caring for the sick, aged, or mentally ill in institutions other than hospitals; 60 hours for agricultural work and is exempt from the overtime provisions of the federal act.

Massachusetts

Mass. Gen. Laws ch. 151, § 1A

Time and a half after x hours per WEEK: 40

Notes: Sunday or holiday: time and a half as overtime unless already paid that rate as part of regular compensation.

Michigan

Mich. Comp. Laws §§ 408.382 and 408.384a

Time and a half after x hours per WEEK: 40

Employment overtime laws apply to: Employers of 2 or more employees.

Minnesota

Minn. Stat. Ann. § 177.25

Time and a half after x hours per WEEK: 48

Mississippi

No state overtime rules that differ from FLSA.

Missouri

Mo. Rev. Stat. §§ 290.500 and 290.505

Time and a half after x hours per WEEK: 40; 52 hours for seasonal amusement or recreation businesses.

Montana

Mont. Code Ann. §§ 39-3-405 and 39-3-406

Time and a half after x hours per WEEK: 40; 48 hours for students working seasonal jobs at amusement or recreational areas.

Nebraska

No state overtime rules that differ from FLSA.

Nevada

Nev. Rev. Stat. Ann. § 608.018

Time and a half after x hours per DAY: Eight, if employee's regular rate of pay is less than 1½ times the minimum wage.

Time and a half after x hours per WEEK: 40

Notes: Employer and employee may agree to flextime schedule of four 10-hour days.

New Hampshire

N.H. Rev. Stat. Ann. § 279.21(VIII)

Time and a half after x hours per WEEK: 40

New Jersey

N.J. Stat. Ann. §§ 34.11-56a4 and 34.11-56a4.1

Time and a half after x hours per WEEK: 40

New Mexico

N.M. Stat. Ann. § 50-4-22(C)

Time and a half after x hours per WEEK: 40

State Overtime Laws (continued)

New York

N.Y. Lab. Law §§ 160(3), 161; N.Y. Comp. Codes R. & Regs. tit. 12, § 142-2.2

Time and a half after x hours per WEEK: 40 for nonresidential workers; 44 for residential workers.

Notes: In some industries, employees must be given 24 consecutive hours off per week. See N.Y. Lab. Law § 161.

North Carolina

N.C. Gen. Stat. §§ 95-25.14, 95-25.4

Time and a half after x hours per WEEK: 40; 45 hours a week in seasonal amusement or recreational establishments.

North Dakota

N.D. Admin. Code § 46-02-07-02(4)

Time and a half after x hours per DAY: 8, if in the health care field and agreed-upon 14-day overtime period instead of seven-day period.

Time and a half after x hours per WEEK: 40; 50 hours per week, cabdrivers.

Ohio

Ohio Rev. Code Ann. § 4111.03

Time and a half after x hours per WEEK: 40

Employment overtime laws apply to: Employers who gross more than $150,000 a year.

Oklahoma

No state overtime rules that differ from FLSA.

Oregon

Or. Rev. Stat. §§ 653.261, 653.265

Time and a half after x hours per WEEK: 40

Notes: Time and a half required after 10 hours a day in canneries, driers, packing plants, mills, factories, and manufacturing facilities.

Pennsylvania

43 Pa. Cons. Stat. Ann. § 333.104(c); 34 Pa. Code § 231.41

Time and a half after x hours per WEEK: 40

Rhode Island

R.I. Gen. Laws §§ 28-12-4.1 and following, 5-23-2(h)

Time and a half after x hours per WEEK: 40

Notes: Time and a half for Sunday and holiday work is required for most retail businesses (these hours are not included in calculating weekly overtime).

South Carolina

No state overtime rules.

South Dakota

No state overtime rules that differ from FLSA.

Tennessee

No state overtime rules.

Texas

No state overtime rules.

Utah

No state overtime rules.

Vermont

Vt. Stat. Ann. tit. 21, §§ 382, 384(b); Vt. Code R. § 24 090 003

State Overtime Laws (continued)

Time and a half after x hours per WEEK: 40

Employment overtime laws apply to:
Employers of 2 or more employees.

Virginia

No state overtime rules.

Washington

Wash. Rev. Code Ann. § 49.46.130

Time and a half after x hours per WEEK: 40

West Virginia

W.Va. Code §§ 21-5c-1(e), 21-5c-3

Time and a half after x hours per WEEK: 40

Employment overtime laws apply to:

Employers of 6 or more employees at one location.

Wisconsin

Wis. Stat. Ann. § 103.01, 103.03; Wis. Admin. Code DWD §§ 274.01, 274.03, 274.04

Time and a half after x hours per WEEK: 40

Employment overtime laws apply to:
Manufacturing, mechanical, or retail businesses; beauty parlors, laundries, restaurants, hotels; telephone, express, shipping, and transportation companies.

Wyoming

No state overtime rules that differ from FLSA.

State Meal and Rest Break Laws

Note: The states of Alabama, Alaska, Arizona, Arkansas, District of Columbia, Florida, Idaho, Iowa, Louisiana, Maryland, Michigan, Mississippi, Missouri, Montana, New Jersey, New Mexico, North Carolina, Ohio, Oklahoma, South Carolina, South Dakota, Texas, Utah, Virginia, and Wyoming are not listed in this chart because they do not have laws or regulations on rest and meal breaks for adults employed in the private sector. Many states also exclude professional, administrative, and executive employees from these rules.

Other exceptions may apply. For example, many states have special break rules for specific occupations or industries, which are beyond the scope of this chart. Check the statute or check with your state department of labor if you need more information. (See Appendix A for contact list.).

California

Cal. Lab. Code §§ 512, 1030; Cal. Code Regs. tit. 8, §§ 11010-11170

Applies to: Employers in most industries.

Exceptions: Motion picture and other occupations. See wage orders, Cal. Code Regs. tit. 8, §§ 11010 to 11160, for additional exceptions.

Meal Break: 30 minutes, unpaid, after 5 hours, except when workday will be completed in 6 hours or less and employer and employee consent to waive meal break. Employee cannot work more than 10 hours a day without a second 30-minute break, except if workday is no more than 12 hours; second meal break may be waived if first meal break was not waived. On-duty paid meal period permitted when nature of work prevents relief from all duties and parties agree in writing.

Rest Break: Paid 10-minute rest period for each 4 hours worked or major fraction thereof; as practicable, in the middle of the work period; not required for employees whose total daily work time is less than 3½ hours.

Breast-feeding: Reasonable time to breast-feed infant or to express breast milk; paid if taken concurrent with other break time; otherwise, unpaid.

Colorado

Colo. Code Regs. tit. 7 § 1103-1(7)-(8)

Applies to: Retail and service, food and beverage, commercial support service, and health and medical industries.

Exceptions: Numerous exceptions are listed in the regulation.

Meal Break: 30 minutes, unpaid, after 5 hours of work; on-duty paid meal period permitted when nature of work prevents break from all duties.

Rest Break: Paid 10-minute rest period for each 4 hours or major fraction worked; if practical, in the middle of the work period.

Connecticut

Conn. Gen. Stat. Ann. §§ 31-51ii, 31-40w

Applies to: All employers, except as noted.

Exceptions: Employers who pay for rest breaks as described below, those with a written agreement providing other break rules, and those granted an exemption for reasons listed in statute.

Meal Break: 30 minutes, unpaid, after first 2 hours of work and before last 2 hours

State Meal and Rest Break Laws (continued)

for employees who work 7½ or more consecutive hours.

Rest Break: As alternative to meal break, a total of 30 minutes paid in each 7½-hour work period.

Breast-feeding: Employee may use meal or rest break for breast-feeding or expressing breast milk.

Delaware

Del. Code Ann. tit. 19, § 707

Applies to: All employers, except as noted.

Exceptions: Employers with alternative written agreement and those granted exemptions specified in statute. Law does not apply to teachers.

Meal Break: 30 minutes, unpaid, after first 2 hours and before the last 2 hours, for employees who work 7½ consecutive hours or more.

Georgia

Ga. Code Ann. § 34-1-6

Applies to: All employers.

Breast-feeding: Reasonable unpaid break time to breast-feed infant or to express breast milk.

Hawaii

Haw. Rev. Stat. § 378-2

Applies to: All employers.

Breast-feeding: Allowed during any break required by law or collective bargaining agreement.

Illinois

820 Ill. Comp. Stat. §§ 140/3, 260/10

Applies to: All employers.

Exceptions: Employees whose meal periods are established by collective bargaining agreement.

Employees who monitor individuals with developmental disabilities or mental illness, or both, and who are required to be on call during an entire 8-hour work period; these employees must be allowed to eat a meal while working.

Meal Break: 20 minutes, no later than 5 hours after the beginning of the shift, for employees who work 7½ or more continuous hours.

Breast-feeding: Reasonable unpaid break time to breast-feed infant or express breast milk.

Indiana

Ind. Code §§ 22-2-14, 5-10-6-2

Applies to: All employers with 25 or more employees.

Breast-feeding: Reasonable unpaid break time to express breast milk.

Kansas

Kan. Admin. Reg. 49-30-3

Applies to: Employees not covered under FLSA.

Meal Break: Not required, but if less than 30 minutes is given, break must be paid.

Kentucky

Ky. Rev. Stat. Ann. §§ 337.355, 337.365;
Ky. Admin. Regs. tit. 803, 1:065 § 4

Applies to: All employers, except as noted.

Exceptions: Written agreement providing different meal period; employers subject to Federal Railway Labor Act.

State Meal and Rest Break Laws (continued)

Meal Break: Reasonable off-duty period close to the middle of the shift; can't be required to take it before the third or after the fifth hour of work.

Rest Break: Paid 10-minute rest period for each 4-hour work period; rest period must be in addition to regularly scheduled meal period.

Maine

Me. Rev. Stat. Ann. tit. 26, § 601

Applies to: Most employers.

Exceptions: Small businesses with fewer than 3 employees on duty who are able to take frequent breaks during the workday; collective bargaining or other written agreement between employer and employee may provide for different breaks.

Meal and Rest Break: 30 minutes, unpaid, after 6 consecutive hours of work, except in cases of emergency.

Breast-feeding: Adequate unpaid time to express breast milk, or employee may use rest or meal time.

Massachusetts

Mass. Gen. Laws ch. 149, §§ 100, 101

Applies to: All employers, except as noted.

Exceptions: Excludes iron works, glass works, paper mills, letterpresses, print works, and bleaching or dyeing works. Attorney general may exempt businesses that require continuous operation if it won't affect worker safety. Collective bargaining agreement may also provide for different breaks.

Meal Break: 30 minutes, if work is for more than 6 hours.

Minnesota

Minn. Stat. Ann. §§ 177.253, 177.254, 181.939

Applies to: All employers.

Exceptions: Excludes certain agricultural and seasonal employees.

A collective bargaining agreement may provide for different rest and meal breaks.

Meal Break: Sufficient unpaid time for employees who work 8 consecutive hours or more.

Rest Break: Paid adequate rest period within each 4 consecutive hours of work to utilize nearest convenient rest room.

Breast-feeding: Reasonable unpaid break time to breast-feed infant or express milk.

Nebraska

Neb. Rev. Stat. § 48-212

Applies to: Assembly plant, workshop, or mechanical establishment.

Exceptions: Other written agreement between employer and employees.

Meal Break: 30 minutes off premises for each 8-hour shift.

Nevada

Nev. Rev. Stat. Ann. § 608.019

Applies to: Employers of two or more employees.

Exceptions: Employees covered by collective bargaining agreement; exemptions for business necessity.

Meal Break: 30 minutes for 8 continuous hours of work.

Rest Break: Paid 10-minute rest period for each 4 hours or major fraction worked; as practicable, in middle of the work period;

State Meal and Rest Break Laws (continued)

not required for employees whose total daily work time is less than 3½ hours.

New Hampshire

N.H. Rev. Stat. Ann. § 275:30-a

Applies to: All employers.

Meal Break: 30 minutes after 5 consecutive hours, unless the employer allows the employee to eat while working and it is feasible for the employee to do so.

New York

N.Y. Lab. Law §§ 162, 206-c

Applies to: Factories, workshops, manufacturing facilities, mercantile (retail and wholesale) establishments.

Meal Break: Factory employees, 60 minutes between 11 a.m. and 2 p.m.; mercantile employees, 30 minutes between 11 a.m. and 2 p.m. If a shift starts before 11 a.m. and ends after 7 p.m., every employee gets an additional 20 minutes between 5 p.m. and 7 p.m. If a shift starts between 1 p.m. and 6 a.m., a factory employee gets 60 minutes, and a mercantile employee gets 45 minutes, in the middle of the shift. Labor commissioner may permit a shorter meal break; the permit must be in writing and posted conspicuously in the main entrance of the workplace.

Breast-feeding: Reasonable unpaid break time to express breast milk for up to three years after child's birth.

North Dakota

N.D. Admin. Code § 46-02-07-02

Applies to: Applicable when two or more employees are on duty.

Exceptions: Waiver by employee or other provision in collective bargaining agreement.

Meal Break: 30 minutes for each shift over 5 hours; unpaid if employee is completely relieved of duties.

Oregon

Or. Admin. R. §§ 839-020-0050, 839-020-0051

Applies to: All employers except as noted.

Exceptions: Agricultural workers and employees covered by a collective bargaining agreement.

Meal Break: 30 minutes for employees who work at least six hours, unpaid if relieved of all duties; paid time to eat if employee cannot be relieved of duty; a 20-minute paid break, if employer can show that it is industry practice or custom. If shift of 7 hours or less, meal break must occur between hours 2 and 5; if shift longer than 7 hours, meal break must be between hours 3 and 6.

Rest Break: Paid 10-minute rest period for each 4 hours or major fraction worked; if practical, in the middle of the work period.

Rest period must be in addition to usual meal break and taken separately; can't be added to meal period or deducted from beginning or end of shift to reduce length of total work period.

Rest period is not required for certain solo adult employees serving the public, although they must be allowed to use rest room.

Breast-feeding: Reasonable unpaid rest period, no greater than 30 minutes for each 4 hours worked, to express milk to child 18 months or younger.

State Meal and Rest Break Laws (continued)

Pennsylvania

43 Pa. Cons. Stat. Ann. § 1301.207

Applies to: Employers of seasonal farmworkers.

Meal Break: 30 minutes after 5 hours.

Rhode Island

R.I. Gen. Laws §§ 28-3-8, 28-3-14, 23-13-2.1

Applies to: Employers with 5 or more employees.

Exceptions: Employers of health care facility or employers with fewer than 3 employees on any shift.

Meal Break: 20 minutes, unpaid, within a 6-hour shift or 30 minutes, unpaid, within an 8-hour shift.

Breast-feeding: Reasonable unpaid break time to breast-feed infant or express breast milk.

Tennessee

Tenn. Code Ann. §§ 50-2-103(h), 50-1-305

Applies to: Employers with 5 or more employees.

Meal and Rest Break: 30 minutes unpaid for employees scheduled to work 6 con-secutive hours or more unless work is such that there is ample time for breaks throughout the day.

Breast-feeding: Reasonable unpaid break time to breast-feed infant or express breast milk, and employer shall make reasonable efforts to provide a space (other than a toilet stall) for employee to express breast milk in privacy.

Vermont

Vt. Stat. Ann. tit. 21, § 304

Applies to: All employers.

Meal Break: Employees must be given reasonable opportunities to eat and use toilet facilities during work periods.

Washington

Wash. Admin. Code §§ 296-126-092, 286-131-020

Applies to: All employers except as noted.

Exceptions: Newspaper vendor or carrier, domestic or casual labor around private residence, sheltered workshop; separate provisions for agricultural labor.

Meal Break: 30-minute break, if work period is more than 5 consecutive hours, not less than 2 hours nor more than 5 hours from beginning of shift. This time is paid if employee is on duty or is required to be at a site for employer's benefit. Employees who work 3 or more hours longer than regular workday are entitled to an additional half hour, before or during overtime.

Agricultural employees: 30 minutes if working more than 5 hours; additional 30 minutes if working 11 or more hours in a day

Rest Break: Paid 10-minute rest break for each 4-hour work period, scheduled as near as possible to midpoint of each work period. Employee cannot be required to work more than 3 hours without a rest break.

Scheduled rest breaks are not required where nature of work allows employee to take intermittent rest breaks equivalent to required standard.

State Meal and Rest Break Laws (continued)

West Virginia

W.Va. Code § 21-3-10a; W.Va. Code St. R. § 42-5-2(2.6)

Applies to: All employers.

Meal Break: At least 20-minute break for each 6 consecutive hours worked, unless employees are allowed to take breaks as needed or to eat lunch while working.

Rest Break: Rest breaks of 20 minutes or less must be counted as paid work time.

Wisconsin

Wis. Admin. Code § DWD 274.02

Applies to: All employers.

Meal Break: Recommended but not required: 30 minutes close to usual meal time or near middle of shift. Shifts of more than 6 hours without a meal break should be avoided. If employee is not free to leave the workplace, meal period is considered paid time.

Family and Medical Leave Act (FMLA)

Statute: 29 U.S.C. § 2601 and following
www.dol.gov/whd/fmla/fmlaAmended.htm

Regulations: 29 C.F.R. § 825.100 and following
www.gpo.gov/fdsys/pkg/CFR-2012-title29-vol3/pdf/CFR-2012-title29-vol3-part825.pdf

Overview of the FMLA

Originally passed in 1993, the Family and Medical Leave Act (FMLA) requires covered employers to allow eligible employees to take up to 12 weeks of unpaid leave per 12-month period for the arrival of a new child through birth, adoption, or *foster care*, to care for a family member who is suffering from a *serious health condition*, or to deal with the employee's own serious health condition. Employees are entitled to continue their health benefits while on leave. Once their leave is over, employees are entitled to reinstatement.

In 2008, Congress amended the FMLA to add two leave rights relating to military service:

- Employees may take FMLA leave for a qualifying exigency relating to a family member's *covered active duty*. This leave counts toward the employee's 12-week total entitlement for all types of FMLA leave.
- Employees may take up to 26 weeks of leave in a single 12-month period to care for certain family members who are *covered servicemembers*. If employees use this leave and regular FMLA leave during the year, they are entitled only to 26 weeks of leave total, and no more than 12 of those weeks may be used for regular FMLA leave.

The FMLA has special rules for employees of public and private schools, which are not covered here.

Regulated Employers

The following employers must comply with the FMLA:

- private employers with 50 or more employees
- the federal government
- state and local governments, and
- public and private elementary schools and secondary schools.

Definitions

Authentication To give a health care provider a copy of the certification and request verification that the information was completed or authorized by the provider who signed the document. No additional medical information may be requested.

Certification A document that employers may require employees to provide when they want to take leave for their own *serious health condition*, a family member's serious health condition, or a *qualifying exigency*, or leave to care for a *covered servicemember* with a *serious illness or injury*.

Clarification To contact a health care provider to understand the handwriting or the meaning of a response on a certification. No additional information may be sought beyond that required by the certification form.

Continuing treatment by a health care provider A period of incapacity of more than three full consecutive days that also involves (1) treatment two or more times within 30 days of the first day of incapacity by a health care provider or a nurse or other provider of health care services under orders of, or on referral by, a health care provider; or (2) at least one treatment by a health care provider that results in a regimen of continuing treatment under the health care provider's supervision.

Covered active duty For a member of a regular component of the armed forces, duty during deployment to a foreign country. For a member of the National Guard or reserves, duty during deployment to a foreign country under call or order to active duty.

Covered servicemember (1) A current member of the armed forces, the National Guard, or reserves, who is undergoing medical treatment, recuperation, or therapy; is otherwise in outpatient status; or is otherwise on the temporary disability retired list, for a serious injury or illness.

(2) A veteran who is undergoing medical treatment, recuperation, or therapy, for a serious injury or illness and who was a member of the armed forces (including a member of the National Guard or reserves) at any time in the previous five years.

Essential duties The fundamental, not marginal, duties of a job.

Definitions (continued)

Fitness for duty certification A document from the employee's health care provider stating that the employee is able to resume work; employers may require employees who take FMLA leave for their own *serious health condition* to provide such a certification before returning to work.

Foster care The 24-hour care for children as a substitute for, and away from, their own parents or guardians. Informal care arrangements don't constitute foster care, which arises only when the government is involved in taking children away from their own families and placing them in another's home.

Intermittent leave Leave that is not taken all at once, but is instead taken piecemeal or results in a reduced work schedule.

Key employee A salaried eligible employee who is among the highest paid 10% of the employer's employees within a 75-mile radius of the site where the employee works.

Next of kin A covered servicemember's nearest blood relative, other than a parent, child, or spouse, in the following order of priority: (1) blood relatives who have been granted legal custody of the servicemember; (2) siblings; (3) grandparents; (4) aunts and uncles; and (5) first cousins. If the covered servicemember has designated a blood relative as next of kin, that designation must be followed. If not, all blood relatives within the same level of the highest-priority relationship are considered the servicemember's next of kin.

Reasonable safety concerns A reasonable belief of significant risk or harm to the employee or others, considering the nature, severity, and likelihood of the potential harm, which gives the employer a right to require more frequent fitness for duty certifications from an employee using intermittent leave.

Definitions (continued)

Serious health condition An illness, injury, impairment, or a physical or mental condition that involves (1) inpatient care (an overnight stay) in a medical facility; (2) incapacity for at least three full, consecutive days with *continuing treatment by a health care provider*; (3) incapacity due to pregnancy or prenatal care; (4) incapacity or treatment for a chronic serious health condition; (5) permanent or long-term incapacity for a condition for which treatment may not be effective (such as a terminal illness); or (6) absence for multiple treatments for either restorative surgery following an injury or accident or a condition that would require an absence of more than three days if not treated.

Serious illness or injury In the case of a current member of the armed forces, National Guard, or reserves, an illness or injury that was incurred in the line of duty on active duty, or that existed before the member's active duty and was aggravated by service in the line of duty on active duty, which may render the member medically unfit to perform the duties of his or her office, grade, rank, or rating. In the case of a veteran, a qualifying injury or illness (as defined in final regulations to be issued by the Department of Labor) that was incurred in the line of duty on active duty, or that existed before the member's active duty and was aggravated by service in the line of duty on active duty, and that manifested itself before or after the member became a veteran.

Total monthly guarantee The minimum number of hours for which an employer has agreed to schedule a flight attendant or flight crew member in a given month, or the number of hours for which an employer has agreed to pay a flight attendant or flight crew member who is on reserve status in a given month, as established by the collective bargaining agreement or in the employer's policies.

Legal Developments

- **Military family leave is expanded.** The National Defense Authorization Act of 2010 included the Supporting Military Families Act, which built on the FMLA's recent provisions for family military leave. The act makes these changes, each discussed in this chapter:
  - Qualifying exigency leave is now available to family members of those in the regular armed forces as well as those in the National Guard and reserves.
  - Qualifying exigency leave is now available to family members of those deployed to a foreign country, not only those serving in support of a contingency operation.
  - Military caregiver leave is now available to family members of veterans who need care and were in the military in the last five years. The types of injuries and illnesses covered are to be determined by regulations to be issued by the Department of Labor.
  - Military caregiver leave is now available for a family member's preexisting serious illness or injury that is aggravated by active duty in the military.
- **Proposed regulations issued on expansion of military family leave.** In 2012, the Department of Labor issued proposed regulations implementing the military family leave changes. Among other things, these proposed regulations tweak the rules for qualifying exigency leave (by, for example, increasing the amount of time an employee can take for a family member's rest and recuperation); explain what constitutes a serious injury for a veteran; modify the certification requirements for military family leave; and seek input on how to define preexisting injuries and illnesses aggravated by active duty. These rules have not been finalized as we go to press, and the Department of Labor has taken the position that employers need not provide military caregiver leave to employees who need time off to care for a veteran until final regulations are issued.
- **Airline employees get coverage.** In December 2009, Congress passed the Airline Flight Crew Technical Corrections Act, a law that lowers the hours-worked requirement for FMLA coverage. Flight attendants and flight crew members are covered if they have worked at least 60% of the *total monthly guarantee* in the past 12 months and have worked or been paid for at least 504 hours (not including leave, vacation, or commute time) during that period.

Covered Workers

To be eligible to take FMLA leave, an employee must:
- have worked for a covered employer for at least 12 months (these months do not have to be consecutive, but the employer does not have to count time worked prior to a break in service of seven years or more in most cases)
- have worked at least 1,250 hours for the employer in the 12 months immediately preceding the leave (flight attendants are covered if they have worked at least 60% of their total monthly guarantee or worked or been paid for at least 504 hours—not including leave, vacation, or commute time—during the previous 12 months), and
- work at a location with 50 or more employees within a 75-mile radius.

Employees who take leave to serve in the U.S. military are entitled to count that time as hours worked for all purposes, including eligibility for the FMLA. (See Chapter 19, on the Uniformed Services Employment and Reemployment Rights Act, for more information.)

Did You Know ...

- The Department of Labor estimates that seven million employees use FMLA leave every year, and that an additional 139,000 employees will take FMLA leave each year under the new provisions relating to military service (for qualifying exigencies and to care for family members injured while on active duty).
- Between September 11, 2001 and October 2012, more than 860,000 Guard members and reservists were mobilized.
- Almost a quarter of the employees who take FMLA leave use at least some of it intermittently.

Major Provisions of the FMLA

12-Week FMLA Leave Provisions

The original FMLA gives an eligible employee the right to take leave to bond with a new child, recover from a serious health condition, or care for a family member with a serious health condition. The 2008 amendments to the FMLA also allow an eligible employee to take leave for a qualifying exigency relating to a family member's *covered active duty*.

Regulated Employers

All regulated employers are subject to these provisions.

Covered Workers

All covered workers are subject to these provisions.

What's Prohibited

Employers may not prevent employees from exercising their FMLA rights, nor may they discriminate or retaliate against employees for exercising their FMLA rights. Employers cannot fire or otherwise retaliate against employees for taking or requesting FMLA leave.

   Employers may not interfere with court proceedings or investigations pertaining to the FMLA. Prohibited interference includes firing or discriminating against someone who plans to testify or give information.

What's Required

Employers must grant leave to an eligible employee in the following circumstances, all discussed in "Reasons Employees May Take Leave," below:
   • to bond with a newborn child, newly adopted child, or a child placed with the employee for foster care
   • to care for a family member with a serious health condition
   • for the employee's own serious health condition that makes the employee unable to work, or
   • for a qualifying exigency relating to a family member's covered active duty.

Amount of Leave

Eligible employees can receive up to 12 workweeks of unpaid leave per every 12-month period of employment. This limit applies to an employee's total leave for all covered situations. For example, an employee who uses eight weeks of leave to care for a new child has only four weeks of leave left in that 12-month period for all types of leave. Special time limits apply to certain types of leave for a qualifying exigency; see "Reasons Employees May Take Leave," below.

An employer can choose any one of the following methods for determining when the 12-month period begins and ends:

- the calendar year
- any fixed 12-month period, such as a fiscal year, a year required by state law, or a year starting on an employee's anniversary date
- a 12-month period beginning on the date the employee first takes FMLA leave, or
- a 12-month period measured backward from the date the employee uses any FMLA leave.

The employer must use the same method of measuring the 12-month period for all employees. An employee who takes leave to bond with a new child must complete that leave within the 12-month period after the child arrives—that is, the day the child is born or placed for adoption or foster care.

Paid or Unpaid Leave

The FMLA requires only unpaid leave. However, an employee may choose, or an employer may require an employee, to use accrued paid leave at the same time as FMLA leave. This rule applies only if the employee meets the criteria and follows the procedures of the employer's paid leave plan. For example, if the employer generally allows employees to use sick leave to care for an ailing family member, an employee may use that leave during FMLA leave to care for a family member with a serious health condition. If the employer allows employees to use sick leave only for their own illnesses, however, an employee may not use that leave when caring for a family member.

The employee must also meet the procedural requirements of the employer's paid leave plan. For example, if the employer's vacation policy requires employees to request vacation time two weeks in advance, an employee must follow that rule to use paid vacation time during FMLA leave. If the employee is unable to follow the rule—for example, because the employee is in an accident and

206 | THE ESSENTIAL GUIDE TO FEDERAL EMPLOYMENT LAWS

needs FMLA leave immediately—then the employee is not entitled to paid leave but is still entitled to unpaid FMLA leave. Using the facts above, an employee who is in an accident and requests paid vacation time on the day of the accident would not be entitled to use vacation days until two weeks have passed; however, those two weeks would still be protected as FMLA leave.

Sometimes, an employee on FMLA leave also receives some wage replacement in the form of disability or workers' compensation benefits. In this situation, substitution of leave is not allowed and may not be required, because the employee is already receiving some pay. However, the employee and employer may agree that the employee can use paid leave to make up the difference between the employee's benefit and the employee's usual salary. For example, if an employee is receiving two-thirds of his or her usual salary in workers' compensation benefits, the employer and employee could agree that the employee may use vacation pay to make up the remaining third.

Benefits While on Leave

Employees may keep their health benefits while on FMLA leave, and the employer must continue to pay whatever premiums it would pay if the employee were not on leave. If the employee voluntarily chooses not to return from leave, however, the employer may require the employee to repay the cost of the health care premiums it paid while the employee was on leave. The employer may not seek reimbursement if the employee fails to return to work for reasons beyond the employee's control (for example, a serious health condition that does not improve enough to allow the employee to return to work).

The employee accrues (or does not accrue, according to the employer's policies) earned benefits such as seniority or paid time off while on FMLA leave in the same manner that employees generally accrue (or do not accrue) these benefits while on other types of unpaid leave.

Reasons Employees May Take Leave

For a New Child

A mother and a father have an equal right to take FMLA leave to bond with a new child, whether the child arrives by birth, adoption, or foster care.

If an employee is unable to work because of pregnancy, she may take FMLA leave before the child is born. However, she still gets only 12 weeks of FMLA leave for the 12-month leave year, so the amount of time she takes off before the birth will count against the amount of time off she may take after the birth if both occur within the same 12-month period. Some states provide additional leave for pregnancy-related disabilities. For information about such laws in your state, see "State Laws Relating to Family and Medical Leave," below, and consult your state fair employment agency or labor department (see Appendix A for contact information).

Employees who are expecting a child through adoption or foster care may take some FMLA leave before the child arrives if the leave is needed to arrange for the child's placement. For example, some courts order parents to undergo counseling before receiving a foster child. The FMLA covers time off from work for that counseling.

Parents can take *intermittent leave* for the arrival of a new child only if the employer agrees.

For a Family Member With a Health Problem

An employee may take FMLA leave to care for a family member who is suffering from a serious health condition. Employers may ask an employee to provide *certification* from a health care provider that the family member is suffering from a serious health condition. (For more information, see "Certification," below.)

If an employee needs leave to care for a family member, the employee may do so on an intermittent schedule. The employee can take intermittent leave both when the family member's health condition is intermittent and when the employee's need to take leave is intermittent (for example, when the employee shares care responsibilities with other people). If the leave is for planned medical treatment, the employer may temporarily assign the employee to a different position with equal pay and benefits to accommodate the intermittent schedule.

Not all members of an employee's family are family members for purposes of this provision of the FMLA. Family members consist of spouses, parents, and children:

- A spouse must be someone whom state law recognizes as being married to the employee. The only exception to this rule is for same-sex spouses. Even though at least some states and foreign countries recognize marriage between same-sex couples, such couples probably won't qualify as "family members" under the FMLA. This is so because a federal law called the Defense of Marriage Act (DOMA) defines marriage for purposes of all federal laws as a union between a man and a woman. The Department of Labor (DOL) has said, in an opinion letter, that DOMA restricts the FMLA definition of "spouse" in this way, and no court has yet contradicted this interpretation.

• A parent must be a biological, adopted, stepparent, or foster parent, or a person who acted as a parent (that is, someone who had the day-to-day responsibility of caring for or financially supporting the employee as a child). Thus, a mother-in-law is not a parent, but an aunt who took in an employee as a child, when the employee's parents were killed or incapacitated, might be.

• A son or daughter is a biological child, adopted child, foster child, stepchild, legal ward, or a child for whom the employee acts as a parent (that is, a child for whom the employee takes day-to-day responsibility for care and financial support). For this provision of the FMLA, the child must be either under the age of 18 or at least 18 years old and incapable of caring for him- or herself.

For Employee's Own Health Problem

To take FMLA leave for his or her own health problem, an employee must:

• be suffering from a serious health condition, and
• be unable to perform one or more of the *essential duties* of his or her job.

An employee can be considered unable to perform his or her job duties because he or she is absent from work for medical treatment. Under certain circumstances, employees may take FMLA leave to treat a substance abuse problem if the condition otherwise meets the definition of a serious health condition.

The employer may require the employee to provide certification from a health care provider that the employee is indeed unable to perform an essential duty of the job. (For more, see "Certification," below.)

If medically necessary, an employee may take FMLA leave on an intermittent schedule for his or her own serious illness. If intermittent leave is necessary for planned medical treatment, the employee must make a reasonable effort to schedule the treatment so as not to unduly disrupt the employer's operations. The employer may temporarily assign the employee to a different position with equal pay and benefits to accommodate the intermittent schedule.

For a Qualifying Exigency

Employees may take FMLA leave while the employee's spouse, child, or parent is on covered active duty for a qualifying exigency. For purposes of this provision, the employee's child may be any age; the child need not be either under the age of 18 or, if 18 or older, incapable of self-care, as is true for other types of 12-week FMLA leave.

This leave is available for exigencies relating to regular members of the armed forces as well as members of the National Guard or reserves and, in certain circumstances, retired members of the regular armed forces or reserves.

Employees may take leave for seven types of qualifying exigencies, as explained below. For some of these exigencies, the amount of leave is limited. In addition to these seven categories, an employee may take qualifying exigency leave for other activities if employer and employee agree that the activity is a qualifying exigency and agree on the timing and duration of leave. The seven categories of qualifying exigencies are:

- **Short-notice deployment.** Leave is available to address any issue arising from the fact that a covered family member is notified of the order or call to active duty within seven calendar days of the date of deployment. Leave may be used for seven calendar days starting on the date the covered family member is notified.
- **Military events and related activities.** Leave may be taken to attend any official ceremony, program, or event sponsored by the military and attend family support and assistance programs and information briefings sponsored or promoted by the military, military service organizations, or the American Red Cross, related to the family member's covered active duty.
- **Child care and school activities.** The employee may take leave to arrange alternative child care if a family member's covered active duty requires a change; to provide child care on an urgent, immediate need basis (not regularly); to enroll in or transfer the child to another school; and to attend meetings with school or day care staff.
- **Financial and legal arrangements.** Leave is available to deal with financial or legal matters necessary to address the family member's absence, such as creating financial and health care powers of attorney; transferring bank account signature authority; enrolling in the Defense Enrollment Eligibility Reporting System (DEERS); getting military ID cards;

preparing a will or living trust; or acting as the family member's representative before a government agency regarding military service benefits, for up to 90 days after termination of the member's active duty status.

- **Counseling.** The employee may take leave to attend counseling for oneself, the family member, or the family member's child, relating to covered active duty.
- **Rest and recuperation.** The employee may take leave to spend time with the family member who is on short-term, temporary rest and recreation leave during deployment. Although current rules limit employees to five days off for each of the family member's rest and recuperation periods, proposed regulations would extend this to a maximum of 15 days.
- **Postdeployment activities.** Leave may be taken to attend arrival ceremonies, reintegration briefings and events, and any other official military ceremony or program for up to 90 days after termination of the family member's active duty. Leave is also available to address issues arising from the member's death, such as recovering the body and making funeral arrangements.

Qualifying exigency leave may be taken intermittently or on a reduced leave schedule. Employers may require employees to submit a certification regarding their qualified exigency leave; see "Certification," below.

Required Notice From the Employer

There are four types of notice an employer may have to give under the FMLA: general notice, eligibility notice, rights and responsibilities notice, and designation notice.

General Notice

An employer must post a notice in its workplace explaining the FMLA. Employers can obtain this notice from the DOL. (See "Agency Resources," below, for details.) The notice can be posted electronically, as long as it is large enough to be easily read, contains fully legible text, and can readily be seen by employees and applicants for employment.

If an employer has any written materials, such as an employee handbook, that explain employee benefits, the employer must include the general notice in those materials or distribute a copy of the general notice to each new employee upon hire. In either situation, the notice may be distributed electronically.

Eligibility Notice

When an employee requests FMLA leave or the employer becomes aware that an employee's leave may qualify for FMLA protection, the employer must notify the employee of his or her eligibility to take FMLA leave. The employer has five business days to provide this eligibility notice, absent extenuating circumstances. This notice may be written or oral. If the employee is not eligible for leave, the notice must state at least one reason for the employee's ineligibility.

All FMLA absences for the same qualifying reason are considered a single leave, and the employee's eligibility to take that leave doesn't change during the applicable 12-month period. If the employee requests leave for a second qualifying reason, and the employee's eligibility has not changed, the employer need not provide a second eligibility notice. However, if the employee's eligibility has changed, the employer must provide notice of the change within five business days, absent extenuating circumstances.

Rights and Responsibilities Notice

The employer must also give employees written notice of their rights and responsibilities under the FMLA. This notice must be provided each time the eligibility notice is provided. This notice must state:

- that the employee's leave may be designated as FMLA leave and counted against his or her entitlement
- whether the employer will require the employee to provide certification (and the consequences of failing to provide the certification)
- the employee's right to use accrued paid time off during the unpaid FMLA leave, whether the employer will require the employee to use accrued paid time off during leave, the conditions related to using accrued paid time off, and the employee's right to take unpaid FMLA leave if the employee doesn't meet the conditions for using paid leave
- how health benefit premiums will be paid and the consequences of failing to pay them
- whether the employee is a key employee and the consequences of that classification (see "Exceptions," below, for more about key employees)
- the employee's right to restoration of benefits and reinstatement to the same or an equivalent job upon return from leave, and

- the employee's potential liability for any health insurance premiums the employer pays while the employee is on FMLA leave, if the employee fails to return to work after FMLA leave.

The DOL has created prototype notice forms that employers may adapt as appropriate to meet their notice requirements; see "Agency Resources," below. The employer may distribute this notice electronically.

Designation Notice

When the employer has enough information to determine whether an employee is taking leave for an FMLA-qualifying reason, the employer must notify the employee whether leave will be designated and counted as FMLA leave. The employer must provide this notice within five business days, absent extenuating circumstances. The employer need provide only one designation notice per qualifying reason per 12-month leave year, whether the leave will be taken intermittently or all at once. If the information in the notice changes, the employer must notify the employee of the change within five business days after receiving the employee's first notice of need for leave following the change, absent extenuating circumstances.

If the employer requires the substitution of paid leave or will count paid leave taken under an existing plan against the employee's FMLA entitlement, the employer must inform the employee with the designation notice. The employer must also inform the employee if it will require a fitness for duty certification to return the employee to work. The employer may require that the fitness for duty certification address the employee's ability to perform the essential functions of his or her position. If the employer imposes this requirement, it must inform the employee in the designation notice and must include a list of the essential functions.

The notice must tell the employee how much leave will be counted against the employee's leave entitlement. If the amount of leave needed is known when the employer designates it as FMLA leave, the employer must include the number of hours, days, or weeks that will be counted against the employee's FMLA entitlement in the designation notice. If it isn't possible to provide this detail (typically, because the employee needs intermittent leave on an unforeseeable basis), the employer must notify the employee of how much leave has been counted against his or her entitlement upon the employee's request, but no more often than once in a 30-day period during which leave was taken. The employer may give this notice orally, but must confirm it in writing no later than the following payday or, if that payday falls less than a week after the oral notice, by the subsequent payday. This written notice may be in any form, including a notation on the employee's pay stub.

Required Notice From the Employee

The employee must give the employer at least 30 days' notice of his or her desire to take leave when the leave is foreseeable (for example, for a planned birth or operation) or as soon as practicable for an unforeseeable event (for example, a sudden heart attack) or for leave that is foreseeable less than 30 days in advance (for example, if the employee is scheduled for surgery the following week). An employee who does not give 30 days' notice must respond to the employer's request to explain why such leave was not practicable. When it is practicable for an employee to give notice depends on the facts and circumstances; ordinarily, it will be practicable for an employee to give notice the same day or following day after learning of the need for leave.

For qualifying exigency leave, the 30-day requirement doesn't apply; employees need only give as much notice as is practicable.

Absent unusual circumstances, employers may require employees to comply with usual notice and other requirements for requesting leave, such as making requests in writing or notifying a particular person; failure to comply absent unusual circumstances that justify the failure may result in delay or denial of leave, unless the employer's policy requires more notice than the FMLA and the employee's notice was timely under the FMLA.

Calling in "sick" without more information is not sufficient notice. The employee must provide enough information so the employer can determine whether the leave is for an FMLA-qualifying reason. The employee must respond to the employer's questions intended to determine whether the leave is protected by the FMLA. Employees seeking more leave for a qualifying reason for which they have already taken leave must specifically refer to either the qualifying reason or the need for FMLA leave.

In addition to the initial notice, the employer can require an employee who is on FMLA leave to report periodically on his or her status and intent to return to work.

Reasons to Delay Leave

An employer may delay an eligible employee's leave in the following circumstances:

- If an employee could have given 30 days' notice, but failed to do so, the employer can delay the leave until 30 days have passed from the date the employee told the employer about the leave.
- If the employee fails to give notice as soon as practicable, the employer may delay the leave for the number of days between when the employee gave notice and when the employee should have given notice.
- If an employee doesn't provide certification, the employer can delay the leave until the employee does provide certification.

Certification

Medical Certification

If an employee requests FMLA leave for his or her own serious health condition or for a family member's serious health condition, the employer may ask the employee to provide documentation from a health care provider certifying the existence of the serious health condition. The employer must make this request within five business days after (1) the employee requests to take leave or (2) the employee's unforeseeable leave begins. When the employer requests the certification, the employer must also inform the employee of the consequences of failing to provide certification.

The employee has 15 calendar days to provide the certification, unless it is not practicable to do so under the circumstances despite the employee's good-faith efforts. When an employee provides certification, the employer must tell the employee if it thinks the certification is incomplete or insufficient, and state in writing what additional information is necessary. The employer must give the employee at least seven calendar days to cure the problem, unless it's not practicable to do so under the circumstances, despite the employee's good-faith efforts.

After giving the employee the opportunity to cure any deficiencies in the certification, the employer may contact the health care provider for purposes of *authentication* or *clarification*. This contact must be made through a health care provider, human resources professional, leave administrator, or management official; the employee's direct supervisor may not contact the employee's health care provider.

The employee may submit a certification from a health care provider in another country if the family member lives or is visiting there or the employee is visiting there when the serious health condition develops. If the certification is not in English, the employee must provide a written translation upon the employer's request.

Certifications must contain very specific and detailed information. The DOL provides two forms that employees can use when obtaining medical certifications, one for the employee's own serious health condition and one for a family member's health condition. Although use of these forms is optional, they are helpful to employers and medical providers because they request the specific information that the FMLA requires. (For more information about these forms, see "Agency Resources," below.)

If an employer doubts the validity of a certification, the employer can request a second opinion at the employer's expense. Although the employer can choose the second health care provider, that person may not be someone who works for the employer on a regular basis. If the first and second opinions differ, the employer can request a third certification—again at the employer's expense. This third health care provider must be someone whom both the employer and the employee agree upon. This third opinion is final and binding.

The employer may also request recertification—a follow-up certification from the same health care provider. The employer may request recertification no more often than every 30 days, and only in connection with an employee's absence, with some exceptions. The employer must wait longer than 30 days to request recertification if the original certification indicates that the serious health condition is expected to last more than 30 days. In this situation, the employer must wait until the estimated duration of the health condition has passed. However, the employer is entitled to request recertification every six months, even if the health condition is expected to last longer than that.

An employer may request a recertification more often than every 30 days if:

- The employee requests an extension of leave.
- The circumstances described in the previous certification have changed significantly (for example, the employee is taking quite a bit more intermittent leave than the certification indicated would be necessary).
- The employer receives information casting doubt on the employee's stated reason for the absence or the continuing validity of the certification.

As part of the recertification process, the employer may give the health care provider a record of the employee's absence pattern and ask whether the serious health condition and need for leave is consistent with that pattern.

Certification of a Qualifying Exigency

When an employee first requests leave for a qualifying exigency, the employer may require the employee to provide a copy of the active duty orders or other documentation issued by the military indicating the family member's covered active duty and the dates of service. The employee need not supply this documentation again unless leave is necessary because of a subsequent active duty or a different family member.

The employer may also require the employee to submit a certification that includes specified information about the exigency and leave. The DOL has developed an optional form employers can use to request this information; see "Agency Resources," below.

If the certification is complete, the employer may not request more information. The employer may contact third parties identified in the certification to verify a meeting or an appointment schedule and find out the nature of the meeting; no additional information may be requested, and the employee's permission is not required. The employer may also contact the Department of Defense (DOD) to request verification that the employee is on covered active duty; no additional information may be requested, and the employee's permission is not required.

An employer may not request recertification of the employee's need for qualifying exigency leave.

Fitness for Duty Certification

If an employee takes FMLA leave for his or her own serious health condition, the employer may require the employee to provide a fitness for duty certification from his or her doctor before returning to work. The employer may request that the fitness for duty certification specifically address the employee's ability to perform the essential functions of the job. To do so, the employer must notify the employee of the requirement and provide the employee with a list of those functions along with the designation notice.

The employer may seek authentication or clarification of the fitness for duty certification, but the employee's return to work may not be delayed while the employer contacts the provider.

The employer may not require a fitness for duty certification for each absence taken intermittently, but may require one up to once every 30 days for such absences if *reasonable safety concerns* exist regarding the employee's ability to perform his or her duties relating to the serious health condition for which leave was taken.

Reinstatement

Following FMLA leave, an employee has the right to be returned to the same position the employee held before or to an equivalent position—one that is nearly identical to the employee's former position in terms of pay, benefits, and working conditions, including privileges, perquisites, and status. The equivalent position must involve the same or substantially similar duties, which must require substantially equivalent skill, effort, responsibility, and authority.

Equivalent pay includes any bonuses or payments that occurred while the employee was on FMLA leave, if those payments were unconditional. Pay increases that depend on seniority, length of service, or work performed must be handled the same way for employees on FMLA leave as for employees who are on leave that doesn't qualify for FMLA protection. A bonus or payment based on the employee's achievement of a goal such as hours worked, products sold, or perfect attendance need not be paid to employees who missed the goal because of FMLA leave, unless such bonuses are paid to employees who missed the goal due to leave that doesn't qualify for FMLA protection.

An employee who accepts a light-duty position while recovering from a serious health condition retains the right to reinstatement to the employee's former position until the end of the leave year.

An employer can delay or deny an employee's return to work in these circumstances:

- The employer can delay reinstatement until the employee provides a fitness for duty certification.
- If the employee could have been legitimately fired or laid off while not on leave, an employer may fire or lay off the employee while he or she is on leave. In such a situation, the employee has no right to reinstatement, continued leave, or continued benefits. For example, if an employee goes on FMLA leave to have a baby and, while the employee is on leave, the employer eliminates the employee's entire department, the employee

does not have a right to reinstatement, because her job no longer exists. Because it is illegal to fire or otherwise retaliate against an employee for taking FMLA leave, however, employers who rely on this provision must make very certain that their reasons for termination are beyond reproach.

- If an employee clearly tells the employer that he or she does not intend to return to work, the employee has no right to reinstatement, continued leave, or continued health benefits.

- If an employee is a key employee, the employer may deny reinstatement in certain circumstances. (See "Exceptions," below, for more about key employees.)

- If an employee obtains FMLA leave fraudulently (for example, by falsely claiming that a family member is seriously ill in order to take an extended vacation), the employee has no right to leave, reinstatement, or continued benefits.

Exceptions

Husband and Wife

If a husband and wife work for the same employer, the employer has the right to limit the total amount of leave the couple can take for the arrival of a new child or for an employee's parent with a serious health condition. In those two circumstances, the employer can limit the employees to a combined total of 12 workweeks of unpaid leave during a 12-month period. For example, if the husband takes four weeks to care for a new child, then the employer may limit the wife to eight weeks to care for the new child. (This limit also applies to the 26-week military caregiver leave provision, as explained below.)

This limitation does not apply when married employees take leave for their own serious health condition or for the serious health condition of a family member other than a parent. Thus, if the husband takes four weeks to care for a new daughter, he may still take eight weeks for his own serious health condition. Similarly, if his wife takes eight weeks to care for the new daughter, she may still take four weeks to care for the couple's son who suffers from a serious health condition.

Key Employees

If an employee is a key employee (see "Definitions," above), the employer may refuse to reinstate the employee if the employee's return would cause "substantial and grievous" economic injury to the employer. This is intended to be a difficult standard to meet (for example, more difficult than proving that a requested accommodation for a disabled employee would be an "undue hardship" on the employer—see Chapter 2.)

In the rights and responsibilities notice, the employer must state whether it considers the employee a key employee and the consequences of that designation. The employer must also notify the employee if and when it decides not to reinstate the employee based on the key employee exception. This notice must explain the basis for the employer's finding that substantial and grievous economic injury will result from reinstatement and, if the employee is already on leave, must give the employee a reasonable time in which to return to work, taking into account the circumstances (for example, why the employee took leave and why the company needs the employee to return).

If the employee does not return to work in response to this notice, he or she is still entitled to take FMLA leave, and to continued health benefits during that leave, until either the employee notifies the employer that he or she will not return to work or the employer refuses to reinstate the employee at the end of the employee's leave. An employee who has been notified that he or she will not be reinstated pursuant to the key employee exception can still request reinstatement at the end of his or her leave. If the employee makes this request, the employer must once again determine whether reinstating the employee would cause substantial and grievous economic injury, based on the circumstances at that time.

26-Week Military Caregiver Leave

As amended in 2008 and 2009, the FMLA also allows eligible employees to take up to 26 weeks of leave in a single 12-month period to care for a covered servicemember with a serious injury or illness. Although many of the rules for military caregiver leave are similar to the rules for other types of FMLA leave, there are also some important differences. This section covers those differences; issues that aren't included here are handled as they are for 12-week FMLA leave, explained above.

Regulated Employers

All regulated employers are subject to these provisions.

Covered Workers

As for other types of FMLA leave, the employee must have worked for at least a year, and at least 1,250 hours in the past year, to be eligible. For this type of leave, the employee must also be the covered servicemember's spouse, child, parent, or next of kin. A "child" of the servicemember may be any age; in other words, the child need not be either under the age of 18 or at least 18 and incapable of self-care.

What's Prohibited

The same prohibitions that apply to the 12-week provisions of FMLA leave also apply to military caregiver leave.

What's Required

Employers must allow eligible employees to take up to 26 weeks of leave in a single 12-month period to care for a covered servicemember who suffers a serious injury or illness. For those who are current members of the armed forces, National Guard, or reserves, a serious illness or injury is one that was incurred in the line of duty on active duty and may render the member medically unfit to perform the duties of his or her office, grade, rank, or rating. Amendments to the FMLA in 2009 added coverage for illnesses or injuries that preexisted the member's active duty and were aggravated by service in the line of duty on active duty.

The 2009 amendments also expanded coverage to include veterans who are undergoing medical treatment, recuperation, or therapy, for a serious injury or illness and who were members of the armed forces (including a member of the National Guard or reserves) at any time in the previous five years. In the case of a veteran, a serious illness or injury is a "qualifying" injury or illness (this term is to be defined in final regulations to be issued by the Department of Labor) that was incurred in the line of duty on active duty, or that existed before the member's active duty and was aggravated by service in the line of duty on active duty. The illness or injury may manifest itself before or after the member became a veteran.

Amount of Leave

Eligible employees may take up to 26 weeks of leave in a single 12-month period. This is a per servicemember, per injury entitlement; it does not automatically renew each year. Any part of the 26 weeks the employee doesn't take during the 12-month period is lost; it doesn't carry over to the following year.

The employee is entitled to only one 26-week leave entitlement unless another covered servicemember for whom the employee is eligible to take leave suffers a serious injury or illness or the same covered servicemember suffers a subsequent serious injury or illness. The Department of Labor's 2012 proposed regulations complicate this a bit by stating that it believes employees could be entitled to two leave periods for the same family member, once while the family member is still in the military and once after the family member becomes a veteran. It isn't clear whether the Department intends that the injury must be different to entitle the employee to a second leave (for example, if the family member suffered a physical injury and then later developed PTSD). This issue should be resolved once final regulations are issued.

Even if an employee has a right to more than one 26-week leave entitlement, the employee may not take more than 26 total weeks of leave in a 12-month period. This is true even if the leave entitlements overlap.

The 12-month period begins on the first day the employee takes military caregiver leave, regardless of how the employer measures the leave year for other types of FMLA leave.

The 26-week entitlement applies to all types of FMLA leave combined. For example, if an employee takes 20 weeks of military caregiver leave, the employee may take only six additional weeks of FMLA leave during that 12-month period for any other purpose. The employee's leave entitlement for other types of FMLA leave remains 12 weeks, even if the employee uses less than 14 weeks of military caregiver leave.

Employers must designate qualifying leave as military caregiver leave in the first instance. For example, if an employee takes time off to care for a covered servicemember who is the employee's spouse, that leave would likely otherwise count as both military caregiver leave and leave to care for a spouse with a serious health condition. The employer may not designate it as both, however; instead, the employer must designate any leave that qualifies for the military caregiver provision as that type of leave.

Military caregiver leave may be taken intermittently or on a reduced schedule if medically necessary.

Certification

The employer may require the employee to submit a certification. Part of the certification is to be completed by one of these health care providers (if the health care provider can't make military-related determinations required by the form, he or she may rely on determinations from an authorized DOD representative):

- DOD health care provider
- Department of Veterans Affairs (VA) health care provider
- DOD TRICARE network authorized private health care provider, or
- DOD nonnetwork TRICARE authorized private health care provider.

The proposed regulations issued in 2012 modify these requirements to reflect that injured service members, and particularly injured veterans, may be seeing private health care providers rather than using the military health care system. However, these regulations have not yet been finalized.

The health care provider may be asked to provide specified information about the covered servicemember's injury or illness, treatment, and need for care. In addition, the employee or covered servicemember must provide information about the servicemember, the care and leave required, and the relationship between the employee and the servicemember. The DOL has created an optional certification form employers can use for this purpose; see "Agency Resources," below.

The employer may seek authentication or clarification, but not recertification or a second or third opinion. The employer may also require the employee to provide confirmation of a covered family relationship to the member.

In lieu of certification, an employer must accept an invitational travel order or invitational travel authorization. For the time specified in that document, the employer may not require additional or separate certification. The employee need not be named in the document. If the time on the document expires, the employer may request certification. The employer may seek authentication or clarification of the document, but not recertification or a second or third opinion.

Exceptions

Husband and Wife

Spouses who work for the same employer may be limited in how much combined leave they may take. The employer has the right to limit the amount of leave the couple can take to bond with a new child, to care for an employee's parent with a serious health condition, and to care for a covered servicemember with a serious illness or injury, to 26 weeks total.

This limitation does not apply to leave married employees take for their own serious health condition or for the serious health condition of a family member other than a parent.

How the FMLA Is Enforced

Individual Complaints

Employees who believe their employers have violated their FMLA rights can file complaints with the DOL within two years of the violations, or they can file private lawsuits. They are not required to file complaints with the DOL before pursuing lawsuits. An employee may file a private lawsuit within two years of the employer's FMLA violation, or within three years if the violation was willful.

Agency Enforcement

The Wage and Hour Division of the DOL investigates FMLA complaints. The DOL can also file lawsuits in court to compel compliance.

Complying With the FMLA

Deadlines

- Employers must give an employee an eligibility notice and a rights and responsibilities notice within five business days after an employee requests leave or the employer learns that the employee's leave may be FMLA qualifying. If the employee's eligibility changes, the employer must notify the employee within *five business days* of the change.

- Employers must give an employee a designation notice within *five business days* after receiving enough information to determine whether an employee's leave is FMLA qualifying. If the information in the designation notice changes, the employer must notify the employee within *five business days* of the employee's first request for leave after the change.

- Employers that will require an employee to submit a certification must inform the employee of this requirement within *five business days* after (1) the employee requests to take leave or (2) the employee's unforeseeable leave begins.

Reporting Requirements

The FMLA imposes no reporting requirements.

Posting Requirements

All covered employers must post a notice approved by the DOL that explains employee rights and responsibilities under the FMLA. To find out how to obtain a copy of that notice, see "Agency Resources," below.

Record-Keeping Requirements

Employers must keep records pertaining to their FMLA obligations. These records include:

- payroll information for each employee, including name, address, job title, rate or basis of pay, terms of compensation, daily and weekly hours worked per pay period, additions to wages, deductions from wages, and total compensation paid (unless the employee is exempt from the Fair Labor Standards Act's record-keeping requirements; see Chapter 7 on the FLSA)

- dates the employee has taken FMLA leave

- if the employee has taken less than a day of FMLA leave, the number of hours of leave taken
- copies of all written notices the employee has given the employer about FMLA leave
- copies of all written notices the employer has given the employee about FMLA leave
- documents describing employee benefits
- documents describing employer policies regarding paid and unpaid leave
- documents recording employer-paid health insurance premiums, and
- records of any disputes between the employer and the employee regarding FMLA leave.

Employers of airline flight crews must also keep on file, with the secretary of labor, information regarding the applicable total monthly guarantee for each category of employee to whom such a guarantee applies.

Penalties

If an employee prevails in a lawsuit against an employer, the employee might be entitled to any or all of the following remedies:

- lost wages
- lost employment benefits
- cost of providing care (for example, the cost of paying a home care provider to care for a seriously ill family member for the period of time when an employee was illegally denied the right to take leave)
- interest on damages
- money damages set by the statute (called liquidated damages)
- reinstatement
- promotion
- attorneys' fees, and
- legal costs.

If an employer fails to post required notices, the DOL can impose a civil fine of up to $110 for each offense. An employer that fails to post required notices may not deny an employee FMLA leave if the employee fails to give the employer advance notice of his or her intent to take FMLA leave.

Agency Resources

- The poster that employers must display alerting employees to their FMLA rights and obligations
  Family and Medical Leave Act (FMLA) Poster
  www.dol.gov/whd/regs/compliance/posters/fmlaen.pdf

- An optional form that employees may use to obtain a medical certification from a health care provider regarding their own serious health condition
  Form WH-380-E: Certification of Health Care Provider for Employee's Serious Health Condition
  www.dol.gov/whd/forms/WH-380-E.pdf

- An optional form that employees may use to obtain a medical certification from a health care provider regarding a family member's own serious health condition
  Form WH-380-F: Certification of Health Care Provider for Family Member's Serious Health Condition
  www.dol.gov/whd/forms/WH-380-F.pdf

- An optional form that employees may use to obtain a certification from a health care provider regarding a covered servicemember's serious illness or injury
  Form WH-385: Certification for Serious Injury or Illness of Covered Servicemember—for Military Family Leave
  www.dol.gov/whd/forms/WH-385.pdf

- An optional form that employees may use to provide certification of their need for qualifying exigency leave
  Form WH-384: Certification of Qualifying Exigency for Military Family Leave
  www.dol.gov/whd/forms/WH-384.pdf

- An optional form employers may use to provide the eligibility notice and rights and responsibilities notice
  Form WH-381: Notice of Eligibility and Rights & Responsibilities
  www.dol.gov/whd/fmla/finalrule/WH381.pdf

- An optional form employers may use to provide designation notice
  Form WH-382: Designation Notice
  www.dol.gov/whd/forms/WH-382.pdf

The DOL has more information and publications available online. For a complete list, visit www.dol.gov/whd/fmla.

State Laws Relating to Family and Medical Leave

Some states also have laws that require employers to provide family and medical leave. These laws may be more extensive than the FMLA—for example, they may apply to smaller employers, allow employees to take leave to care for a broader range of family members (such as siblings or domestic partners), or provide time off to attend a child's school function or take a family member to medical appointments.

The chart below provides basic information about these state laws, but does not address every aspect of the law, such as notice requirements, medical certification rules, or reinstatement procedures. For more information, contact your state's department of labor (see Appendix A for contact information).

Family and Medical Leave Laws

California

Cal. Gov't. Code §§ 12945 and 12945.2; Cal. Lab. Code §§ 230 and following; Cal. Unemp. Ins. §§ 3300 and following

Employers Covered: For pregnancy leave: employers with 5 or more employees; for domestic violence leave and school activity leave: employers with 25 or more employees; for family medical leave: employers with 50 or more employees; for paid family and disability leave: employers whose employees contribute to state temporary disability insurance (SDI) fund.

Eligible Employees: For pregnancy, domestic violence, or school activity leave: all employees; for family medical leave: employee with more than 12 months of service with the employer, and who has at least 1,250 hours of service with the employer during the previous 12-month period; for paid family and disability leave benefits program: employees who contribute to SDI fund.

Family Medical Leave: Up to 4 months for disability related to pregnancy (in addition to 12 weeks under family leave law). Up to 12 weeks of leave per year to care for seriously ill family member, for employee's own serious illness, or to bond with new child. Employees who contribute to SDI fund may receive paid family leave benefits for up to 6 weeks of leave per year to care for a seriously ill family member (including a registered domestic partner) or bond with a new child; up to 52 weeks of leave paid by state fund for own short-term disability.

School Activities: 40 hours per year, not more than 8 hours per calendar month.

Domestic Violence: Reasonable time for issues dealing with domestic violence or sexual assault, including health, counseling, and safety measures. Family member or domestic partner of a victim of a felony may take leave to attend judicial proceedings related to the crime.

Colorado

Colo. Rev. Stat. §§ 19-5-211; 24-34-402.7

Employers Covered: For adoption leave: all employers who offer leave for birth of a child; for domestic violence leave and school activities leave: employers with 50 or more employees.

Eligible Employees: For adoption leave and school activities leave: all employees; for domestic violence leave: employees with one year of service.

Family Medical Leave: Employee must be given same leave for adoption as allowed for childbirth (doesn't apply to stepparent adoption).

School Activities: 18 hours per year, no more than 6 hours per month, to attend parent teacher conferences and meetings relating to special education, truancy, attendance, discipline, drop-out prevention, or response to intervention.

Domestic Violence: Up to 3 days' leave in any 12-month period to seek restraining order, obtain medical care or counseling, relocate, or seek legal assistance for victim of domestic violence, sexual assault, or stalking.

Family and Medical Leave Laws (continued)

Connecticut

Conn. Gen. Stat. Ann. §§ 31-51kk to 31-51qq; 46a-60

Employers Covered: For pregnancy leave: employers with 3 or more employees; for family medical or serious health leave: employers with 75 or more employees; for paid sick leave: service-industry employers with at least 50 employees.

Eligible Employees: For pregnancy leave and paid sick leave: all employees; for family medical or serious health condition leave: any employee with one year and at least 1,000 hours of service in last 12 months.

Family Medical Leave: Reasonable amount of pregnancy leave required. 16 weeks per any 24-month period for childbirth, adoption, employee's serious health condition, care for family member with serious health condition, or bone marrow or organ donation. 26 weeks per 12-month period for each family member who is also a current member of the armed forces and is undergoing medical treatment. For paid sick leave: one hour of paid sick leave for every 40 hours worked, up to 40 hours accrued per year, for the employee's own medical needs or to care for an ill family member.

District of Columbia

D.C. Code Ann. §§ 32-501 and following; 32-1202, 32-131.01 and following

Employers Covered: Employers with 20 or more employees.

Eligible Employees: Employees who have worked at company for at least one year and at least 1,000 hours during the previous 12 months.

Family Medical Leave: 16 weeks per any 24-month period for childbirth, adoption, pregnancy/maternity, domestic violence, or care for family member with serious health condition; additional 16 weeks per any 24-month period for employee's serious health condition; paid leave for the employee's or family member's physical or mental illness, injury, or medical condition; for the employee's or family member's medical care, diagnosis, or preventive medical care. Amount of paid leave depends on employer size: Employers with 100 or more employees must provide at least one hour of paid leave for every 37 hours worked, up to seven days of leave per year; employers with 25 to 99 employees must provide at least one hour of paid leave for every 43 hours worked, up to five days of leave per year; employers with fewer than 25 employees must provide at least one hour of paid leave for every 87 hours worked, up to three days of leave per year.

School Activities: Up to 24 hours of unpaid leave per year (all employees, all employers).

Domestic Violence: Paid leave, described under "Family Medical Leave," may also be used for employee or family member who is a victim of stalking, domestic violence, or abuse to get medical attention, get services, seek counseling, relocate, take legal action, or take steps to enhance health and safety.

Florida

Fla. Stat. § 741.313

Employers Covered: Employers with at least 50 employees.

Family and Medical Leave Laws (continued)

Eligible Employees: Employees with at least 3 months of employment.

Domestic Violence: Up to 3 working days in any 12-month period if employee or family/household member is victim of domestic violence, with or without pay at discretion of employer.

Hawaii

Haw. Rev. Stat. §§ 398-1 to 398-11; 378-1, 378-71 to 378-74

Employers Covered: For childbirth, adoption, and serious health condition leave: employers with 100 or more employees; for pregnancy leave, temporary disability, and domestic violence leave: all employers.

Eligible Employees: For childbirth, adoption, and serious health condition leave: employees with 6 months of service; for pregnancy, domestic violence, and temporary disability leave: all employees.

Family Medical Leave: 4 weeks per calendar year for childbirth, adoption, or care for family member with serious health condition; "reasonable period" of pregnancy/maternity leave required by discrimination statute and case law. Up to 26 weeks of temporary disability leave paid by state insurance program.

Domestic Violence: Employer with 50 or more employees must allow up to 30 days' unpaid leave per year for employee who is a victim of domestic or sexual violence or if employee's minor child is a victim. Employer with 49 or fewer employees must allow up to 5 days' leave.

Illinois

820 Ill. Comp. Stat. §§ 147/1 and following; 180/1 and following

Employers Covered: Employers with 15 or more employees.

Eligible Employees: For school activities leave: employees who have worked at least half-time for 6 months; for domestic violence leave: all employees.

School Activities: Eight hours per year (no more than 4 hours per day); required only if employee has no paid leave available.

Domestic Violence: If employer has at least 50 employees, up to 12 weeks' unpaid leave per 12-month period for employee who is a victim of domestic violence or sexual assault or for employee with a family or household member who is a victim; if employer has at least 15 but not more than 49 employees, up to 8 weeks' unpaid leave during any 12-month period.

Iowa

Iowa Code § 216.6

Employers Covered: Employers with 4 or more employees.

Eligible Employees: All employees.

Family Medical Leave: Up to 8 weeks for disability due to pregnancy, childbirth, or related conditions.

Kentucky

Ky. Rev. Stat. Ann. § 337.015

Employers Covered: All employers.

Eligible Employees: All employees.

Family Medical Leave: Up to 6 weeks for adoption of a child under 7 years old.

Family and Medical Leave Laws (continued)

Louisiana

La. Rev. Stat. Ann. §§ 23:341 to 23:342; 23:1015 and following; 40:1299.124

Employers Covered: For pregnancy/maternity leave: employers with 25 or more employees; for leave to donate bone marrow: employers with 20 or more employees; for school activities leave: all employers.

Eligible Employees: For pregnancy/maternity or school activities leave: all employees; for leave to donate bone marrow: employees who work 20 or more hours per week.

Family Medical Leave: "Reasonable period of time" for pregnancy disability and childbirth, not to exceed 6 weeks for normal pregnancy and 4 months for more disabling pregnancies; up to 40 hours' paid leave per year to donate bone marrow.

School Activities: 16 hours per year.

Maine

Me. Rev. Stat. Ann. tit. 26, §§ 843 and following

Employers Covered: For domestic violence leave: all employers; for family medical leave: employers with 15 or more employees at one location.

Eligible Employees: All employees for domestic violence leave; employees with at least one year of service for family medical leave.

Family Medical Leave: 10 weeks in any two-year period for childbirth, adoption (for child 16 or younger), employee's serious health condition, care for family member with serious health condition, or

death or serious health condition of family member suffered while on active military duty.

Domestic Violence: "Reasonable and necessary" leave for employee who is victim of domestic violence, sexual assault, or stalking, or whose parent, spouse, or child is a victim, to prepare for and attend court, for medical treatment, and for other necessary services.

Maryland

Md. Code Ann., Lab. & Empl. § 3-801, 3-802

Employers Covered: Employers with 15 or more employees.

Eligible Employees: All employees.

Family Medical Leave: Employee must be given same leave for adoption as allowed for childbirth.

Massachusetts

Mass. Gen. Laws ch. 149, §§ 52D, 105D; ch. 151B, § 1(5)

Employers Covered: For maternity and adoption leave: employers with 6 or more employees; for school activities leave: employers with 50 or more employees.

Eligible Employees: For maternity and adoption leave: full-time female employees who have completed probationary period, or 3 months of service if no set probationary period; for all other leave: employees who are eligible under FMLA.

Family Medical Leave: Eight weeks total for childbirth/maternity or adoption of child younger than 18 (younger than 23 if disabled); additional 24 hours total per year (combined with school activities

Family and Medical Leave Laws (continued)

leave) to accompany minor child or relative age 60 or older to medical and dental appointments.

School Activities: 24 hours per year total (combined with medical care).

Minnesota

Minn. Stat. Ann. §§ 181.940 and following

Employers Covered: For childbirth/ maternity and adoption leave: employers with 21 or more employees at one site; for bone marrow donation: employers with 20 or more employees; for school activities: employers with 2 or more employees.

Eligible Employees: For maternity leave: employees who have worked at least half-time for one year; for bone marrow donation: employees who work at least 20 hours per week; for school activities: employees who have worked at least one year.

Family Medical Leave: Six weeks for childbirth/maternity or adoption; up to 40 hours paid leave per year to donate bone marrow; parent can use accrued sick leave to care for sick or injured child. Up to ten days if family member is killed or injured in active military service (all employers).

School Activities: 16 hours in 12-month period; includes activities related to child care, preschool, or special education.

Montana

Mont. Code Ann. §§ 49-2-310, 49-2-311

Employers Covered: All employers.

Eligible Employees: All employees.

Family Medical Leave: Reasonable leave of absence for pregnancy disability and childbirth.

Nebraska

Neb. Rev. Stat. § 48-234

Employers Covered: Employers that allow workers to take leave for the birth of a child.

Eligible Employees: All employees.

Family Medical Leave: Employee must be given same leave as allowed for childbirth to adopt a child, unless child is over 8 (or over 18 for special needs child); does not apply to stepparent or foster parent adoptions.

Nevada

Nev. Rev. Stat. Ann. §§ 392.920, 613.335, 392.4577

Employers Covered: All employers.

Eligible Employees: All employees.

Family Medical Leave: Same sick or disability leave policies that apply to other medical conditions must be extended to pregnancy, miscarriage, and childbirth.

School Activities: Employers may not fire or threaten to fire a parent, guardian, or custodian for attending a school conference or responding to a child's emergency. Employers with 50 or more employees must provide parent with a child in public school a leave of 4 hours per school year, which must be taken in increments of at least 1 hour, to attend parent-teacher conferences, attend school related activities during regular school hours, attend school sponsored events, or volunteer or be involved at the school.

Family and Medical Leave Laws (continued)

New Hampshire

N.H. Rev. Stat. Ann. § 354-A:7(VI)

Employers Covered: Employers with 6 or more employees.

Eligible Employees: All employees.

Family Medical Leave: Temporary disability leave for pregnancy/childbirth or related medical condition.

New Jersey

N.J. Stat. Ann. §§ 34:11B-1 and following; 43-21-1 and following

Employers Covered: Employers with 50 or more employees; for paid family and temporary disability leave, employers subject to the New Jersey Unemployment Compensation Law.

Eligible Employees: Employees who have worked for at least one year and at least 1,000 hours in previous 12 months; for paid family and temporary disability leave benefits program: employees who worked 20 calendar weeks in covered New Jersey employment; or earned at least 1000 times New Jersey minimum wage during 52 weeks preceding leave.

Family Medical Leave: 12 weeks (or 24 weeks reduced leave schedule) in any 24-month period for pregnancy/ maternity, childbirth, adoption, or care for family member with serious health condition. Employees may receive paid family leave benefits for up to 6 weeks of leave per year to care for a seriously ill family member (including a registered domestic partner) or bond with a new child. Employee may receive temporary disability benefits while the employee is unable to work, up to 26 weeks.

New Mexico

N.M. Stat. Ann. § 50-4A-1 and following

Employers Covered: All employers.

Eligible Employees: All employees.

Domestic Violence: Employer must provide intermittent paid or unpaid leave time for up to fourteen days in any calendar year, taken by an employee for up to eight hours in one day, to obtain or attempt to obtain an order of protection or other judicial relief from domestic abuse or to meet with law enforcement officials, to consult with attorneys or district attorneys' victim advocates or to attend court proceedings related to the domestic abuse of an employee or an employee's family member.

New York

N.Y. Lab. Law §§ 201-c; 202-a

Employers Covered: Employers that allow workers to take leave for the birth of a child must allow adoption leave; employers with 20 or more employees at one site must allow leave to donate bone marrow; employers with at least one employee for 30 days are covered by the state's temporary disability program 4 weeks later.

Eligible Employees: All employees are eligible for adoption leave; employees who work at least 20 hours per week are eligible for leave to donate bone marrow; employees who have worked for a covered employer for at least 4 consecutive weeks are eligible for temporary disability benefits.

Family and Medical Leave Laws (continued)

Family Medical Leave: Employees must be given same leave as allowed for childbirth to adopt a child of preschool age or younger, or no older than 18 if disabled; up to 24 hours' leave to donate bone marrow. Temporary disability insurance benefits available for up to 26 weeks while employee is unable to work.

North Carolina

N.C. Gen. Stat. §§ 95-28.3, 50B-5.5

Employers Covered: All employers.

Eligible Employees: All employees.

School Activities: Parents and guardians of school-aged children must be given up to 4 hours of leave per year.

Domestic Violence: Reasonable time off from work to obtain or attempt to obtain relief from domestic violence and sexual assault.

Oregon

Or. Rev. Stat. §§ 659A.029, 659A.150 and following, 659A.312, 659A.270 and following

Employers Covered: For childbirth, adoption, and serious health condition leave: employers with 25 or more employees; for domestic violence leave: employers with 6 or more employees; for leave to donate bone marrow: all employers.

Eligible Employees: For childbirth, adoption, serious health condition or domestic violence leave: employees who have worked 25 or more hours per week for at least 180 days; for leave to donate bone marrow: employees who work an average of 20 or more hours per week.

Family Medical Leave: 12 weeks per year for pregnancy disability; additional 12 weeks per year for parental leave, serious health condition, care for family member with serious health condition, or care for child who has an illness, injury, or condition that requires home care; employee who takes 12 weeks of parental leave may take an additional 12 weeks to care for a sick child. Up to 40 hours or amount of accrued paid leave (whichever is less) to donate bone marrow.

Domestic Violence: Reasonable leave for employee who is victim of domestic violence, sexual assault, or stalking, or whose minor child is a victim, to seek legal treatment, medical services, counseling, or to relocate/secure existing home.

Rhode Island

R.I. Gen. Laws §§ 28-48-1 and following

Employers Covered: For Family medical leave: employers with 50 or more employees.

Eligible Employees: For family medical leave: employees who have worked an average of 30 or more hours a week for at least 12 consecutive months; for school activities leave: all employees; for temporary disability leave: all employees who meet the earning requirements.

Family Medical Leave: 13 weeks in any two calendar years for childbirth, adoption of child up to 16 years old, employee's serious health condition, or care for family member with serious health condition. While temporarily unable to work due to disability (including pregnancy), employees can collect benefits from state insurance fund for up to 30 weeks.

Family and Medical Leave Laws (continued)

School Activities: Up to 10 hours a year.

South Carolina

S.C. Code Ann. § 44-43-80

Employers Covered: Employers with 20 or more workers at one site in South Carolina.

Eligible Employees: Employees who work an average of at least 20 hours per week.

Family Medical Leave: Up to 40 hours paid leave per year to donate bone marrow—employers are not required to grant such leave.

Tennessee

Tenn. Code Ann. § 4-21-408

Employers Covered: Employers with 100 or more employees.

Eligible Employees: Employees who have worked 12 consecutive months as full-time employees.

Family Medical Leave: Up to 4 months of unpaid leave for pregnancy, childbirth, nursing, and adoption; employee must give 3 months' notice unless a medical emergency requires the leave to begin sooner; these laws must be included in employee handbook.

Vermont

Vt. Stat. Ann. tit. 21, §§ 471 and following

Employers Covered: For childbirth and adoption leave: employers with 10 or more employees; for family medical and school activities leave: employers with 15 or more employees.

Eligible Employees: Employees who have worked an average of 30 or more hours per week for at least one year.

Family Medical Leave: 12 weeks per year for pregnancy, childbirth, adoption of child age 16 or younger, employee's serious health condition, or care for family member with a serious health condition; combined with school activities leave, additional 4 hours of unpaid leave in a 30-day period (up to 24 hours per year) to take a family member to a medical, dental, or professional well-care appointment or respond to a family member's medical emergency.

School Activities: Combined with leave described above, 4 hours' total unpaid leave in a 30-day period (up to 24 hours per year) to participate in child's school activities.

Washington

Wash. Rev. Code Ann. §§ 49.78.010 and following, 49.12.265 and following, 49.12.350 and following, 49.76.010 and following, 49.86.005 and following

Employers Covered: All employers must provide domestic violence leave; employers with 8 or more employees must provide pregnancy disability leave; employers with 50 or more employees must provide leave to care for newborn, adopted, or foster child, or family member with serious health condition.

Eligible Employees: All employees who accrue paid sick leave may use it to care for sick family members (including state registered domestic partners); employees who have worked at least 1,250 hours in the previous year are eligible for parental leave to care for newborn, adopted, or foster child, or leave to care for a family

Family and Medical Laws (continued)

member with serious health condition.

Family Medical Leave: In addition to any . leave available under federal FMLA and state law, employee may take leave for the period of time when she is temporarily disabled due to pregnancy or childbirth; employers with 50 or more employees must allow up to 12 weeks during any 12-month period for the birth or placement of a child, employee's serious health condition, or care for a family member with a serious health condition; all employees can use paid sick leave to care for a sick family member.

Domestic Violence: Reasonable leave from work, with or without pay, for employee who is victim of domestic violence, sexual assault, or stalking, or whose family member is a victim, to prepare for and attend court, for medical treatment, and for other necessary services.

Wisconsin

Wis. Stat. Ann. § 103.10

Employers Covered: Employers with 50 or more employees.

Eligible Employees: Employees who have worked at least one year and 1,000 hours in the preceding 12 months.

Family Medical Leave: 6 weeks per 12-month period for pregnancy/maternity, childbirth, or adoption; additional 2 weeks per 12-month period to care for family member (including domestic partner) with a serious health condition; additional 2 weeks per 12-month period to care for the employee's own serious health condition.

Genetic Information Nondiscrimination Act (GINA)

Statute: 42 U.S.C. § 2000ff and following
http://eeoc.gov/laws/statutes/gina.cfm

Regulations: 29 C.F.R. 1635
www.gpo.gov/fdsys/pkg/CFR-2012-title29-vol4/pdf/CFR-2012-title29-vol4-part1635.pdf

Overview of GINA

The most recent civil rights law on the books is the Genetic Information Nondiscrimination Act (GINA), enacted in 2008. GINA prohibits health insurers from using genetic information to deny insurance coverage or determine premiums. It also prohibits covered employers from making employment decisions based on an applicant or employee's genetic information, and requires employers to keep employee genetic information confidential.

Regulated Employers

The following employers must comply with GINA:
- private employers with 15 or more employees
- the federal government
- state governments
- private and public employment agencies
- labor organizations, and
- joint labor-management committees.

Legal Developments

- **Genetic discrimination charges at the EEOC.** In 2011, the EEOC received 245 charges of discrimination under GINA. Most of the cases were resolved, netting $500,000 in monetary benefits (not including any damages awarded in litigation).
- **First publicized GINA charge involves the BRCA2 gene.** In 2010, Pamela Fink filed the first publicized EEOC charge alleging wrongful termination in violation of GINA. Fink claimed that she told her supervisors that she carried the BRCA2 gene and had undergone a voluntary double mastectomy after her two sisters were diagnosed with breast cancer. Upon returning from surgery, Fink claims that her job duties were taken away, she was demoted, and then was fired. Her case has settled out of court, according to news reports.

Definitions

Family medical history Information about the manifestation of a disease or disorder in a person's family members. To be manifested, a disease or disorder must be capable of diagnosis by a health care professional with appropriate training and expertise in the field; if the diagnosis is based principally on genetic information, the condition is not manifested.

Family member A dependent of an employee or applicant, or a first-degree, second-degree, third-degree, or fourth-degree relative of an employee, applicant, or the employee's or applicant's dependent.

Genetic information Information about (1) a person's genetic tests, (2) the genetic tests of a person's family members, (3) the manifestation of a disease or disorder in the person's family members, (4) any requests for or receipt of genetic services, or participation in clinical research that includes genetic services, by the person or his or her family members, and (5) genetic information of a fetus the person or a family member is carrying or of any embryo legally held by the person or a family member using assisted reproductive technology. Genetic information does not include information about the sex or age of the person or family members, or information about the race or ethnicity of the person or family members that is not derived from a genetic test.

Genetic monitoring The periodic examination of employees to evaluate acquired modifications to their genetic material, such as chromosomal damage or evidence of increased occurrence of mutations, caused by exposure to toxic substances in performing their jobs, in order to identify, evaluate, and respond to those effects or to control adverse environmental exposures in the workplace.

Genetic services A genetic test, genetic education, or genetic counseling (including the gathering, interpretation, and assessment of genetic information).

Genetic test An analysis of human DNA, RNA, chromosomes, proteins, or metabolites, that detects genotypes, mutations, or chromosomal changes.

Covered Workers

GINA protects all prospective and current employees of a covered employer.

Did You Know ...

- Federal employees have been protected from discrimination based on genetic information since February 2000, when President Clinton signed Executive Order 13145.
- More than 30 states have laws that prohibit genetic discrimination. (To find out whether your state is one of them, see "State Laws Prohibiting Discrimination in Employment," in Chapter 18.
- According to a survey conducted in 2007 by the Genetics and Public Policy Center, 93% of respondents said that employers should not be able to make employment decisions based on genetic information; 76% of respondents expressed support for a law prohibiting employers from doing so.

Major Provisions of GINA

Discrimination

Employers may not use genetic information as a basis for employment decisions.

Key Facts: Discrimination

- Employers may not make employment decisions based on genetic information about an employee, an applicant, or a family member of an employee or applicant.
- Employers may not retaliate against an employee or applicant who complains about a violation of GINA or participates in a hearing or investigation of such a violation.
- Disparate impact claims—in which an employee alleges that a seemingly neutral employment practice has had a disproportionately negative effect on a protected group—are not allowed under GINA.

Regulated Employers

All regulated employers are subject to GINA's antidiscrimination provisions.

Covered Workers

All covered workers are subject to GINA's antidiscrimination provisions.

What's Prohibited

Employers may not discriminate against any employee or applicant based on genetic information. Like Title VII (see Chapter 18), GINA prohibits discrimination in every aspect of employment, including hiring, firing, compensation, benefits, job classifications, and any other terms, conditions, or privileges of employment.

GINA also prohibits retaliation against an employee who has opposed any act the law prohibits or who has made a charge, testified, assisted, or participated in any other way in an investigation, proceeding, or hearing.

Unlike Title VII, GINA does not allow disparate impact claims, in which an employee alleges that a neutral employment practice had a disproportionately negative effect on a protected group. (For more on Title VII and disparate impact claims, see Chapter 18.) However, the law provides for the creation of a commission, six years after the date GINA was enacted, to study the issue and make recommendations to Congress as to whether disparate impact claims should be allowed.

Exceptions

It is not a violation of GINA for an employer to make decisions based on genetic information if it is required to do so by a law or regulation that mandates genetic monitoring, such as certain OSHA regulations.

Acquisition of Genetic Information

With a few exceptions, GINA prohibits employers from requiring or asking workers to provide genetic information.

Key Facts: Acquisition of Genetic Information

- Employers may not require employees, applicants, or their family members to provide genetic information.
- Employers may not purchase genetic information about employees, applicants, or their family members.
- There are a handful of exceptions to this rule; if one of them applies, the employer is obligated to treat any genetic information it receives as a confidential medical record.

Regulated Employers

All regulated employers are subject to these provisions.

Covered Workers

All covered workers are subject to these provisions.

What's Prohibited

Employers may not ask or require employees to provide genetic information about themselves or a family member. For example, an employer may not require employees to take a genetic test. Employers also may not purchase genetic information about employees or their family members.

This prohibition applies to otherwise lawful medical examinations relating to employment, such as fitness for duty exams. In this case, the employer must tell the health care provider not to collect or provide genetic information, and must take reasonable steps if it learns that such information is nonetheless being requested or provided, such as switching health care providers.

An employer that lawfully requests, requires, or purchases information about a manifested disease, disorder, or pathological condition of an employee's family member who works for the same employer has not violated this prohibition. For example, it doesn't violate the law if an employee's sibling applies for a job and is asked to take a post-offer medical examination, or works for the same employer and is receiving voluntary genetic services.

Exceptions

There are six exceptions to the general prohibition on acquiring genetic information from employees and their family members. Even if one of these exceptions applies, however, employers may not use the genetic information acquired as a basis for employment decisions. Employers must also safeguard the confidentiality of the information, as provided in "Confidentiality of Genetic Information," below.

It isn't illegal for an employer to obtain genetic information on an employee or family member in any of the following circumstances.

The employer inadvertently requests or requires genetic information from an employee or family member. This might happen if a supervisor hears of genetic information during a casual conversation, in response to an expression of concern, without have sought or solicited the information, or on a social networking site (if, for example, the supervisor and employee are Facebook friends and the employee posts genetic information). This exception doesn't apply if the employer seeks the information by, for example, searching online for genetic information about an employee, eavesdropping on conversations, searching someone's personal belongings, or asking pointed follow-up questions in a conversation about a family member's health.

If an employer receives genetic information in response to a lawful request for medical information, it will be considered inadvertent (and therefore be covered by this exception) if the employer tells the information provider not to give genetic information. This part of the exception applies to, for example, requests for documentation to support a request for reasonable accommodation under the ADA or other disability laws, a request pursuant to the FMLA or other leave laws, or a request for leave under the employer's own policies. The regulations provide the following suggested language, which may be provided in writing (or orally if the employer requests the medical information orally):

> The Genetic Information Nondiscrimination Act of 2008 (GINA) prohibits employers and other entities covered by GINA Title II from requesting or requiring genetic information of an individual or family member of the individual, except as specifically allowed by this law. To comply with this law, we are asking that you not provide any genetic information when responding to this request for medical information. "Genetic information" as defined by GINA, includes an individual's family medical history, the results of an individual's or family member's genetic tests, the fact that an individual or an individual's family member sought or received genetic services, and genetic information of a fetus carried by an individual or an individual's family member or an embryo lawfully held by an individual or family member receiving assistive reproductive services.

The employer offers health or genetic services, including as part of a voluntary wellness program. This exception applies only if all of the following are true:

- Providing genetic information is voluntary, meaning that employees are not required to provide it or penalized for choosing not to provide it. If an employer offers financial inducements to employees who participate (for example, by completing a health risk assessment), the employer must make clear that the inducement will be available whether or not the employee provides genetic information. An employer may offer financial inducements for employees who have voluntarily provided genetic information indicating a heightened risk of acquiring a health condition in the future to participate in programs that promote healthy lifestyles or to meet particular health goals, as long as the programs are also offered to those whose current health conditions or lifestyle choices put them at heightened risk of developing the condition.

- The employee gives prior knowing, voluntary, and written authorization, on a form that is written so the employee is likely to understand it, describes the type of genetic information that will be obtained and the purposes for which it will be used, and describes the restrictions on disclosure of genetic information. This authorization may be electronic.
- Only the employee or family member receiving services, along with the health care professional or board certified genetic counselor involved in providing the services, receive individually identifiable genetic information; this information may not be accessible to managers, supervisors, others who make employment decisions, or anyone else in the workplace.
- Any individually identifiable genetic information resulting from the services is available only for purposes of those services and is not disclosed to the employer except in aggregate terms that don't reveal the identity of any person. This requirement is not violated if the employer receives information that, for reasons outside of its control or the control of the information provider (such as a small sample size), makes the genetic information of a particular person readily identifiable with no effort on the employer's part.

The employer requests family medical history to comply with the certification requirements of the FMLA (see Chapter 8), state or local family medical leave laws, or employer policies that permit the use of leave to care for a sick family member.

The employer acquires genetic information from documents that are commercially and publicly available. This exception applies if, for example, the employer reads a newspaper or magazine article about an employee's struggle with a genetic disorder. It does not apply to medical databases, court records, or scientific research databases available to scientists on a restricted basis, nor to information acquired through sources with limited access, such as social networking sites that require permission to access from a particular person or that allow access only to members of a particular group. It also doesn't apply if the employer accessed commercially and publicly available documents with the intent of gathering employee genetic information, or if the employer was likely to acquire genetic information from viewing them (for example, if an employer visits an online discussion group about genetic testing or discrimination).

The information acquired is to be used for genetic monitoring of the biological effects of toxic substances in the workplace. This exception applies only if all of the following are true:

- The employer provides written notice of the monitoring to the employee.
- The monitoring is required by federal or state law, or the employee gives prior knowing, voluntary, and written authorization to the monitoring on a form that is written so the employee is likely to understand it, describes the type of genetic information that will be obtained, and describes the restrictions on disclosure of genetic information.
- The employee is informed of the results.
- The monitoring complies with federal or state genetic monitoring regulations (depending on whether the state has its own genetic monitoring program under the authority of the OSH Act).
- Other than any licensed health care professional or genetic counselor involved in the program, the employer receives results from the program only in aggregate form, which does not disclose the identity of individual employees.

The employer conducts DNA analysis for law enforcement purposes as a forensic laboratory or to identify human remains, and requests or requires genetic information from employees only for analysis of DNA identification markers as a means of detecting sample contamination.

Confidentiality of Genetic Information

Employers that have genetic information about an employee must keep it in separate files and treat it confidentially.

Key Facts: Confidentiality of Genetic Information

- An employer that has genetic information about an employee must keep it on separate forms and in separate files.
- Such information must be treated as confidential medical information, which may be disclosed only if an exception applies.

Regulated Employers

All regulated employers that possess genetic information about an employee are subject to these provisions.

Covered Workers

All covered workers are subject to these provisions.

What's Required

Employers that have genetic information about employees must keep it separately, on separate forms and in separate files. Employers must treat this information as a confidential medical record. GINA provides that employers comply with this requirement if they treat genetic information as they treat confidential medical records under the Americans with Disabilities Act (ADA). This means the information must be kept separately from regular personnel files with restricted access.

An employer that receives genetic information orally (for example, in casual conversation with an employee) need not reduce it to writing, but still must keep it confidential. An employer need not go through its personnel files and remove genetic information that predates the effective date of GINA, but it may not use or disclose that information except in accordance with the law. Genetic information that an employer acquires through commercially and publicly available sources (in accordance with an exception to the prohibition on acquiring genetic information discussed above) need not be treated as confidential, but the employer may not discriminate based on that information.

Exceptions

An employer may disclose genetic information about an employee in the following circumstances:

- to the employee or family member, upon his or her written request
- to an occupational or health researcher, for research conducted in compliance with Part 46 of Title 45 of the Code of Federal Regulations (the Department of Health and Human Service's rules for the protection of human research subjects)

- in response to a court order, only the genetic information expressly authorized by that order. If the court order was obtained without the employee or family member's knowledge, the employer must notify the employee or family member of the order and of any genetic information that was disclosed as a result.
- to government officials investigating compliance with GINA, if the information is relevant to the investigation
- in connection with the employee's compliance with the certification requirements of the FMLA or a similar state law
- to a federal, state, or local public health agency, an employer may disclose only information about the manifestation of a disease or disorder in an employee's family member if that information concerns a contagious disease that presents an imminent hazard of death or life-threatening illness. The employer must notify the employee of the disclosure.

How GINA Is Enforced

Individual Complaints

The enforcement provisions of Title VII apply to GINA. (See Chapter 18.)

Agency Enforcement

The enforcement provisions of Title VII apply to GINA. (See Chapter 18.)

Complying With GINA

Posting Requirements

Employers must post a notice about federal laws prohibiting discrimination, including GINA. See Chapter 18 for information on getting the required poster from the EEOC.

Penalties

The penalties for violating GINA are the same as those for violating Title VII. (See Chapter 18.)

Agency Resources

- Information for employers on genetic information discrimination
  Genetic Information Discrimination
  www.eeoc.gov/laws/types/genetic.cfm
- FAQs for small businesses regarding GINA
  Questions and Answers for Small Businesses: EEOC Final Rule on Title II of the Genetic Information Nondiscrimination Act of 2008
  www.eeoc.gov/laws/regulations/gina_qanda_smallbus.cfm

State Laws Relating to Genetic Discrimination

See "State Laws Prohibiting Discrimination in Employment," in Chapter 18, for information on state laws relating to all forms of employment discrimination, including discrimination on the basis of genetic information.

Immigration Reform and Control Act of 1986 (IRCA)

Statute: 8 U.S.C. § 1324a and 1324b

http://uscode.house.gov/download/pls/08C12.txt

Regulations: 8 C.F.R. § 274a

www.gpo.gov/fdsys/pkg/CFR-2012-title8-vol1/pdf/CFR-2012-title8-vol1-part274a.pdf

28 C.F.R. § 44

www.gpo.gov/fdsys/pkg/CFR-2012-title28-vol2/pdf/CFR-2012-title28-vol2-part44.pdf

Overview of IRCA

When the Immigration Reform and Control Act of 1986 (IRCA) was passed in 1986, it was the most sweeping immigration law enacted by Congress in more than 35 years. IRCA addresses many immigration issues, but this chapter focuses on the law's regulation of the employment relationship. This discussion does not cover the rules that apply to agricultural workers, nor does it cover the steps potential employers can take to secure temporary employment visas (such as H-B1 visas) for foreign workers whom they wish to hire.

The IRCA has three major provisions affecting nonagricultural employment:

- **Verification.** Employers must verify that all employees are legally *authorized to work in the United States*. IRCA makes it illegal for an employer to knowingly hire, recruit, or refer for employment an unauthorized alien.
- **Record keeping.** Employers must keep forms verifying that employees are legally authorized to work in the United States.
- **Antidiscrimination.** Employers may not discriminate based on citizenship status or national origin.

Regulated Employers

The verification and record-keeping provisions of IRCA cover all employers regardless of size, including:

- private employers
- the federal government
- state governments
- local governments, and
- persons or entities that refer workers to employers for a fee.

The antidiscrimination provision of IRCA applies to the following employers only:

- private employers with four or more employees
- the federal government
- state governments, and
- local governments.

Definitions

Authorized to work in the United States Legally permitted to hold a job in the United States. The following categories of people are authorized to work in the United States:

- U.S. citizens
- lawful permanent resident aliens
- lawful temporary resident aliens
- aliens paroled into the United States as refugees (but only for the specified period) aliens granted asylum (but only for the specified period)
- aliens admitted into the United States as nonimmigrant fiancées and fiancés (but only for the specified period)
- citizens of Micronesia and the Marshall Islands
- aliens granted suspension of deportation, and
- aliens granted extended voluntary departure as members of certain nationality groups, by request of the secretary of state.

Date of hire The date on which the employee actually starts working for wages or other remuneration. The date of hire is not necessarily the date a job offer is made or accepted (although it can be, if the employee starts work that same day).

Independent contractor Someone who carries on an independent business, contracts to do a piece of work according to his or her own means or methods, and is subject to the control of the person or business who contracted for the work only as to results. Other federal and state laws have somewhat different definitions, but those do not apply here.

Unauthorized alien A person who is not a U.S. citizen and who is neither (1) an alien lawfully admitted into the United States for permanent residence, nor (2) an alien authorized to be employed in the United States.

Legal Developments

- **Employers can check work authorization online.** A USCIS program allows employers to use the Internet to verify that new hires are authorized to work in the United States. (This program was once called Basic Pilot; now it's called E-Verify.) Employers can check Social Security Administration and Department of Homeland Security databases to verify the employment authorization of new hires. Although the program is voluntary for most employers, federal contractors are required to use it, under an Executive Order signed by President Bush in 2008. In addition, some states require employers to use E-Verify.

- **Supreme Court decides two IRCA cases on Arizona immigration laws.** In the past couple of years, the Supreme Court has twice considered whether Arizona's notoriously strict immigration laws are valid, with mixed results. The Court upheld Arizona's requirement that all employers in the state must use E-Verify, and the state's penalty of suspending or revoking the business licenses of employers in the state who intentionally or knowingly employ unauthorized workers. (*Chamber of Commerce v. Whiting*, 131 S.Ct. 1968 (2011).) A year later, however, the Court struck down several other parts of Arizona's law, finding that the state could not criminalize someone's failure to possess and carry registration papers or someone's efforts to get work as an employee or contractor without proper work authorization (among other things). (*Arizona v. United States*, 132 S.Ct. 2492 (2012).) The Court found that these provisions were preempted by IRCA.

- **Changes proposed to the I-9 Form.** The USCIS has proposed some changes to Form I-9. These changes would, among other things, revise the layout of the form, expand the instructions, and allow for the inclusion of employee telephone numbers and email addresses. The USCIS has not yet finalized the form. It has advised employers to continue using the version of the form that expired in August 2012 until the new form is available.

Covered Workers

The verification and record-keeping provisions of IRCA cover all employees of regulated employers, including:

- U.S. citizens and nationals, and
- aliens who are legally authorized to work in the United States.

The antidiscrimination provision of IRCA covers the following workers:

- citizens and nationals of the United States
- aliens lawfully admitted for permanent residence
- aliens lawfully admitted for temporary residence
- aliens admitted as refugees, and
- aliens granted asylum.

None of IRCA's employment-related provisions cover independent contractors or people who provide domestic service (for example, baby-sitting or housecleaning) in a private home and whose service is sporadic, irregular, or intermittent. If, however, the domestic worker's service is regular (for example, once a week or twice a month), then the worker is covered by IRCA.

Did You Know ...

- The U.S. Immigration and Naturalization Service (INS) changed its name on March 1, 2003 to the U.S. Citizenship and Immigration Services (USCIS), when it became part of the Department of Homeland Security. Former duties of the INS were divided among other organizations, including the USCIS and the new U.S. Immigration and Customs Enforcement (ICE).
- ICE has stepped up its worksite enforcement. In 2009, the agency reported that it would focus its enforcement efforts on employers, not employees. The press release on the enforcement plan said that worksite enforcement resources would be focused on the criminal prosecution of employers who knowingly hire unauthorized workers, "to target the root cause of illegal immigration." Managers, supervisors, and HR personnel have all faced criminal charges as a result of worksite enforcement actions.
- Various estimates place the current number of undocumented workers in the United States at between six and eight million people.

Major Provisions of IRCA

Verification

Employers must verify that the people who work for them are legally authorized to work in the United States.

Key Facts: Verification

- Employers may not knowingly hire, recruit, or refer unauthorized aliens for employment in the United States, and may not continue to employ someone after discovering that he or she is an unauthorized alien.
- To verify the employee's work authorization, employers must examine certain documents within three days of hiring an employee or by the end of the first day of work, if the employee will work for fewer than three days. If the employee's authorization to work in this country has an expiration date, the employer must reverify the employee's work eligibility when that authorization has expired.
- If the documents the employee presents reasonably appear genuine and reasonably appear to refer to the person who presented them, the employer may not ask the employee for additional identity and work authorization documents.
- Employers who fail to properly verify work authorization face civil and criminal penalties and fines.

Regulated Employers

All regulated employers are subject to these provisions.

Covered Workers

All covered workers are subject to these provisions.

What's Prohibited

Employers may not:

- knowingly hire, recruit, or refer for a fee an unauthorized alien for employment in the United States
- continue to employ a person after discovering that he or she is an unauthorized alien, or
- ask an employee for additional identity and work authorization documents if the documents the employee presents reasonably appear genuine and reasonably appear to refer to the person who presented them (see "Record Keeping," below, for a list of acceptable documents that establish identity and authorization).

What's Required

Employers must do all of the following:

- Within three business days of the employee's date of hire, the employer must physically examine documents presented by the employee to establish the employee's identity and authorization to work in the United States. (See "Record Keeping," below, for a list of acceptable documents that establish identity and authorization.)
- If the employer is hiring the employee for fewer than three days total, the employer must examine the documents before the end of the employee's first day of work.
- If the employee's authorization to work in the United States is temporary, the employer must reverify the employee's employment eligibility on or before the date when the original authorization expires. The employer may do this by completing Section 3 of the original Form I-9, or by completing a new Form I-9.

Record Keeping

Employers must keep records to prove that they verified the legality of their workers.

Key Facts: Record Keeping

- After examining the necessary documents to verify work authorization, employers must complete Form I-9 for each employee they hire, including their own relatives.
- Only certain documents are acceptable to verify employment authorization. (See "Acceptable Documents," below.)
- Employers must keep an employee's Form I-9 for three years or one year after the employee's termination, whichever is later. Employers need not file the forms with any agency but must keep them and make them available for inspection by federal agencies.

Regulated Employers

All regulated employers are subject to these provisions.

Covered Workers

All covered workers are subject to these provisions.

What's Prohibited

Employers may not use their copies of an employee's verification documents for any purpose other than complying with IRCA. Employers may copy any of the documents presented by the employee for verification purposes, but only if the copy is kept with Form I-9, the document that employers must complete to verify that they have checked the legality of their workers. (See "What's Required," below, for more about Form I-9.)

What's Required

Employers must do all of the following:
- Within three business days of the date of hire, the employer must verify under penalty of perjury that the employee is a U.S. citizen or an authorized alien by completing Form I-9. Employers must do this

for all employees, including employees who are relatives or personal acquaintances.

- If the employer is hiring the employee for fewer than three days, then the employer must complete Form I-9 before the end of the employee's first day of work.
- The employer must make sure that the employee completes his or her portion of the USCIS Form I-9 within one day of the date of hire.
- The employer may complete "Section 3: Updating and Reverification" of the employee's original Form I-9, rather than generating a new Form I-9, if:
  - the employee changes his or her name
  - the employee is rehired within three years of the date the original form was completed, and continues to be eligible for employment on the same basis, or
  - the employee's original work authorization has expired or will soon do so.
- Employers must keep the Form I-9 for three years after the date of hire or one year after the date of termination, whichever is later. Employers may store these forms electronically.
- Employers must make all I-9 forms available for inspection by the USCIS, ICE, the Office of the Special Counsel for Immigration-Related Unfair Employment Practices (OSC), or the U.S. Department of Labor (DOL).

Acceptable Documents

To satisfy the law's verification and record-keeping requirements, employers may view one document or a combination of documents, depending on the nature of a document.

Documents that are acceptable under IRCA fall into one of three categories:

- those that verify both identity and authorization to work in the United States (see List A, below)
- those that verify only identity (see List B, below), and
- those that verify only employment authorization (see List C, below).

If an employee submits a document from List A, no other documents are necessary. Otherwise, an employee must submit one document each from List B and List C. To get the most up-to-date information regarding acceptable documents, refer to the USCIS website. (See Appendix A for contact information.)

List A. The following documents establish both identity and employment authorization:

- U.S. passport or passport card
- permanent resident card or alien registration receipt card (Form I-151 or I-551)
- foreign passport with a temporary I-551 stamp or temporary I-551 printed notation on a machine-readable immigrant visa
- employment authorization document that includes a photograph (Form I-766)
- for a nonimmigrant alien authorized to work for a particular employer incident to status, a foreign passport with Form I-94 or Form I-94A bearing the same name as the passport and containing an endorsement of the holder's nonimmigrant status, as long as the endorsement period has not expired and the proposed employment does not conflict with any restrictions or limitations listed on the form, or
- a passport from Micronesia (FSM) or the Marshall Islands (RMI) with Form I-94 or Form I-94A indicating nonimmigrant admission under the Compact of Free Association Between the United States and the FSM or RMI.

List B. The following documents establish identity only:

- driver's license or identification card issued by a state or outlying possession of the United States, as long as it contains a photograph or identifying information such as name, date of birth, sex, height, eye color, and address
- identification card issued by a federal, state, or local government agency or entity, provided it contains a photograph or identifying information such as name, date of birth, sex, height, eye color, and address
- school identification card with a photograph
- voter's registration card
- U.S. military card or draft record
- military dependent's identification card
- U.S. Coast Guard Merchant Mariner card
- Native American tribal document
- driver's license issued by a Canadian government authority, or

- for those younger than 18 who can't present any of the documents above, a school report or report card; a clinic, doctor, or hospital record; or a day care or nursery school record.

List C. The following documents establish work authorization only:

- U.S. Social Security card issued by the Social Security Administration (other than a card stating that it is not valid for employment)
- certification of birth abroad issued by the Department of State (Form FS-545 or Form DS-1350)
- original or certified copy of a birth certificate issued by a state, county, municipal authority, or outlying possession of the United States bearing an official seal
- Native American tribal document
- U.S. citizen identification card (Form I-197)
- identification card of a resident citizen in the United States (Form I-179), or
- unexpired employment authorization document issued by the Department of Homeland Security (other than those listed under List A, above).

In certain circumstances, an employer may accept a document called a receipt in place of one of the acceptable documents listed above—for example, when the employee presents a receipt showing application for a replacement document. For details on when receipts are an acceptable substitute for the specified documents, refer to USCIS's publications and website. (See "Agency Resources," below.)

Antidiscrimination

IRCA protects certain workers from discrimination based on citizenship or national origin.

Key Facts: Antidiscrimination

- Employers may not discriminate in any aspect of employment based on citizenship status or national origin unless a federal law specifically allows them to do so.
- Employers who discriminate can be investigated by the Office of the Special Counsel for Immigration-Related Unfair Employment Practices (OSC) and/or the EEOC and face fines and lawsuits.

Regulated Employers

All regulated employers are subject to these provisions.

Covered Workers

All covered workers are subject to these provisions.

What's Prohibited

Employers may not discriminate against employees on the basis of citizenship status or national origin unless a federal law explicitly allows them to do so because U.S. citizenship has been declared an essential requirement of the job. This prohibition applies to all phases of the employment relationship, including hiring, promotion, pay, job assignment, discipline, and termination. For example, an employer may not refuse to hire a worker because the worker's authorization document has a future expiration date.

Employers may not retaliate against workers for asserting their rights under IRCA.

Exceptions

IRCA's antidiscrimination provisions do not protect the following types of aliens:

- one who fails to apply for naturalization within six months of the date he or she first becomes eligible to apply for naturalization, or
- one who has applied on a timely basis, but who has not been naturalized as a citizen within two years after the date of the application (excluding

the time government agencies spend processing the application), unless the alien can establish that he or she is actively pursuing naturalization.

If two applicants are equally qualified for a position, an employer may give preference to a citizen or national of the United States. However, an employer may not institute a blanket policy of preferring U.S. citizens for all job openings.

How IRCA Is Enforced

Individual Complaints

Anyone may file a complaint with the USCIS if he or she thinks an employer is violating the record-keeping or verification provisions of the law. Employees who want to complain about discrimination can complain to either the OSC or the EEOC, depending on the type of discrimination and the size of the employer:

- Employees who think that they are being discriminated against on the basis of citizenship status—and who work for an employer with four or more employees—can file a charge with the OSC.
- Employees who think that they are being discriminated against on the basis of national origin—and who work for an employer with four to 14 employees—can file a charge with the OSC.
- Employees who think that they are being discriminated against on the basis of national origin—and who work for an employer with 15 or more employees—can file a charge with the EEOC. (For more about the EEOC and national origin discrimination, see Chapter 18.)

Agency Enforcement

The Department of Homeland Security (DHS), which includes USCIS and ICE, has the authority to investigate discrimination complaints and inspect employers' I-9 forms.

The OSC has the authority to investigate an employee's or applicant's complaint that an employer has violated IRCA. The OSC may file a complaint against the employer before an administrative law judge. The OSC also has the power to initiate independent investigations of an employer based on information obtained in other investigations or on information provided by members of the public.

The EEOC has the authority to investigate charges and file complaints against employers in a court of law. Like the OSC, the EEOC also has the power to initiate independent investigations.

Complying With IRCA

Deadlines

Employers must verify an employee's authorization to work in the United States *within three days of hiring the employee,* or *by the end of the employee's first day of work if the employee will work for fewer than three days.*

Reporting Requirements

IRCA imposes no reporting requirements.

Posting Requirements

IRCA imposes no posting requirements.

Record-Keeping Requirements

IRCA's record-keeping requirements are discussed in "Record Keeping," above.

Penalties

The penalties for violating IRCA depend on the provision violated.

Employers who knowingly hire an unauthorized alien or who knowingly continue to employ an unauthorized alien face both criminal and civil penalties:

- **Criminal penalties.** Employers can be fined up to $3,000 for each unauthorized worker or imprisoned for up to six months or both.
- **Civil penalties.** Employers can be ordered to cease violating the law and to pay a fine according to the following schedule:

- first offense: $375 to $3,200 for each unauthorized alien
- second offense: $3,200 to $6,500 for each unauthorized alien, and
- more than two offenses: $4,300 to $16,000 for each unauthorized alien.

Employers who fail to comply with IRCA's verification requirements must pay a fine of $110 to $1,100 for each unauthorized alien whose identity and work authorization they fail to verify.

Employers who refuse to honor acceptable documents presented to them, ask for more documents than necessary to follow the law, or fail to keep I-9s for the required period must pay a civil penalty of between $100 and $1,000 for each violation.

Employers who violate IRCA's antidiscrimination provisions may face a hearing in front of an administrative law judge or a civil trial in federal court and may be assessed the following penalties:

- an order to reinstate the aggrieved employee(s) with or without back pay
- if the employer has never been found guilty before, a civil fine of between $375 and $3,200 for each aggrieved employee or applicant
- if the employer has been found guilty once before, a civil fine of between $3,200 and $6,500 for each aggrieved employee or applicant
- if the employer has previously been found guilty two or more times, a civil fine of between $4,300 and $16,000 for each aggrieved employee or applicant, and
- an order to pay the attorneys' fees of the employee(s) or applicant(s) who brought suit.

Employers who have more than 14 employees and have been found guilty of national origin discrimination also face penalties under Title VII. (For more, see Chapter 18.)

Agency Resources

- USCIS Form I-9
  www.uscis.gov/files/form/i-9.pdf
- Guide for employers on completing the i-9 form
  How Do I Complete Form I-9, Employment Eligibility Verification?
  www.uscis.gov/USCIS/Resources/E3en.pdf

- A comprehensive manual on completing and storing I-9 forms
  Handbook for Employers: Instructions for Completing Form I-9
  www.uscis.gov/files/form/m-274.pdf
- Article on verification procedures
  Verifying the Legal Status of Your Employees Without Committing Unlawful Discrimination
  www.justice.gov/crt/about/osc/htm/article.php
- Employer guide to immigration-related discrimination
  Look at the Facts, Not at the Faces
  www.justice.gov/crt/about/osc/pdf/publications/EmployGuideJul09.pdf

State Laws Relating to Immigration

To find out if your state has a law relating to immigration, contact your state fair employment practices agency and/or state labor department. (See Appendix A for contact details.)

National Labor Relations Act (NLRA)

Statute: 29 U.S.C. §§ 151–169
http://uscode.house.gov/download/pls/29C7.txt

Regulations: 29 C.F.R. §§ 100.101–103.100 (National Labor Relations Board)
www.gpo.gov/fdsys/pkg/CFR-2012-title29-vol2/pdf/CFR-2012-title29-vol2-subtitleB-chapl.pdf29

C.F.R. §§1400 and following (Federal Conciliation and Mediation Service)
www.gpo.gov/fdsys/pkg/CFR-2012-title29-vol4/pdf/CFR-2012-title29-vol4-subtitleB-chapXII.pdf

Overview of the NLRA

The National Labor Relations Act (NLRA) establishes what unions and management can and can't do in their dealings with each other and with individual employees. When it became law in 1935, the NLRA voiced strong support for workers' rights to organize and bargain collectively with their employer. The law outlawed certain employer efforts to prevent union organizing and bust up existing unions. Subsequent amendments to the NLRA (particularly the Labor Management Relations Act, commonly known as the Taft-Hartley Act) are more supportive of employers, declaring certain union actions to be illegal and upholding a worker's right not to support a union.

The law includes provisions on:

- **Organizing and representation elections.** The NLRA sets the guidelines for employer and union conduct during organizing campaigns and elections held to determine whether a union should represent a group of workers.
- **Unfair labor practices.** The NLRA prohibits employers and unions from engaging in certain acts toward each other and toward individual employees.

This book does not cover the Labor Management Reporting and Disclosure Act, commonly known as the Landrum-Griffin Act (29 U.S.C. §§ 401-531), which imposes a number of procedural requirements on unions and establishes certain rights that unions must provide to their members.

Definitions

Bargaining unit A group of employees whom a union represents (or seeks to represent) in its dealings with an employer. Workers in a bargaining unit must have similar job duties, skills, or working conditions and have common concerns about wages and hours. Usually, professional and nonprofessional employees will not be combined in a single bargaining unit. A single workplace may contain more than one bargaining unit (for example, the butchers, checkers, and janitors in a grocery store might all be members of different bargaining units). A bargaining unit can include workers from different facilities (for example, all of the cashiers in a chain of retail stores).

Definitions (continued)

Collective bargaining agreement The contract between the union (on behalf of the bargaining unit it represents) and the employer that governs the terms and conditions of the workers' employment.

Federal Mediation and Conciliation Service An agency of the federal government that helps parties to a labor dispute reach a resolution through negotiation and mediation.

Health care institution A hospital, convalescent hospital, health maintenance organization, health clinic, nursing home, extended care facility, or another institution devoted to providing care for the sick, infirm, or aged.

Hot cargo agreement An agreement between an employer and a union in which the employer promises to stop doing business with another employer, typically one with whom the union has a dispute.

Manager A worker who represents the company's interests by taking or recommending actions that control or implement company policy.

Protected concerted activities Action taken by two or more employees to improve, protest, or otherwise change the terms and conditions of their employment (such as wages, benefits, work environment, supervision, productivity requirements, or workplace rules). Workers may not be disciplined or retaliated against for engaging in protected concerted activities, in union or nonunion companies.

Supervisor An employee who has the authority, in the interests of the employer, to hire, transfer, suspend, lay off, recall, promote, discharge, assign, reward, discipline, responsibly direct, or adjust the grievances of other employees, or to effectively recommend any of those actions. The authority granted the supervisor must not be only routine or clerical, but must require the supervisor to exercise independent judgment. Supervisors may spend most of their time doing the same work as the employees they supervise, as long as they spend 10% to 15% of their time on the supervisory tasks described above.

Regulated Employers

The NLRA applies to all private employers whose operations affect commerce between states—that is, whose employees handle, sell, produce, or otherwise work on goods or materials that have come from or will go to another state, or whose employees use the mail, telephone, or other equipment to communicate across state lines. The law would reach virtually every employer if not for the jurisdictional standards noted below.

The NLRA does not apply to:
- federal, state, or local governments
- religious schools, and
- any employer subject to the Railway Labor Act (45 U.S.C. §§ 151-188), which governs labor relations in the railroad and airline industries.

Jurisdictional Standards

Although the National Labor Relations Board (NLRB) has the right to act to enforce the NLRA whenever the employer's enterprise affects interstate commerce, the NLRB has decided to intervene only in larger disputes. In its discretion, the NLRB has set minimum business volume requirements, which it calls "jurisdictional requirements," that an employer's business must meet before the NLRB will step in. Jurisdictional limits for some common industries are as follows:

- **Nonretail businesses:** at least $50,000 in direct sales of goods or services to consumers in other states, indirect sales (through other sellers), direct purchases of goods or services from suppliers in other states, or indirect purchases (through other purchasers)
- **Retail enterprises:** at least $500,000 in total gross annual business volume
- **Management and operation of office buildings and shopping centers:** at least $100,000 in total annual revenue, of which $25,000 or more must come from organizations that meet any of the other jurisdictional standards (except the indirect sale or purchase of goods for nonretail businesses)
- **Newspapers:** at least $200,000 in total annual business volume
- **Radio, telegraph, television, and telephone companies:** at least $100,000 in total annual business volume
- **Hotels, motels, and residential apartment buildings:** at least $500,000 in total annual business volume

- **Privately operated health care institutions:** at least $250,000 in total annual business volume for hospitals; $100,000 for nursing homes, visiting nurses associations, and related facilities
- **Private universities and colleges:** at least $1,000,000 in gross annual revenue from all sources (except contributions not available for operating expenses at the grantor's request)
- **Law firms and legal assistance programs:** at least $250,000 in gross annual revenue
- **Employers that provide social services (such as groups that solicit and distribute charitable contributions):** at least $250,000 in gross annual revenue, and
- **National defense:** any enterprise affecting commerce whose operations have a substantial impact on national defense.

This is not an exhaustive list: The NLRB has standards for a variety of enterprises, including taxi companies, symphony orchestras, casinos, and cemeteries.

If an employer won't give the NLRB the information it needs to figure out whether the employer meets one of these standards, the NLRB can disregard the standards altogether and get involved in a dispute involving that employer.

Legal Developments

- **NLRB rule changing election procedures is enjoined.** The NLRB issued a final regulation in 2011, modifying the process by which union elections are held in the workplace. These controversial rules were intended to speed up election proceedings by, among other things, limiting the legal challenges an employer may bring before the election is held and giving the officers who hear such preelection challenges greater discretion to streamline the proceedings by restricting the issues to be heard and limiting written briefs. Although the new procedures were scheduled to become effective in April 2012, they didn't: A federal district court found that the NLRB lacked the necessary quorum to adopt the final regulation, which was therefore invalid. The NLRB has appealed this decision, but for the time being, the new rules are on hold.

Legal Developments (Continued)

- **NLRB posting rule never goes into effect.** In 2011, the NLRB issued regulations requiring employers to post a notice of employee rights under the law. This new rule was set to go into effect in April 2012, but opponents filed a lawsuit to block implementation of the rule until a court could consider its legality. The federal Court of Appeals for the D.C. Circuit issued an injunction preventing the rule from going into effect while that Court hears arguments about the rule. As we go to press, that injunction is still in effect, so employers do not yet have to post the notice.

- **Social media policies in the spotlight—and on the hot seat.** Recently, the NLRB has come down hard on employers with social media policies that might restrict discussion of working conditions. Policy language that many companies have used for years has been struck down as too likely to lead employees to believe that they may not criticize the company's policies and practices online, in violation of the right employees have to freely discuss working conditions with each other and plan to take action to improve their situation.

- **May companies ban employees from using email for personal messages under the NLRA?** In December 2007, the NLRB decided that a company may ban employees from sending any personal messages or place other limits on use of the company's email system—for example, prohibiting solicitations or messages sent on behalf of outside organizations—without violating the law, as long as the rule doesn't explicitly prohibit only union-related messages. In 2009, however, the federal Court of Appeals for the D.C. Circuit took another look at the facts in this case and found that the employer had, in fact, singled out union messages for discipline by selectively enforcing its "no solicitations" rule only to union-related communications. *Guard Publishing Co. v. NLRB*, 571 F.3d 53 (D.C. Cir. 2009).

Covered Workers

The NLRA generally covers all employees of a regulated employer, except:
- agricultural workers
- domestic servants

- anyone employed by a parent or spouse
- independent contractors
- *managers*
- *supervisors*
- government employees, and
- workers whose employers are subject to the Railway Labor Act.

Did You Know ...

- The NLRA applies even to nonunion companies. For example, a nonunion company must follow the legal rules for union elections, employee discussions or actions regarding the terms and conditions of their employment, and work rules that could inhibit employee rights to organize and act collectively.
- When the NLRA was passed, fewer than 14% of American workers were union members. Five years after the NLRA became law, that number had doubled. Today, union membership has once again declined, to 11.8% of all employees in 2011. More than a third (37%) of public employees belong to a union, compared to only 6.9% of the private sector workforce.
- For 2011, the median weekly earnings for a union member were $209 more than for an employee who was not represented by a union. This adds up to a wage differential of more than $10,000 a year.

Major Provisions of the NLRA

Organizing and Representation Elections

The NLRA establishes workers' basic right to organize—to form, join, or assist a union; to choose their own representatives to negotiate with their employer about terms and conditions of employment; and to engage in other collective efforts to improve their work situations. The law also establishes procedures for determining whether a particular union should have the right to represent a group of workers.

Key Facts: Organizing and Elections

- Employers may not use threats or coercion to influence the outcome of a union election, nor may they unfairly influence their workers' decision to join or form a union.
- Employers may not adopt policies or take actions that unfairly inhibit their employees' rights to discuss the terms and conditions of their employment or union issues. However, employers have the right to prohibit all nonwork discussions at certain times and places.
- An employer and a union may enter into a union security agreement, which requires all workers—even those who choose not to join the union—to make certain payments to the union as a condition of getting or keeping a job. However, states have the right to prohibit these agreements, and some of them have. Also, employees who object to paying dues on religious or political grounds are entitled to pay the same amount to certain types of charity organizations rather than to a union.

The Election Process

In order to represent workers in negotiations with an employer, a union must have the support of a majority of workers in an appropriate *bargaining unit*. Unions generally demonstrate this support by asking workers to sign authorization cards, which are forms that each worker signs to indicate a desire to be represented by the union in dealings with the employer.

If the union gets the support of a majority of bargaining unit workers, it will often ask the employer to recognize the union voluntarily. If the employer agrees, the union will be the official bargaining representative of the unit, and employer and union can begin negotiating a *collective bargaining agreement*.

If the employer refuses to recognize the union—for example, if the employer believes the bargaining unit is improper or believes the union's support is not genuine—the workers or union can file a petition with the NLRB, asking it to hold an election. Their petition must be supported by authorization cards or other signed statements of union support from at least 30% of the workers in the proposed bargaining unit. After the NLRB investigates and tries to resolve any disputes between the parties over the scope of the bargaining unit and the time and place of the election, the NLRB will hold a secret election. If the union receives a majority of the votes cast, it will be certified as the bargaining representative of the unit.

An employer may also petition the NLRB for an election if one or more individuals or unions claims the right to represent a particular bargaining unit.

In 2011, the NLRB issued a final rule proposing changes to the election process. Sometimes referred to as the "speedy election" rule, these regulations have been very controversial, so much so that they were challenged—successfully—before they went into effect. After a federal district court found that the NLRB didn't have the necessary quorum to approve the final regulations, they are now on hold, pending the NLRB's appeal of that decision. Unless and until a higher court determines that the rule was properly promulgated, these new procedures will not go into effect.

Some of the proposed changes would simply bring the agency up to technological speed or otherwise streamline the process. For example, parties would be able to file documents with the NLRB electronically, and would receive certain basic information and forms when an election petition is filed. The rule would also bring together all of the NLRB's regulations on elections in one place, to minimize confusion and possible contradictions.

However, a number of the changes would speed up the election process, both by shortening the period between when an election petition is filed and when the election is actually held, and by eliminating or postponing certain procedures and challenges until the election is over. These proposals have been very controversial, in part because they shorten the time during which employers can try to defeat an organization campaign. Union advocates claim that employers have used this window (between the filing of a petition and the actual election) to intimidate employees into opposing the union; employer advocates counter that the more employees learn about unions, the more likely they are to vote against representation. Whether this time is used for legitimate communication or unfair tactics, both sides agree that speeding up the election process will benefit unions, not employers. Stay tuned to find out if and when the final rule goes into effect.

Regulated Employers

All regulated employers are subject to these provisions.

Covered Workers

All covered workers are subject to these provisions.

What's Prohibited: Employers

The NLRA prohibits employers from unfairly influencing their workers' decision to join or form a union and from using threats or other coercive tactics to influence the outcome of an election. However, employers still have free speech rights. Many of the tactics that the NLRA prohibits employers from using during an election process are discussed as unfair labor practices, below.

If the NRLB finds that an employer has unfairly influenced the outcome of an election, it can set aside a vote rejecting the union or declare the union the victor by default. Here are some examples of prohibited employer conduct:

- **Punishing union supporters.** An employer may not retaliate or discriminate against workers who support the union.
- **Threats.** An employer cannot threaten to fire, demote, or take any other negative job action against workers because they support a union, nor can it threaten to shut down or move the business if the union wins the election.
- **Inducements.** An employer cannot promise or give benefits to workers who oppose the union. Once an organizing campaign has begun, an employer may not increase workers' benefits to discourage them from forming or joining a union.
- **Infiltration.** An employer may not conduct surveillance or otherwise spy on union meetings or on employees who support the union.
- **Interrogation.** An employer may not question workers about their union membership, union meetings, or their support for the union; nor may it ask employees to report on union activities or their coworkers' union views.

What's Prohibited: Unions

Like employers, unions are prohibited from unfairly influencing a worker's decision to support or reject the union or the outcome of an election. The list of prohibited actions for unions is similar to the list for employers. Here are some examples:

- **Threats.** A union may not threaten workers with job loss or other negative job actions for failing to support the union, nor may a union cause an employer to take negative job actions against such workers.

- **Takeovers.** A union may not enter into an agreement with an employer that recognizes the union as the exclusive bargaining representative of a bargaining unit if it does not have the support of a majority of unit employees.
- **Inducements.** A union may not promise or grant benefits to workers for supporting the union.
- **Violence.** A union may not use or threaten physical force against workers to influence their votes.

Exceptions

Union Security Agreements

Although the NLRA protects a worker's right to freely choose whether to join or support a union, it also allows a union and an employer to enter into a contract, called a union security agreement, requiring workers to make certain payments (called "agency fees") to the union as a condition of getting or keeping a job. If a union and an employer have entered into a union security agreement, all workers must either join the union or pay agency fees to the union as a condition of employment. If a worker refuses to pay up or join, the employer must fire the worker.

The NLRA allows states to prohibit union security agreements, and many have. In these states (called "right-to-work" states), workers who decide not to join the union cannot be required to pay any fees to the union and can't be fired or otherwise penalized for failing to do so. (See "State Right-to-Work Laws," at the end of this chapter, for a list of states that have adopted these laws.)

Dues Objectors

Workers who object to paying agency fees either on religious grounds or because they don't support the union's political or other activities can make alternative arrangements, even if they work in a state that allows union security agreements. A worker who has religious reasons for refusing to pay fees may be required to make a similar contribution to a nonlabor, nonreligious charity group.

In states that allow union security agreements, nonunion workers who object to the union's use of their fees for political or other purposes are entitled to a refund of the portion of their dues spent for those purposes. However, they still have to pay their fair share of union money spent on representing the bargaining unit's workers. Some states require unions to get workers' permission before even collecting any fees for activities other than representing workers.

Unfair Labor Practices

In addition to the rules governing union organizing campaigns and elections, the NLRA prohibits a number of activities—called unfair labor practices—by employers and unions. Some of these rules apply to the interactions between employer and union; others protect individual workers from unfair treatment by an employer or a union.

Key Facts: Unfair Labor Practices

- The NLRA prohibits employers from taking certain actions tending to inhibit employees' right to organize, including:
  - banning workplace discussions about union issues or working conditions (for example, wages) while allowing workplace conversations about other nonwork topics
  - retaliating against an employee for filing a complaint with the NLRB
  - refusing to bargain collectively with a union
  - unilaterally changing a workplace rule or policy that covers a topic that the employer is required to bargain over with the union, and dominating a union or creating a sham union.
- The NLRB has found that certain voluntary workplace committees composed of workers and management might be sham unions, if the group is dominated by management and deals with issues that must be collectively bargained.
- Strikes are protected under the NLRA only if employees are striking over issues of wages, hours, or terms and conditions of employment, or to protest an unfair labor practice by the employer. However, a strike for any reason will not be protected under the NLRA if it violates a no-strike clause in the collective bargaining agreement.

Regulated Employers

All regulated employers are subject to these provisions.

Covered Workers

All covered workers are subject to these provisions.

What's Prohibited: Employers

In addition to the prohibitions discussed in "Organizing and Representation Elections," above, the NLRA prohibits employers from:

- interfering with an employee's right to organize, join, or assist a union; engage in collective bargaining; or engage in *protected concerted activities* (see "Banning Union Discussions in the Workplace," below)
- dominating or providing illegal assistance or support to a labor union (see "Company Unions," below)
- discriminating against employees to encourage or discourage member-ship in a labor organization, or replacing workers who strike to protest an unfair labor practice (see "Replacing Workers During a Protected Strike," below)
- retaliating against an employee for filing a charge with or giving testimony to the NLRB
- refusing to engage in good-faith collective bargaining (see "What's Required: Employers and Unions," below), and
- making a *hot cargo agreement* with a union.

Banning Union Discussions in the Workplace

An employer may not completely prohibit union discussions—including discussions that occur before workers are unionized, such as conversations about whether to form or join a union—in the workplace. Instead, employers must treat union-related communications like any other matter not related to work. The specific rules depend on the employer's general rules on nonwork communications:

- An employer may prohibit workers from talking about union matters in work areas during work hours, but only if the employer prohibits workers from talking about other nonwork issues as well.
- An employer must allow workers to talk about union matters outside of work hours in nonwork areas (like a lunchroom or locker room).

- An employer may prohibit union discussions outside of work hours in work areas only if such a rule is necessary to maintain productivity or discipline and the rule applies to all nonwork topics.
- An employer may prohibit distribution of union literature (such as pamphlets or fact sheets) in work areas at all times, as long as the ban applies to all nonwork literature.
- An employer may not prohibit workers from wearing clothing bearing a pro-union message or logo, unless that apparel creates a safety hazard or other special circumstances override the workers' right to communicate their support for the union.

These rules apply equally to union and nonunion workplaces, and they cover discussions that are explicitly about unions or unionizing as well as discussions in which employees act together to change their wages, working conditions, or other terms and conditions of their employment. (Such discussions are protected concerted activities under the NLRA.) Employers may not prevent employees from exercising these rights by, for example, prohibiting employees from talking about wages.

Email is now subject to a different set of rules. As explained in "Legal Developments," above, the NLRB recently issued a decision regarding employee use of company email for union messages. Employers may not single out union-related email or messages regarding wages, working conditions, or other terms of employment for prohibition, either by written rule or by practice. However, the Board held that companies may adopt and enforce rules that prohibit personal use of email, prohibit certain uses of email (for example, solicitation), or even prohibit only certain types of messages (for example, allowing solicitation for charitable causes only or allowing personal messages but prohibiting messages on behalf of outside organizations), as long as union-related communications aren't singled out. In reaching this decision, the Board essentially decided to treat email like any other type of company equipment or resource, rather than as a workplace discussion.

Social Media Policies and Practices

In the last few years, the NLRB has become extremely active in going after employers who fire or discipline employees for posting critical comments about the company on social media sites or blogs. For example:

- A collections agency was found to have illegally fired an employee for Facebook posts complaining about her transfer. The employee swore and said she was done being a good employee; her coworkers who were Facebook friends posted comments expressing support, criticizing the employer, and suggesting a class action lawsuit. Because the employees were discussing taking action regarding the terms of their employment, the NLRB concluded that they were engaged in protected concerted activity.
- An employee at a veterinary hospital posted to her Facebook page after being denied a promotion. Several coworkers responded to the post, and engaged in a conversation in which they complained about the person who received the promotion, the company's practices regarding raises and reviews, and so on. The NLRB found it illegal when the employee and one friend were fired, and the other two participants in the conversation disciplined.
- A group of employees took to Facebook to complain about a coworker who they felt had been criticizing their performance. A conversation about the employer's policies towards its clientele ensued, then five of the employees were fired. The NLRB found the firings illegal, because the employees were discussing the terms of their employment and considering how to raise those concerns with their employer.

As part of these enforcement actions, the NLRB often finds that the employer's social media and posting policy is too broad, because it would tend to discourage employees from exercising their right to engage in Section 7 activity. The Board has objected to policies that prohibit disparagement or criticism of others; policies that require employees not to post "confidential" or "non-public" information (unless the policy illustrates the types of information covered, so as not to dissuade employees from discussing wages or other terms of employment); policies that require employees to avoid picking fights or discussing topics that are objectionable or inflammatory; and policies that require employees to check with a supervisor before posting.

Company Unions

Employers may not establish, dominate, or interfere with any labor organization. This rule exists to outlaw so-called sham unions—company groups that appear to represent employees' interests but are really controlled by the employer. To figure out whether an employer unfairly controls a particular workplace group, the NLRB looks at all the circumstances, including:

- whether the employer started the group
- whether the employer played a role in organizing the group and deciding how it will function
- whether management actually attends the group's meetings or otherwise tries to set the group's agenda
- the group's purpose, and
- how the group makes decisions.

The NLRB has held that workplace employee-management committees—informal groups in which workers and management meet to resolve workplace problems—violate this rule if they are dominated by management and if they resolve topics that must be collectively bargained (such as wages, hours, or working conditions; see "What's Required: Employers and Unions," below).

Replacing Workers During a Protected Strike

The NLRA limits employers' right to replace workers who go out on strike for a protected purpose. Generally, a strike has a protected purpose if workers are striking regarding wages, hours, or terms and conditions of employment or to protest an unfair labor practice by the employer (like discriminating against union members or refusing to bargain with the union). Strikes that don't fall within these categories are not protected by the NLRA, nor are strikes in violation of a no-strike provision in the collective bargaining agreement or strikes in which the strikers engage in serious misconduct. (See "Unlawful Strikes," in "What's Prohibited: Unions," below, for examples.)

An employer may not fire or hire permanent replacements for workers who strike to protest an unfair labor practice. These workers are entitled to reinstatement once the strike is over.

However, workers who strike for other protected reasons can be replaced permanently. Once the strike is over, they are entitled to their former jobs only if the employer did not hire permanent replacements. If the employer hired permanent replacements, the workers who went on strike are only entitled to be called back for job openings as those jobs become available, and only if they are unable to find regular and substantially similar work elsewhere.

What's Prohibited: Unions

In addition to the rules discussed in "Organizing and Representation Elections," above, the NLRA prohibits unions from:

- restraining or coercing employees in the free exercise of their right not to support a union (for example, by threatening employees who don't want a union or expelling members for crossing an illegal picket line)
- restraining or coercing an employer in its choice of a bargaining representative (by insisting on meeting only with a particular management employee or refusing to bargain with the representative the employer chooses)
- causing or trying to cause an employer to discriminate against an employee for the purpose of encouraging or discouraging union membership (for example, convincing an employer to penalize employees who engage in antiunion activities)
- refusing to engage in good-faith collective bargaining (for example, refusing to come to the bargaining table or listen to any of the employer's proposals) (see "What's Required: Employers and Unions," below)
- engaging in strikes, boycotts, or other coercive action for an illegal purpose (see "Unlawful Strikes," below)
- charging excessive or discriminatory membership fees
- getting or trying to get an employer to agree to pay for work that is not performed (this practice is called featherbedding)
- for a union that is not certified to represent a group of workers, picketing or threatening to picket an employer in order to force the employer to recognize or bargain with the union or force the workers to accept the union as their representative if (1) another union already represents the workers, (2) a valid representation election was held in the past year, or (3) the union does not file a petition for an election with the NLRB within 30 days after the picketing starts
- making a hot cargo agreement, and
- striking, picketing, or otherwise engaging in a collective work stoppage at any *health care institution* without giving at least ten days' written notice both to the institution and the *Federal Mediation and Conciliation Service.*

Unlawful Strikes

A union may not strike, boycott, or use other means of persuasion or coercion for prohibited purposes. Such prohibited purposes include:

- forcing or requiring an employer to assign particular work to employees in a particular union, trade, craft, or class
- forcing or requiring an employer to recognize or bargain with a particular union if another union has been duly certified as the representative of its employees
- forcing or requiring any person to stop doing business with any other business or to stop using, selling, or transporting the products of any other business (such strikes or boycotts against a business other than the employer are called secondary strikes), and
- forcing or requiring an employer or self-employed person to join any labor or employer organization or enter into a hot cargo agreement.

Even a strike with a lawful purpose might not be protected under the NLRA if the workers strike in violation of a no-strike provision in the collective bargaining agreement or if the strikers engage in serious misconduct (like violence).

What's Required: Employers and Unions

Once a union has been elected, the NLRA requires employer and union to engage in collective bargaining. Collective bargaining is the negotiation process between the union (on behalf of the bargaining unit it represents) and the company to work out an agreement that will govern wages, work hours, and other terms and conditions of the workers' employment. These topics are called mandatory subjects of bargaining. The two sides don't have to reach an agreement, but they have to bargain in good faith.

Before an employer changes a workplace rule or policy that implicates a mandatory subject of bargaining, it must ask the union to negotiate the issue—even if the change will provide an overall benefit to workers. An employer that makes unilateral changes regarding mandatory bargaining issues commits an unfair labor practice.

How the NLRA Is Enforced

Individual Complaints

An employee, an employer, or a union that believes an unfair labor practice has been committed may file a charge with the NLRB. Unfair labor practice charges must be filed within six months of the incident alleged to be unfair.

If a dispute arises over whether employees want a particular union to represent them, then an employee, an employer, or a union may file a petition asking the NLRB to hold an election. The NLRB's procedures for handling charges and petitions are described below.

The NLRA cannot be enforced through private lawsuits; violations of the NLRA must be challenged through the NLRB.

Agency Enforcement

The NLRB handles two issues: representation questions (disputes over whether employees want a union) and unfair labor practices.

Representation Questions

Representation questions are brought to the NLRB when an employee, an employer, or a union files a petition with the agency. If a union or an employee files the petition, it must show that at least 30% of the affected workers want an election. An employer may petition the NLRB for an election only if one or more individuals or unions claim the right to represent a particular bargaining unit.

Once a petition is filed, the NLRB will investigate if the employer in question meets the NLRB's jurisdictional standards (see "Jurisdictional Standards," above). If it finds that the petition has merit, it will try to hammer out an agreement between the employees and employer regarding election issues like the scope of the bargaining unit and the time and place of the election. The NLRB will then order an election by secret ballot and certify a union if it receives a majority of votes cast. If a union is certified, it becomes the workers' representative and is entitled to bargain with the employer. If a union is not certified, it does not have the right to represent the workers.

Unfair Labor Practices

Unfair labor practices come to the NLRB when an employee, an employer, or a union files a charge with the agency. The NLRB will investigate the charge if the employer in question meets the NLRB's jurisdictional standards. (See "Jurisdictional Standards," above.) If the NLRB finds reason to believe that the NLRA has been violated, the agency will try to get the parties to settle their differences. If this fails, the NLRB will hold a hearing before an administrative law judge, who will issue a written decision. This decision may be appealed within the NLRB, and if either party is dissatisfied with the NLRB's final decision, it may appeal the matter to the federal courts.

Complying With the NLRA

Reporting Requirements

The NLRA imposes no reporting requirements. However, employers and unions have reporting requirements under the Labor Management Reporting and Disclosure Act.

Posting Requirements

Once the NLRB gets involved in a representation dispute or an unfair labor practice complaint, it can require employers to post various notices relating to elections or the resolution of a particular charge of unfair labor practices.

Pursuant to Executive Order 13201, federal contractors and subcontractors must post a notice that employees do not have to join or maintain membership in a union to keep their jobs, and that employees may object to the use of the agency fees for anything other than the costs of representation. (See "Exceptions" under "Organizing and Representation Elections," above, for information on these rules.) This poster, often referred to as the *Beck* poster after the NLRB decision that established these rights, is available from the Department of Labor (see "Agency Resources," below).

The NLRB issued a final regulation in 2011, requiring employers to post a workplace notice of employee rights under the National Labor Relations Act. This rule would have required posting as a matter of course, not just after the

NLRB is called in to handle a dispute. However, before the rule went into effect in April 2012, it was enjoined by a federal court of appeals. For now, the rule is ineffective, unless and until the injunction is lifted and the court allows the rule to go into effect.

Record-Keeping Requirements

The NLRA does not impose record-keeping requirements.

Penalties

If an employer, a union, or an employee files a petition seeking an election, there are no penalties awarded. The NLRB simply holds an election and certifies the results.

If the NLRB finds that an employer has committed an unfair labor practice during an organizing campaign or at any other time, the employer may be required to do any or all of the following:

- pay any compensation, benefits, or other monetary losses, plus interest, the employee suffered as a result of the unfair practice
- take action to remedy the problem by reinstating an employee, changing workplace rules, stopping an illegal practice, or recognizing a union
- pay attorneys' fees and costs (with some limitations), and/or
- post a notice in the workplace regarding the unfair practice.

Agency Resources

- A tool to help you find NLRB offices
  Regional Offices
  www.nlrb.gov/who-we-are/regional-offices
- A comprehensive resource on the NLRA's provisions
  Basic Guide to the National Labor Relations Act
  www.nlrb.gov/sites/default/files/documents/224/basicguide.pdf
- The *Beck* poster (federal contractors and subcontractors only)
  Notice to Employees
  www.dol.gov/olms/regs/compliance/BeckPosterWithNLRB.pdf

State Right-to-Work Laws

As noted under "Exceptions" in "Organizing and Representation Elections," above, the NLRA allows states to prohibit union security agreements, which require employees to pay fees to a union as a condition of getting or keeping a job. The chart below lists the states that have prohibited union security agreements and provides a citation to the relevant state statute. In these states (called "right-to-work" states), workers who decide not to join the union cannot be required to pay any fees to the union and cannot be fired or otherwise penalized for failing to do so.

State Right-to-Work Laws	
Alabama	Ala. Code §§ 25-7-30 to 25-7-36
Alaska	No right-to-work law
Arizona	Ariz. Const. art. 25; Ariz. Rev. Stat. §§ 23-1301 to 23-1307
Arkansas	Ark. Const. amend. 34 § 1; Ark. Code Ann. §§ 11-3-301 to 11-3-304
California	No right-to-work law
Colorado	No right-to-work law
Connecticut	No right-to-work law
Delaware	No right-to-work law
Dist. of Columbia	No right-to-work law
Florida	Fla. Const. art. 1, § 6; Fla. Stat. Ann. § 447.17
Georgia	Ga. Code Ann. §§ 34-6-20 to 34-6-28
Hawaii	No right-to-work law
Idaho	Idaho Code §§ 44-2001 to 44-2013
Illinois	No right-to-work law
Indiana	Ind. Code Ann. 22-6-6-8
Iowa	Iowa Code § 731.1 to 731.9
Kansas	Kan. Const. art. 15 § 12; Kan. Stat. Ann. §§ 44-808(5), 44-831
Kentucky	No right-to-work law
Louisiana	La. Rev. Stat. Ann. §§ 23:981 to 23:987 (all workers) and 23:881 to 23:889 (agricultural workers)
Maine	No right-to-work law
Maryland	No right-to-work law
Massachusetts	No right-to-work law
Michigan	2012 Mich. Legis. Serv. P.A. 348 (S.B. 116) (WEST)
Minnesota	No right-to-work law
Mississippi	Miss. Const. Art. 7, § 198-A; Miss. Code Ann. § 71-1-47
Missouri	No right-to-work law

State Right-to-Work Laws (continued)	
Montana	No right-to-work law
Nebraska	Neb. Const. art XV, §§ 13 to 15; Neb. Rev. Stat. § 48-217 to 48-219
Nevada	Nev. Rev. Stat. Ann. §§ 613.230 to 613.300
New Hampshire	No right-to-work law
New Jersey	No right-to-work law
New Mexico	No right-to-work law
New York	No right-to-work law
North Carolina	N.C. Gen. Stat. §§ 95-78 to 95-84
North Dakota	N.D. Cent. Code §§ 34-01-14
Ohio	No right-to-work law
Oklahoma	Okla. Const. Art. 23, § 1A
Oregon	No right-to-work law
Pennsylvania	No right-to-work law
Rhode Island	No right-to-work law
South Carolina	S.C. Code Ann. §§ 41-7-10 to 41-7-100
South Dakota	S.D. Const. art. VI, § 2; S.D. Codified Law Ann. §§ 60-8-3 to 60-8-8
Tennessee	Tenn. Code Ann. §§ 50-1-201 to 50-1-206
Texas	Tex. Lab. Code Ann. §§ 101.051 to 101.053
Utah	Utah Code Ann. §§ 34-34-1 to 34-34-17
Vermont	No right-to-work law
Virginia	Va. Code Ann. §§ 40.1-59 to 40.1-69
Washington	No right-to-work law
West Virginia	No right-to-work law
Wisconsin	No right-to-work law
Wyoming	Wyo. Stat. §§ 27-7-108 to 27-7-115

Occupational Safety and Health Act (OSH Act)

Statute: 29 U.S.C. § 651 and following
http://uscode.house.gov/download/pls/29C15.txt

Regulations: 29 C.F.R. § 1900 and following
www.gpo.gov/fdsys/pkg/CFR-2012-title29-vol9/pdf/CFR-2012-title29-vol9-subtitleB-chapXVII.pdf

Overview of the OSH Act

Congress passed the Occupational Safety and Health Act (the OSH Act) in 1970 to ensure safe working conditions for all American workers. The act requires employers to provide hazard-free working conditions and imposes stiff penalties on those who fail to do so.

The OSH Act has four main provisions:

- **Compliance.** Employers must comply with standards issued by the Occupational Safety and Health Administration (OSHA) or, if they are in a *state plan state*, by the state agency.
- **Safety.** Employers must keep their workplaces free of *recognized hazards*.
- **Inspection.** Employers must submit to inspections from OSHA inspectors or, if they are in a state plan state, from OSHA-approved state inspectors.
- **Employee rights.** The OSH Act gives employees the right to request information about workplace hazards, refuse to work in hazardous environments, and otherwise get involved in workplace safety issues without employer retaliation.

In addition, employers must maintain accurate records of all work-related accidents and diseases and inform employees of their protections and duties under the law.

The OSH Act has literally thousands of pages of regulations, covering everything from proper use of ladders to handling radioactive substances. The type of business a company engages in will determine which of these regulations it has to follow. This discussion addresses only general employer duties under the OSH Act; it cannot begin to cover all of the industry-specific regulations that may apply to a particular company. To find out about these rules, refer to the "Agency Resources" section, below.

Issues relating to multiemployer responsibility are also not covered here.

Regulated Employers

The OSH Act covers virtually all private businesses, regardless of size, as long as they employ at least one person and are located in one of the 50 states, the District of Columbia, the Virgin Islands, American Samoa, Puerto Rico, the Trust Territory of the Pacific Islands, the Canal Zone, the Outer Continental Shelf, Wake Island, or Johnson Island.

Definitions

Imminent danger Any condition or practice that could reasonably be expected to cause death or serious physical harm either immediately or before the danger can be eliminated through OSHA enforcement procedures.

Longshoring The loading, unloading, moving, or handling of a ship's cargo, stores, gear, and so on.

Recognized hazard A workplace hazard that an employer is, or should be, aware of. Recognized hazards encompass not only working conditions and the workplace environment, but also workplace practices.

State plan state A state that has submitted a workplace safety plan to the secretary of labor for approval. If the secretary approves the plan, the state can retain control of work-related health and safety issues within its borders.

Some employers that are subject to the OSH Act are required to follow their state's occupational health and safety laws rather than the federal law. The OSH Act allows states to enact their own occupational health and safety laws, and many states have done so. Employers in these states (called state plan states) must follow state regulations instead of OSH Act regulations. (See "State Laws Relating to Occupational Safety and Health," below, for more about this issue.)

The OSH Act does not apply to businesses regulated under the Atomic Energy Act or under job safety rules of federal agencies other than the U.S. Department of Labor (DOL). For example, the Federal Aviation Administration has its own regulations on how to transport radioactive materials on airplanes. Those rules supersede OSHA regulations about radioactive hazards for airline workers. There has been much dispute over which federal regulations fit within this exception and which do not; because these rules are quite complicated, they aren't covered here.

The OSH Act does not apply to local governments and their political subdivisions. It also does not apply to state governments and their political subdivisions. However, if a state wants to take advantage of the state plan option, its plan must cover state employers. Thus, in all of the state plan states, state employers are subject to the state's equivalent of the OSH Act.

Legal Developments

- **OSHA warns employers not to punish safety whistleblowers.** In a memo released in March of 2012, OSHA offered advice to employers that penalizing employees for safety violations could be illegal retaliation. OSHA pointed out that employers who routinely discipline employees who are injured on the job, regardless of fault, are violating the law. It also warned employers against policies that punish employees for failing to follow the proper procedures to report injuries or punish employees for failing to follow safety rules, if the policies cross the line of punishing employees for making safety problems known. Finally, the memo warns that employers who reward for safe practices could inadvertently discourage whistleblowing.

- **OSHA moves toward consistent labeling of hazardous chemicals.** In March of 2012, OSHA announced changes to its Hazard Communication Rule. The change would align the rule with the United Nations' global chemical labeling system, which will allow for more consistency in communication of workplace dangers. OSHA estimates that the change will prevent 43 deaths and 585 injuries and illnesses per year.

- **Getting out of the Severe Violator Enforcement Program (SVEP).** In 2010, OSHA introduced the SVEP, with the purpose of focusing its enforcement efforts on those employers who have demonstrated their "indifference" to the OSH Act through repeated, willful, and failure-to-abate violations. Employers in the SVEP face enhanced follow-up inspections, inspections of related workplaces nationwide, more publicizing of violations (through sending citations to the company's headquarters and officers, as well as issuing news releases), and heightened requirements in settlement agreements, intended to ensure future compliance. As explained in an August 2012 memorandum, SVEP employers may be removed from the program, at the discretion of the Regional Administrator, once three years have passed since the final disposition of the inspection citation items. The employer must have abated all hazards, paid all penalties, abided by all settlement provisions, and avoided any further serious citations. The employer will also be subject to a final inspection before exiting the program.

The OSH Act does not apply to the federal government and its political subdivisions. However, it does require each federal agency to devise health and safety standards that are consistent with the OSH Act. In addition, an executive order issued by President Carter protects federal workers by requiring federal agencies to comply with OSH Act standards, provide workplaces free of recognized hazards, and submit to inspections from the DOL. The order also protects workers from retaliation for filing reports about unsafe working conditions.

Covered Workers

The OSH Act applies to any employee of a covered employer, regardless of the employee's title, status, or classification. Thus, the law applies to managers, supervisors, partners, stockholders, officers, and family member employees as well as to rank-and-file employees.

The OSH Act does not apply to independent contractors or to the immediate family members of a farm operator.

Did You Know ...

- In 2011, there were 4,609 fatal work injuries according to the Bureau of Labor Statistics.
- Some of the most common causes of fatal workplace injuries are transportation incidents (such as car crashes or being struck by a vehicle), and violent acts (by people or animals), machine-related injuries, and falls.
- OSHA offers Voluntary Protection Programs (VPP) to promote health and safety at company worksites. VPP invites companies to apply to be assessed against its criteria for managed safety and health systems. Approval requires application review, vigorous inspection, annual self-evaluation, and periodic reevaluation. But OSHA claims that, by reducing injuries and illnesses among employees, participating companies can reduce workers' compensation premiums and other costs. For more information, visit www.osha.gov/dcsp/vpp/index.html.

Major Provisions of the OSH Act

Compliance

Since its inception in 1970, OSHA has been issuing workplace safety standards. These standards fall into four broad categories: general industry, maritime and *longshoring*, construction, and agricultural. Covered employers must follow the safety standards that apply to their business. This is referred to as "pre-inspection compliance," because employers must comply with the safety regulations before they are specifically told to do so by an OSHA inspector. Failure to comply may result in fines and penalties.

If an employer operates in a state plan state, then it must follow its state plan standards rather than the OSH Act standards. (See "State Laws Relating to Occupational Safety and Health," below, for information about state plan states.)

Key Facts: Compliance

- Employers must determine which standards—under the federal OSH Act or an applicable state plan—apply to their industry, their specific business, and their operations, and then strictly comply with those standards.
- Employers must train and supervise their employees appropriately and adequately under the OSH Act or applicable state plan.
- Employers must provide safe tools and equipment, as well as proper safety equipment, for all of their workers.

Regulated Employers

All regulated employers are subject to these provisions.

Covered Workers

All covered workers are subject to these provisions.

What's Required

Employers must follow the standards that apply to their industry:

- **General industry.** As a general rule, all covered employers must follow the general industry standards, unless the standard itself specifies the type of workplace to which it applies. (For example, one set of general industry standards applies only to bakeries.) The general industry standards cover such things as safe operation of machinery, exit routes, fire safety, how materials must be handled and stored, walkways and work surfaces, ventilation, exposure to noise, use of forklifts, and personal protective gear.
- **Construction.** As the name suggests, construction standards apply to covered employers with employees who do construction work, including construction, alteration, repair, painting, and decorating.
- **Maritime and longshoring.** These standards apply to covered employers with employees involved in ship repairing, shipbuilding, shipbreaking, and longshoring.
- **Agricultural.** These standards apply to any employer with employees involved in growing or harvesting crops, raising livestock or poultry, or related activities on sites such as farms, ranches, orchards, or dairies.

Within each broad category are additional categories and levels of standards—and sometimes, two or more standards may apply to the same activity. Thus, finding out which standards apply to any one business or to any one operation can be daunting. OSHA and the state plan states provide resources to help employers understand which standards they must follow. (To find out more, see "Agency Resources" and "State Laws Relating to Occupational Safety and Health," below.)

The standards are meant to be taken literally. Whether or not an accident has occurred is irrelevant to determining whether a covered employer has violated the compliance provision. An employer can have no accidents for decades and still violate the OSH Act (or its state equivalent) if it doesn't follow the standard. Similarly, an employer can have a number of accidents and be in full compliance as long as it follows the standard (although workplace accidents may place the employer in violation of the OSH Act's safety provisions or the safety provisions of its state equivalent; see "Safety," below).

The OSH Act requires employers to train employees adequately for their jobs. Some of the standards specify the type of training employees must receive. In addition, covered employers must adequately supervise their employees.

Employers have a general duty to provide employees with tools and equipment that are in safe condition. Many of the standards require that employers provide their employees with specific types of safety equipment; with very few exceptions, employers have to pay for this equipment. Some of the standards require employers to protect employees from health hazards, such as asbestos and lead.

There are a number of defenses that employers can raise if they are accused of failing to follow the standards. Those are beyond the scope of this discussion.

Safety

Covered employers have a general duty to provide their employees with work and a workplace free of recognized hazards. Congress enacted this provision to cover serious hazards to which no OSHA standard applies. If an OSHA standard does cover a hazard, then that hazard does not fall under the general safety provision.

If an employer operates its business in a state plan state, then it must follow its state plan standards, not the OSH Act standards. (See "State Laws Relating to Occupational Safety and Health," below, for information about state plan states.)

Key Facts: Safety

- Employers must provide their employees with work and a workplace free of recognized hazards that could cause death or serious physical injury.

Regulated Employers

All regulated employers are subject to these provisions.

Covered Workers

All covered workers are subject to these provisions.

What's Required

Covered employers must provide work and a place of employment free of recognized hazards that are causing or are likely to cause death or serious physical injury to employees. This duty extends beyond the four walls of a company's business to any location where an employee performs work for an employer.

It can be difficult to determine which hazards are recognized hazards. Obviously, a hazard that an employer knows about is recognized, as is one that is common knowledge in the employer's industry. A hazard will also be a recognized hazard if the employer could easily detect it simply by walking through the workplace and using the five senses. Many courts have also held that hazards that the employer could detect through instruments are recognized.

Inspections

The chief way in which OSHA enforces the OSH Act is through on-site inspections. These inspections may be conducted at random, or OSHA may inspect a particular worksite because it has received a complaint of unsafe conditions.

Employers who operate their businesses in state plan states face inspection from state inspectors, not OSHA inspectors.

Key Facts: Inspections

- OSHA inspectors (or state plan inspectors, where applicable) enforce the OSH Act (or state law) through random on-site inspections or inspections in response to complaints.
- Employers can demand that an inspector have or obtain a warrant before conducting an inspection. But once the investigator provides a warrant, an employer must allow the inspection.

Regulated Employers

All regulated employers are subject to these provisions.

Covered Workers

All covered workers are subject to these provisions.

What's Required

If OSHA presents an employer with an inspection warrant, the employer must submit to the inspection. If OSHA appears without a warrant, however, the employer can either consent to the inspection or demand that OSHA get a warrant before entering the worksite.

Employee Rights

The OSH Act gives employees various ways to take action to ensure that their workplace is safe. If an employee works for an employer that operates in a state plan state, the employee's rights may be slightly different from the ones described in this section.

Key Facts: Employee Rights

- Under the OSH Act, employees have the right to ensure that their workplaces are safe in a variety of ways, including participating in setting safety standards and notifying or complaining to authorities about unsafe working conditions or OSH Act violations.
- Employees also have a right to get information about hazards in their workplaces.
- Employees may refuse to work when they face an imminent danger in the workplace that the employer refuses to correct, if the condition is so dangerous that it could harm the employee before OSHA can respond to an employee's request for an investigation.

The OSH Act gives employees a number of important rights, including the right to:

- petition OSHA to adopt a safety standard
- file a complaint with OSHA about unsafe working conditions or other OSH Act violations
- where an *imminent danger* exists, seek a court order compelling the secretary of labor to conduct an inspection
- participate in the inspection and conferences relating to the inspection
- oppose settlements and withdrawals of contested cases
- inspect their employer's log of occupational injuries and illnesses, and
- request a government determination as to whether there are any toxic substances in the workplace.

The Act also gives employees the right to receive or request certain information about workplace hazards. For example, employers whose operations require them to monitor employee exposure to toxic substances must:

- inform employees of the presence of certain toxic substances in the workplace
- allow employees to participate in the monitoring
- give employees all of the information obtained in the monitoring
- inform employees when they are being exposed to dangerous levels of toxins, and
- give employees access to exposure records and their own medical records.

Although the OSH Act does not expressly allow employees to refuse to work in dangerous conditions, OSHA regulations do allow it when employees are faced with imminent danger. An employer may not discipline an employee for refusing to work if:

- The employee has a reasonable and good-faith belief that performing the work presents a real danger of death or serious physical injury.
- The employer will not correct the danger.
- There isn't enough time to eliminate the danger through other channels, such as requesting an OSHA inspection.

In the case of a toxic substance or another health hazard, the worker must reasonably believe that the toxic substance or hazard is present and will shorten life or substantially reduce physical or mental efficiency. The harm itself does not have to happen immediately.

State plan states and unionized workplaces with collective bargaining agreements may have different rules about when employees can refuse to work because of workplace hazards.

How the OSH Act Is Enforced

Individual Complaints

Employees can complain to OSHA, or to the OSHA-approved agency in their state if they work in a state plan state, about safety hazards and violations. Employees cannot sue their employers directly for violations of the OSH Act.

Agency Enforcement

Except in state plan states, the OSH Act is enforced by OSHA, a division of the Department of Labor. (See Appendix A for information on how to contact OSHA.) In state plan states, the law is enforced by an OSHA-approved state equivalent.

The principal enforcement method is inspections by federal OSHA inspectors or by OSHA-authorized state inspectors in state plan states. Often, the agency will not inspect in person, but instead will call the employer and follow up with a letter describing the unsafe conditions that have been alleged. If the employer responds quickly and provides detailed facts showing either that the hazard does not exist or that it will be remedied soon, that might end the matter.

If, however, the employer's response does not satisfy the agency, or the agency decides that the allegations are serious enough to warrant an on-site inspection (for example, because an imminent danger is alleged or the employer has a history of OSH Act violations), the company can expect visitors. If the inspectors find violations, they will issue a citation to the employer along with a proposed penalty. Usually, the citation will also order the employer to cure the violation within a certain time period.

If the employer disagrees with the citation or wants to do something different from what the citation orders, the employer must say so within 15 days. If the employer doesn't act within 15 days, the citation becomes final. If the employer disputes the citation, then it doesn't have to pay penalties or cure the alleged violation until an administrative law judge decides the matter.

Complying With the OSH Act

Reporting Requirements

All covered employers must report to OSHA, *within eight hours*, any accident that results in one or more deaths or the hospitalization of three or more employees. This requirement applies even to employers that are exempt from OSHA's record-keeping requirements (see "Record-Keeping Requirements," below).

Posting Requirements

All covered employers must post:
- an OSHA poster informing employees of their rights and obligations under the OSH Act (see "Agency Resources," below)
- a log and summary of occupational illnesses and injuries (unless the employer is not required to keep these records—see "Record-Keeping Requirements," below)
- current citations that OSHA inspectors have issued to the employer, and
- any petitions that the employer has filed for modification or abatement.

Employers may be required to post additional industry-specific notices, depending on the type of business that they run. Employers that operate in a state plan state may have different posting responsibilities than the ones described above.

Record-Keeping Requirements

The OSH Act has numerous record-keeping regulations. Generally speaking, however, covered employers must maintain:
- records of their efforts to comply with the law and to prevent occupational injuries and illnesses
- records of work-related deaths, injuries, and illnesses, and

- records of employee exposure to potentially toxic substances or harmful physical agents.

Not all covered employers have to keep all of these records, however. Employers with ten or fewer employees do not have to keep OSHA illness and injury records, nor do employers in certain low-hazard retail and service industries, such as art galleries, advertising agencies, banks, computer and data processing companies, insurance agencies, and restaurants.

Employers must allow OSHA inspectors access to their logs and records and must transmit certain information about workplace health and safety to OSHA. Employers must use OSHA forms to keep their records.

Employers must also participate in any surveys that the Bureau of Labor Statistics sends to them.

Companies that operate in state plan states may have to follow different record-keeping rules. Those employers should contact their state agency (see "State Laws Relating to Occupational Safety and Health," below, for more information).

Penalties

Employers face civil penalties and criminal prosecution for violating the OSH Act. These penalties can be as high as $70,000 for each willful or repeated violation.

In addition, some state prosecutors have charged employers with such things as manslaughter, murder, and aggravated assault when employees have been severely injured or killed by unsafe working conditions. Sometimes, prosecutors introduce OSH Act violations as evidence in these prosecutions.

In addition, workers and their families can sometimes sue employers outside of the workers' compensation system for injuries and deaths caused by unsafe workplaces.

Agency Resources

- Workplace safety poster that employers are required to display
  Job Safety and Health: It's the law!
  www.osha.gov/Publications/osha3165.pdf

- A concise summary of employer responsibilities under the OSH Act
  Employer Responsibilities
  www.osha.gov/as/opa/worker/employer-responsibility.html

- Information about OSHA's consultation program for small businesses
  On-site Consultation
  www.osha.gov/dcsp/smallbusiness/consult.html

- A guide to the OSH Act's record-keeping requirements
  OSHA Recordkeeping Handbook
  www.osha.gov/recordkeeping/handbook/index.html

- A list of the industries, by SIC (Standard Industrial Classification) code
  number, that are exempt from OSHA's record-keeping requirements
  Partially Exempt Industries
  www.osha.gov/recordkeeping/ppt1/RK1exempttable.html

The National Institute for Occupational Safety and Health (NIOSH) is part of the Centers for Disease Control and Prevention in the U.S. Department of Health and Human Services. It researches health and safety problems and develops criteria that OSHA can use when promulgating standards designed to cure those problems. As part of its research, NIOSH can inspect workplaces, issue subpoenas, and interview employers and workers. NIOSH also conducts training and educational programs. The NIOSH website (www.cdc.gov/niosh) offers lots of information about workplace hazards and safety strategies.

State Laws Relating to Occupational Safety and Health

When it was passed, the OSH Act preempted all state job safety and health laws. Each state then had the option of submitting a plan to the secretary of labor for approval. If the secretary found the plan acceptable, then the state's law could stand. Below is a list of states that have exercised this state plan option for both public and private workplaces as of October 2012. For the most up-to-date list and contact information for each of the state plan organizations, visit www.osha.gov/dcsp/osp/index.html.

State Plan States

Alaska	Kentucky	North Carolina	Vermont
Arizona	Maryland	Oregon	Virginia
California	Michigan	Puerto Rico	Washington
Hawaii	Minnesota	South Carolina	Wyoming
Indiana	Nevada	Tennessee	
Iowa	New Mexico	Utah	

In addition, Connecticut, Illinois, New Jersey, New York, and the Virgin Islands have state plans that cover public sector employment only.

If a state has an approved state plan, then that state can govern workplace health and safety with its own laws, regulations, and standards.

If a state does not have an approved plan, then the federal law preempts state laws, regulations, and standards relating to job health and safety—except in cases where the federal law doesn't cover an issue. For example, the federal law does not have standards relating to elevators. Therefore, states can have their own standards relating to elevators, even if they did not exercise the state plan option.

In addition, all states—even those that aren't state plan states—can enforce laws, such as fire codes, that protect a wider class of people than just employees. All states can also train and educate and consult on job safety and health issues. And all states can have laws protecting state and local government employees.

Older Workers Benefit Protection Act (OWBPA)

Statute: 29 U.S.C. § 651 and following
http://uscode.house.gov/download/pls/29C15.txt

Regulations: 29 C.F.R. § 1900 and following
www.gpo.gov/fdsys/pkg/CFR-2012-title29-vol4/pdf/CFR-2012-title29-vol4-part1625.pdf

Overview of OWBPA

Passed in 1990, the Older Workers Benefit Protection Act (OWBPA) gives guidance to courts that have to decide whether the benefits employers offer to older workers are equal to the benefits offered to younger workers, which is a requirement under the Age Discrimination in Employment Act (ADEA). (See Chapter 1 for more information on the ADEA.) OWBPA also regulates *waivers* and requires employers to take certain steps to make sure that waivers are knowing and voluntary.

The OWBPA includes provisions on:

- **Benefits.** Employers must offer older workers benefits that are equal to or, in some cases, cost the employer as much as, the benefits offered to younger workers. The rules for determining whether benefits are equal depend on the type of benefit offered.
- **Waivers.** A waiver of the right to sue for age discrimination is valid only if it meets certain standards designed to ensure that the waiver is knowing and voluntary.

Although technically an amendment to the ADEA, OWBPA addresses issues that were not covered in the original ADEA. For this reason, human resources professionals and lawyers generally refer to it by its own name as a separate law—as do we.

Definitions

Applicable defined benefit plan A defined benefit plan in which the accrued benefit, or any portion of it, is calculated as the balance of a hypothetical account maintained for the participant or as an accumulated percentage of the participant's final average compensation.

Bona fide employee benefit plan A benefit plan that has been accurately described, in writing, to all employees and that actually provides the benefits promised.

Definitions (continued)

Defined benefit plan A type of pension plan in which participants do not receive an individual account and benefits are not based solely on contributions to that account. Instead, a defined benefit plan guarantees participants a specified pension benefit defined either as a particular dollar amount or as a set formula (for example, 1% of final average salary per year of service).

Early retirement incentive plan A voluntary program in which employers offer employees the opportunity to retire early—before they reach normal retirement age under the employer's pension or other retirement plan—in exchange for additional benefits to which they would not otherwise have been entitled. Many employers credit employees who agree to retire early with additional years of service for purposes of pension accrual, so the employee will be eligible to receive an immediate *unreduced pension.*

Exit incentive program A voluntary program offered to a group or class of at least two employees, whereby the employees are offered something of value (such as enhanced benefits or compensation) in exchange for their decision to resign and sign a *waiver.*

Other employment termination program A program by which a group or class of at least two employees are terminated involuntarily (through a layoff or reduction in force, for example) and are offered something of value in exchange for their decision to sign a *waiver.*

Unreduced pension The full pension amount an employee will receive under an employer's pension plan if the employee works until normal retirement age.

Waiver A legal agreement or contract between an employer and an employee in which the employee gives up ("waives") the right to sue the employer for specified claims. Generally, a waiver may cover every potential legal claim an employee might have against an employer or may be limited to only certain claims. The requirements of the OWBPA apply only to waivers of claims for age discrimination under the Age Discrimination in Employment Act (ADEA). A waiver is sometimes also referred to as a "release" or "release of claims."

Regulated Employers

OWBPA applies to all employers covered by the ADEA. (See Chapter 1.)

Legal Developments

- **EEOC guidance for employees on waivers and releases.** In 2009, the EEOC issued enforcement guidance for employees with questions about releases and severance agreements. As the guidance states, the economic downturn led to an increase in employee reductions and terminations, which have led more employees to question their rights when asked to sign a waiver. Although the guidance is written for employees, it includes good information on the OWBPA's waiver requirements, along with a sample release to be used in a group layoff situation that meets the OWBPA's requirements.
- **EEOC wins showdown with AARP over retiree health benefits.** In 2004, the EEOC drafted regulations stating that it is not age discrimination for an employer to reduce, alter, or even eliminate retiree health benefits once they are eligible for Medicare. The AARP sued to prevent the EEOC from finalizing these regulations. After much wrangling, the EEOC won in the federal Court of Appeals and issued final regulations in 2007.
- **Pension system may benefit younger employees in certain situations.** In 2008, the Supreme Court upheld Kentucky's pension system for employees in hazardous positions who suffer a disability on the job. An employee who had not yet served enough years to qualify for retirement received credit for the additional years necessary upon suffering a disability. Because of the way the system was set up, it could result in younger workers being credited with more years—and, therefore, receiving higher pension payments—than older employees. The Court nonetheless upheld the system, finding that Kentucky did not intend to discriminate based on age. (*Kentucky Retirement Systems v. Equal Employment Opportunity Commission*, 128 S.Ct. 2361 (2008).)

Covered Workers

OWBPA protects all employees and job applicants covered by the ADEA. (See Chapter 1.) Like the ADEA, it applies only to those who are at least 40 years old.

Did You Know ...

- Congress passed the OWBPA to overturn a U.S. Supreme Court case called *Public Employees Retirement System of Ohio v. Betts.* (492 U.S. 158 (1989).) In *Betts,* the Supreme Court found that bona fide employee benefit plans were not covered by the ADEA—that is, employees could not claim that such a plan was discriminatory—unless the plan was a subterfuge for illegal age discrimination in some other aspect of employment. (As an example, the Court said that a company that cut all employee salaries while simultaneously providing substantially increased benefits only to younger workers might be using its benefit plan as a subterfuge for age discrimination.) Congress found that this interpretation ignored its intent to prohibit discrimination in the provision of benefits except when justified by "significant cost considerations."

Major Provisions of OWBPA

Benefits

Congress passed OWBPA to prohibit age discrimination in the provision of fringe benefits (such as life insurance, health insurance, disability benefits, pensions, and retirement benefits) but allow employers to reduce benefits to older workers when justified by significant cost considerations. In most situations, employers must provide equal benefits to older and younger workers. For some types of benefits, however, employers can meet this nondiscrimination requirement by spending the same amount on the benefit provided to each group, even if older workers receive lesser benefits. Employers are also allowed, in some circumstances, to provide lesser benefits to older workers if the older workers receive additional benefits (from the employer or the government) to make up the difference.

As you'll see, these rules are detailed, and applying them can be fairly complicated. If you need help determining whether your company's plans offer equal benefits to older and younger workers, consult with an enrolled actuary.

Key Facts: Benefits

- Generally, a company must provide equal benefits to older and younger workers. However, for some benefits, an employer may offer benefits of equal cost to older and younger workers without violating OWBPA, even if the older workers receive lesser benefits as a result.
- In some situations, an employer may count other benefits older workers receive, from the employer or from the government, toward the equal benefit obligation. As long as the older workers' total benefits are equal to the total benefits younger workers receive, the employer has not violated OWBPA. However, this rule applies only to certain benefits.
- Special rules apply to some early retirement incentive plans, pension plans, hybrid pension plans, long-term disability plans, and employee contribution plans.

Regulated Employers

All regulated employers are subject to these provisions.

Covered Workers

All covered employees are subject to these provisions.

What's Prohibited

Employers may not rely on the provisions of a benefit plan to:
- refuse to hire anyone based on the person's age, or
- require anyone to retire involuntarily because of that person's age.

What's Required

Employers are not always required to provide precisely the same benefits to older workers as they provide to younger workers. In some cases, an employer may comply with OWBPA by showing that although the benefits to each group aren't identical, the employer paid the same amount for benefits to older and younger workers. This is called the equal cost defense. In some other cases, employers may comply with OWBPA by showing that any shortfall in benefits to older workers was made up (offset) by additional benefits from the employer or the government.

Below, we explain how these defenses work, then explain a few special rules that apply to certain types of benefits.

The Equal Cost Defense

An employer may offer a lesser benefit to older workers if it costs the same as the benefit offered to younger workers. However, this rule applies only to certain types of benefits and is subject to several conditions. An employer may use the equal cost defense only if all of the following are true:

- **The benefit is one that becomes more costly to provide as workers grow older.** This is often true of life insurance, health insurance, and disability insurance, for example. As workers age, it becomes more likely that they will use these benefits, and insurers often charge more for coverage to guard against this possibility. Because benefits such as severance pay or paid vacations do not cost more to provide to older workers, the equal cost defense does not apply to these benefits.
- **The benefit is not a retirement benefit (to which the equal cost defense does not apply).**
- **The benefit is provided as part of a *bona fide employee benefit plan*.**
- **The benefit plan explicitly requires lower benefits for older workers.** An employer cannot use the equal cost defense if the benefit plan gives the employer discretion to provide lower benefits to older workers if it chooses; the plan must require benefits to diminish for older workers.
- **The employer pays the same amount (as a premium, for example) for coverage for older and younger workers.** This is the equal cost requirement.
- **Benefit levels for older workers have not been reduced more than is necessary to achieve equal cost for coverage of older and younger workers.**

- **When comparing coverage costs, the employer has not used age brackets of more than five years.** That is, an employer who wishes to reduce a benefit for workers ages 61 through 65 must compare the cost of covering those workers to the cost of covering workers ages 56 through 60—not the cost of covering workers in their 20s or 30s.

Offsets

In some cases, employers may offer older employees lesser benefits if those employees receive additional benefits from the employer or the government that make up the difference. The employer may use these additional benefits to offset the shortfall and bring the older workers' benefits up to the same level offered to younger employees.

Offsets may be used only in the following circumstances:

- Employers can use government-provided disability benefits to offset disability benefits or disability retirement benefits provided by the employer. For example, if a disabled employee collects workers' compensation or Social Security disability payments, the employer can count that money toward the total disability benefit it offers older workers for purposes of the equal benefit rule.
- Employers can use the portion of an older worker's pension benefit that is attributable to employer contributions to offset long-term disability benefits if:
  - the worker voluntarily elects to receive the pension (at any age), or
  - the worker has reached the later of age 62 or the pension plan's normal retirement age and is eligible for an *unreduced pension.*
- Employers can use retiree health benefits provided to an employee to offset severance benefits if (1) the retiree actually receives the health benefit coverage (if an employer offers the benefit but the retiree turns it down, this requirement has not been met), (2) the retiree health benefits are at least comparable to Medicare benefits in type and value, or to the value of Medicare benefits, if the retiree is over the age of 64, and (3) the retiree is eligible for an immediate pension. If these requirements are met, the employer may take the following offsets:
  - For health benefits provided for an unlimited time period (for example, for the rest of the employee's lifetime), the employer may offset $48,000 if the employee is younger than 65, and $24,000 if the

employee is 65 or older at the time of retirement.

- For benefits of limited duration, the employer may deduct $3,000 per year of benefits paid before the employee reaches the age of 65, and $750 per year once the employee reaches 65.

- Employers can use additional pension benefits to offset severance benefits if the following are true:

  - The additional pension benefits are made available solely because of the employee's separation from employment.

  - Counting the additional pension benefit, the employee is eligible for an immediate and unreduced pension.

- Employers who increase the value of a pension benefit for employees who work beyond normal retirement age may use that increased value to offset the employee's pension accrual. For example, if a pension accrues a benefit of $50 per year of service but pays employees $75 for each year of work beyond normal retirement age, the employer is not required to pay both amounts. The $75 increased value offsets the $50 benefit.

- Employers who begin pension payments while an employee is still working may use the actuarial value of those payments to offset the employee's pension accrual. For example, if an employee works for one year beyond normal retirement age and receives $10,000 in pension payments during that time, the employer may use the actuarial value of those payments (what that amount would be worth to the employee per month over the course of the employee's lifetime) to offset pension accrual (how much the employee is entitled to earn per year of service).

- Employers may use Social Security Old Age benefits to offset pension benefits, in some cases.

Special Rules for Certain Benefits

OWBPA places special requirements on certain types of benefits.

Employee Contribution Plans. If an employee contributes a portion of the costs of a required benefit (for example, an employee pays part of a health insurance or life insurance premium for a benefit that all employees are required to have), the employer may not require an older employee, as a condition of employment, to pay a higher contribution than younger employees. However, the employer may require an older employee to contribute more to participate in a voluntary benefit plan, as long as that higher contribution is justified by the equal cost defense. The employer may also allow older workers to pay more to maintain their benefit at the same level provided to younger employees.

Benefit Packages. The equal cost approach applies to benefit packages as well as to individual benefits. An employer may offer a different total benefit package to older employees than to younger employees, as long as the difference is justified by the equal cost defense. However, the following requirements apply:

- Only those benefits that become more costly to provide with increasing age may be included in the benefits to which the equal cost defense is applied. Retirement or pension plans may not be included.

- Employers may not use the benefit package approach to reduce health benefits beyond what would be allowed under an individual benefit comparison. Any reductions in health insurance must be justified by the increased cost to the employer of providing that benefit alone.

- If an older worker is deprived of a particular benefit because of the increased cost of providing that benefit as workers age, the worker must receive additional benefits in exchange. Considered as a whole, the entire benefit package for older workers must be no worse than they would have received had the employer compared benefits individually under the equal cost defense.

Long-Term Disability Benefits. OWBPA provides a safe harbor for employers who offer long-term disability benefits. Under this rule, an employer may stop disability benefits at age 65 for an employee who is disabled at the age of 60 or younger and may stop disability benefits five years after the disability is incurred for workers who become disabled past the age of 60.

Retiree Health Benefits. Employers who provide health benefits to retirees may alter, reduce, or eliminate those benefits once the recipient is eligible for Medicare health benefits. These employers are exempt from the equal cost/equal benefit rules that would otherwise apply. This exemption, finalized by the EEOC in 2007, is intended to encourage employers to provide retiree health benefits by allowing them to coordinate those benefits with Medicare (and thereby reduce the costs of providing such benefits).

Pension Benefits. An employer who offers pension benefits is legally allowed to set a normal or early retirement age for receipt of benefits, require a specified number of years of service before an employee will be eligible to retire and receive benefits, and limit the total amount of benefits provided or the total number of years of service that will be credited in calculating pension benefits. However, employers may not:

- prevent an employee from participating in a pension plan solely because that employee is near the plan's normal retirement age when hired
- discontinue benefit accrual based on an employee's age, or
- stop contributing to an employee's pension account because of the employee's age.

Early Retirement Incentive Plans. Early retirement incentive plans sometimes provide a greater benefit to younger employees: If the plan offers an unreduced pension benefit to employees who have not yet reached normal retirement age, the youngest employees benefit the most from such a plan. Nevertheless, an early retirement incentive plan that doesn't provide equal benefits to older and younger employees is legal if it is voluntary (that is, it does not require any employee to retire) and it meets at least one of these additional requirements:

- The incentive plan subsidizes a retirement plan by paying employees who agree to retire additional pension benefits. An employer may pay retiring employees an additional subsidy to bring their retirement benefits up to the level of an unreduced pension.
- The incentive plan provides Social Security supplements to retiring employees who are not yet eligible for Social Security, as long as the payments do not exceed the amount that would be paid if the employee received Social Security. Such payments must stop when the employee becomes eligible for Social Security.
- The plan is offered by an institution of higher education to tenured faculty, as long as the plan does not reduce or eliminate other benefits or repackage benefits that were already offered to the retiring employees during the year prior to the incentive.
- The plan otherwise treats employees equally without regard to age. For example, an employer may offer employees additional compensation to retire (a set dollar amount, additional money based on years of service, a percentage or set dollar increase in pension benefits, or credit for additional years of service) as long as the same benefits are offered to all employees eligible for the retirement incentive.

Applicable Defined Benefit Plans. The Pension Protection Act of 2006 creates special rules for certain hybrid pension plans, a type of defined benefit pension plan that can be less beneficial to older employees because of the way benefits are calculated. In a cash balance hybrid plan, for example, an employee's benefit is expressed as the balance in a hypothetical individual account. Each year, the employee's "account" receives a pay credit, based on the employee's compensation for that year, and an interest credit, representing the earnings of the entire account balance for the year based on a stated interest rate. Because younger employees will earn interest on their account balances for a longer period of time, their benefit might be more valuable than an older employee's benefit. This issue has led to litigation, particularly by older employees whose employers converted, during their employment, from a traditional defined benefit plan to a cash balance plan.

The Pension Protection Act amends the OWBPA to provide that defined benefit plans in which the benefit is calculated as the balance of a hypothetical account for a participant or as an accumulated percentage of the participant's final average compensation won't be considered discriminatory if a participant's accrued benefit under the plan is at least equal to the accrued benefit of any other younger participant who is similarly situated except for age. These plans must also meet these additional requirements to pass muster under the OWBPA and the ADEA (additional requirements may apply under ERISA):

- Any "interest credit" portion of the benefit must be calculated at an interest rate that is no greater than the market rate of return. An interest rate of less than zero may not reduce the account value below the total amount of contributions credited to the account.
- If an employer converts to a hybrid plan, a participant's benefit may not be less than his or her total benefit under the old plan before the conversion plus his or her total benefit under the new plan since the conversion.
- If the plan uses a variable rate to calculate interest credits, and the plan terminates, it must calculate interest using the average rate used by the plan over the five years preceding its termination.

Waivers

Under OWBPA, a waiver of the right to sue for age discrimination is valid only if it is knowing and voluntary.

Key Facts

- An employee's waiver of the right to sue for age discrimination must be knowing and voluntary. To meet this standard, the waiver must meet certain requirements.
- Although an employer generally is required to give employees 21 days to consider a waiver and seven days to revoke the waiver after signing it, these requirements do not apply if the employee has already filed an EEOC charge or a lawsuit alleging age discrimination.
- If the waiver is offered as part of an exit incentive program or another employment termination program, the employer must provide specific information to the employee about the program and the employees to whom it was offered.
- The employer may not stop providing any continuing benefits (for example, severance payments or health insurance benefits) because an employee files a lawsuit despite the waiver.

Regulated Employers

All regulated employers must comply with these provisions when seeking waivers of ADEA claims from their employees.

Covered Workers

These provisions protect all covered workers whose employers ask them to waive ADEA claims.

What's Required

A waiver is valid only if it is knowing and voluntary. Because these terms are open to interpretation, Congress decided that a waiver will not be considered knowing and voluntary unless it meets certain minimum requirements. (See "Requirements for a Knowing and Voluntary Agreement," below.)

Waivers that do not meet these requirements are invalid. This means that a court will not enforce the waiver, and the worker will be able to sue for age discrimination despite having signed the waiver.

Even if a waiver meets these minimum standards, a court still might find it invalid if other evidence demonstrates that the worker did not knowingly and voluntarily agree to the waiver. For example, if the waiver is misleading or omits important information, a court might throw out the waiver, even if it meets the specifications listed below.

Requirements for a Knowing and Voluntary Agreement

A waiver will be considered knowing and voluntary only if it:
- is part of a written agreement between the employer and the employee
- is written in language understandable to the employee (or, in the case of an offer made to a group, understandable to the average employee eligible to participate)
- specifically refers to the worker's rights or claims under the ADEA
- does not require the employee to waive any rights or claims that may arise after the agreement is signed, and
- gives the employee something of value (such as cash or continued benefits) in exchange for the waiver, over and above anything to which the employee is already entitled. For example, if all employees receive a set amount of severance pay, the employer must give an employee who signs an ADEA waiver something in addition to that pay.

In addition, employers must:
- advise the employee, in writing, to consult with an attorney before signing the agreement
- give the employee at least 21 days to consider the agreement, or 45 days if the waiver is requested in connection with an *exit incentive program* or *another employment termination program* offered to a group of employees (the employee can accept the agreement after a shorter period of deliberation, as long as the employee had the opportunity to take as long as the law allows), and
- give the employee at least seven days after signing to revoke the agreement.

Additional Rules for Exit Incentive or Other Employment Termination Programs

If the waiver is requested in connection with an exit incentive program or another employment termination program offered to a group of employees, the employer must also inform the employee, in writing, of:

- any class, unit, or group of individuals covered by the program, any eligibility rules for the program, and any time limits applicable to the program, and
- the job titles and ages of all individuals eligible or selected for the program, and the ages of all individuals in the same job classification or organizational unit who are not eligible or selected for the program.

Rules for Waivers to Settle an EEOC Charge or Lawsuit

If an employee has already filed a charge of age discrimination with the EEOC or filed a lawsuit against the employer for age discrimination, the rules for waivers are less strict. In these situations, the employer does not have to allow a revocation period of seven days, provide 21 or 45 days for the employee to consider the agreement, or give the additional information (on eligible employees—their ages and so on) required for a group exit program.

However, the waiver must meet the other requirements listed above. In addition, the employee must be given a reasonable period of time to consider the settlement.

Lawsuits Filed After a Waiver: The Tender-Back Rule

If a worker tries to sue an employer after signing a waiver, traditional legal principles require that worker to first give back whatever he or she received (for example, severance pay or continued benefits) in exchange for giving up the right to sue. This requirement, referred to as the tender-back rule, requires workers to put their money where their mouths are: In order to argue that the waiver should not prevent a lawsuit, the worker must give up his or her rights under the waiver.

However, the tender-back rule does not apply to workers who file age discrimination lawsuits. Older workers may keep their release money **and** file an ADEA claim. If the worker wins the lawsuit, the employer is entitled to reimbursement of the money paid for the release. The employer can recover either the full amount paid for the release or the full amount the worker wins in the lawsuit, whichever is less.

The waiver may not include any penalty for filing a lawsuit. For example, some waivers require an employee to pay the employer's attorneys' fees if the employee files a lawsuit—such a requirement is illegal. Employers also may not stop fulfilling their obligations under a waiver if a lawsuit is filed. For example, many waivers provide that an employee will be paid a monthly severance check or will receive certain retirement benefits for a period of time. The employer cannot stop honoring these agreements simply because the employee files a lawsuit claiming the waiver is invalid.

How OWBPA Is Enforced

Individual Complaints

Employees may file a complaint (also called a charge) of age discrimination with the EEOC. The deadlines for filing a charge depend on whether the state where the discrimination charge will be filed also has an antidiscrimination law. In states without antidiscrimination laws, an employee has 180 days from the date of the discriminatory act to complain. In states with an antidiscrimination law, this deadline is extended to 300 days. (See Chapter 18 for information on state antidiscrimination laws.)

An employee may also file a lawsuit for age discrimination under the OWBPA. However, the employee must file a charge of discrimination with the EEOC and get a "right to sue" letter first. An employee must file the lawsuit within 90 days of receiving a right to sue letter from the EEOC.

Agency Enforcement

The federal agency responsible for investigating OWBPA complaints is the EEOC. An employee usually initiates the process by filing a charge (complaint) with the EEOC, although the agency can also act on its own initiative. The EEOC has the power to investigate, negotiate with employers, and bring lawsuits against employers to stop discriminatory practices.

Complying With OWBPA

Reporting Requirements

OWBPA imposes no reporting requirements.

Posting Requirements

OWBPA has no posting requirements separate from those required by the ADEA, which are covered in Chapter 1.

Record-Keeping Requirements

OWBPA has no record-keeping requirements separate from those required by the ADEA, which are covered in Chapter 1.

Penalties

The penalties for violating OWBPA are the same as those for violating the ADEA, which are covered in Chapter 1.

Agency Resources

- Information on waivers of ADEA and other discrimination claims
  Understanding Waivers of Discrimination Claims in Employee Severance Agreements
  www.eeoc.gov/policy/docs/qanda_severance-agreements.html
- Detailed explanations and examples of OWBPA's benefits rules
  EEOC Compliance Manual: Employee Benefits
  www.eeoc.gov/policy/docs/benefits.html

State Laws Relating to Age Discrimination

At the end of Chapter 18, you'll find a chart of state laws relating to fair employment, which includes laws prohibiting age discrimination.

Personal Responsibility and Work Opportunity Reconciliation Act (PRWORA)

Statute: 29 U.S.C. § 651 and following
http://uscode.house.gov/download/pls/29C15.txt

Regulations: 29 C.F.R. § 1900 and following
www.gpo.gov/fdsys/pkg/CFR-2012-title29-vol4/pdf/CFR-2012-title29-vol4-part1625.pdf

Overview of PRWORA

Passed in 1996 as part of former President Clinton's welfare reform effort, the Personal Responsibility and Work Opportunity Reconciliation Act (PRWORA) enlists employers in the effort to help parents collect child support. The law requires employers to report all new hires to a state registry, which uses this information to try to track down parents who aren't meeting their child support obligations.

PRWORA is a broad welfare law, with provisions on nutrition programs, teen pregnancy prevention, welfare-to-work requirements, and more. This book discusses only employers' responsibilities under the law's child support collection provision.

Definitions

Date of hire The first day on which an employee performs services for wages; in other words, an employee's first actual work day. The date of hire is not the same as the day on which a job offer is made or accepted, unless the employee begins work that day.

Independent contractor Someone who performs services for another person or business under contract, rather than as an employee. PRWORA uses the Internal Revenue Service's definitions of employee and independent contractor. Under these rules, a worker will usually be classified as an independent contractor if the person paying the worker has the right to control or direct only the result of the work, not the means or methods by which that result is to be accomplished.

Multistate employer An employer that has employees working in more than one state.

Regulated Employers

The law covers:
- state and local governments
- the federal government

- all private employers
- union hiring halls, if they retain an employment relationship with the workers whom they refer for jobs (for example, if the union rather than the company pays the worker's wages)
- unions that employ workers for wages (as paid organizers or administrative workers, for example), and
- temporary or placement agencies that retain an employment relationship with the workers whom they place (for example, agencies that collect an hourly rate from the companies in which workers are placed, then pay a portion of that rate to the workers as wages).

Employers on Native American reservations and lands are not required to comply with the law, unless the tribe has entered into an agreement with the state to do so.

Did You Know ...

- More than $27 billion was collected for child support in 2011; 70% of those dollars were submitted by employers through wage withholding, and an additional 5% were withheld from unemployment benefits.
- Through 2011, total child support arrearages—child support that was owed and not paid—exceeded $111 billion. Arrearages in California were the highest by far, at more than $18 billion.

Covered Workers

PRWORA applies to all newly hired employees, including:

- former employees who are rehired
- agricultural and domestic workers (housekeepers and child care workers, for example), and
- short-term employees (workers who quit or are fired before the 20-day deadline for reporting new hires has passed; see "What's Required," below, for more on this deadline).

PRWORA does not cover:

- employees acquired through a merger or reorganization. For example, if one company buys another company and acquires the purchased company's workers, the purchasing company usually does not have to report those employees as new hires. However, if the employees complete new IRS W-4 forms after the merger, then the company must report them as new hires.
- independent contractors. Some states require employers to report *independent contractors*, but PRWORA does not.
- employees working outside of the United States. PRWORA does not cover employees that work in another country, even if they work for an American employer.
- employees of a federal or state agency who perform intelligence or counterintelligence functions. Such employees are not covered if the head of the agency determines that reporting them as new hires could endanger the employees' safety or compromise an ongoing investigation or intelligence mission.

Key Facts

- Employers must report new hires to a state agency, which uses the information to find parents who are not paying child support.
- Some states require employers to provide more information on new hires than PRWORA requires or to submit information on workers who are not covered by PRWORA.
- Employers that do business in more than one state can designate one state to which they will send all new hire reports, even for employees who do not work in that state.

What's Required

Employers must report all new hires to a state agency called the State Directory of New Hires (PRWORA requires each state to establish such an agency). Employers must submit this information to the state agency in the state where the employee works, except that *multistate employers* may designate one state as the recipient of all new hire reports. (See "Exceptions," below).

Required Information

The employer must submit the following information every time it hires a new employee:
- employee's name
- employee's address
- employee's Social Security number
- employer's name
- employer's address, and
- employer's federal employer identification number.

The employer may comply with this requirement by submitting the employee's IRS W-4 form or by supplying the information in a different format.

PRWORA allows states to require employers to submit additional information on new hires, such as the *date of hire* and the employee's birth date.

Deadlines for Submitting Information

Employers must submit the required information within 20 days after a new employee's date of hire. Employers who choose to report new hire information electronically or by magnetic media (on a magnetic tape, for example) must report at least twice a month (if necessary). These reports must be no less than 12, and no more than 16, days apart.

Information Requested for Employees Called to Active Duty

In addition to the required information on new hires, the federal Office of Child Support Enforcement asks employers to submit additional information for current employees who are called to active military duty. This is a request, not a requirement: Employers are not legally obligated to submit this information.

For employees serving in the reserves, employers are asked to:
- contact the child support agency that issued the wage withholding order
- tell the agency that the employee has been called to active duty, and
- provide the date of the employee's activation.

This will allow the agency to issue a new withholding order to the military, so the employee's child support payments will continue uninterrupted while he or she is on active duty.

Exceptions

The law does not require multistate employers to report each new hire to the state agency where the employee works. Instead, a multistate employer can designate one state agency as the recipient of all new hire reports, regardless of where these employees actually work. To use this exception, the multistate employer must:

- choose a state where it employs workers
- submit its new hire information electronically or by magnetic media (on tape)
- follow that state's reporting laws for all employees (for example, if the state requires employers to report information for independent contractors, then the employer must submit information on all independent contractors, including contractors who work in other states), and
- tell the office of the Secretary of Health and Human Services, in writing, which state it has designated to receive new hire reports.

How PRWORA Is Enforced

Under PRWORA, state agencies are responsible for policing an employer's compliance with PRWORA's reporting requirement. Although the federal Office of Child Support Enforcement (OCSE), a division of the Administration for Children and Families, which is part of the Department of Health and Human Services, oversees the entire program, each state is responsible for making sure that employers within its borders comply with PRWORA. (See Appendix A for information on how to contact the OCSE.)

Individuals may not sue an employer for failing to comply with PRWORA.

Complying With PRWORA

Deadlines

- Employers must report new hires within 20 days after their date of hire.
- Employers who report new hire information electronically or by magnetic media must report at least twice a month (if necessary), no less than 12 days apart and no more than 16 days apart.

Reporting Requirements

The law is essentially a reporting requirement. See "What's Required," above, for details.

Record-Keeping Requirements

PRWORA imposes no special record-keeping requirements on employers. There is no requirement that employers keep a copy of the information they send to the state directory of new hires for any length of time, for example.

Penalties

PRWORA authorizes states to impose penalties on employers who fail to report new hires as required by the law. If a state chooses to impose such a penalty, it may not exceed:

- $25 for each new hire whom the employer fails to report, or
- if the employer and employee conspire in the failure to report (for example, if an employer agrees to an employee's request that it not file the report so that the employee can evade child support obligations), $500 for each new hire.

Agency Resources

- A list of ACF's regional offices
  Offices
  www.acf.hhs.gov/about/offices

- An employer's guide to complying with PRWORA's reporting requirements
  New Hire Reporting
  www.acf.hhs.gov/programs/css/employers/new-hire-reporting
- A list of each state's new hire reporting requirements, including contact information and websites for state child support enforcement offices
  State New Hire Reporting Information
  www.acf.hhs.gov/sites/default/files/ocse/state_new_hire_reporting_contacts_and_program_information.pdf
- A form multistate employers can use to designate the state to which they will submit new hire information
  Multistate Employer Notification Form for New Hire Reporting
  www.acf.hhs.gov/sites/default/files/ocse/mse_form.pdf
- Information on how to respond to a wage-withholding order
  Income Withholding for Support (IWO) for Private Employers
  www.acf.hhs.gov/programs/css/resource/income-withholding-for-support-iwo-for-private-employers

State Laws Relating to New Hire Reporting

PRWORA gives states the leeway to impose stricter requirements on employers. For example, although the federal law doesn't require it, states may choose to enact laws requiring employers to:

- report independent contractors as well as employees
- submit new hire information within a shorter time limit than the 20 days allowed under PRWORA
- provide more information about new hires than the federal law requires, and
- pay penalties for failing to comply with the law.

You can find information on each state's requirements, as well as citations to your state's law and the address of your state's enforcement agency, at the OCSE's website; see "Agency Resources," above.

Pregnancy Discrimination Act (PDA)

Statute: 42 U.S.C. § 2000e(k)

http://uscode.house.gov/download/pls/42C21.txt

Regulations: 29 C.F.R. § 1604 and Appendix to Part 1604

www.gpo.gov/fdsys/pkg/CFR-2012-title29-vol4/pdf/CFR-2012-title29-vol4-part1604.pdf

Overview of the Pregnancy Discrimination Act

The Pregnancy Discrimination Act (PDA) prohibits discrimination on the basis of pregnancy, childbirth, and related medical conditions in employment, health insurance plans, disability insurance plans, and sick leave plans. Under the PDA, discrimination based on pregnancy, childbirth, and/or related medical conditions is impermissible sex-based discrimination under Title VII of the Civil Rights Act of 1964 (Title VII). (Chapter 18 covers Title VII in detail.)

Definitions

Definitions for the Pregnancy Discrimination Act are the same as those for Title VII. See "Definitions," in Chapter 18.

Regulated Employers

The PDA covers:
- private employers with 15 or more employees
- the federal government
- state and local governments
- private and public employment agencies
- labor organizations, and
- joint labor/management committees.

Covered Workers

The PDA protects all prospective and current employees of a covered employer.

Legal Developments

- **EEOC focuses on pregnancy discrimination.** In 2012, the EEOC released its strategic enforcement plan for the next four years. This plan establishes the agency's priorities moving forward, and pregnancy is decidedly on the docket. The plan identifies failure to accommodate pregnancy as an emerging enforcement issue, particularly when women are forced to take unpaid leave when an employer denies them accommodations that are made available to other temporarily disabled employees. Shortly after releasing the plan, the EEOC further signaled its interest in this area by filing several pregnancy discrimination cases.

- **Pregnant Workers Fairness Act would require accommodations.** In its last session, Congress considered the Pregnant Workers Fairness Act, a bill that would require employers to provide reasonable accommodations for pregnant employees. The bill would also prohibit employers from refusing to hire a pregnant applicant because she needed such an accommodation, forcing a pregnant employee to accept an accommodation she didn't want, or forcing a pregnant employee to take leave if a reasonable accommodation could have been provided.

- **Pension payments based on discriminatory systems that predated the PDA are not illegal.** Before 1977 (when the PDA became law), AT&T employees who took pregnancy leave were credited with a maximum of 30 days of service (later raised to six weeks), no matter how much time they took off. Employees who took disability leave for any other reason received full credit for all of the time they took off, without limit. Once the PDA passed, AT&T changed its system, but a group of female employees who were subject to this rule sued after retiring, claiming that AT&T's service credit policy was discriminatory and left them with lower pensions than employees who took leave for other disabilities. The Supreme Court rejected their arguments, however, because the system was legal when it was in place, and Congress did not make the PDA retroactive. *AT&T Corp. v. Hulteen*, 129 S.Ct. 1962 (2009).

Did You Know ...

- Congress passed the PDA in 1978 in direct response to the U.S. Supreme Court's ruling in the case of *General Electric Co. v. Gilbert*, 429 U.S. 125 (1976), in which the Court held that pregnancy-related discrimination was not necessarily sex discrimination—and, therefore, was not necessarily illegal under Title VII.
- There were more than 5,700 pregnancy discrimination claims filed with the U.S. Equal Employment Opportunity Commission in 2011. Not including cases that actually went to court, the EEOC obtained more than $17 million in compensation for workers whose pregnancy discrimination claims it settled in 2011.
- In the ten years before the advent of the PDA, more than half of employed women quit their jobs when they became pregnant. That number dropped to 26.9% by the early 1990s.

What's Prohibited

The PDA prohibits employers from discriminating against prospective and current employees on the basis of pregnancy, childbirth, or related medical conditions. The PDA applies to all terms and benefits of employment, including:

- hiring
- firing
- compensation and benefits
- job assignment
- employee classification
- transfer
- promotion
- layoff or recall
- training and apprenticeship programs
- use of company facilities
- retirement plans, and
- time off.

The PDA also prohibits employers from retaliating against those who complain or who otherwise assert their rights under the law. For example, an employer cannot fire someone for complaining about pregnancy discrimination. (For more, see "Retaliation," in Chapter 18.)

Key Facts

- Under the PDA, discrimination based on pregnancy, birth, or related medical conditions in any aspect of employment is illegal sex-based discrimination under Title VII of the Civil Rights Act of 1964. (See Chapter 18 for more on Title VII.)
- The PDA is part of Title VII; as such, the PDA's requirements, prohibitions, and complaint and enforcement procedures are the same as those for Title VII.
- Employers must treat workers with pregnancy-related disabilities just as they treat workers with any other temporary disability—for example, a worker who broke a leg or had a heart attack.

Related Medical Conditions

Unfortunately, the PDA does not define the term "related medical condition," so the task of giving this term meaning has been left to the courts. Although different courts define the term differently, there are a few bright-line rules. If, as a direct result of pregnancy or childbirth, a woman suffers from a medical complication or disability that requires medical treatment, then her condition is a related medical condition. For example, recovery from childbirth (even if the birth was uneventful) and recovery from miscarriage or abortion fall within this category.

Women are also protected from discrimination based on their potential to become pregnant. For example, an employer cannot exclude all women of childbearing years from jobs that require contact with toxic chemicals or other substances that could lead to birth defects.

On the other end of the spectrum, breast-feeding and child care are not considered related medical conditions and are therefore not protected by the

PDA. Note, however, that some states require employers to accommodate their employees' desire to breast-feed their children, as does the federal health care reform law (by requiring lactation breaks).

Courts are divided as to whether infertility is a related medical condition, generally depending on the facts of the case. Several courts have held that penalizing female employees who are seeking fertility treatment in order to become pregnant is impermissible under the PDA. Yet other courts have also held that, because infertility can affect both men and women, denying health care coverage for infertility treatments cannot give rise to a claim of sex discrimination under the PDA.

What's Required

If an employee is temporarily disabled by pregnancy, childbirth, or a related medical condition, the employer must treat the employee the same way the employer would treat any other temporarily disabled employee—for example, by temporarily modifying the job, providing disability leave, or providing unpaid leave. Similarly, rules pertaining to benefit accrual, seniority, vacation calculation, pay increases, and other benefits must be applied the same way to employees on pregnancy disability leave as to employees on any other disability leave.

If an employee is absent because of pregnancy, childbirth, or a related medical condition, the employer must hold the employee's job open for the same amount of time that the employer would hold open the job of an employee who is on leave for illness or disability. This requirement may also be affected by the Family and Medical Leave Act. (See Chapter 8 for more information.)

Employers must allow pregnant employees to work for as long as they are able to do their jobs. For example, an employer cannot require a pregnant employee to go on leave—whether paid or unpaid—prior to the baby's birth if the employee is able to work and does not want to go on leave.

If the employer provides health insurance as a benefit to employees, the policy must cover expenses for pregnancy, childbirth, and related medical conditions to the same extent that it covers expenses for other medical conditions. However, employers do not have to provide benefits to pay for an abortion unless the life of the mother would be endangered if she carried the fetus to term. If a woman does have an abortion, the employer's health benefits must cover any medical complications arising from that abortion, whether or not the benefits paid for the abortion in the first place.

If the male spouses or partners of a company's employees get comprehensive medical benefits as dependents of employees, then the female spouses or partners must also get comprehensive medical benefits as dependents—including benefits for pregnancy and so on.

Employees who are pregnant or new parents may also have rights under the Family and Medical Leave Act. (See Chapter 8 for more information.)

Exceptions

The exceptions to the PDA are the same as those for Title VII. (See Chapter 18.)

How the Pregnancy Discrimination Act Is Enforced

Individual Complaints

The enforcement provisions of Title VII apply to the PDA. (See Chapter 18.)

Agency Enforcement

The enforcement provisions of Title VII apply to the PDA. (See Chapter 18.)

Complying With the Pregnancy Discrimination Act

Reporting Requirements

The reporting requirements for the PDA are the same as those for Title VII. (See Chapter 18.)

Posting Requirements

The PDA is among the laws covered in the general antidiscrimination poster required by Title VII. You can order a copy of this poster from the EEOC; see Appendix A for contact information.

Record-Keeping Requirements

The record-keeping requirements for the PDA are the same as those for Title VII. (See Chapter 18.)

Penalties

The penalties for violating the PDA are the same as those for violating Title VII. (See Chapter 18.)

Agency Resources

- Information about pregnancy discrimination
  Pregnancy Discrimination
  www.eeoc.gov/laws/types/pregnancy.cfm

- A fact sheet on the relationship between the Family and Medical Leave Act, the Americans with Disabilities Act, and Title VII's protections against pregnancy and sex discrimination
  The Family and Medical Leave Act, the Americans with Disabilities Act, and Title VII of the Civil Rights Act of 1964
  www.eeoc.gov/policy/docs/fmlaada.html

State Laws Relating to Pregnancy Discrimination

See "State Antidiscrimination Laws," in Chapter 18, for information on state laws relating to all forms of employment discrimination, including pregnancy and gender discrimination.

Sarbanes-Oxley Act of 2002 (SOX)

Statute: 15 U.S.C. §§ 78j-1(m); 18 U.S.C. § 1514A

http://uscode.house.gov/download/pls/15C2B.txt

http://uscode.house.gov/download/pls/18C73.txt

Regulations: 17 C.F.R. § 240.10A-3; 29 C.F.R. § 1980

www.gpo.gov/fdsys/pkg/CFR-2012-title17-vol3/pdf/CFR-2012-title17-vol3-sec240-10A-3.pdf

www.gpo.gov/fdsys/pkg/CFR-2012-title29-vol9/pdf/CFR-2012-title29-vol9-part1980.pdf

Overview of SOX

I n the wake of corporate scandals involving WorldCom, Enron, and other large companies accused of defrauding shareholders, Congress passed the Sarbanes-Oxley Act of 2002 (SOX). The stated purpose of SOX is to protect investors by improving the accuracy and reliability of corporate disclosures, and much of the law seeks to further this goal by imposing strict rules for audits and auditors of publicly traded companies, preventing insider trading and deals, requiring companies to adopt strict internal controls, and increasing the penalties for white-collar crimes relating to investor fraud. Because these provisions don't directly implicate employment issues, they aren't covered here.

SOX also creates employee whistle-blower protections: Employees who complain of, or provide information about, actions they believe to be shareholder fraud are protected from discrimination and retaliation. The law also obligates covered companies to create procedures by which employees can report concerns about audits or accounting procedures.

In 2010, Congress passed the Dodd-Frank Act, also called the Wall Street Reform and Consumer Protection Act, a response to the financial collapse that began in late 2007. Among many other things, this law adds a number of new whistle-blower protections for those who raise concerns about the conduct of financial firms, ratings agencies, and so on. It also amends SOX in several important aspects, all of which are covered in this chapter.

Regulated Employers

SOX generally applies only to *public companies* (which includes their subsidiaries and affiliates). However, its whistle-blower provisions also apply to *company representatives*, which could include people or businesses that have neither issued stock nor gone public. For example, the whistle-blower provisions could apply to a private company that contracts to do work for public companies.

SOX creates personal liability for company representatives, including employees who are in a position to retaliate against other employees who raise concerns about corporate misfeasance. This means that managers and supervisors who violate SOX by retaliating against whistle-blowers may be held personally liable—and have to pay any judgment awarded to the employee.

Although SOX's prohibition on retaliation for whistle-blowing and the penalties for violating that provision apply only to public companies and their representatives, SOX also includes a criminal provision that applies more broadly. Anyone who intentionally harms someone else for providing truthful information to a law enforcement officer relating to the commission of any federal offense faces up to ten years in prison. (18 U.S.C. § 1513(e).) Because the law defines harm to include interference with the employment or livelihood of the informant, this provision could apply to anyone who retaliates against a whistle-blower, whether or not the perpetrator works for or has any association with a public company.

Definitions

Audit committee A committee of members of the board of directors of a *public company*, formed to oversee the company's audits and accounting and financial reporting processes. The audit committee has a number of legal obligations under SOX. If a public company does not establish a separate audit committee, the entire board of directors is responsible for seeing that these obligations are met.

Company representative Any officer, contractor, subcontractor, agent, or employee of a company.

Public company Any company that has a class of securities registered with the Securities and Exchange Commission (SEC) under 15 U.S.C. § 78l or that is required to file periodic reports with the SEC under 15 U.S.C. § 78o(d). As amended by the Dodd-Frank Act, this includes any subsidiary or affiliate whose financial information is included in the consolidated financial statements of such a company.

Legal Developments

- **Whistle-blowers may be entitled to a bounty.** Someone who reports possible violations of federal security laws directly to the Securities and Exchange Commission (SEC) may be entitled to a share of what the agency recovers. To qualify, the whistle-blower must voluntarily provide the SEC with original information that leads to a successful enforcement action resulting in an award of more than $1 million in monetary sanctions. The bounty payment ranges from 10% to 30%, depending on a number of factors; if the whistle-blower is an employee of the company, a higher amount may be awarded to someone who first tried to use the company's internal complaint process before going to the SEC.

- **OSHA introduces pilot ADR program.** In October of 2012, OSHA announced that it would begin an alternative dispute resolution (ADR) pilot program in two of its regions for whistle-blower complaints. The program will use mediation to try to resolve complaints outside of the formal legal system. After 120 days, the regions are to submit data on their experience and the program will be evaluated.

- **In 2010, Congress passed the Wall Street Reform and Consumer Protection Act,** informally called the Dodd-Frank Act, after its two sponsors. This law is a broad-ranging response to the financial collapse that began in late 2007. Along with the accompanying regulations, Dodd-Frank amends SOX to:
  - include subsidiaries and affiliates in the definition of public companies
  - protect against retaliation by nationally recognized statistical rating organizations
  - allow complaints to be made orally, in any language, and/or filed by someone else on the employee's behalf (with the employee's consent)
  - extend the statute of limitations for whistle-blowing complaints to 180 days
  - allow a jury trial for those who bring a SOX lawsuit, and
  - provide that predispute arbitration agreements are not enforceable for SOX claims.

Covered Workers

All employees who work for public companies are covered by SOX's whistle-blower provisions. Not every employee qualifies as a whistle-blower, however. To be protected, an employee must either:

- make a complaint to specific groups or people about certain types of misconduct, or
- participate in certain types of proceedings relating to shareholder misconduct.

Did You Know ...

- Human resources professionals are finding themselves responsible for SOX compliance in areas outside of their traditional employee relations function. For example, many HR experts are responsible for—or assist in—implementing Section 404 of the law, which requires companies to have strict internal controls to ensure the accuracy of their financial numbers. Because salaries, benefits, recruiting, and other costs of hiring and managing employees are the largest component of many companies' budgets, HR experts are often involved in developing and implementing ways to verify that the company—and, more importantly for purposes of SOX, its shareholders—are getting their money's worth.
- From the beginning of FY 2005 through the first half of FY 2012, OSHA's whistle-blower office had received more than 1,700 complaints of SOX violations.
- According to statistics reported by the Center for Public Integrity in July 2010, the Department of Labor (DOL) has upheld 25 whistle-blower complaints under SOX since the law passed—and thrown out 1,066 claims. In other words, whistle-blowers prevailed in just over 2% of the cases that have been decided.

Protected Complaints

To qualify as a protected whistle-blower, an employee must provide information, cause information to be provided, or assist in an investigation or a proceeding regarding conduct that the employee reasonably believes violates (1) 18 U.S.C. § 1341, 1343, 1344, or 1348 (statutes that criminalize mail fraud, wire fraud, bank fraud, and shareholder fraud); (2) any rule or regulation of the SEC; or (3) any federal law relating to shareholder fraud. The employee must raise these concerns with particular people or organizations in order to be protected.

Conduct Relating to Shareholder Fraud

An employee is protected under SOX only for providing information about conduct that he or she reasonably believes violates the federal laws enumerated above, SEC regulations, or federal laws against shareholder fraud. Employees who complain of violations of state law are not protected, nor are employees who complain of violations of internal company policies or procedures (unless the violation also could mislead shareholders).

There is some uncertainty over what types of complaints are covered. Clearly, if an employee complains that the company failed to disclose material information to its shareholders, the complaint would be protected. The rules are less clear, however, if the employee complains of other allegedly illegal activities that could potentially affect the company's bottom line.

There is also some uncertainty about whether an employee has to specifically state, when reporting concerns or making a complaint, that he or she believes the law was violated. Some judges have found that an employee who only questions certain conduct or complains about the conduct without raising the possibility of shareholder fraud is not protected by SOX. And some judges have found that an employee is protected only if the employee raises a concern that the action is illegal.

The employee's claim of shareholder fraud does not have to be correct. Rather, the employee must show only that he or she had a reasonable belief that the conduct constituted fraud. An employee whose complaint is based on a feeling or hunch, in the absence of any evidence, is not protected. However, an employee who reasonably believes that the company has overstated income, filed false reports, or engaged in accounting fraud is protected, even if the company's actions turn out to be perfectly legal.

Recipients of the Complaint or Assistance

An employee cannot claim the protections of SOX unless he or she provides information to, causes information to be provided to, or assists in an investigation conducted by:

- a federal regulatory or law enforcement agency (such as the SEC)
- a member or committee of Congress, or
- a person who either has supervisory authority over the employee or has the authority to investigate, discover, or terminate the alleged misconduct.

Key Facts:

- SOX prohibits retaliation against an employee who provides information or assists in an investigation regarding conduct that the employee reasonably believes to be a violation of specified federal statutes that prohibit mail fraud, wire fraud, bank fraud, and securities fraud; any rule or regulation of the Securities and Exchange Commission (SEC); or any federal law relating to shareholder fraud.
- To be protected, the employee must provide the information to, or assist in an investigation by, a federal agency, a member or committee of Congress, or a person who either supervises the employee or has the authority to investigate or put a stop to the alleged misconduct.
- The law also prohibits retaliation against an employee who files or participates in an enforcement proceeding relating to shareholder fraud.
- SOX requires companies to adopt procedures for receiving, handling, and retaining complaints about their accounting, auditing, or internal controls. Companies must also establish a way for employees to submit confidential, anonymous complaints of questionable accounting or auditing practices.

Protected Proceedings

There are two types of proceedings that are protected under SOX: investigations and legal proceedings.

Employees are protected if they assist in an investigation into conduct that they reasonably believe constitutes shareholder fraud by any of the complaint recipients listed in "Recipients of the Complaint or Assistance," above. An employee does not have to provide the information that leads to the investigation; an employee who acts as a witness in or provides information to an ongoing investigation is also protected.

Employees are also protected if they file, cause to be filed, testify in, participate in, or otherwise assist in a proceeding that has been filed or is about to be filed relating to an alleged violation of SEC regulations or federal laws relating to shareholder fraud.

What's Prohibited

Public companies and company representatives may not retaliate against an employee in the terms or conditions of his or her employment because the employee provided information, participated in an investigation, or participated in a proceeding relating to shareholder fraud.

SOX states that termination, demotion, suspension, threats, and harassment all constitute retaliation. However, judges are divided as to whether actions that don't cause a tangible job consequence count. Some cases have held that giving a negative performance evaluation, moving the employee to a work space with fewer amenities, or taking away the employee's "officer" status did not constitute retaliation, because they were unaccompanied by any tangible consequences such as a demotion or decrease in pay. On the other hand, other cases have held that taking away job responsibilities, changing the employee's performance improvement plan, and placing the employee on a layoff list (although he or she is never actually laid off) are all sufficient to constitute retaliation.

What's Required

The *audit committee* of a public company must establish procedures for:
- receiving, keeping, and handling complaints the company receives regarding its accounting, auditing, or internal accounting controls, and
- allowing employees to submit confidential, anonymous complaints and concerns about questionable accounting or auditing matters.

The SEC regulations do not require companies to follow particular procedures for taking employee complaints (such as setting up an ethics hotline or a Web-based complaint system).

How SOX Is Enforced

Individual Complaints

An employee who wishes to bring a lawsuit claiming that he or she was discriminated or retaliated against in violation of SOX's whistle-blower protections must first file a complaint with the Occupational Safety and Health Administration (OSHA) within 180 days. (See Appendix A for information on how to contact OSHA.) If OSHA does not issue a final decision on the employee's complaint within 180 days after the complaint is filed, the employee can file a lawsuit in federal district court.

However, 15 days before filing the lawsuit, the employee must file a notice with the administrative law judge assigned to the original complaint (or to the Administrative Review Board, if the case is pending before it) that the employee intends to file such a lawsuit. The employee must also serve this notice on the other parties to the dispute (the employer and any other companies or individuals whom the employee accuses of retaliation). (For more detailed information about OSHA's investigation and hearing procedures, see "Agency Enforcement," below.)

There is no avenue for employee complaints regarding a public company's failure to adopt an appropriate system for confidential employee complaints. This provision is enforced by the SEC only.

Agency Enforcement

Whistle-Blower Protections

The whistle-blowing provisions of SOX are enforced by OSHA, a division of the Department of Labor (DOL). After an employee files a complaint (as described in "Individual Complaints," above), OSHA will investigate if the complaint shows that:

- the employee engaged in protected activity (that is, provided information or participated in a proceeding covered by SOX)
- the person accused of retaliation knew of the activity
- the employee suffered an adverse employment action, and
- the circumstances create an inference that the adverse employment action was due, at least in part, to the employee's protected activity.

Even if the employee provides evidence of the points listed above, OSHA will not proceed if the company or person named in the complaint can show, by clear and convincing evidence, that it would have taken the same action against the employee even in the absence of the employee's protected activity. The company or person must present its evidence within 20 days after it receives notice of the complaint.

If OSHA investigates, it will issue findings and a preliminary order within 60 days after the complaint is filed. Either party may object to these findings and request a hearing within 30 days after receiving the findings and order. If a hearing is requested, it will be held before an administrative law judge, who will issue a decision and order. Either party may request a review of the judge's decision by filing a petition with the Administrative Review Board within ten days after the date on the judge's order. The board can either adopt the judge's decision as its own or review the case itself. Once the board issues its decision, the parties have 60 days in which to file an appeal with the U.S. Court of Appeals.

Internal Complaint Procedures

The requirement that public companies create procedures for anonymous employee complaints is enforced by the SEC. The SEC has issued rules requiring the national securities exchanges and associations to delist the stock of companies that fail to comply with this requirement (see "Penalties," below), which effectively enlists the securities exchanges and associations as the primary enforcers of this provision.

Complying With SOX

Deadlines

- The employer has 20 days to respond to an employee's complaint to OSHA.
- The employer has 30 days to object to the administrative law judge's findings and request a hearing.
- The employer has 60 days to appeal the board's decision to the U.S. Court of Appeals.

Reporting Requirements

The financial safeguards imposed by SOX include numerous reporting requirements, but there are no reporting requirements associated solely with its whistle-blower provisions.

The rules of the national securities exchanges and commissions may require public companies to report on the complaint policies adopted by their audit committees.

Posting Requirements

SOX imposes no posting requirements relating to its whistle-blowing provisions. However, posting could be one component of a company's complaint system.

Record-Keeping Requirements

SOX requires public companies to develop a system for retaining complaints regarding auditing or accounting procedures.

Penalties

Whistle-Blower Protections

Public companies and company representatives who violate the whistle-blower protections of SOX may be ordered to:
- reinstate the worker to the same position, with the same benefits, responsibilities, and seniority, that the worker would have had absent the retaliation
- pay the worker all compensation and benefits lost as a result of the retaliation, with interest, and
- pay the employee's attorneys' fees and court costs.

Courts and judges are divided as to whether SOX allows damages for emotional distress, damage to reputation, pain and suffering, and similar types of harm.

Complaint Procedures

A public company that fails to adopt the complaint procedures mandated by SOX can have its stock delisted by the national securities exchanges and associations.

Agency Resources

- A detailed discussion of SOX whistle-blower cases decided by the DOL
  Sarbanes-Oxley Act (SOX) Whistleblower Digest
  www.oalj.dol.gov/PUBLIC/Whistle-blower/REFERENCES/
  REFERENCE_WORKS/SOX_DIGEST.HTM

- A tool to help you find local OSHA offices
  Regional & Area Offices
  www.osha.gov/html/RAmap.html

- A page of links to newsletters, cases decided by administrative law judges, and other resource materials on SOX
  OALJ Whistleblower Collection
  www.oalj.dol.gov/LIBWHIST.HTM

State Laws Relating to Whistle-Blowers

Some states have laws that protect whistle-blowers from retaliation for reporting particular types of misconduct, such as dangerous work conditions or violations of child labor laws. In some states, courts recognize an employee's legal right to sue for wrongful termination "in violation of public policy" if he or she was fired in retaliation for reporting illegal or unethical conduct. The requirements for these types of claims vary from state to state. For information on your state's whistle-blower protections (if any), contact your state labor department. (You can find contact information in Appendix A.)

Civil Rights Act of 1866 (Section 1981)

Statute: 15 U.S.C. §§ 78j-1(m); 18 U.S.C. § 1514A

http://uscode.house.gov/download/pls/15C2B.txt

http://uscode.house.gov/download/pls/18C73.txt

Regulations: 17 C.F.R. § 240.10A-3; 29 C.F.R. § 1980

www.gpo.gov/fdsys/pkg/CFR-2012-title17-vol3/pdf/CFR-2012-title17-vol3-sec240-10A-3.pdf

www.gpo.gov/fdsys/pkg/CFR-2012-title29-vol9/pdf/CFR-2012-title29-vol9-part1980.pdf

Overview of Section 1981

The Civil Rights Act of 1866 declares African Americans to be citizens, entitled to a series of rights previously reserved to white men. This law is known as Section 1981 because of its location in the United States Code.

Section 1981 confers a number of rights, including the right to sue or be sued in court, to give evidence in a lawsuit, and to purchase property. This book discusses only one of the law's protections: the right to make and enforce contracts, which courts have found prohibits racial discrimination in the employment relationship.

Although the law's original purpose was to protect African Americans, courts have interpreted it to protect people of all races from discrimination and harassment.

Definitions

At-will employee An employee who can quit or be fired at any time, for any reason that is not illegal. In every state but Montana, a worker is employed at will unless he or she has an employment contract that limits the employer's right to fire. Such an employment contract may be written, oral, or implied from the conduct of the employer and employee.

Regulated Employers

Section 1981 applies to:

- state and local governments, and
- private employers of any size.

Section 1981 also applies to some entities that are not employers in the legal sense, but have a contractual relationship with people performing work for them. For example, partners in a partnership are covered by Section 1981, but not by other federal antidiscrimination statutes, such as Title VII, the Age Discrimination in Employment Act, or the Americans with Disabilities Act.

Most courts have also found that firms hiring independent contractors are covered by Section 1981. (See "Covered Workers," below.)

Legal Developments

- **Supreme Court decides that retaliation is covered by Section 1981.** In 2008, the U.S. Supreme Court found that an employee may bring a retaliation claim under Section 1981. In that case, the employee had claimed race discrimination and retaliation under both Title VII and Section 1981, but his Title VII claims were dismissed. The Supreme Court found that its previous decision interpreting 42 U.S.C. § 1982, a provision similar to Section 1981 but dealing with the right to own property, had led most lower federal courts to conclude that retaliation was also prohibited under Section 1981, and that there was no reason to disturb this precedent. (*CBOCS West, Inc. v. Humphries*, 553 U.S. 442 (2008).)
- **Employees have up to four years to file lawsuits alleging violations of Section 1981.** Because Section 1981 doesn't include its own statute of limitations (the time limit for filing lawsuits claiming violations of the law), courts had traditionally applied the statute of limitations for similar claims in the state where the plaintiff brought the lawsuit. In 2004, however, the U.S. Supreme Court decided that cases that were made possible by the Civil Rights Act of 1991—that is, cases alleging discrimination or harassment during the employment relationship, not discriminatory refusal to enter into an employment contract—should be governed by a four-year federal statute of limitations. (*Jones v. R.R. Donnelly & Sons*, 541 U.S. 369 (2004).) This ruling means that employees will have much longer to file certain claims under Section 1981 than they would under other federal antidiscrimination statutes.

Covered Workers

All private employees and employees of state and local governments are covered by Section 1981. In addition, the law covers partners in a partnership.

At-Will Employees

Section 1981 protects the right to make and enforce contracts, including employment contracts. Most federal courts that have considered this issue—including several federal courts of appeal—have decided that *at-will employees* may sue an employer for violating Section 1981, even though they do not have employment contracts limiting the employer's right to fire them. These courts reasoned that at-will employees have very basic employment contracts (covering, for example, wages and work to be performed), although those contracts offer no job protection. The Supreme Court has not yet considered this issue explicitly. However, the Court found in favor of an employee claiming retaliation in violation of Section 1981 in the case of *CBOCS West, Inc. v. Humphries*, 553 U.S. 442 (2008); according to the federal Court of Appeals opinion in that case, Mr. Humphries was an at-will employee.

Independent Contractors

Section 1981 protects independent contractors from race discrimination by their hiring firm. However, at least one court has decided that this protection does not extend to claims of race harassment. The U.S. Supreme Court has not yet considered this issue.

Contractors who have incorporated their businesses cannot personally sue another company for race discrimination in contracting, however. In *Domino's Pizza v. McDonald*, 546 U.S. 470 (2006), the U.S. Supreme Court rejected a black contractor's Section 1981 claim that Domino's Pizza had broken several contracts with his corporation because of his race. Although the contractor was the sole shareholder of his corporation and entered into the contracts on its behalf, the Court found that he had no right to sue because the contracts were between Domino's and his corporation, not him personally.

Federal Employees

The Supreme Court has found that federal applicants and employees must use Title VII (and its separate enforcement scheme for federal agencies) to raise any claims that are covered by that statute. Because Title VII prohibits employment discrimination on the bases of race and national origin (among other things), most courts have found that federal employees cannot use Section 1981 for employment-related claims.

Did You Know ...

- Section 1981 was passed over the veto of President Andrew Johnson. His opposition to this and other Reconstruction-era efforts to grant civil rights to the former slaves was one of the major issues that led to his eventual impeachment.
- A primary purpose of Section 1981 was to undermine the so-called Black Codes, state laws adopted after the Civil War that restricted the rights of newly freed slaves to own property, make contracts, or leave a job, among other things.
- Although Title VII of the Civil Rights Act of 1964 (see Chapter 18) also prohibits race discrimination, many workers sue under Section 1981 instead, because it applies to all employers regardless of size, it does not require workers to file an administrative charge with the EEOC before bringing a lawsuit, it gives workers a longer deadline for filing cases, and it doesn't impose a limit on the money damages an employee can win in a successful lawsuit.

What's Prohibited

Section 1981 prohibits discrimination on the basis of race in the making or enforcement of employment contracts. This language has been interpreted broadly to prohibit any intentional workplace discrimination—including harassment—on the basis of race. Some courts have also found that Section 1981 prohibits discrimination and harassment on the basis of ethnicity, at least where that ethnicity has a racial component. (See "Race and Ethnicity," below.) Section 1981 also prohibits retaliation against those who complain of race discrimination.

Key Facts

- Section 1981 prohibits discrimination on the basis of race and ethnicity in every aspect of employment. It also prohibits retaliation against those who assert their rights under the statute.
- Unlike Title VII (see Chapter 18), Section 1981 applies to all private employers, regardless of size.
- Employees do not have to file a charge of discrimination with the EEOC before bringing a lawsuit under Section 1981.

Covered Employment Practices

Employers may not discriminate on the basis of race in any aspect of employment, including:

- hiring
- promotions
- employment benefits
- pay
- time off, and
- firing.

Racial Harassment

Today, it is undisputed that Section 1981 prohibits racial harassment. However, this issue was fiercely contested at one time, in a battle between Congress and the Supreme Court.

In 1989, the U.S. Supreme Court decided that Section 1981 covered only the right to enter into a contract in the first place and did not extend to any problems or issues—such as harassment—that might later arise in the employment relationship. (*Patterson v. McClean Credit Union*, 491 U.S. 164.) In response to this and several other Supreme Court decisions that narrowed employees' rights, Congress passed the Civil Rights Act of 1991. Among other things, this law overruled *Patterson* and amended Section 1981 so that it now clearly prohibits racial harassment.

An employee claiming racial harassment in violation of Section 1981 must show that he or she was subjected to unwelcome racial comments or offensive conduct that was severe or pervasive enough to alter the conditions of employment. This test is the same as that used under Title VII. (See Chapter 18 for more information on what constitutes harassment.)

Race and Ethnicity

Although Section 1981 was originally intended to protect newly freed slaves, courts have consistently interpreted the law to protect people of any race (including white people) from intentional race discrimination.

Some courts have also found that Section 1981 prohibits discrimination on the basis of ethnicity, but only if that discrimination is racial in character. For example, courts have held that discrimination against Latin Americans, Arab Americans, and Asian Americans violates Section 1981, but discrimination against persons of Slavic or Italian origin does not.

In deciding whether ethnic discrimination constitutes race discrimination under Section 1981, courts have looked at several factors, including:

- whether the discriminator perceived or characterized the victim as belonging to a separate race because of his or her ethnicity
- whether the victim belongs to an ethnicity that is perceived as "nonwhite"
- whether the victim belongs to an ethnicity that has traditionally been subject to discrimination, and
- whether the victim is claiming discrimination based on characteristics commonly associated with national origin (country of birth, language fluency, and surname, for example), which is not a violation of Section 1981; or on characteristics commonly associated with race (physical characteristics or skin color, for example), which is.

Exceptions

Other Types of Discrimination

Section 1981 prohibits only discrimination based on race or ethnicity. It does not prohibit discrimination based on sex, religion, disability, or age.

Unintentional Discrimination

Only intentional race discrimination violates Section 1981. Unintentional discrimination—such as the use of seemingly neutral hiring criteria that disproportionately weed out applicants of a particular race—does not violate the law. Lawsuits for unintentional discrimination (called "disparate impact" lawsuits) are allowed under other antidiscrimination laws, such as Title VII. (See Chapter 18.)

How Section 1981 Is Enforced

Individual Complaints

Employees or applicants who believe that their rights under Section 1981 have been violated may file a lawsuit in state court or in a federal district court.

No government agency takes complaints about violations of Section 1981. Therefore, an employee's only official avenue of redress is through the courts.

If an employer is covered by Title VII (see Chapter 18), the employee can also file a charge of race discrimination with the Equal Employment Opportunity Commission (EEOC). However, the EEOC will only enforce rights under Title VII, not Section 1981 rights.

Agency Enforcement

Section 1981 is enforced only through private lawsuits, not through agency action.

Complying With Section 1981

Reporting Requirements

Section 1981 imposes no reporting requirements.

Posting Requirements

Posting is not required under Section 1981.

Record-Keeping Requirements

Section 1981 does not require employers to keep any particular records.

Penalties

If an employee wins a lawsuit for violation of Section 1981, the employer may be required to:
- pay the employee back pay and benefits lost as a result of the discrimination or harassment
- pay the employee compensatory damages for emotional distress, such as pain and suffering
- pay punitive damages, a sum of money intended to punish the employer for violating the law
- take action to remedy the discrimination, such as promoting, hiring, or reinstating a worker who was discriminated against, and
- pay the employee's attorneys' fees and court costs.

State Laws Relating to Race Discrimination

You'll find a chart of state laws prohibiting discrimination, including race discrimination, at the end of Chapter 18.

Title VII of the Civil Rights Act of 1964 (Title VII)

Statute: 42 U.S.C. § 2000e
http://uscode.house.gov/download/pls/42C21.txt

Regulations: 29 C.F.R. §§ 1600–1609
www.gpo.gov/fdsys/pkg/CFR-2012-title29-vol4/pdf/CFR-2012-title29-vol4-subtitleB-chapXIV.pdf

Overview of Title VII

Signed by President Lyndon B. Johnson in 1964, the landmark Civil Rights Act outlaws discrimination and segregation in public establishments, schools, and federally funded programs. Title VII of the Civil Rights Act—so named for its location in the law—prohibits employment discrimination based on race, color, religion, sex, and national origin.

Regulated Employers

Title VII covers the following employers:
- private employers with 15 or more employees
- the federal government
- state and local governments
- private and public employment agencies
- labor organizations, and
- joint labor/management committees.

Title VII covers multinational employers with operations in the United States or its territories, unless the employer is covered by a treaty or another binding international agreement that dictates otherwise—for example, a treaty permitting the company to prefer its own citizens for specific jobs.

Title VII covers an employer with operations in other countries if the employer is incorporated in the United States, based in the United States, or controlled by a U.S. company. However, an employer is exempt from Title VII's requirements if complying with Title VII would violate a law of the country in which it operates.

Definitions

Bona fide occupational qualification (BFOQ) An exception to Title VII's general prohibition of discrimination, BFOQs allow employers to discriminate (except on the basis of race) when the very nature of the job requires them to do so.

Disparate impact A type of unlawful discrimination that occurs when a seemingly neutral policy disproportionately affects members of a *protected class*.

Harassment Work conditions or behavior by coworkers, superiors, managers, or others that subjects employees who are members of a *protected class* to a work environment that is hostile, intimidating, or offensive.

Protected class A group specifically protected by Title VII. For example, because Title VII prohibits discrimination based on sex, both men and women fall within protected classes. People with cats, however, are not members of a protected class because there is no ban against discrimination based on pet ownership.

Quid pro quo A Latin term meaning "this for that," which refers to a type of sexual harassment in which a supervisor demands sexual favors from a subordinate in exchange for a promotion, positive performance evaluation, or another job benefit, or in which a supervisor threatens *adverse action* if the subordinate does not comply with a sexual demand.

Retaliation Adverse action taken by an employer or someone who works for the employer against an employee for complaining, participating in an investigation or another proceeding, or otherwise opposing *harassment* or discrimination.

Sexual harassment Any unwelcome sexual advance or conduct on the job that creates an intimidating, hostile, or offensive working environment.

Legal Developments

- **Employers can be liable for discrimination even if the decision maker doesn't have discriminatory intent.** In this so-called "cat's paw" situation, one supervisor has a discriminatory motive, but a different supervisor makes the adverse decision (for example, to fire an employee). In a case involving discrimination against an employee because of his military service, the Supreme Court found that an employer is liable if a supervisor takes action with the intent of causing negative treatment of an employee, and that supervisor's action is the proximate cause of such negative treatment. In other words, if the supervisor's discriminatory motive taints the decision-making process and ultimately causes the employee to be mistreated, the company is liable. (*Staub v. Proctor Hospital,* 131 S.Ct. 1186 (2011).)

- **What is illegal retaliation?** In *Burlington Northern & Santa Fe Railway v. White* (548 U.S. 53 (2006)), the Supreme Court found that only "materially adverse" actions—those harmful enough to deter a reasonable worker from complaining of discrimination or harassment—could be actionable retaliation. A change in work duties, shift change, or other alteration in the employee's job might be illegal retaliation, depending on the circumstances. This case was the first in a series of recent Supreme Court cases addressing retaliation, including *CBOCS West, Inc. v. Humphries*, 128 S.Ct. 1951 (2007) (addressing retaliation under Section 1981); *Gomez-Perez v. Potter*, 128 S.Ct. 1931 (2008) (addressing retaliation against federal employees who complain of age discrimination); *Thompson v. North American Stainless*, 131 S.Ct. 863 (2011) (employee can sue for retaliation based on his fiancé's legal claims against their mutual employer); and *Kasten v. Saint-Gobain Performance Plastics Corp.* 131 S.Ct. 1325 (2011) (employee who made oral complaints may sue for retaliation under Fair Labor Standards Act).

- **Retaliation against witnesses is also prohibited.** Title VII prohibits employers from retaliating against an employee for opposing illegal practices under the law, such as discrimination and harassment. Clearly, this protects employees who make a complaint, whether to the employer or to an outside agency, such as the Equal Employment Opportunity Commission. The U.S. Supreme Court recently held that witnesses and others who speak out against illegal practices during a workplace investigation are also protected, even if they aren't the original source of the complaint. *Crawford v. Metropolitan Government of Nashville and Davidson County, Tennessee*, 129 S.Ct. 846 (2009).

Covered Workers

Title VII protects all prospective and current employees of a covered employer, including foreign nationals working for a covered employer, even if the employee is not authorized to work in the United States. Such an employee still has rights under Title VII, although his or her available remedies may be limited. For example, although reinstatement is a common remedy for an unlawfully fired employee, a foreign national may not be reinstated to a job in the United States if he or she is not authorized to work in the United States.

Title VII also protects U.S. citizens working outside the United States for employers that are incorporated in the United States, based in the United States, or controlled by a U.S. employer.

Did You Know ...

- Before it was passed in 1964, Title VII was the subject of the longest debate in Congressional history.
- Sexual harassment was not recognized as a form of sex discrimination until 1977—13 years after Congress passed Title VII.
- In 2011, retaliation was the single most common allegation in EEOC charges, more common than any type of discrimination. More than a third (37%) of all charges alleged retaliation. In 2009, more charges included retaliation claims than claims of race discrimination for the first time since the EEOC began keeping track; that trend continued in 2010 and 2011.

What's Prohibited

Title VII prohibits employers from discriminating against prospective and current employees on the basis of race, color, religion, sex, and national origin. (For detailed information about each, see "Protected Classes," below.)

Title VII was amended in 1978 to add pregnancy as a *protected class*. To learn more about pregnancy discrimination, see Chapter 15, which covers the Pregnancy Discrimination Act (PDA).

Title VII prohibits discrimination and *harassment* in all aspects of employment, including:

- hiring
- firing
- compensation and benefits
- job assignment
- employee classification
- transfer
- promotion
- layoff or recall
- training and apprenticeship programs
- use of company facilities
- retirement plans, and
- time off.

Title VII also prohibits employers from retaliating against those who complain or who otherwise assert their rights under the law. For example, an employer cannot fire someone for complaining about race discrimination. (For more, see "Retaliation," below.)

Key Facts

- Title VII prohibits employment discrimination and harassment based on race, color, religion, sex, and national origin.
- An employer may not retaliate (take adverse action) against a prospective or current employee who complains in good faith of discrimination or harassment, even if the original complaint itself is found to be baseless.
- Seemingly neutral employment policies that have a disproportionately negative impact on members of a protected class may violate Title VII, even if the employer did not intend to discriminate.

Discrimination

Unlawful discrimination includes the following practices:

- giving some people preferential treatment over others based on their membership in a protected class
- treating some people worse than others based on their membership in a protected class
- harassing people because of their membership in a protected class (see "Harassment," below)
- physically isolating or segregating employees because of their membership in a protected class
- coding resumes or employment applications to indicate race, color, gender, national origin, or religion
- asking questions in an interview to elicit information about an applicant's race, color, gender, national origin, or religion
- making decisions based on stereotypes about people of a protected class (for example, refusing to hire a woman as a police officer because of a belief that women are too emotional and not tough enough to do the job), and
- treating people differently because of their marriage to or association with members of a protected class (for example, refusing to hire a white man because he is married to an Asian American woman).

Title VII outlaws both intentional discrimination and practices that have a discriminatory effect even if the employer did not intend to discriminate. The discriminatory effect of neutral employment practices is called *disparate impact*, and it happens when a practice that seems neutral actually affects a protected class in a disproportionate and unfair way. Unless the employer has a legitimate and nondiscriminatory business reason for using that practice, the law will view that practice as unlawful. For example, if an employer refuses to hire people who don't meet minimum strength requirements, the employer could be discriminating against women, who will be disproportionately affected by this rule. The rule will pass legal muster only if the employer can show that it is clearly related to the physical demands of the particular job— heavy lifting in a warehouse, for example.

Harassment

Harassment occurs when employees are forced to endure a work environment that is hostile, intimidating, or offensive to them because of their membership in a protected class. Harassing acts can include:

- slurs
- offensive "jokes"
- offensive remarks based on a protected characteristic
- drawings or pictures that depict people with a protected characteristic in an unfavorable light
- threats
- intimidation
- hostile demeanor, and
- physical violence.

Sexual Harassment

Sexual harassment is a type of gender discrimination. It is unwelcome sexual conduct that is so severe or pervasive that it affects the terms and conditions of the victim's employment—either because the victim's submission or failure to submit to the behavior is the basis for job-related decisions (this is sometimes referred to as *quid pro quo* harassment) or because the victim reasonably finds the workplace intimidating, hostile, or abusive as a result of the harassment. Examples of sexual harassment include unwelcome sexual advances, fondling, requests for sexual favors, making sexual remarks or jokes, sending sexually explicit email messages, commenting on the employee's sex life, and posting pornographic images in the workplace.

The harasser can be the victim's supervisor, manager, or coworker. The harasser can even be a nonemployee—for example, a customer or vendor—if the person is on the premises with the employer's permission.

Both men and women can be sexual harassers, and both men and women can be the victims of sexual harassment. Women may sexually harass other women, and men may sexually harass other men. However, most allegations of sexual harassment are made by women against men.

Harassment based on gender can also constitute sexual harassment, even if it is not sexual in nature. In these cases, the harasser is not interested in having a sexual relationship with the victim or otherwise "sexualizing" the workplace with inappropriate jokes and comments, but instead wants to make the workplace hostile for workers of a particular gender (almost always women). The harassment in these claims, typically complained of by women working in traditionally male professions, might involve sabotaging the tools, vehicles, or work of female employees; defacing women's workspaces, lockers, or restroom facilities; subjecting women to dangerous working conditions; making comments about women's ability to do the job; or displaying cartoons or telling jokes that depict violence toward women.

Retaliation

An employer retaliates when it takes negative action against an employee for opposing harassment or discrimination—for example, by filing a complaint or giving evidence as a witness in a lawsuit, an administrative proceeding, or an internal investigation. Any action harmful enough to deter a reasonable worker from asserting his or her rights qualifies as illegal retaliation (see "Legal Developments," above).

Any action an employer or manager takes against an employee because that employee has made a complaint could conceivably be illegal retaliation, even if the employer did not intend to harm the employee. For example:

- A female employee complains that her supervisor is sexually harassing her. In response, the employer moves the employee who complained from the day shift to the night shift, so she doesn't have to work with that supervisor any more. Even though the employer didn't intend to hurt the employee, this action could be retaliatory if the employee preferred the day shift.
- An African American employee complains to his employer that the store in which he works is racially hostile toward him because his coworkers tell racial jokes and refer to him with racially derogatory names. In response, the employer transfers him to another store. This action could be retaliatory if the new store is farther from the employee's home or is less desirable in some other way.

Protected Classes

Race

Title VII doesn't only prohibit discrimination against specific races. It also forbids discriminating against people because they have certain physical characteristics associated with people of a certain race, such as skin color, hair texture, or other physical features.

Color

Discrimination based on color is prohibited by Title VII, even if that discrimination is not also race based. For example, it is illegal to favor a light-skinned employee over one with darker skin color, even if both employees are African American.

Religion

Title VII both prohibits employers from making decisions based on a person's religion and requires employers to make decisions based on a person's religion.

This seeming contradiction comes from the fact that religion is more than just a characteristic: It is also a set of practices and beliefs. The law prohibits employers from discriminating based on the fact of someone's religion (for example, because an employee is Jewish, Catholic, or Muslim), and it requires employers to make allowances for a person's religious practices and beliefs (for example, that an employee needs time after lunch to pray or needs Saturdays off to observe the Sabbath).

The first part is fairly simple. Employers can't refuse to hire someone because he or she is Jewish; they can't promote someone because he or she is Muslim. Employers must make those decisions for nondiscriminatory reasons.

The second part is more complicated. Employers must work with their employees to make it possible for the employees to practice their religious beliefs—within reason. This might mean agreeing not to schedule an employee to work on his or her Sabbath day or relaxing a dress code so that an employee can wear religious garments. In legal parlance, these allowances are called accommodations.

Employers must accommodate an employee's religious practice unless doing so would cause the business to suffer undue hardship. Although this term is used in other employment laws, such as the Americans with Disabilities Act (covered in Chapter 2) and the Uniformed Services Employment and Reemployment Rights Act (covered in Chapter 19), it is typically easier for an employer to show that a particular religious accommodation creates an undue hardship. For instance, an employer need not depart from its established seniority system to accommodate an employee's religious practice if doing so would deprive another employee of his or her rights under the system. Similarly, an employer doesn't have to pay more than minimal administrative costs—for example, the cost of adjusting its scheduling documents and payroll—to provide a religious accommodation.

National Origin

The prohibition against national origin discrimination generally means that employers cannot make employment decisions based on:

- birthplace
- ancestry
- culture
- native language
- English language proficiency (unless lack of proficiency affects the person's ability to perform the job)
- accent (unless it affects the person's ability to perform the job)
- marriage or association with people of a national ethnic group
- membership in or association with an ethnic cultural organization
- attendance or participation in schools, churches, temples, or mosques that are generally associated with a specific ethnic group, or
- a name that is associated with a specific ethnic group.

A rule requiring employees to speak only English at work may violate Title VII unless the employer can show that the rule is necessary for the safe or efficient operation of its business.

National origin and citizenship status discrimination is also prohibited by the federal Immigration Reform and Control Act (IRCA). (For more on IRCA, see Chapter 10.)

Sex

Title VII's prohibition against sex discrimination protects both men and women from discrimination and harassment based on gender. Title VII also prohibits discrimination against pregnant employees. (See Chapter 15 for information on the Pregnancy Discrimination Act, which amended Title VII to explicitly prohibit discrimination based on pregnancy and associated conditions.)

Sex discrimination includes decisions based on someone's failure to conform to gender stereotypes. For example, a restaurant may not refuse to hire a woman as a waitress or bartender because she isn't feminine enough. However, courts have upheld dress and grooming rules that require female employees to wear make-up and style their hair, as long as the rules have parallel dress and grooming requirements for men (for example, short hair styles, no facial hair, and trimmed fingernails). If dress codes and grooming rules impose greatly unequal burdens on either men or women, however, they may violate Title VII.

Title VII does not prohibit discrimination based on sexual orientation. However, many states have explicitly added this protection to their own fair employment laws. (See "State Antidiscrimination Laws," below, for information on the types of discrimination each state prohibits.)

What's Required

Employers must provide their employees with a workplace free of unlawful discrimination and harassment. This means that employers must act when they learn that an employee, customer, vendor, manager, or supervisor is discriminating against or harassing another employee or group of employees. Employers must take effective and immediate action to stop such conduct. This action might include investigating the situation and disciplining (up to and including firing) the offender.

Exceptions

In a very rare and narrow exception to Title VII, employers can discriminate against people on the basis of gender, religion, and national origin (but not race or color) if the very nature of the job requires them to do so. This rule, called the *bona fide occupational qualification (BFOQ)* exception, reflects Congress's recognition that some jobs must be filled by people who have certain characteristics—even though the law would ordinarily prohibit the employer from discriminating on that basis.

In order to use this exception, the employer must prove that the discriminatory policy is reasonably necessary to the operation of its business—in other words, that the essence of the operation would be undermined if the employer had to do away with its discriminatory policy. The employer must also show that there is no reasonable alternative to its policy.

Although it can be very hard to defend, there are times when an employer has no choice but to use the BFOQ exception. Sometimes this is necessary for reasons of authenticity. For example, a director casting the role of Hamlet's mother could refuse to consider men for the part. Sex-based BFOQ exceptions have also been allowed for positions like bathroom attendant and prison guard, on the grounds of protecting privacy.

How Title VII Is Enforced

Individual Complaints

A person may file a complaint (also called a charge) of discrimination, harassment, or retaliation with the U.S. Equal Employment Opportunity Commission (EEOC). (For contact information, see Appendix A.) The complaint must be filed with the EEOC within 300 days of the alleged incident in states that have an antidiscrimination law. In states without an antidiscrimination law, the complaint must be filed within 180 days of the incident. (To find out about your state's law, see "State Antidiscrimination Laws," below.)

Individuals may also file a lawsuit. However, they must first file a complaint with the EEOC or their state fair employment office (if their state has one), and then receive what is called a "right to sue" letter. Once they receive that letter, they have 90 days to file suit.

Agency Enforcement

The EEOC may act on its own initiative or after receiving a complaint. It has the authority to investigate a complaint, negotiate a settlement, mediate the complaint, and bring a suit in federal court. The EEOC also issues regulations and other forms of guidance interpreting Title VII. Even if an aggrieved employee has signed an arbitration agreement limiting his or her rights to sue, the EEOC may still sue on the employee's behalf.

Complying With Title VII

Reporting Requirements

Large private employers (those with 100 or more employees) and certain companies with federal contracts must file annual reports with the EEOC.

The requirements of these reports—called Standard Form 100, but commonly referred to as the EEO-1 Form—are beyond the scope of this chapter.

Posting Requirements

Employers must post a notice about federal laws prohibiting discrimination. The notices must be posted in locations easily accessible to employees. (For information on how to obtain a copy of the poster, see "Agency Resources," below.)

Record-Keeping Requirements

EEOC regulations require employers to keep personnel and employment records for at least one year. If an employer terminates someone's employment, the employer must keep that employee's records for a year after the termination.

Penalties

If an employer is found guilty of discrimination, harassment, or retaliation, the penalties might include the following:

- paying lost wages
- hiring the aggrieved employee(s)
- promoting the aggrieved employee(s)
- reinstating the aggrieved employee(s)
- paying for pain and suffering
- paying punitive damages (these damages are capped at an amount between $50,000 and $300,000, depending on the size of the employer; this cap includes any damages awarded for pain and suffering—in other words, the cap applies to the total combined punitive damages and damages for pain and suffering)
- providing a reasonable accommodation
- taking corrective and preventive measures to cure discrimination in the workplace, and/or
- paying attorneys' fees, expert witness fees, and court costs.

Agency Resources

The EEOC has a publications Web page from which you can download or order many informative publications in multiple languages. From this Web page, you can also order copies of any publications not available online. Among the publications included are fact sheets on all types of discrimination and the laws the EEOC enforces. Visit www.eeoc.gov for the complete list.

Employers must display a poster informing employees of their rights under federal antidiscrimination laws. The poster is available online at www.eeoc.gov/employers/poster.cfm.

State Antidiscrimination Laws

Almost every state has its own antidiscrimination law, and many of these laws are more restrictive than Title VII. For example, some state laws apply to smaller employers or prohibit additional types of discrimination. The chart below provides basic information on these state laws. If you need to know more, contact your state fair employment practices agency (see Appendix A for contact information).

State Laws Prohibiting Discrimination in Employment

Alabama

Ala. Code §§ 25-1-20, 25-1-21

Law applies to employers with: 20 or more employees

Private employers may not make employment decisions based on:
- Age (40 and older)

Alaska

Alaska Stat. §§ 18.80.220, 47.30.865

Law applies to employers with: One or more employees

Private employers may not make employment decisions based on:
- Age
- Ancestry or national origin
- Physical or mental disability
- AIDS/HIV
- Gender
- Marital status, including changes in status
- Pregnancy, childbirth, and related medical conditions, including parenthood
- Race or color
- Religion or creed
- Mental illness

Arizona

Ariz. Rev. Stat. §§ 41-1461, 41-1463, 41-1465

Law applies to employers with: 15 or more employees

Private employers may not make employment decisions based on:
- Age (40 and older)
- Ancestry or national origin
- Physical or mental disability
- AIDS/HIV
- Gender
- Race or color
- Religion or creed
- Genetic testing information

Arkansas

Ark. Code Ann. §§ 16-123-102, 16-123-107, 11-4-601, 11-5-403

Law applies to employers with: Nine or more employees

Private employers may not make employment decisions based on:
- Ancestry or national origin
- Physical, mental, or sensory disability
- Gender
- Pregnancy, childbirth, and related medical conditions
- Race or color
- Religion or creed
- Genetic testing information

California

Cal. Gov't. Code §§ 12920, 12926.1, 12940, 12941, 12945; Cal. Lab. Code § 1101

Law applies to employers with: Five or more employees

Private employers may not make employment decisions based on:
- Age (40 and older)
- Ancestry or national origin
- Physical or mental disability
- AIDS/HIV
- Gender
- Marital status
- Pregnancy, childbirth, and related medical conditions
- Race or color
- Religion or creed

State Laws Prohibiting Discrimination in Employment (continued)

- Sexual orientation
- Genetic testing information
- Gender identity
- Medical condition
- Political activities or affiliations

Colorado

Colo. Rev. Stat. §§ 24-34-301, 24-34-401, 24-34-402, 24-34-402.5, 27-65-115; Colo. Code Regs. 708-1:60.1, 708-1:80.8

Law applies to employers with: One or more employees

Private employers may not make employment decisions based on:

- Age (40 to 70)
- Ancestry or national origin
- Physical, mental, or learning disability
- AIDS/HIV
- Gender
- Pregnancy, childbirth, and related medical conditions
- Race or color
- Religion or creed
- Sexual orientation, including perceived sexual orientation
- Lawful conduct outside of work
- Mental illness
- Transgender status

Connecticut

Conn. Gen. Stat. Ann. §§ 46a-51, 46a-60, 46a-81a, 46a-81c, 25-4-1401

Law applies to employers with: Three or more employees

Private employers may not make employment decisions based on:

- Age
- Ancestry or national origin

- Present or past physical, mental, learning disability, or mental retardation
- AIDS/HIV
- Gender
- Marital status, including civil unions
- Pregnancy, childbirth, and related medical conditions
- Race or color
- Religion or creed
- Sexual orientation, including having a history of being identified with a preference
- Genetic testing information
- Gender identity or expression

Delaware

Del. Code Ann. tit. 19, §§ 710, 711, 724

Law applies to employers with: Four or more employees

Private employers may not make employment decisions based on:

- Age (40 and older)
- Ancestry or national origin
- Physical or mental disability
- Gender
- Marital status
- Pregnancy, childbirth, and related medical conditions
- Race or color
- Religion or creed
- Sexual orientation
- Genetic testing information

District of Columbia

D.C. Code Ann. §§ 2-1401.01, 2-1401.02, 2-1401.05, 2-1402.82, 7-1703.03, 32-131.08

Law applies to employers with: One or more employees

State Laws Prohibiting Discrimination in Employment (continued)

Private employers may not make employment decisions based on:
- Age (18 and older)
- Ancestry or national origin
- Physical or mental disability
- Gender
- Marital status, including domestic partnership
- Pregnancy, childbirth, and related medical conditions, including parenthood and breast-feeding
- Race or color
- Religion or creed
- Sexual orientation
- Genetic testing information
- Enrollment in vocational, professional, or college education
- Family duties
- Source of income
- Place of residence or business
- Personal appearance
- Political affiliation
- Victim of intrafamily offense
- Gender identity or expression
- Status as unemployed
- Any reason other than individual merit
- Tobacco use

Florida

Fla. Stat. Ann. §§ 760.01, 760.02, 760.10, 760.50, 448.075

Law applies to employers with: 15 or more employees

Private employers may not make employment decisions based on:
- Age
- Ancestry or national origin
- "Handicap"
- AIDS/HIV
- Gender
- Marital status
- Race or color
- Religion or creed
- Sickle cell trait

Georgia

Ga. Code Ann. §§ 34-1-2, 34-5-1, 34-5-2, 34-6A-1 and following, 45-19-20 and following

Law applies to employers with: 15 or more employees (disability); 10 or more employees (gender)

Private employers may not make employment decisions based on:
- Age (40 to 70)
- Ancestry or national origin
- Physical, mental, or learning disability or mental retardation
- Gender (wage discrimination only)
- Race or color
- Religion or creed
- Domestic and agricultural employees are not protected.

Hawaii

Haw. Rev. Stat. §§ 378-1, 378-2, 378-2.5; Hawaii Admin. Rules § 12-46-182

Law applies to employers with: One or more employees

Private employers may not make employment decisions based on:
- Age
- Ancestry or national origin
- Physical or mental disability
- AIDS/HIV
- Gender
- Marital status

State Laws Prohibiting Discrimination in Employment (continued)

- Pregnancy, childbirth, and related medical conditions, including breast-feeding
- Race or color
- Religion or creed
- Sexual orientation
- Genetic testing information
- Arrest and court record (unless there is a conviction directly related to job)
- Credit history or credit report, unless the information in the individual's credit history or credit report directly relates to a bona fide occupational qualification

Idaho

Idaho Code §§ 39-8303, 67-5902, 67-5909, 67-5910

Law applies to employers with: Five or more employees

Private employers may not make employment decisions based on:
- Age (40 and older)
- Ancestry or national origin
- Physical or mental disability
- Gender
- Pregnancy, childbirth, and related medical conditions
- Race or color
- Religion or creed
- Genetic testing information

Illinois

410 Ill. Comp. Stat. § 513/25; 775 Ill. Comp. Stat. §§ 5/1-102, 5/1-103, 5/1-105, 5/2-101, 5/2-102, 5/2-103; 820 Ill. Comp. Stat. §§ 105/4, 180/30; Ill. Admin. Code tit. 56, § 5210.110

Law applies to employers with: 15 or more employees; one or more employees (disability)

Private employers may not make employment decisions based on:
- Age (40 and older)
- Ancestry or national origin
- Physical or mental disability
- Gender
- Marital status
- Pregnancy, childbirth, and related medical conditions
- Race or color
- Religion or creed
- Sexual orientation
- Genetic testing information
- Citizenship status
- Military status
- Unfavorable military discharge
- Gender identity
- Arrest record
- Victims of domestic violence
- Order of protection status

Indiana

Ind. Code Ann. §§ 22-9-1-2, 22-9-2-1, 22-9-2-2, 22-9-5-1 and following

Law applies to employers with: Six or more employees

Private employers may not make employment decisions based on:
- Age (40 to 75—applies to employers with one or more employees)
- Ancestry or national origin
- Physical or mental disability (15 or more employees)
- Gender
- Race or color
- Religion or creed
- Off-duty tobacco use

State Laws Prohibiting Discrimination in Employment (continued)

Iowa

Iowa Code §§ 216.2, 216.6, 729.6, 216.6A

Law applies to employers with: Four or more employees

Private employers may not make employment decisions based on:
- Age (18 or older)
- Ancestry or national origin
- Physical or mental disability
- AIDS/HIV
- Gender
- Pregnancy, childbirth, and related medical conditions
- Race or color
- Religion or creed
- Sexual orientation
- Genetic testing information
- Gender identity
- Wage discrimination

Kansas

Kan. Stat. Ann. §§ 44-1002, 44-1009, 44-1112, 44-1113, 44-1125, 44-1126, 65-6002(e)

Law applies to employers with: Four or more employees

Private employers may not make employment decisions based on:
- Age (40 or older)
- Ancestry or national origin
- Physical or mental disability
- AIDS/HIV
- Gender
- Race or color
- Religion or creed
- Genetic testing information
- Military service or status

Kentucky

Ky. Rev. Stat. Ann. §§ 207.130, 207.135, 207.150, 342.197, 344.010, 344.030, 344.040

Law applies to employers with: Eight or more employees

Private employers may not make employment decisions based on:
- Age (40 or older)
- Ancestry or national origin
- Physical or mental disability
- AIDS/HIV
- Gender
- Pregnancy, childbirth, and related medical conditions
- Race or color
- Religion or creed
- Occupational pneumoconiosis with no respiratory impairment resulting from exposure to coal dust
- Off-duty tobacco use

Louisiana

La. Rev. Stat. Ann. §§ 23:301 to 23:368

Law applies to employers with: 20 or more employees

Private employers may not make employment decisions based on:
- Age (40 or older)
- Ancestry or national origin
- Physical or mental disability
- Gender
- Pregnancy, childbirth, and related medical conditions (applies to employers with 25 or more employees)
- Race or color
- Religion or creed
- Genetic testing information
- Sickle cell trait

State Laws Prohibiting Discrimination in Employment (continued)

Maine

Me. Rev. Stat. Ann. tit. 5, §§ 19302, 4552, 4553, 4571 to 4576, 23; tit. 26, § 833; tit. 39-A, § 353

Law applies to employers with: One or more employees

Private employers may not make employment decisions based on:

- Age
- Ancestry or national origin
- Physical or mental disability
- Gender
- Pregnancy, childbirth, and related medical conditions
- Race or color
- Religion or creed
- Sexual orientation, including perceived sexual orientation
- Genetic testing information
- Gender identity or expression
- Past workers' compensation claim
- Past whistle-blowing
- Medical support notice for child

Maryland

Md. Code, State Government, §§ 20-101, 20-601 to 20-608

Law applies to employers with: 15 or more employees

Private employers may not make employment decisions based on:

- Age
- Ancestry or national origin
- Physical or mental disability
- Gender
- Marital status
- Pregnancy, childbirth, and related medical conditions

- Race or color
- Religion or creed
- Sexual orientation
- Genetic testing information
- Civil Air Patrol membership

Massachusetts

Mass. Gen. Laws ch. 149 § 24A, ch. 151B, §§ 1, 4; Code of Massachusetts Regulations 804 CMR 3.01

Law applies to employers with: Six or more employees

Private employers may not make employment decisions based on:

- Age (40 or older)
- Ancestry or national origin
- Physical or mental disability
- Gender
- Marital status
- Race or color
- Religion or creed
- Sexual orientation
- Genetic testing information
- Military service
- Arrest record
- Gender identity

Michigan

Mich. Comp. Laws §§ 37.1103, 37.1201, 37.1202, 37.2201, 37.2202, 37.2205a, 750.556

Law applies to employers with: One or more employees

Private employers may not make employment decisions based on:

- Age
- Ancestry or national origin
- Physical or mental disability
- AIDS/HIV

State Laws Prohibiting Discrimination in Employment (continued)

- Gender
- Marital status
- Pregnancy, childbirth, and related medical conditions
- Race or color
- Religion or creed
- Genetic testing information
- Height or weight
- Misdemeanor arrest record

Minnesota

Minn. Stat. Ann. §§ 144.417, 181.81, 181.974, 363A.03, 363A.08

Law applies to employers with: One or more employees

Private employers may not make employment decisions based on:
- Age (18 to 70)
- Ancestry or national origin
- Physical, sensory, or mental disability
- Gender
- Marital status
- Pregnancy, childbirth, and related medical conditions
- Race or color
- Religion or creed
- Sexual orientation, including perceived sexual orientation
- Genetic testing information
- Gender identity
- Member of local commission
- Receiving public assistance

Mississippi

Miss. Code Ann. § 33-1-15

Law applies to employers with: One or more employees

Private employers may not make employment decisions based on:
- Military status
- No other protected categories unless employer receives public funding

Missouri

Mo. Rev. Stat. §§ 191.665, 213.010, 213.055, 375.1306

Law applies to employers with: Six or more employees

Private employers may not make employment decisions based on:
- Age (40 to 70)
- Ancestry or national origin
- Physical or mental disability
- AIDS/HIV
- Gender
- Race or color
- Religion or creed
- Genetic testing information

Montana

Mont. Code Ann. §§ 49-2-101, 49-2-303, 49-2-310

Law applies to employers with: One or more employees

Private employers may not make employment decisions based on:
- Age
- Ancestry or national origin
- Physical or mental disability
- Gender
- Marital status
- Pregnancy, childbirth, and related medical conditions
- Race or color
- Religion or creed

State Laws Prohibiting Discrimination in Employment (continued)

Nebraska

Neb. Rev. Stat. §§ 20-168, 48-236, 48-1001 to 48-1010, 48-1102, 48-1104

Law applies to employers with: 15 or more employees

Private employers may not make employment decisions based on:
- Age (40 or older—applies to employers with 20 or more employees)
- Ancestry or national origin
- Physical or mental disability
- AIDS/HIV
- Gender
- Marital status
- Pregnancy, childbirth, and related medical conditions
- Race or color
- Religion or creed
- Genetic testing information (applies to all employers)

Nevada

Nev. Rev. Stat. Ann. §§ 613.310 and following

Law applies to employers with: 15 or more employees

Private employers may not make employment decisions based on:
- Age (40 or older)
- Ancestry or national origin
- Physical or mental disability
- Gender
- Pregnancy, childbirth, and related medical conditions
- Race or color
- Religion or creed
- Sexual orientation, including perceived sexual orientation
- Genetic testing information
- Use of service animal
- Gender identity or expression
- Opposing unlawful employment practices

New Hampshire

N.H. Rev. Stat. Ann. §§ 141-H:3, 354-A:2, 354-A:6, 354-A:7

Law applies to employers with: Six or more employees

Private employers may not make employment decisions based on:
- Age
- Ancestry or national origin
- Physical or mental disability
- Gender
- Marital status
- Pregnancy, childbirth, and related medical conditions
- Race or color
- Religion or creed
- Sexual orientation
- Genetic testing information

New Jersey

N.J. Stat. Ann. §§ 10:5-1, 10:5-4.1, 10:5-5, 10:5-12, 10:5-29.1, 34:6B-1, 43:21-49

Law applies to employers with: One or more employees

Private employers may not make employment decisions based on:
- Age (18 to 70)
- Ancestry or national origin
- Past or present physical or mental disability
- AIDS/HIV
- Gender

State Laws Prohibiting Discrimination in Employment (continued)

- Marital status, including civil union or domestic partnership status
- Pregnancy, childbirth, and related medical conditions
- Race or color
- Religion or creed
- Sexual orientation, including affectional orientation and perceived sexual orientation
- Genetic testing information
- Atypical heredity cellular or blood trait
- Accompanied by service or guide dog
- Military service
- Gender identity
- Unemployed status

New Mexico

N.M. Stat. Ann. §§ 24-21-4, 28-1-2, 28-1-7, 50-4A-4; N.M. Admin Code 9.1.1

Law applies to employers with: Four or more employees

Private employers may not make employment decisions based on:
- Age (40 or older)
- Ancestry or national origin
- Physical or mental disability
- Gender
- Marital status (applies to employers with 50 or more employees)
- Pregnancy, childbirth, and related medical conditions
- Race or color
- Religion or creed
- Sexual orientation, including perceived sexual orientation (applies to employers with 15 or more employees)
- Genetic testing information

- Gender identity (employers with 15 or more employees)
- Serious medical condition
- Domestic abuse leave

New York

N.Y. Exec. Law §§ 292, 296; N.Y. Lab. Law § 201-d

Law applies to employers with: Four or more employees

Private employers may not make employment decisions based on:
- Age (18 and over)
- Ancestry or national origin
- Physical or mental disability
- Gender
- Marital status
- Pregnancy, childbirth, and related medical conditions
- Race or color
- Religion or creed
- Sexual orientation, including perceived sexual orientation
- Genetic testing information
- Lawful recreational activities when not at work
- Military status or service
- Observance of Sabbath
- Political activities
- Use of service dog
- Arrest or criminal accusation
- Domestic violence victim status

North Carolina

N.C. Gen. Stat. §§ 95-28.1, 95-28.1A, 127B-11, 130A-148, 143-422.2, 168A-5

Law applies to employers with: 15 or more employees

State Laws Prohibiting Discrimination in Employment (continued)

Private employers may not make employment decisions based on:
- Age
- Ancestry or national origin
- Physical or mental disability
- AIDS/HIV
- Gender
- Race or color
- Religion or creed
- Genetic testing information
- Military status or service
- Sickle cell or hemoglobin C trait

North Dakota

N.D. Cent. Code §§ 14-02.4-02, 14-02.4-03, 34-01-17

Law applies to employers with: One or more employees

Private employers may not make employment decisions based on:
- Age (40 or older)
- Ancestry or national origin
- Physical or mental disability
- Gender
- Marital status
- Pregnancy, childbirth, and related medical conditions
- Race or color
- Religion or creed
- Lawful conduct outside of work
- Receiving public assistance
- Keeping and bearing arms (as long as firearm is never exhibited on company property except for lawful defensive purposes)

Ohio

Ohio Rev. Code Ann. §§ 4111.17, 4112.01, 4112.02

Law applies to employers with: Four or more employees

Private employers may not make employment decisions based on:
- Age (40 or older)
- Ancestry or national origin
- Physical, mental, or learning disability
- Gender
- Pregnancy, childbirth, and related medical conditions
- Race or color
- Religion or creed
- Armed services
- Caring for a sibling, child, parent, or spouse injured while in the armed services

Oklahoma

Okla. Stat. Ann. tit. 25, §§ 1301, 1302; tit. 36, § 3614.2; tit. 40, § 500; tit. 44, § 208

Law applies to employers with: 15 or more employees

Private employers may not make employment decisions based on:
- Age (40 or older)
- Ancestry or national origin
- Physical, mental, or learning disability
- Gender
- Pregnancy, childbirth, and related medical conditions (except abortions where the woman is not in "imminent danger of death")
- Race or color
- Religion or creed

State Laws Prohibiting Discrimination in Employment (continued)

- Genetic testing information
- Military service

Oregon

Or. Rev. Stat. §§ 25-337, 659A.030, 659A.122 and following, 659A.303

Law applies to employers with: One or more employees

Private employers may not make employment decisions based on:
- Age (18 or older)
- Ancestry or national origin
- Physical or mental disability (applies to employers with 6 or more employees)
- Gender
- Marital status
- Pregnancy, childbirth, and related medical conditions
- Race or color
- Religion or creed
- Sexual orientation
- Genetic testing information
- Parent who has medical support order imposed by court
- Domestic violence victim status
- Refusal to attend an employer-sponsored meeting with the primary purpose of communicating the employer's opinion on religious or political matters
- Credit history

Pennsylvania

43 Pa. Cons. Stat. Ann. §§ 954–955

Law applies to employers with: Four or more employees

Private employers may not make employment decisions based on:
- Age (40 to 70)
- Ancestry or national origin
- Physical or mental disability
- Gender
- Pregnancy, childbirth, and related medical conditions
- Race or color
- Religion or creed
- Relationship or association with disabled person
- GED rather than high school diploma
- Use of service animal

Rhode Island

R.I. Gen. Laws §§ 12-28-10, 23-6.3-11, 28-5-6, 28-5-7, 28-6-18, 28-6.7-1

Law applies to employers with: Four or more employees; one or more employees (gender-based wage discrimination)

Private employers may not make employment decisions based on:
- Age (40 or older)
- Ancestry or national origin
- Physical or mental disability
- AIDS/HIV
- Gender
- Pregnancy, childbirth, and related medical conditions
- Race or color
- Religion or creed
- Sexual orientation, including perceived sexual orientation
- Genetic testing information
- Domestic abuse victim
- Gender identity or expression
- Homelessness

State Laws Prohibiting Discrimination in Employment (continued)

South Carolina

S.C. Code §§ 1-13-30, 1-13-80

Law applies to employers with: 15 or more employees

Private employers may not make employment decisions based on:
- Age (40 or older)
- Ancestry or national origin
- Physical or mental disability
- Gender
- Pregnancy, childbirth, and related medical conditions
- Race or color
- Religion or creed

South Dakota

S.D. Codified Laws Ann. §§ 20-13-1, 20-13-10, 60-2-20, 60-12-15, 62-1-17

Law applies to employers with: One or more employees

Private employers may not make employment decisions based on:
- Ancestry or national origin
- Physical or mental disability
- Gender
- Race or color
- Religion or creed
- Genetic testing information
- Preexisting injury

Tennessee

Tenn. Code Ann. §§ 4-21-102, 4-21-401 and following, 8-50-103, 50-2-201, 50-2-202

Law applies to employers with: Eight or more employees; one or more employees (gender-based wage discrimination)

Private employers may not make employment decisions based on:
- Age (40 or older)
- Ancestry or national origin
- Physical, mental, or visual disability
- Gender
- Pregnancy, childbirth, and related medical conditions (refer to chart on Family and Medical Leave)
- Race or color
- Religion or creed
- Use of guide dog
- Volunteer rescue squad worker responding to an emergency

Texas

Tex. Lab. Code Ann. §§ 21.002, 21.051, 21.082, 21.101, 21.106, 21.402

Law applies to employers with: 15 or more employees

Private employers may not make employment decisions based on:
- Age (40 or older)
- Ancestry or national origin
- Physical or mental disability
- Gender
- Pregnancy, childbirth, and related medical conditions
- Race or color
- Religion or creed
- Genetic testing information

Utah

Utah Code Ann. §§ 26-45-103, 34A-5-102, 34A-5-106

Law applies to employers with: 15 or more employees

State Laws Prohibiting Discrimination in Employment (continued)

Private employers may not make employment decisions based on:
- Age (40 or older)
- Ancestry or national origin
- Physical or mental disability
- AIDS/HIV
- Gender
- Pregnancy, childbirth, and related medical conditions
- Race or color
- Religion or creed
- Genetic testing information

Vermont

Vt. Stat. Ann. tit. 21, § 495, 495d; tit. 18, § 9333

Law applies to employers with: One or more employees

Private employers may not make employment decisions based on:
- Age (18 or older)
- Ancestry or national origin
- Physical, mental, or emotional disability
- AIDS/HIV
- Gender
- Race or color
- Religion or creed
- Sexual orientation
- Genetic testing information
- Gender identity
- Place of birth
- Credit report or credit history

Virginia

Va. Code Ann. §§ 2.2-3900, 2.2-3901, 40.1-28.6, 40.1-28.7:1, 51.5-41

Law applies to employers with: One or more employees

Private employers may not make employment decisions based on:
- Age
- Ancestry or national origin
- Physical or mental disability
- Gender
- Marital status
- Pregnancy, childbirth, and related medical conditions
- Race or color
- Religion or creed
- Genetic testing information

Washington

Wash. Rev. Code Ann. §§ 38.40.110, 49.44.180, 49.60.040, 49.60.172, 49.60.180, 49.12.175, 49.44.090, 49.76.120, 49.60.030; Wash. Admin. Code § 162-30-020

Law applies to employers with: Eight or more employees; one or more employees (gender-based wage discrimination)

Private employers may not make employment decisions based on:
- Age (40 or older)
- Ancestry or national origin
- Physical, mental, or sensory disability
- AIDS/HIV
- Gender
- Marital status
- Pregnancy, childbirth, and related medical conditions, including breast-feeding
- Race or color
- Religion or creed
- Sexual orientation
- Genetic testing information
- Hepatitis C infection
- Member of state militia

State Laws Prohibiting Discrimination in Employment (continued)

- Use of service animal
- Gender identity
- Domestic violence victim

West Virginia

W.Va. Code §§ 5-11-3, 5-11-9, 16-3C-3, 21-5B-1, 21-5B-3

Law applies to employers with: 12 or more employees; one or more employees (gender-based wage discrimination)

Private employers may not make employment decisions based on:
- Age (40 or older)
- Ancestry or national origin
- Physical or mental disability, or blindness
- AIDS/HIV
- Gender
- Race or color
- Religion or creed

Wisconsin

Wis. Stat. Ann. §§ 111.32 and following

Law applies to employers with: One or more employees

Private employers may not make employment decisions based on:
- Age (40 or older)
- Ancestry or national origin
- Physical or mental disability
- Gender

- Marital status
- Pregnancy, childbirth, and related medical conditions
- Race or color
- Religion or creed
- Sexual orientation, including having a history of or being identified with a preference
- Genetic testing information
- Arrest or conviction record
- Member of National Guard/state defense force/military reserve
- Declining to attend a meeting or to participate in any communication about religious matters or political matters

Wyoming

Wyo. Stat. §§ 27-9-102, 27-9-105, 19-11-104

Law applies to employers with: Two or more employees

Private employers may not make employment decisions based on:
- Age (40 or older)
- Ancestry or national origin
- Disability
- Gender
- Pregnancy, childbirth, and related medical conditions
- Race or color
- Religion or creed
- Military service or status

Uniformed Services Employment and Reemployment Rights Act (USERRA)

Statute: 42 U.S.C. § 2000e

http://uscode.house.gov/download/pls/42C21.txt

Regulations: 29 C.F.R. §§ 1600–1609

www.gpo.gov/fdsys/pkg/CFR-2012-title29-vol4/pdf/CFR-2012-title29-vol4-subtitleB-chapXIV.pdf

Overview of USERRA

Since 1940, federal law has guaranteed certain employment rights to workers who are in the *uniformed services*. In 1994, following the Persian Gulf War, Congress substantially revised this law, now called the Uniformed Services Employment and Reemployment Rights Act (USERRA). The law includes provisions on:

- **Antidiscrimination.** Employers may not discriminate against members of the uniformed services.
- **Reinstatement.** Employers must reinstate employees upon their return from up to five years of leave for *service in the uniformed services*.
- **Benefits.** Employers must restore all benefits to returning servicemembers. For purposes of benefit eligibility, accrual of seniority-based benefits, and vesting (that is, rules providing that employees are not entitled to collect or use benefits until they have worked for a certain period of time), time spent on leave for service in the uniformed services must be treated as time worked.
- **Job security.** Employers may not fire returning service members except for *cause* for up to one year after they return from military duty.

Definitions

Cause A legitimate, nondiscriminatory reason for firing or laying off an employee. There are two types of cause recognized by USERRA: misconduct by the employee (stealing from the employer, for example) and legitimate business reasons unrelated to the employee's military service (such as companywide layoffs).

Escalator position The position an employee would have attained had he or she not taken time off to serve in the *uniformed services*. The escalator position includes any promotions, pay raises, increased responsibilities, and other benefits the employee ordinarily would have attained; it could also include demotion, transfer, or layoff, if those events would have occurred if the employee had not taken leave.

Service in the uniformed services Voluntary or involuntary performance of duties in the *uniformed services*, including:
- active duty

Definitions (continued)

- active duty for training
- initial active duty for training
- inactive duty training
- full-time National Guard duty
- absence for an examination to determine a worker's fitness for any of the above types of duty
- funeral honors duty performed by National Guard or reserve members, or
- service as an intermittent, disaster response appointee of the National Disaster Medical System, when federally activated or attending authorized training.

We sometimes refer to this as "military service."

Successor employer A company that takes over or acquires the company for which the employee worked.

Undue hardship An action requiring significant difficulty or expense for the employer, in light of:

- the nature and cost of the action
- the overall financial resources of the particular facility where the action would be taken
- the number of workers at the facility
- how the action would affect the facility's operation, including expenses and resources
- the overall financial resources and size of the employer, including the location, number, and nature of its facilities, and
- the type of operations in which the employer engages.

Uniformed services The following branches of the U. S. military:

- Army
- Navy
- Marine Corps
- Air Force
- Coast Guard
- Reserves
- Army or Air National Guard, and
- Commissioned Corps of the Public Health Service.

Regulated Employers

USERRA covers all employers of all sizes, including:
- all private employers, including foreign employers doing business in the United States
- American businesses that operate either directly or through an entity under their control in a foreign county (unless complying with USERRA would violate the laws of that country)
- hiring halls operated by a union or an employer association, if they perform hiring and job assignment functions for the employer
- the federal government, and
- state and local governments.

USERRA also covers *successor employers*. If a company takes over another company through a merger or an acquisition, for example, the new company may be considered a successor to the former employer and have to comply with USERRA for employees of the former employer. This issue typically comes up when the original employer is acquired while an employee is serving in the military: If the new company is a successor employer, it will have to reinstate the employee according to USERRA's provisions. Whether a company is a successor depends on:
- whether there is substantial continuity in business operations from the former to the current employer
- whether the current employer uses the same or similar facilities, machinery, equipment, and methods of production
- whether the current employer uses many of the same employees, managers, and/or supervisors
- whether the jobs and working conditions are similar, and
- whether the products or services offered are similar.

Covered Workers

Everyone who performs or has performed service in the uniformed services has USERRA rights. However, only a person who is employed, was employed, or seeks initial employment as an applicant can invoke those rights. A company does not have USERRA obligations to those who perform services for the company as independent contractors.

Legal Developments

- **Time served is time worked.** The Department of Labor has issued guidance on the effect of military leave on an employee's rights under the Family and Medical Leave Act (FMLA). (See Chapter 8 for more information on the FMLA.) Because time an employee spends on military leave must be counted as hours worked for purposes of eligibility for and accrual of benefits (see "Benefits," below), such time also must be counted as hours worked for purposes of coverage under the FMLA.

- **Courts are enforcing arbitration agreements for USERRA claims.** Several federal courts have found that employers can compel arbitration of USERRA claims if the employee has signed a valid arbitration agreement. In these cases, the employees had signed agreements to arbitrate employment-related disputes rather than taking them to court. The courts in these cases generally found that requiring employees to arbitrate these claims did not violate their rights under USERRA, but instead merely required them to submit disputes over those rights to a different forum (that is, to an arbitrator rather than a federal court). (See, for example, *Landis v. Pinnacle Eye Care, LLC*, 537 F.3d 559 (6th Cir. 2008); *Garrett v. Circuit City Stores, Inc.*, 449 F.3d 672 (5th Cir. 2006).)

- **No USERRA amendments so far.** In each of the last three Congressional sessions, the Servicemembers Access to Justice Act has been introduced. Among other things, the act would prohibit predispute arbitration agreements of USERRA claims, increase the damages available to employees who win USERRA claims, clarify who counts as a successor employer, and make clear that USERRA prohibits wage discrimination. So far, however, the act hasn't made it out of committee in either the House or Senate. If a later Congress succeeds in passing the act, President Obama is likely to sign: He was one of the original sponsors of the act in the Senate in 2008.

An employee's entitlement to the protections of USERRA's various provisions depends on several factors, including length of military service. For details, see "Major Provisions of USERRA," below.

An employee's entitlement to the reinstatement, benefits, and job security rights provided by USERRA terminates if the employee:

- is separated from a uniformed service under other than honorable conditions (such as a dishonorable discharge, a bad conduct discharge, or an "other than honorable" discharge), or
- in the case of a commissioned officer, is dropped from the military rolls because of an absence without authority of more than three months or imprisonment by a civilian court, is dismissed from the uniformed service in a court martial, or is dismissed by order of the president in time of war.

Did You Know ...

- As of 2011, half of our country's total military power comes from the Guard and reserves.
- According to a 2012 report to Congress, more than 1,500 USERRA claims were reviewed by the DOL in 2011. However, many more problems were handled informally: The Employer Support for the Guard and Reserve (ESGR), a Department of Defense organization, reported that it received more than 29,000 contacts regarding USERRA in the same time frame, and that 2,884 of those contacts turned into USERRA cases for which ESGR provided ombudsmen services.
- The same 2012 report reveals that the vast majority of USERRA complaints reviewed by the DOL involved discrimination based on the employee's military obligations.

Major Provisions of USERRA

Antidiscrimination

Employers may not discriminate against members of the uniformed services or retaliate against workers who exercise their rights under USERRA.

Key Facts: Antidiscrimination

- Members of the military and those who take leave under USERRA are protected from employment discrimination.
- Employers may not take adverse action against an employee for exercising his or her rights under USERRA or participating in a USERRA investigation or enforcement proceeding.

Regulated Employers

All regulated employers are subject to this provision.

Covered Workers

All members of, and applicants for membership in, the uniformed services are covered by this provision. In addition, any person who participates in a proceeding to enforce USERRA rights (a witness in an investigation, a hearing, or a lawsuit, for example) is protected from retaliation, whether or not the person is a member of the uniformed services.

What's Prohibited

Employers may not take any negative job action against an employee or job applicant based on that person's membership, or application for membership, in the uniformed services. Negative job actions include:
- firing
- demoting
- reducing pay or benefits

- transferring, and
- refusing to hire.

Employers also may not retaliate (by taking any negative job action, as described above) against any person who:

- takes action to enforce USERRA rights
- testifies or makes a statement in connection with any USERRA enforcement proceeding
- participates in an investigation of a USERRA violation, or
- exercises his or her rights under USERRA.

Reinstatement

Employers must reinstate employees upon their return from up to five years of leave for service in the uniformed services.

Key Facts: Reinstatement

- Employers must reinstate returning servicemembers to the positions they would have held had they been not been on leave, unless the employers' circumstances have changed so much that reemployment is impossible or unreasonable.
- If an employee is not qualified for an escalator position, the employer must make reasonable efforts to help the employee qualify. If these efforts fail, the employer may reinstate the employee to the position he or she held before taking leave for military service.
- An employer must reinstate an employee only if the employee:
  - notifies the employer that the leave was for military service
  - spends no more than five years, total, on leave (with a few exceptions)
  - is released from military service under honorable conditions, and
  - reports back to work within specified time limits.

Regulated Employers

All regulated employers are subject to these provisions.

Covered Workers

Reinstatement rights are available only to employees who have been absent from employment due to service in the uniformed services. In addition, employees are eligible for reinstatement only if all of the following are true:

- The employee gave the employer notice, before taking leave, that the leave was for military service. This notice may be oral or written. If military necessity prevented the employee from giving notice or it was otherwise impossible or unreasonable to give notice under the circumstances (for example, because the employee was ordered to report for service immediately), this requirement doesn't apply.
- The employee spent no more than five years, cumulatively, on leave for military service. This time limit may be extended in some circumstances. (See "Exceptions," below.)
- The employee was released from military service under honorable conditions.
- The employee reports back or applies for reinstatement within specified time limits. These limits vary depending on the length of the employee's leave and whether the employee suffered or aggravated a disability while serving. (See "What's Required," below.)

What's Required

An employer must reinstate workers who have taken up to a total of five years of leave from a position with that employer to serve in the uniformed services. Reinstated employees are entitled to be returned to the "escalator position": the position they would have held had they been continuously employed. They are entitled to any promotions, raises, and other seniority-based benefits they would have received had they not taken leave. (See "Benefits," below.)

The employee is not entitled to be placed in a better position than he or she would have had if he or she had not taken leave. If, for example, an employer transfers the employee's entire department to another facility while the employee is on leave, the employee is entitled only to that transferred position; the employee is not entitled to be reinstated at the original facility while the rest of the department works elsewhere.

Returning employees are entitled to "prompt" reinstatement. The DOL interprets this to mean that employees must be reinstated within two weeks of the employee's application for reemployment, absent unusual circumstances. What constitutes prompt reinstatement will depend on the circumstances, such as how long the employee has been gone, whether the employee's return date was known to the employer, what staffing or other changes will be required to reinstate the employee, and so on.

Reinstatement of an Unqualified Worker

If the worker is not qualified for the *escalator position*, the employer must make reasonable efforts to help the employee qualify (by offering training, for example). If the employee still isn't qualified, the employer's obligations depend on the length of the employee's service:

- If the employee served for up to 90 days, the employer may reinstate him or her to the position held prior to starting military service.
- If the employee served for more than 90 days, the employer may reinstate him or her to either the position held prior to starting military service or a position that nearly approximates the previously held position.

Time Limits for Reinstatement

Absent unusual circumstances, the employer must reemploy a returning servicemember within two weeks after he or she applies for reinstatement. The time limits for reporting back or applying for reinstatement depend on how long the worker was out on leave:

- **Workers who were on leave for 30 or fewer days** must report back on the first regularly scheduled workday after their service is complete, allowing for safe transportation home and an additional eight-hour period.
- **Workers who were on leave for more than 30 but fewer than 181 days** must submit an application for reemployment within 14 days of completing their service. If it is impossible or unreasonable for the employee to report within 14 days, through no fault of his or her own, the employee must report for work on the next calendar day when it becomes possible to do so.
- **Workers who were on leave for more than 181 days** must submit a written or oral application for reemployment within 90 days after their period of service is complete.

- **Workers who are injured or become ill while performing service** must report to the employer or submit an application for reemployment once they have recovered. This recovery period may not exceed two years.

Documentation

If an employee served for more than 30 days, the employer can ask the employee to provide documents showing that:
- The employee's application for reinstatement is timely.
- The employee's service did not exceed the five-year limit.
- The employee was separated or discharged from service under honorable conditions.

However, the employee's inability to provide this documentation doesn't relieve the employer of the obligation to return the employee to work. The employer must reinstate the employee pending availability of these documents. If the documents don't exist, the employee needn't provide them. If, however, documentation later becomes available showing that the employee didn't meet one or more of the requirements for reinstatement, the employer may fire the employee.

Exceptions

Exceptions to the Reinstatement Right

An employer does not have to reinstate an employee in any of the following situations:
- The employer's circumstances have changed so much that reemployment is impossible or unreasonable.
- The job was for a brief, nonrecurrent period, and the worker had no reasonable expectation that the job would continue indefinitely or for a significant length of time.
- The employee is not qualified for the position and helping the employee qualify for reinstatement would impose an *undue hardship* on the employer.

Exceptions to the Five-Year Service Limit

An employee who takes more than a total of five years of leave is still entitled to reinstatement if:

- The employee's initial service obligation exceeds five years. (For example, some military specialties require members to serve an initial term of more than five years.)
- The employee is unable to obtain a release from duty within five years. (This exception applies to service members who are involuntarily retained on active duty after their initial service obligation ends.)
- The employee takes time off for reserve or National Guard training, or for other training as determined and certified by a proper military authority as necessary to complete skill training, for retraining, or for the employee's professional development. This training does not count toward the five-year limit.
- The employee is ordered to remain or go on active duty during a domestic emergency, a national security situation, or a war or national emergency declared by the president or Congress.
- The employee performs service while ordered to, or retained on, active duty in the following capacities:
  - involuntary active duty by a military retiree or retired Coast Guard member
  - retention on active duty while held captive
  - involuntary active duty of a critical person in a time of crisis
  - voluntary active duty by a retired Coast Guard officer or enlistee
  - involuntary active duty by the Coast Guard reserves during disasters, or
  - involuntary retention of Coast Guard members on active duty.
- The employee volunteers for active duty in support of an operational mission for which members of the Selected Reserve have been involuntarily ordered to active duty. (Examples of this exception are workers who volunteered to support operational missions in Bosnia.)
- The employee volunteers for active duty in support of a critical mission or requirement (as certified by the secretary of the uniformed service involved), when no war or national emergency has been declared and no involuntary call-up is in effect.
- The employee is a member of the National Guard called into federal service by the president to suppress an insurrection, repel an invasion, or execute the laws of the United States.

Benefits

Employers must make certain employment benefits available to workers who take leave for service in the uniformed services. In addition, returning workers are entitled to have their benefits restored.

Key Facts: Benefits

- Employers are required to provide health insurance continuation for up to 24 months while an employee is on leave.
- Employees on leave are entitled to the same benefits that are provided to employees who take a leave of absence for other reasons.
- An employee who returns from military leave is entitled to the seniority and all rights and benefits based on seniority that he or she would have accrued if not for taking leave.
- An employee who has been on leave must be allowed to make up any missed employee contributions to a pension plan. An employer must match these contributions to the same extent that it matches contributions from other employees, and must make any required contributions for the period when the employee was on leave.

Regulated Employers

All regulated employers are subject to these provisions.

Covered Workers

Workers who take leave from work for service in the uniformed services are eligible for benefits continuation while on leave. Only workers who are entitled to reinstatement following service in the uniformed services are eligible for benefits reinstatement. (See "Reinstatement," above.)

What's Required

Benefits During Leave

While a worker is on leave, the employer has the following obligations, depending on the type of benefit:

- **Health insurance.** Employers must continue to provide health insurance for up to 24 months after a worker goes on leave for service in the uniformed services. If the worker is absent for up to 30 days, the employer may not require the worker to pay more than the usual employee share (if any) for such coverage. If the worker is absent for more than 30 days, the employer may require the worker to pay up to 102% of the full premium for such coverage.
- **Paid time off.** Employers must allow servicemembers to use accrued vacation time for military service. However, an employer may not require a servicemember to use vacation time for this purpose.
- **Other benefits.** The employer must give the worker the same benefits that are generally provided to a worker in a similar position who takes a leave of absence. If such workers are required to continue to pay the employee cost of a funded benefit, workers on leave for military service may also be required to pay.

Benefits After Reinstatement

Once a worker is reinstated following leave for service in the uniformed services, all benefits must be restored. Additional obligations depend on the type of benefit.

Health Insurance. If the worker's health insurance coverage was terminated while he or she was on leave, this coverage must be reinstated without an exclusion or a waiting period for the worker and any others (spouse and dependents, for example) covered under the worker's insurance. However, the health plan can impose an exclusion or a waiting period as to illnesses or injuries that the Secretary of Veterans Affairs office determines were caused or aggravated by the employee's military service.

Seniority-Based Benefits. Reinstated workers are entitled to the seniority, and any rights and benefits based on seniority, that they would have attained had they been continuously employed. For example, time the employee spent on leave must be counted as time worked for purposes of determining whether the employee is eligible for FMLA leave. (For more on the FMLA's eligibility requirements, see Chapter 8.)

Benefits Not Based on Seniority. A reinstated worker is entitled to the same benefits not based on seniority that are generally provided to employees who take a leave of absence for nonmilitary reasons.

Pension Plans. USERRA provides detailed rules for the treatment of pension plans. A reinstated worker's time on leave must not be treated as a break in service for purposes of an employer-maintained pension plan. For purposes of vesting and benefit accrual, time the worker spends in military service and any time the worker is legally allowed to take off before applying for reinstatement must be considered service with the employer.

If the employee is not required or permitted to contribute to the pension plan (that is, if the plan is funded entirely by the employer), the employer must contribute the amount attributable to the time the employee spent on leave not later than 90 days after the employee is reinstated or when contributions are ordinarily made for the years in which the employee was on leave, whichever is later.

The employee must be allowed to make up any employee contributions he or she missed because of service in the uniformed services, and the employer must match these contributions to the same extent it matches contributions by other employees. The worker has up to three times the length of his or her military service, or five years, whichever is shorter, to make these contributions. If the employee received a distribution from the plan while on leave, the employee must be allowed to repay this amount, with interest.

Job Security

Employers may not fire an employee, except for *cause*, for up to one year after he or she returns to work after service in the uniformed services. The length of time of the job security provision depends on the length of the employee's military service.

Key Facts: Job Security

- Employers must have cause to fire an employee for a limited time after he or she returns from military service. An employer may fire an employee during this protected period, but the employer must show that it had cause to terminate the worker's employment, that it acted reasonably, and that the employee had notice that his or her conduct was cause for discharge.
- Employees are entitled to this protection only if they served for at least 31 days in the uniformed services. Employees who served for up to 180 days are protected from being fired at will for 180 days after returning to work; employees with longer terms of service are protected for one year after returning to work.

Regulated Employers

All regulated employers are subject to these provisions.

Covered Workers

Only employees who served for at least 31 days in the uniformed services are covered by the job protection provision.

What's Prohibited

Employers are prohibited from firing an employee who returns to work after service in the uniformed services, except for cause, for:

- 180 days after the worker is reinstated, if the worker served in the uniformed services for 31 to 180 days, or
- one year after the worker is reinstated, if the worker served in the uniformed services for more than 180 days.

During USERRA's required period of job security, an employer who fires a protected employee must show that the discharge was reasonable and that the employee had notice that his or her conduct was cause for discharge. The employer bears the burden of proving that it acted legally.

How USERRA Is Enforced

Individual Complaints

An employee whose USERRA rights have been violated has several choices. The employee may try to resolve the problem informally, with the assistance of the Department of Defense's Employer Support for the Guard and Reserve (ESGR) ombudsmen services. The ESGR offers information and mediation services to assist the employer and employee in resolving disputes.

The employee may also file a complaint with the Veterans Employment and Training Service (VETS), an agency within the Department of Labor, which will investigate and attempt to resolve the complaint. (For information on contacting VETS, see Appendix A.)

An employee does not have to complain to the ESGR or VETS, however. The employee can go directly to federal district court and file a lawsuit against the employer. USERRA has no statute of limitations; this means that, in theory at least, employees may file a lawsuit no matter how much time has passed since their employer violated USERRA. However, some courts have applied a four-year statute of limitations to USERRA claims. Also, if the employee unreasonably delays bringing a lawsuit, and this delay prejudices the employer's ability to defend itself, a judge might throw out the case.

Agency Enforcement

VETS has the authority to investigate complaints of USERRA violations. Once it has investigated, it will attempt to resolve the complaint. However, VETS cannot force an employer to comply with the law, nor can it impose penalties or fines on an employer that refuses to comply. If VETS's efforts at resolution are unsuccessful, it will inform the complaining employee, in writing, of the results of the investigation and of the employee's right to continue to press the complaint.

If VETS has investigated and unsuccessfully attempted to resolve a USERRA complaint, an employee can either file a lawsuit or ask VETS to refer the complaint to the U.S. attorney general's office.

If the attorney general's office decides that the complaint has merit, a lawyer from that office may bring a lawsuit against the employer to enforce the complaining employee's USERRA rights. If the attorney general's office decides not to take the case, the employee can still file a private lawsuit.

Complying With USERRA

Deadlines

Many of USERRA's deadlines apply to employees only—for example, the requirement that employees must report or return to work within a specified time (see "Reinstatement," above) and make up missed pension plan contributions within a specific timeframe.

Here are the deadlines that apply to employers:

- Employers generally must reemploy returning service members within *two weeks* after the employee reports or applies for reinstatement.
- Employers must make up their contributions to a pension plan for the period the employee spent in military service within *90 days* after the employee is reinstated or by the deadline for making contributions for the years when the employee was serving in the military, whichever is later.

Reporting Requirements

USERRA imposes no reporting requirements.

Posting Requirements

Employers are required to notify employees of their USERRA rights. They can meet this obligation by posting a notice created by the Department of Labor. (See "Agency Resources," below, for information on getting this poster.)

Record-Keeping Requirements

USERRA does not require employers to keep any particular records.

Penalties

Employers who violate USERRA may be required to:

- comply with the law (for example, by reinstating a worker or restoring a worker's benefits)
- pay the worker for any benefits or wages lost because of the employer's violation, and
- pay the worker's attorneys' fees and court costs.

If a court finds that the employer knew, or should have known, that its acts were against the law, the employer can also be ordered to pay twice the amount of the worker's lost benefits and wages.

Agency Resources

- A directory of VETS offices nationwide

    VETS Staff Directory

    www.dol.gov/vets/aboutvets/contacts/main.htm

- A fact sheet about USERRA's basic provisions

    Employment Law Guide: Uniformed Service Members

    www.dol.gov/compliance/guide/userra.htm

- An interactive guide to USERRA

    Elaws—USERRA Advisor

    www.dol.gov/elaws/userra.htm

- The USERRA poster

    Your Rights Under USERRA

    www.dol.gov/vets/programs/userra/USERRA_Poster.pdf

State Laws Relating to Military Service

Many states have laws that protect employees who take time off to serve in the state National Guard or militia. Some of these laws are similar to USERRA, in that they provide a right to reinstatement and prohibit discrimination against those in the military. Others provide additional rights, such as a minimum number of days off per year to attend training or educational activities.

The chart below provides some basic information about these state laws. If you need more information, contact your state labor department (you can find contact information in Appendix A).

State Laws on Military Leave

Alabama

Alabama Stat. §§ 31-12-1 to 31-12-4

Alabama National Guard members called to active duty for at least 30 consecutive days or for federally funded duty for service other than training have the same leave and reinstatement rights and benefits guaranteed under USERRA.

Alaska

Alaska Stat. § 26.05.075

Employees called to active service in the state militia are entitled to unlimited unpaid leave and reinstatement to their former or a comparable position, with the pay, seniority, and benefits the employee would have had if not absent for service. Employee must return to work on next workday, after time required for travel. Disabled employee must request reemployment within 30 days of release; if disability leaves the employee unable to do the job, employee must be offered a position with similar pay and benefits.

Arizona

Ariz. Rev. Stat. §§ 26-167, 26-168

Members of the National Guard, Arizona National Guard, and U.S. armed forces reserves called to active duty have the same leave and reinstatement rights and benefits guaranteed under USERRA. Members of the National Guard called to participate in maneuvers or drills are entitled to unlimited unpaid leave and reinstatement to their former or a higher position with the same seniority and vacation benefits. Employer may not dissuade employees from enlisting in state or national military forces by threatening economic reprisal.

Arkansas

Ark. Code Ann. § 12-62-413

Employees called to active state duty as a member of the armed forces (which includes the National Guard and other types of armed forces) of Arkansas or any other state have the same leave and reinstatement rights and benefits guaranteed under USERRA.

California

Cal. Mil. & Vet. Code §§ 394, 394.5, 395.06

Members of the California National Guard called to active duty are entitled to unlimited unpaid leave and reinstatement to their former position or to a position of similar seniority, status, and pay without loss of retirement or other benefits, unless the employer's circumstances have so changed as to make reinstatement impossible or unreasonable. Employee must apply for reinstatement within 40 days of discharge, and cannot be terminated without cause for one year. Employees in the U.S. armed forces reserves, National Guard, or Naval Militia are entitled to 17 days' unpaid leave per year for training or special exercises. Employer may not terminate employee or limit any benefits or seniority because of a temporary disability resulting from duty in the National Guard or Naval Militia (up to 52 weeks). Employer cannot discriminate against employee because of membership in the military services.

Colorado

Colo. Rev. Stat. §§ 28-3-609, 28-3-610.5

Employees who are members of

State Laws on Military Leave (continued)

Colorado National Guard or U.S. armed forces reserves are entitled to 15 days' unpaid leave per year for training and reinstatement to their former or a similar position with the same status, pay, and seniority. Employees called to active service in the Colorado National Guard are entitled to unlimited unpaid leave and reinstatement to their former or comparable position, with the pay, seniority, and benefits the employee would have had if not absent for service.

Connecticut

Conn. Gen. Stat. Ann. §§ 27-33a, 27-34a

Members of the Connecticut National Guard ordered into active duty are entitled to the same rights and benefits guaranteed under USERRA, except those pertaining to life insurance. Employees who are members of the military are entitled to take leave to attend military reserve or National Guard meetings or drills that take place during regular work hours, without loss or reduction of vacation or holiday benefits. Employer may not discriminate in terms of promotion or continued employment.

Delaware

Del. Code Ann. tit. 20 § 905

National Guard members who are called to state active duty shall be entitled to the same rights, privileges, and protections as they would have had if called for military training under federal law protecting reservists and National Guard members.

Florida

Fla. Stat. Ann. §§ 250.482, 627.6692(5)

Employees who are members of the Florida National Guard and are called into active duty may not be penalized for absence from work. Employees not covered by COBRA whose employment is terminated while on active duty are entitled to a new 18-month benefit period beginning when active duty or job ends, whichever is later. Upon return from service, employee is entitled to reinstatement with full benefits unless employer's circumstances have changed to make reinstatement impossible or unreasonable or impose an undue hardship. Employee cannot be terminated without cause for one year after reinstatement.

Georgia

Ga. Code Ann. § 38-2-280

Members of U.S. uniformed services or Georgia National Guard called into active federal or state service are entitled to unlimited unpaid leave for active service and up to 6 months' leave in any 4-year period for service school or annual training. Employee is entitled to reinstatement with full benefits unless employer's circumstances have changed to make reinstatement impossible or unreasonable. Employee must apply for reinstatement within 90 days of discharge or within 10 days of completing school or training.

Hawaii

Haw. Rev. Stat. § 121-43

Members of the National Guard are entitled to unlimited unpaid leave and reinstatement to the same or a position comparable in seniority, status, and pay.

State Laws on Military Leave (continued)

If an employee is not qualified for his or her former position because of a disability sustained during service but is qualified for any other position, the employee is entitled to the position that is most similar to his or her former position, unless employer's circumstances have changed to make reinstatement impossible or unreasonable. Employee cannot be terminated without cause for one year after reinstatement. Employer cannot discriminate against employee because of any obligation as a member of the National Guard.

Idaho

Idaho Code §§ 46-224, 46-225, 46-407

Members of Idaho National Guard or National Guard of another state ordered to active duty may take up to one year of unpaid leave and are entitled to reinstatement to former position or a comparable position with like seniority, status, and pay. If an employee is not qualified for his or her former position because of a disability sustained during service but is qualified for another position, the employee is entitled to the position that is most similar to his or her former position in seniority, status, and pay. Employee must apply for reinstatement within 30 days of release. Returning employees may not be fired without cause for one year. Members of the National Guard and U.S. armed forces reserves may take up to 15 days' leave per year for training without affecting the employee's right to receive normal vacation, sick leave, bonus, advancement, and other advantages of employment. Employee must give 90 days' notice of training dates.

Illinois

20 Ill. Comp. Stat. §§ 1805/30.15, 1805/30.20; 330 Ill. Comp. Stat. § 60/4

Members of the National Guard are entitled to unlimited leave and reinstatement with the same increases in status, seniority, and wages that were earned during the employee's military duty by employees in like positions, or to a position of like seniority, status, and pay, unless employer's circumstances have changed so that reinstatement would be unreasonable or impossible or impose an undue hardship. If employee is no longer qualified for the position because of a disability acquired during service but is qualified for any other position, then the employee is entitled to the position that will provide like seniority, status, and pay. If reasonably possible, employee must give advance notice of military service. Members of the National Guard must submit request for reemployment the day after finishing duty if duty lasted less than 31 days, within 14 days if duty lasted longer than 30 days, or within 90 days if duty lasted longer than 180 days. Members of the U.S. uniformed services must submit request for reemployment within 90 days. Employee can't be discharged without cause for one year.

Indiana

Ind. Code Ann. §§ 10-17-4-1 to 10-17-4-5

Members of U.S. armed forces reserves may take up to 15 days' unpaid (or paid at employer's discretion) leave per year for training. Employee must provide evidence of dates of departure and return, and

State Laws on Military Leave (continued)

proof of completion of the training upon return. Leave does not affect vacation, sick leave, bonus, or promotion rights. Employee must be reinstated to former or a similar position with no loss of seniority or benefits.

Iowa

Iowa Code § 29A.43

Members of the U.S. armed forces reserves, National Guard, or the Civil Air Patrol called into temporary duty are entitled to reinstatement to former or a similar position. Leave does not affect vacation, sick leave, bonuses, or other benefits. Employee must provide proof of satisfactory completion of duty and of qualifications to perform the job's duties.

Kansas

Kan. Stat. Ann. §§ 48-517, 48-222

Members of state military forces called into active duty by the state are entitled to reinstatement to the same position or a comparable position with like seniority, status, and pay. If an employee is not qualified for his or her former position because of a disability sustained during service but is qualified for another position, the employee is entitled to the position that is most similar to his or her former position in seniority, status, and pay. Employee must report to work within 72 hours of release from duty or recovery from service-related injury or illness. Reemployment not required if employer's circumstances have changed so as to make reemployment impossible/unreasonable or if reemployment would impose undue

hardship on employer. In addition to unlimited leave for active duty, employees are entitled to 5 to 10 days' leave each year to attend Kansas National Guard training camp.

Kentucky

Ky. Rev. Stat. Ann. §§ 38.238, 38.460

Members of National Guard are entitled to unlimited unpaid leave for active duty or training and reinstatement to former position with no loss of seniority or benefits. Employer may not in any way discriminate against employee or use threats to prevent employee from enlisting in the Kentucky National Guard or active militia.

Louisiana

La. Rev. Stat. Ann. §§ 29:38, 29:38.1, 42:394

Employees called into active duty in National Guard, state militia, or any branch of the state military forces are entitled to reinstatement to same or comparable position with same seniority, status, benefits, and pay. If employee is not qualified for former position because of disability sustained during active duty, but is otherwise qualified to perform another position, employer or successor shall employ person in other or comparable position with like seniority, status, benefits, and pay provided the employment does not pose a direct threat or significant risk to the health and safety of the individual or others that cannot be eliminated by reasonable accommodation. Employees on leave are entitled to the benefits offered to employees who take leave for other

State Laws on Military Leave (continued)

reasons. Employee must report to work within 72 hours of release or recovery from service-related injury or illness and cannot be fired, except for cause, for one year after reinstatement. Employees in the U.S. National Guard or military reserves are entitled to 15 days of paid leave annually for training. Employer cannot discriminate against employee because of any obligation as a member of the state military forces.

Maine

Me. Rev. Stat. Ann. tit. 37-B, § 342

Employer may not discriminate against employee for membership or service in National Guard or United States armed forces reserves.

Maryland

Md. Code Ann. [Public Safety] § 13-705

Members of the state National Guard and Maryland Defense Force ordered to military duty have the same leave and reinstatement rights and benefits guaranteed under USERRA.

Massachusetts

Mass. Gen. Laws ch. 149, § 52A

Employees who are members of armed forces reserves may take up to 17 days per year for training. Leave does not affect vacation, sick leave, bonus, or promotion rights. Employee who is qualified must be reinstated to former or a similar position. Employee must give employer notice of departure and anticipated return date.

Michigan

Mich. Comp. Laws §§ 32.271 to 32.274

Members of state or U.S. uniformed services called into active state or federal duty may take unpaid leave; employee may also take unpaid leave to take a physical, enlist, be inducted, or attend training. Returning employee must generally be reinstated to former position. Employee must apply for reinstatement within 45 days of release from service, or 90 days if service was more than 180 days. Employer may not in any way discriminate against employee or use threats to prevent employee from enlisting in the state armed forces.

Minnesota

Minn. Stat. Ann. § 192.34

Employer may not discharge employee, interfere with military service, or dissuade employee from enlisting by threatening employee's job. Applies to employees who are members of the U.S., Minnesota, or any other state military or naval forces.

Mississippi

Miss. Code Ann. §§ 33-1-19, 33-1-21

Members of U.S. armed forces reserves or U.S. military veterans are entitled to unpaid leave for military training or duty. If still qualified to perform job duties, employee entitled to reinstatement to previous or similar position. Employee must give evidence of completion of training.

Missouri

Mo. Rev. Stat. § 41.730

Employer may not discharge employee, interfere with employee's military service, or use threats to dissuade employee from

State Laws on Military Leave (continued)

enlisting in the state militia or U.S. armed forces.

Montana

Mont. Code Ann. §§ 10-1-1005, 10-1-1006, 10-1-1007

Members of the state-organized militia called to active service during a state-declared disaster or emergency are entitled to leave for duration of service. Leave may not be deducted from sick leave, vacation, or other leave, although employee may voluntarily use that leave. Returning employee is entitled to reinstatement to same or similar position with the same seniority, status, pay, health insurance, pension, and other benefits. Employer may not in any way discriminate against employee or dissuade employee from enlisting.

Nebraska

Neb. Rev. Stat. § 55-161

Employees who are members of the Nebraska National Guard and are called into active state duty have the same leave and reinstatement rights and benefits guaranteed under USERRA.

Nevada

Nev. Rev. Stat. Ann. §§ 412.139, 412.606

Employers may not discriminate against members of the Nevada National Guard and may not discharge any employee because he or she assembles for training, participates in field training, or is called to active duty.

New Hampshire

N.H. Rev. Stat. Ann. §§ 110-B:65, 110-C:1

Members of the state National Guard or militia called to active duty have the same leave and reinstatement rights and benefits guaranteed under USERRA. Employer may not discriminate against employee because of connection or service with National Guard; may not dissuade employee from enlisting by threatening job.

New Jersey

N.J. Stat. Ann. § 38:23C-20

An employee is entitled to take unpaid leave for active service in the U.S. or state military services. Upon return, employee must be reinstated to the same or a similar position, unless employer's circumstances have changed to make reinstatement impossible or unreasonable. If same or similar position is not possible, employer shall restore such person to any available position, if requested by such person, for which the person is capable and qualified to perform the duties. Employee must apply for reinstatement within 90 days of release from service. Employee may not be fired without cause for one year after returning from service. Employee is also entitled to take up to 3 months' leave in 4-year period for training or assemblies relating to military service. Employee must apply for reinstatement within 10 days.

New Mexico

N.M. Stat. Ann. §§ 28-15-1, 28-15-2, 20-4-6

Members of the U.S. armed forces, National Guard, or organized reserve may take unpaid leave for service (or for up to one

State Laws on Military Leave (continued)

year of hospitalization after discharge). Employee who is still qualified must be reinstated in former or similar position with like status, seniority, pay unless employer's circumstances have changed to make reinstatement impossible or unreasonable. Employee may not be fired without cause for one year after returning from service. Employee must request reinstatement within 90 days. Employer may not discriminate against or discharge employee because of membership in the National Guard; may not prevent employee from performing military service.

New York

N.Y. Mil. Law §§ 317, 318

Members of the U.S. armed forces or organized militia are entitled to unpaid leave for active service; reserve drills or annual training; service school; initial full-time or active duty training. Returning employee is entitled to reinstatement to previous position, or to one with the same seniority, status, and pay, unless the employer's circumstances have changed and reemployment is impossible or unreasonable. Employee must apply for reinstatement within 90 days of discharge from active service, 10 days of completing school or annual training, or 60 days of completing initial training. Employers may not discriminate against persons subject to military duty.

North Carolina

N.C. Gen. Stat. §§ 127A-201, 127A-202, 127A-202.1, 127B-14

Members of the North Carolina National Guard called to active duty by the governor are entitled to take unpaid leave. Unless the employer's circumstances now make it unreasonable: returning employee must be restored to previous position or one of comparable seniority, status, and salary; if no longer qualified, employee must be placed in another position with appropriate seniority, status, and salary. Employee must apply for reinstatement, in writing, within 5 days of release or recovery from service-related injury or illness. Employer may not discriminate against or discharge an employee because of membership in the National Guard or discharge an employee called up for emergency military service.

North Dakota

N.D.C.C. §§ 37-29-01, 37-29-03

Employers cannot terminate, demote, or discriminate against volunteer members of the North Dakota army National Guard, North Dakota air National Guard, or volunteer civilian members of the Civil Air Patrol for being tardy to or absent from work because they were responding to a disaster or emergency.

Ohio

Ohio Rev. Code Ann. § 5903.02

Employees who are members of the Ohio organized militia or National Guard called for active duty or training; members of the commissioned public health service corps; or any other uniformed service called up in time of war or emergency have the same leave and reinstatement rights and benefits guaranteed under USERRA.

State Laws on Military Leave (continued)

Oklahoma

Okla. Stat. Ann. tit. 44, §§ 71, 208.1

Employees called to duty in the Oklahoma National Guard have the same leave and reinstatement rights and benefits guaranteed under USERRA. Members of the National Guard may take leave to attend state National Guard drills, ceremonies, exercises, or other duties.

Oregon

Or. Rev. Stat. § 659A.086

Members of Oregon or other states' organized militias called into active duty may take unpaid leave for term of service. Returning employee is entitled to reinstatement with no loss of seniority or benefits including sick leave, vacation, or service credits under a pension plan. Employee must return to work within 7 calendar days of release from service.

Pennsylvania

51 Pa. Cons. Stat. Ann. §§ 7302 to 7309

Employees who enlist or are drafted during a time of war or emergency called by the president or governor, along with reservists or members of Pennsylvania National Guard called into active duty, are entitled to unpaid military leave. Leave expires 90 days after enlistment/draft period, 90 days after military duty for reservists, 30 days after state duty for Pennsylvania National Guard members. Returning employee must be reinstated to same or similar position with same status, seniority, and pay. If no longer qualified due to disability sustained during military duty, employer must restore to position with like seniority, status, and pay unless employer or successor's circumstances have changed so as to make it impossible or unreasonable to do so. Employers may not discharge or discriminate against any employee because of membership or service in the military. Employees called to active duty are entitled to 30 days' health insurance continuation benefits at no cost.

Rhode Island

R.I. Gen. Laws §§ 30-11-2 to 30-11-9; 30-21-1

Members of state military forces and Rhode Island National Guard members on state active duty have the same leave and reinstatement rights and benefits guaranteed under USERRA. Members of the National Guard or U.S. armed forces reserves are entitled to unpaid leave for training and are entitled to reinstatement with the same status, pay, and seniority. Employees in the U.S. armed forces are entitled to reinstatement to the same position or a position with similar seniority, status, and pay unless the employer's circumstances make reinstatement impossible or unreasonable. Employee must request reinstatement within 40 days. Employer may not discriminate against or discharge employee because of membership in the military reserves, interfere with employee's military service, or dissuade employee from enlisting by threatening employee's job.

South Carolina

S.C. Code Ann. §§ 25-1-2310 to 25-1-2340

Members of the South Carolina National Guard and State Guard called to state

State Laws on Military Leave (continued)

duty by the governor are entitled to unpaid leave for service. Unless employer's circumstances make reinstatement unreasonable: returning employee must be reinstated to previous position or one with same seniority, status, and salary; if no longer qualified, must be given another position. Employee must apply for reinstatement in writing, within 5 days of release from service or related hospitalization.

South Dakota

S.D. Codified Laws Ann. § 33-17-15.1

Members of the South Dakota National Guard ordered to active duty by governor or president have the same leave and reinstatement rights and benefits guaranteed under USERRA.

Tennessee

Tenn. Code Ann. § 58-1-604

Employer may not terminate or refuse to hire an employee because of Tennessee National Guard membership or because employee is absent for a required drill or annual training.

Texas

Tex. Gov't. Code Ann. § 431.006

Members of the Texas or other military forces called to active duty or training are entitled to reinstatement to the same position with no loss of time, efficiency rating, vacation, or benefits unless employer's circumstances have changed so that reemployment is impossible or unreasonable.

Utah

Utah Code Ann. § 39-1-36

Members of U.S. armed forces reserves who are called to active duty, active duty for training, inactive duty training, or state active duty may take up to 5 years of unpaid leave. Upon return, employee is entitled to reinstatement to previous employment with same seniority, status, pay, and vacation rights. Employer may not discriminate against an employee based on membership in armed forces reserves.

Vermont

Vt. Stat. Ann. tit. 21, § 491, Vt. Stat. Ann. tit. 20, § 608

Employees who are members of U.S. armed forces reserves, an organized unit of the National Guard, or the ready reserves and are called to active duty or training are entitled to 15 days per year of unpaid leave. Returning employee must be reinstated to former position with the same status, pay, and seniority, including any seniority that accrued during the leave of absence. Employer may not discriminate against an employee who is a member or an applicant for membership in the state or federal National Guard. Members of the Vermont National Guard ordered to state active duty have the right to take unpaid leave from civilian employment, and cannot be required to exhaust their vacation or other accrued leave.

Virginia

Va. Code Ann. §§ 44-93.2 to 44-93.4

Members of the Virginia National Guard, Virginia State Defense Force, or naval

State Laws on Military Leave (continued)

militia called to active duty by the governor are entitled to take unpaid leave and may not be required to use vacation or any other accrued leave (unless employee wishes). Returning employee whose absence does not exceed five years must be reinstated to previous position or one with same seniority, status, and pay; if position no longer exists, then to a comparable position unless employer's circumstances would make reemployment unreasonable. Employee must apply for reinstatement, in writing, within (a) 14 days of release from service or related hospitalization if service length did not exceed 180 days, or (b) 90 days of release from service or related hospitalization if service length exceeded 180 days. Employer cannot discriminate against employees because of membership in state military service.

Washington

Wash. Rev. Code Ann. §§ 73.16.032 to 73.16.035

Unless the employer's circumstances have changed so that reinstatement is impossible or unreasonable or would be an undue hardship: members of the uniformed services are entitled to reinstatement to the same position or a position of like seniority, status, and pay; if the employee is no longer qualified for the position because of a disability sustained during service, but is qualified for another position, the employee is entitled to a position with the same seniority, status, and pay. Time limits set forth governing written application for reinstatement based on length of uniformed service. Employer cannot discriminate against

employees because of membership in uniformed services.

West Virginia

W.Va. Code § 15-1F-8

Employees who are members of the organized militia in active state service have the same leave and reinstatement rights and benefits guaranteed under USERRA.

Wisconsin

Wis. Stat. Ann. § 321.64

Employees who enlist, are inducted, or are ordered to serve in the U.S. armed forces for 90 days or more, or civilians requested to perform national defense work during an officially proclaimed emergency, may take up to 5 years' leave for military service and/or training unless period of service is extended by law. Returning employee is entitled to reinstatement to previous position, or to one with the same seniority, benefits, and pay, unless the employee is no longer qualified or the employer's circumstances have changed and reemployment is impossible or unreasonable. Employee must apply for reinstatement within 90 days of release or 6 months of release from service-related hospitalization and must present evidence of completion of training or service. Employee may not be fired without cause for one year after returning from service.

Wyoming

Wyo. Stat. §§ 19-11-103, 19-11-104, 19-11-107, 19-11-111

Employees who are members of, or who

State Laws on Military Leave (continued)

apply for membership in, the uniformed services; employees who report for active duty, training, or a qualifying physical exam; or who are called to state duty by the governor, may take up to 5 years' leave of absence. Employee must give advance notice of service. Employee may use vacation or any other accrued leave but is not required to do so. Returning employee is entitled to reemployment with the same seniority, rights, and benefits, plus any additional seniority and benefits that employee would have earned if there had been no absence, unless employer's circumstances have changed so that reemployment is impossible or unreasonable or would impose an undue hardship. Time limits set forth governing written application for reinstatement based on length of uniformed service. Employee is entitled to complete any training program that would have been available to employee's former position during period of absence. Employee may not be terminated without cause for one year after returning to work. Employer cannot discriminate against applicant or member of the uniformed services.

Worker Adjustment and Retraining Notification Act (WARN)

20

Statute: 42 U.S.C. § 2000e

http://uscode.house.gov/download/pls/42C21.txt

Regulations: 29 C.F.R. §§ 1600–1609

www.gpo.gov.fdsys/pkg/CFR-2012-title20-vol3/pdf/CFR-2012-title20-vol3-part639.pdf

Overview of WARN

The Worker Adjustment and Retraining Notification Act (WARN) requires certain larger employers to give some advance notice of an impending plant closing or mass layoff that will result in employment loss for a specified number or percentage of employees. The law was passed to help ease the transition for workers who lose their jobs in these circumstances. WARN requires employers to give notice not only to employees and unions that will be affected by the job cuts, but also to state government agencies that provide assistance to dislocated workers.

Definitions

Affected employees Employees who may reasonably be expected to suffer an *employment loss* as a result of a proposed *plant closing* or *mass layoff* by their employer.

Employment loss An employment loss is:
- an employment termination for reasons other than cause, voluntary departure, or retirement
- a layoff of longer than six months, or
- a reduction of more than 50% in an employee's work hours for six consecutive months.

An employee has not suffered an employment loss if the employer conducted a *plant closing* or *mass layoff* as part of a relocation or consolidation of its business and either:
- prior to the closing or layoff, offered to transfer the employee to a different employment site within a reasonable commuting distance with no more than a six-month break in employment, or
- offered to transfer the employee to any other employment site (regardless of commuting distance) with no more than a six-month break in employment, and the employee accepted this offer within 30 days of the offer or 30 days of the closing or layoff, whichever is later.

Facility A building or buildings in which an employer operates.

Definitions (continued)

Mass layoff A reduction in force that is not the result of a *plant closing* and results in an *employment loss* at a *single site of employment* during any 30-day period for:

- 500 or more employees (excluding *part-time employees*), or
- 50 to 499 employees (excluding *part-time employees*), if the number of employees laid off makes up at least 33% of the employer's active workforce.

Operating unit An organizationally or operationally distinct product, operation, or specific work function within or across *facilities* at a *single site of employment* (for example, a sales force or production line).

Part-time employee An employee who:

- works, on average, fewer than 20 hours per week, or
- has been employed for fewer than six of the 12 months preceding the date on which notice would be required under WARN.

Plant closing The permanent or temporary shutdown of a *single site of employment*, or one or more *facilities* or *operating units* within a *single site of employment*, which results in an employment loss for 50 or more employees (excluding *part-time employees*), during any 30-day period.

Single site of employment One geographical location of an employer's operations. A single site may consist of one building, an office or a suite of offices in a building, or a group of buildings that form a campus or an industrial park, for example. Separate buildings or areas that are not in immediate proximity may nonetheless constitute a single site of employment if they:

- are reasonably close together
- are used for the same purpose, and
- share the same staff and equipment (for example, two warehouses might be a single site if the employer rotates employees from one to the other).

Regulated Employers

Only large private employers must comply with WARN, and then only if they engage in a plant closing or mass layoff as defined above.

Federal, state, and local governments are not covered by WARN and need not comply with its requirements.

Private employers are covered if:

- they have 100 or more employees, not counting part-time employees, or
- they have 100 or more employees (including part-time employees) who work a combined 4,000 or more hours per week.

In deciding whether they meet these eligibility requirements, employers do not have to count independent contractors as employees. However, they must count workers who are on temporary layoff or on leave, if those workers have a reasonable expectation of being recalled or otherwise returning to work. For example, an employee who is taking family medical leave should be counted, because he or she is entitled to be reinstated under the Family and Medical Leave Act (FMLA). (See Chapter 8 for detailed information on the FMLA.)

Layoffs Covered by WARN

Not every reduction in force by a covered employer triggers WARN's notice requirements. An employer must comply with WARN only if it plans to conduct a:

- plant closing
- mass layoff, or
- plant closing or mass layoff that occurs in stages over any 90-day period.

For example, an employer with 150 employees would not have to comply with WARN if it laid off 20 workers in a 30-day period, because this would not constitute a mass layoff as defined by WARN. However, if the same employer laid off 20 more workers in each of the two following months, these combined layoffs would total more than 33% of its workforce—and thus constitute a mass layoff as defined by WARN. This rule is intended to prevent employers from getting around WARN's requirements by conducting a series of smaller layoffs.

Legal Developments

- **Federal government will pick up the WARN tab in case of sequestration.** In September of 2012, the White House issued a memo to federal agencies regarding the looming sequestration: the across-the-board budget cuts scheduled to hit in 2013 if Congress can't come up with a budget deal. Earlier in the year, the Department of Labor had issued an opinion telling federal contractors that they had no obligation to provide WARN notices based on the sequestration, both because those cuts might not happen and because, if they did, it isn't clear which contractors and employees would be affected. Despite this advice, some contractors were still planning to issue notices, just in case. The White House memo tried to reassure contractors by pledging that the government would pay the damages, court costs, and attorney fees for WARN liability, as awarded by a court.

- **Congress considers amendments to WARN.** As the economic downturn results in increasing numbers of jobs lost, Congress has looked at amending the WARN Act to protect more workers. For example, the Alert Laid-off Employees in Reasonable Time (ALERT) Act would expand the definition of a mass layoff to include combined job losses at more than one employment site, and would increase the damages available to employees. The Federal Oversight, Reform and Enforcement of the WARN Act (FOREWARN Act) would apply to employers with at least 75 employees (down from the current minimum of 100), lower the number of employees who must lose their jobs to qualify as a mass layoff or plant closing, and increase the amount of notice required from 60 to 90 days, among other things.

Covered Workers

All *affected employees* are entitled to notice under WARN. Part-time employees are entitled to notice, even though they are not counted in determining whether WARN applies.

Independent contractors are not covered by WARN: They do not count toward the plant closing or mass layoff minimum thresholds, nor are they entitled to notice.

Did You Know ...

- According to the Bureau of Labor Statistics (BLS), more than 235,000 workers were laid off in September 2008, the highest level since the layoffs following the World Trade Center attack on September 11, 2001. (The BLS defines a layoff differently from WARN: To the BLS, a layoff has occurred if an establishment has at least 50 new claims for unemployment filed against it in a five-week period.)
- A study by the General Accountability Office (GAO) found that the issues most likely to be litigated in a WARN case are: (1) whether the job loss in question qualifies as a "mass layoff," and (2) whether the unforeseeable business circumstances exception applies. (This exception allows employers to give less than 60 days' notice; see "Exceptions," below.)

What's Prohibited

WARN prohibits an employer from carrying out a plant closing or mass layoff until 60 days after the employer gives written notice of its plans (see "What's Required," below).

What's Required

If a layoff is covered by WARN, the employer must give written notice of the layoff, 60 days in advance.

Who Is Entitled to Notice

An employer must provide written notice to:
- each affected employee, except those who are union members
- the bargaining representative(s) of all union members who are affected employees
- the state's dislocated worker unit (sometimes called the rapid response coordinator), and
- the local government in the area where the layoff will occur.

Key Facts

- WARN applies only to companies that have at least 100 full-time workers, or that have at least 100 workers (including part-time employees) who work a combined total of at least 4,000 hours a week.
- WARN applies only to large job losses: plant closings, in which an entire single site of employment, facility, or operating unit is shut down and at least 50 employees lose their jobs; or mass layoffs, in which either 500 employees or one-third of the company's workforce—at least 50 employees—lose their jobs.
- An employer can give less than 60 days' notice, or no notice at all, in certain limited circumstances.
- Employers who violate WARN can be required to pay up to 60 days' wages and benefits to employees who lost their jobs, but this amount can be reduced by any wages the employees earned during that time and any amounts the employer paid voluntarily and unconditionally.

Notice Contents

The employer's notice must be based on the best information available when the notice must be given. If that information proves to be wrong because of subsequent changes in events or inadvertent errors, the employer will not be liable.

The legally required contents of the written notice vary depending on the recipient:

- **Affected employees who are not union members** must be given a notice that states whether the planned action is expected to be permanent or temporary; whether an entire plant is to be closed; the expected date when the layoff or plant closing will begin; the expected date when the employee receiving the letter will be terminated; whether the employee will have bumping rights (that is, whether the employee can take the job of a less-senior employee who isn't targeted for layoff); and the name and telephone number of a company official the employee can contact for more information. This notice must be written in language understandable to the employees.
- **Bargaining representatives** must receive written notice stating the name and address of the employment site where the layoff or plant closing will

occur; the name and address of a company official to contact for more information; whether the planned action is expected to be permanent or temporary; whether an entire plant is to be closed; the expected date of the first termination; the expected schedule for the remaining terminations; the job titles of positions expected to be affected; and the names of the workers holding those positions.

- **State dislocated worker units and local governments** must receive a written notice that states the name and address of the employment site where the layoff or plant closing will occur; the name and address of a company official to contact for more information; the expected date of the first termination; and the number of affected employees. In addition, the employer must include the following information in the notice or maintain this information on site and make it available to the dislocated worker unit and local government agency on request: whether the planned action is expected to be permanent or temporary; whether an entire plant is to be closed; the anticipated schedule for making terminations; whether bumping rights exist; the job titles of positions expected to be affected; the names of the workers holding those positions; the name of each union representing affected employees; and the name and address of the chief elected officer of each union. (See "Agency Resources," below, for contact information for state dislocated worker units.)

Exceptions

In certain circumstances, an employer does not have to give notice, or can give notice less than 60 days before a mass layoff or plant closing.

No Notice Required

WARN does not apply—and therefore, an employer need not give advance notice of a mass layoff or plant closing—in these circumstances:

- **Temporary facilities or projects.** If an employer closes a *facility* that was intended to be open only temporarily or lays off workers who were hired only for a specific project that is complete, no notice is required. However, this exception applies only if the laid-off workers understood when they were hired that their employment was limited to the duration of the facility or project.

- **Strikes and lockouts.** If a plant closing or mass layoff results from a union strike or an employer lockout, no notice is required.

Notice of Less Than 60 Days Allowed

An employer may comply with WARN by giving as much notice as possible under the circumstances—even if the employer can't give 60 days' notice—in some cases. If an employer relies on one of these exceptions, it must give as much notice as it can and state (as part of the written notice requirement) why it didn't give the full 60 days' notice that would otherwise be required:

- **Natural disasters.** If a natural disaster forces a mass layoff or plant closing, an employer may give less than 60 days' notice.
- **Unforeseeable business circumstances.** If the plant closing or mass layoff is caused by business circumstances that were not reasonably foreseeable at the time the employer should have given 60 days' notice, a shorter notice period is allowed.
- **Faltering company.** If a company is struggling financially at the time it should have given 60 days' notice of a plant closing, it can give a shorter period of notice. However, the company must show that it was actively seeking business or money that would have allowed it to avoid or postpone the closing, and that it reasonably believed, in good faith, that giving 60 days' notice would have precluded it from obtaining the necessary business or money. This exception does not apply to mass layoffs.

How WARN Is Enforced

Individual Complaints

The only way affected employees, union representatives, or local government units can assert their right to notice under WARN is by filing lawsuits in federal district court.

Agency Enforcement

Although the Department of Labor published the regulations that interpret and explain WARN, Congress gave that agency no power to administer or enforce the law. Therefore, there is no administrative agency available to accept or investigate complaints of WARN violations.

Complying With WARN

Deadlines

Employers must provide the required written notice 60 days before a mass layoff or plant closing covered by WARN, unless an exception applies.

Reporting Requirements

WARN requires reporting to state dislocated worker units and local governments, as explained in "What's Required," above.

Posting Requirements

WARN does not impose any posting requirements.

Record-Keeping Requirements

WARN does not impose any special record-keeping requirements on employers other than those records that must be kept on-site and available for state dislocated worker units and local governments to inspect (see "What's Required," above, for more information).

Penalties

Employers who violate WARN (by conducting a plant closing or mass layoff without giving appropriate notice) may be ordered to:

- pay affected workers for all pay and benefits lost for the period of violation, up to 60 days. Some courts calculate the damages period as 60 calendar days, which works out to roughly 42 days of pay; others use 60 workdays as a measure, which results in larger damages awards. This amount may be reduced by any wages the employees were paid by the employer during that period and by any payments the employer made to the employees voluntarily and unconditionally. Payments the employer is already obligated to make—such as paying out accrued vacation time in states that require employers to do so—cannot be used to offset the damages amount, nor can wages earned from another employer (for example, if the employee immediately gets another job).

- pay a fine of up to $500 for each day of violation, if the employer fails to give notice as required to the state's dislocated worker unit, and
- pay the attorneys' fees and court costs of affected workers who sue the employer successfully for violating WARN.

Agency Resources

- A fact sheet explaining WARN's requirements and coverage
  Fact Sheet: The Worker Adjustment and Retraining Notification Act
  www.doleta.gov/programs/factsht/warn.htm

- A list of the name, address, telephone number, and email address of the coordinator of each state's dislocated worker unit
  State Rapid Response Coordinators
  www.doleta.gov/layoff/rapid_coord.cfm

- A detailed explanation of the rights and obligations created by WARN
  Employer's Guide to Advance Notice of Closings and Layoffs
  www.doleta.gov/layoff/pdf/EmployerWARN09_2003.pdf

- An explanation of the benefits available through state dislocated worker programs
  Rapid Response Services for Employers
  www.doleta.gov/layoff/employers.cfm

State Laws Relating to Plant Closings

Many states have also passed laws relating to plant closings and layoffs. The chart below provides basic information on these laws. If you need more information, contact your state labor department (see Appendix A for contact details).

State Layoff and Plant Closing Laws

Alabama

Ala. Code § 25-3-5

When law applies: Substantial layoff or closing of any plant or industry

State assistance for employees: Commissioner of labor to provide seminars to unemployed or underemployed employees on legal rights regarding debts. To lessen the financial burden of closure or layoffs, commissioner may meet with management and with labor or other organizations, may facilitate communication with creditors, and may set up programs to provide financial assistance. No employer or employee group may be required to contribute to or participate in these programs.

Alaska

Alaska Stat. § 23.15.635

State assistance for employees: Department of Labor offers employment and training programs to workers who are liable to be displaced because of reductions in workforce or job elimination.

California

Cal. Lab. Code § 1401

When law applies: Mass layoff, relocation, or closing of any industrial or commercial facility with at least 75 employees

Notification requirements: Employer must give employees at least 60 days' advance notice in writing before mass layoff, relocation, or termination. Employer must also notify the Employment Development Department, the local workforce investment board, and the chief elected official of each city and county government within which the termination, relocation, or mass layoff occurs. Notice shall include the elements required by the federal WARN Act.

Colorado

Colo. Rev. Stat. § 23-60-306

When law applies: Plant closings; workers displaced by technological changes

State assistance for employees: Workers who have lost their previous jobs because of plant closings are eligible for retraining for new jobs through customized training programs provided by the State Board for Community Colleges and Occupational Education.

Connecticut

Conn. Gen. Stat. Ann. §§ 31-51n, 31-51o

When law applies: Permanent shutdown or relocation of facility out of state

Employers affected by requirements: Employers with 100 or more employees at any time during the previous 12-month period

Severance requirements: Employer must pay for existing group health insurance coverage for terminated employee and dependents for 120 days or until employee is eligible for other group coverage, whichever comes first.

Exceptions: Facility closure due to bankruptcy

District of Columbia

D.C. Code Ann. §§ 32-101, 32-102

When law applies: When a new contractor takes over a service contract

State Layoff and Plant Closing Laws (continued)

Employers affected by requirements: Contractors and subcontractors who employ 25 or more nonprofessionals as food service, health service, or janitorial or building maintenance workers

Severance requirements:

- Within 10 days after a new contract is awarded, previous contractor must give new contractor names of all employees. New contractor must hire all employees who have worked for past 8 months for a 90-day transition period. After 90 days must give each employee a written performance evaluation and retain all employees whose performance is satisfactory.
- Contractor whose contract is not renewed and who is awarded a similar contract within 30 days must hire at least 50% of the employees from the former sites.

Florida

Fla. Stat. Ann. §§ 288.972, 379.2352, 446.60

When law applies: Job loss or displacement due to industry changes

State assistance for employees:

- Department of Labor and Employment Security established Workforce Florida, which provides counseling, training, and placement services to displaced workers in the defense industry and local telecommunications exchange workers.
- State agencies must give priority hiring to anyone who loses full-time employment in the commercial saltwater fishing industry because of the constitutional amendment limiting the use of nets to harvest marine species.

Hawaii

Haw. Rev. Stat. §§ 394B-1 to 394B-13

When law applies: Permanent or partial closing of business; relocation of all or substantial portion of business operations out of state

State assistance for employees: Dislocated workers' program in Department of Labor and Industrial Relations provides assistance and training for workers who have lost their jobs or received a notice of termination.

Employers affected by requirements: Employers with 50 or more employees at any time during the previous 12-month period

Severance requirements: Employer must provide 4 weeks' dislocated worker allowance as a supplement to unemployment compensation; amount is the difference between the weekly former wage and the unemployment benefit. Employers who do not follow notice and severance requirements are liable to each employee for 3 months of compensation.

Notification requirements: Employer must provide each employee with written notice 60 days in advance of closing or relocation.

Illinois

820 Ill. Comp. Stat. §§ 65/1 to 65/99

When law applies: Mass layoff, relocation, or employment loss

Employers affected by requirements: Any business enterprise that employs 75 or more full-time employees or 75 or more

State Layoff and Plant Closing Laws (continued)

employees who in the aggregate work at least 4,000 hours per week (not counting overtime)

Notification requirements: Employer must give 60 days' written notice to affected employees and representatives of affected employees, and to both the Department of Commerce and Economic Opportunity and the chief elected official of each municipal and county government within which the employment loss, relocation, or mass layoff occurs.

Exceptions: Employer seeking capital in good faith; completion of explicitly temporary project; unforeseen circumstances; strike or lockout; physical calamity or war

Penalties: Up to 60 days of back pay and the value of benefits for that time; up to $500 per day civil penalty, unless employer pays the back pay within 3 weeks of announced layoffs; federal penalty payments count toward state penalty

Iowa

Iowa Code §§ 84C.2, 84C.3

When law applies: An employer who plans a business closing (permanent or temporary shutdown) or a mass layoff that will affect twenty-five or more full-time employees

Employers affected by requirements: Employers with 25 or more full-time employees

Notification requirements: Notice period in collective bargaining agreement; otherwise, 30 days

Kansas

Kan. Stat. Ann. §§ 44-603, 44-616

When law applies: Employers involved in manufacture, transportation, or preparation of food products or clothing; fuel mining or production; public utilities, or transportation must apply to state Secretary of Labor for approval before limiting or discontinuing business operations.

Louisiana

La. Rev. Stat. Ann. §§ 23:1842 to 23:1846

When law applies: Job loss related to state environmental protection laws

State assistance for employees: Workers who have lost jobs because employer has relocated to another state to avoid compliance with state environmental protection laws or instituted technological changes because of laws are eligible for services through the Displaced Worker Retraining Program administered by the Department of Workforce Development.

Maine

Me. Rev. Stat. Ann. tit. 26, § 625-B

When law applies: Discontinuation or relocation of business operations at least 100 miles from original location

Employers affected by requirements: Employers with 100 or more employees at any time during the previous 12-month period

Severance requirements: Employer must give severance pay of one week for each year of employment to all employees

State Layoff and Plant Closing Laws (continued)

who have worked for at least 3 years; pay due within one regular pay period after employee's last full day of work.

Notification requirements: Employer must give employees at least 60 days' advance notice in writing before relocating a plant. Employer must also notify the director of the Bureau of Labor Standards and municipal officials where the plant is located. Within 7 days, if employer lays off 100 or more employees, employer must report to the director the expected duration of the layoff and if the layoff is definite or indefinite.

Maryland

Md. Code Ann. [Lab. & Empl.] §§ 11-301 to 11-304

When law applies: Shutdown of workplace or a portion of the operations that results in layoffs of at least 25% of workforce or 15 employees, whichever is greater, over any 3-month period

State assistance for employees: Department of Labor will provide on-site unemployment insurance bulk registration (when more than 25 workers are laid off), retraining, job placement, and job-finding services.

Employers affected by requirements: Employers with 50 or more employees who have been in business at least one year

Severance requirements: Employers are encouraged to follow Department of Labor voluntary guidelines for severance pay, continuation of benefits, and notification.

Notification requirements: 90 days whenever possible

Exceptions: Bankruptcy, seasonal factors common to industry, labor disputes, temporary workplaces, or construction sites

Massachusetts

Mass. Gen. Laws ch. 149, §§ 179B, 182, 183; ch. 151A, §§ 71A to 71H

When law applies:

- Permanent cessation or reduction of business operations which results or will result in the permanent separation of at least 90% of the employees within 6 months
- Sale or transfer of ownership of a business with 50 or more employees

State assistance for employees:

- Reemployment assistance programs which provide counseling, placement, and training are available through the employment and training division of the Department of Workforce Development.
- Employees who have worked for a company for at least one year are eligible for up to 13 weeks of reemployment assistance benefits.

Employers affected by requirements:

- Employers receiving assistance from state business financing or development agencies
- Employers with 50 or more employees who sell or transfer control of a business

Severance requirements:

- Employers receiving state agency assistance must make a good-faith effort to provide 90 days' group health insurance coverage for employees and dependents, at the same payment terms as before plant closing.

State Layoff and Plant Closing Laws (continued)

- When a company with 50 or more employees is sold or changes hands, new owner must give severance pay of 2 weeks' compensation for every year of service to employees who have worked at least 3 years. Employees terminated within 2 years of the sale are due severance within one regular pay period after last day of work; employees terminated within one year of sale are due severance within 4 pay periods after the sale.

Notification requirements:
- Employers receiving state agency assistance are expected to provide 90 days' notice.
- Employers with 12 or more employees must notify the Director of Labor and Workforce Development when business changes location.
- New owner of business with 50 or more employees must provide written notice of rights to each employee and to any collective bargaining representative within 30 days of completion of sale.

Michigan

Mich. Comp. Laws §§ 450.731 to 450.737

When law applies: Permanent shutdown of operations at any establishment with 25 or more employees

State assistance for employees: Department of Labor may study the feasibility of the employees establishing an employee-owned corporation to continue the business.

Notification requirements: Department of Labor encourages businesses that are closing or relocating to give notice

as soon as possible to the Department, the employees and any organization representing them, and the community.

Minnesota

Minn. Stat. Ann. §§ 116L.17, 116L.976

When law applies:
- Plant closing: Announced or actual permanent shutdown of a single site
- Substantial layoff: Permanent reduction in workforce (not due to plant closing) at a single site which results in job loss for at least 50 full-time employees during any 30-day period

Notification requirements: Employers are encouraged to give 60 days' notice to the Department of Trade and Economic Development. If federal WARN Act requires notice, then employer must report to state commissioner of employment and economic development the occupations of workers being terminated.

State assistance for employees: Department of Trade and Economic Development offers rapid response assistance to employees and businesses through the dislocated worker program. May include on-site emergency assistance, information about state and other agency resources, and help in setting up an employee-management committee.

Missouri

Mo. Rev. Stat. § 409.516(5)

When law applies: Any company making a business takeover offer

Notification requirements: Company making offer must file a registration statement with the state securities commission

State Layoff and Plant Closing Laws (continued)

disclosing any plans to liquidate, merge, or consolidate the target company, sell its assets, or make any other major change to its business, corporate structure, management, or employment policies.

Montana

Mont. Code Ann. § 39-51-2116

When law applies: Job loss due to a separation from a declining occupation or from employment due to permanent reduction of operations

State assistance for employees: Workers who have lost their jobs due to separation from a declining occupation or permanent reduction in operations may be eligible for training benefits.

Nebraska

Neb. Rev. St. § 48-628.05

When law applies: Involuntary separation from employment as a result of a permanent reduction in operations or separation from a declining occupation

State assistance for employees: Employees who have lost their jobs due to involuntary separation from employment as a result of a permanent reduction in operations or separation from a declining occupation may be eligible for 26 more weeks of additional unemployment benefits.

New Hampshire

N.H. Rev. Stat. Ann. § 421-A:4(IV)

When law applies: Any company making a business takeover offer

Notification requirements: Company making offer must file a registration statement with the secretary of state and

with the target company disclosing any plans to liquidate, merge, or consolidate the target company, sell its assets, or make any other major change to its business, corporate structure, management, or employment policies.

New Jersey

N.J. Stat. Ann. §§ 34:1B-30, 52:27H-95

When law applies: Potential plant closings

State assistance for employees: Department of Labor and other agencies mandated to assist workers who want to establish employee ownership plans to save jobs threatened by plant closure. If plant closure would cause significant employment loss to an economically distressed municipality, the commissioner of commerce may fund a profitability study of an employee stock ownership plan.

New York

N.Y. Lab. Law §§ 835 to 849; Pub. Auth. Law §§ 1836-a to 1836-g; Bus. Corp. Law § 1603(5)

When law applies:

- Plant closing: Permanent or temporary shutdown of a single site or one or more facilities or operating units within a single site which results in job loss for at least 25 full-time employees during any 30-day period. (If shutdown causes job losses at other sites, they also count toward the 25.)
- Substantial layoff: Reduction in workforce (not due to shutdown) at a single site which results in job loss for at least 33% full-time and 50 part-time employees or 500 full-time employees during any 30-day period

442 | THE ESSENTIAL GUIDE TO FEDERAL EMPLOYMENT LAWS

State Layoff and Plant Closing Laws (continued)

- Any company making a business takeover offer

State assistance for employees:
- The Department of Labor, in coordination with the Department of Economic Development and the dislocated worker unit, provides rapid response services after a plant closure, including: on-site intervention within 48 hours; basic emergency readjustment services; information about retraining, unemployment insurance, and technical assistance.
- The Job Development Authority encourages employees of plants that are about to be closed or relocated to continue to operate them as employee-owned enterprises; state assistance is available.

Notification requirements: Company making offer must file a registration statement with the attorney general's New York City office and with the target company disclosing plans for plant closures or major changes in employment policies.

Ohio

Ohio Rev. Code Ann. §§ 122.13 to 122.136

When law applies: Permanent shutdown of operations at a business with at least 25 employees; relocation of all or substantial portion of operations at least 100 miles from original location

State assistance for employees: Department of Development has an employee ownership assistance program that provides technical assistance and counseling; will conduct a feasibility study for workers who want to establish employee ownership

plans to continue running a business threatened by plant closure.

Oklahoma

Okla. Stat. Ann. tit. 71, § 453(F)(3)

When law applies: Any company making a business takeover offer

Notification requirements: Company making offer must file a registration statement with the state securities commission disclosing plans to close or relocate facilities or to make major changes in employment policies.

Oregon

Or. Rev. Stat. §§ 285A.510 to 285A.522, 657.335 to 657.340

When law applies
- Plant closing: Permanent or temporary shutdown of a single site or one or more facilities or operating units within a single site which results in job loss for at least 50 full-time employees during any 30-day period.
- Mass layoff: Reduction in workforce at a single site not due to shutdown which results in job loss for at least 33% of the workforce and 50 full-time employees, or for 500 full-time employees during any 30-day period

State assistance for employees: State assistance and professional technical training available to dislocated workers. Workers who are in training are entitled to unemployment compensation and related benefits.

Employers affected by requirements: Employers with 100 or more full-time employees

State Layoff and Plant Closing Laws (continued)

Notification requirements: Employers must notify the Department of Community Colleges & Workforce Development of plant closings or mass layoffs.

Pennsylvania

43 Pa. Cons. Stat. Ann. §§ 690a.1 to 690a.6; 70 PCSA §§ 74; 75(4)

When law applies: Jobs or industries which are being rendered technologically obsolete; any company making a business takeover offer

State assistance for employees: Workers employed in jobs or industries which are being rendered technologically obsolete are eligible for customized job training program through the Department of Labor & Industry and are eligible for assistance to support them while in training.

Notification requirements: Company making offer must file a registration statement 20 days in advance with the state securities commission, the target company, and the collective bargaining agent. Must disclose plans for closing down the target company, making major changes in employment policies, or changing any collective bargaining agreements.

Rhode Island

R.I. Gen. Laws § 27-19.1-1

When law applies: Involuntary layoff; permanent reduction of workforce

Severance requirements: Employees and dependents are entitled to at least 18 months' continuation of health care coverage at own expense; premium rate must be the same as the one offered under the group plan. (Length of coverage cannot

exceed time of continuous employment.)

South Carolina

S.C. Code Ann. § 41-1-40

Employers affected by requirements: Employers who require employees to give notice before quitting work

Notification requirements: Employers must give same amount of notice they require of employees or at least 2 weeks' warning. Notice must be in writing and posted in every room of the work building. Employers who do not comply are liable to every employee for any damages that result from failure to give notice.

Tennessee

Tenn. Code Ann. §§ 50-1-601 to 50-1-604

When law applies: Closing, modernization, relocation, or new management policy of a workplace or a portion of the operations that permanently or indefinitely lays off 50 or more employees during any three-month period

Employers affected by requirements: Employers with 50 to 99 full-time employees within the state

Notification requirements: Employer must first notify employees who will lose their jobs due to a reduction in operations and then notify the Commissioner of Labor and Workforce Development. Must give circumstances of closing and number of employees laid off. Toll-free telephone line established to encourage employer compliance.

Exceptions: Construction sites; seasonal factors common to industry

State Layoff and Plant Closing Laws (continued)

Texas

Tex. Govt. Code Ann. §§ 2310.001, 2310.102, 2310.301 to 2310.308; Tex. Util. Code Ann. §§ 39.002, 39.906

When law applies: Industry restructuring or plant o r facility closing

Employers affected by requirements: Private employers who contract with Department of Defense or whose business is directly affected by defense-related economic factors, and certainly utility companies

State assistance for employees:
- Through defense readjustment projects, state provides funding to communities, programs, and businesses that assist or hire dislocated defense workers.
- Public Utility Commission allows employers to recover reasonable transition costs for severance, retraining, early retirement, out-placement, and related expenses for employees affected by electric utility industry restructuring.

Utah

Utah Code Ann. § 67-1-12

When law applies: Defense industry layoffs

State assistance for employees: Workers in defense or defense-related jobs who are laid off may apply to the Office of Job Training for assistance in retraining or reeducation for job skills in demand.

Vermont

21 Vt. Stat. Ann. § 1471

When law applies: Involuntary separation from employment as a result of a permanent reduction in operations or separation from a declining occupation

State assistance for employees: Employees who have lost their jobs due to involuntary separation from employment as a result of a permanent reduction in operations or separation from a declining occupation may be eligible for training benefits.

Washington

Wash. Rev. Code Ann. §§ 50.04.075, 50.12.280, 50.20.042, 50.20.043, 50.70.030 to 50.70.050

When law applies: Employees who have been terminated or received a notice of termination and are unlikely to return to work at their principal occupations or previous industries

State assistance for employees: The Department of Employment Security offers special training and counseling programs for dislocated workers in aerospace, thermal electric generation, and forest products industries in addition to any regular unemployment compensation.

Wisconsin

Wis. Stat. Ann. §§ 106.15, 109.07

When law applies:
- Business closing: Permanent or temporary shutdown of an employment site or of one or more facilities or operating units at a site or within one town that affects 25 or more employees
- Mass layoff: Reduction in workforce that is not the result of a business closing and that affects at least 25% or 25 employees, whichever is greater, or at least 500 employees

State Layoff and Plant Closing Laws (continued)

- Employees who have worked at least 6 of the previous 12 months and who work at least 20 hours/week

Employers affected by requirements: Employers with 50 or more employees in the state

Notification requirements: An employer who has decided upon a business closing or mass layoff in Wisconsin must give at least 60 days' written notice to:

- the Dislocated Worker Committee in the Department of Workforce Development
- every affected employee
- the employees' collective bargaining representative, and
- the highest official of the municipality where the business is located.

Employer must also include contact information for the local workforce development board. Employer who does not comply is liable to employees for pay and for the value of benefits employees would have received if closing or layoff did not take place, from the day that notice was required to the day notice was actually given or business closing or mass layoff occurred, whichever is earlier.

Wyoming

Wyo. Stat. §§ 27-13-101 to 27-13-103

When law applies: Workers unemployed due to plant closings or in substantial plant layoffs

State assistance for employees: Department of Employment, in conjunction with the Department of Education, the University of Wyoming, and the Community College Commission, offers occupational transfer and retraining programs and services for displaced workers.

Federal and State Agencies

Federal Agencies

This section includes contact information for the federal agencies that enforce the laws covered in this book. You can find more information on each agency's authority, enforcement powers, and resources for employers in the chapter that covers the law the agency administers.

Department of Health and Human Services

Administration for Children & Families (ACF)
Office of Child Support Enforcement
370 L'Enfant Promenade SW
Washington, DC 20447
Phone: 202-401-9323
www.acf.hhs.gov/programs/cse

The ACF enforces PRWORA.

Department of Justice

Civil Rights Division
Office of the Special Counsel for Immigration-Related Unfair Employment
 Practices (OSC)
950 Pennsylvania Avenue, NW
Washington, DC 20530
Employer Hotline: 800-255-8155
TDD: 800-237-2515
ww.justice.gov/crt/about/osc

The OSC enforces the antidiscrimination provisions of IRCA.

Department of Labor

Employee Benefits Security Administration (EBSA)

Frances Perkins Building
200 Constitution Avenue, NW
Washington, DC 20210
Phone: 866-444-EBSA (3272)
www.dol.gov/ebsa

The EBSA shares enforcement responsibility for COBRA with the IRS.

Employment and Training Administration (DOLETA)

Office of National Response
200 Constitution Avenue, NW
Washington, DC 20210
Phone: 877-872-5627
www.doleta.gov/layoff

DOLETA issued the regulations interpreting WARN, and has some explanatory resources available.

Occupational Safety & Health Administration (OSHA)

200 Constitution Avenue, NW
Washington, DC 20210
Phone: 800-321-OSHA
TTY: 877-889-5627
www.osha.gov

OSHA enforces the OSH Act and the whistle-blower provisions of Sarbanes-Oxley (SOX).

Veterans Employment and Training Service (VETS)

200 Constitution Avenue, Room S-1325
Washington, DC 20210
Phone: 202-693-4701
www.dol.gov/vets

The VETS enforces USERRA.

Wage and Hour Division (WHD)

Employment Standards Administration
200 Constitution Avenue, NW
Washington, DC 20210
Phone: 866-487-9243
TTY: 877-889-5627
www.dol.gov/whd

The WHD enforces the EPPA, FLSA, and FMLA.

Equal Employment Opportunity Commission (EEOC)

131 M Street, NE
Washington, DC 20507
Phone: 800-669-4000
TTY: 800-669-6820
www.eeoc.gov

The EEOC enforces the ADA, ADEA, EPA, OWBPA, PDA, and Title VII.

Federal Trade Commission (FTC)

600 Pennsylvania Avenue, NW
Washington, DC 20580
Phone: 202-326-2222
www.ftc.gov

The FTC enforces the FCRA.

Internal Revenue Service (IRS)

U.S. Treasury Department
1500 Pennsylvania Avenue, NW
Washington, DC 20220
Phone: 800-829-4933 (for businesses)
TDD: 800-829-4059
www.irs.gov

The IRS shares enforcement responsibility for COBRA with the EBSA.

National Labor Relations Board (NLRB)

1099 14th Street, NW
Washington, DC 20570
Phone: 866-667-6572
TTY: 866-315-NLRB (866-315-6572)
www.nlrb.gov

The NLRB enforces the NLRA.

Securities and Exchange Commission (SEC)

100 F Street, NE
Washington, DC 20549
Phone: 888-SEC-6585
www.sec.gov

The SEC enforces the complaint procedures provision of Sarbanes-Oxley (SOX).

U.S. Citizenship and Immigration Services (USCIS)

111 Massachusetts Avenue, NW
Washington, DC 20539
Phone: 800-375-5283
TDD: 800-767-1833
www.uscis.gov

The USCIS enforces the employment verification provisions of IRCA.

State Agencies

State Labor Departments

Note: Phone numbers listed are for each department's headquarters. Check the website for regional office locations and numbers.

Departments of Labor

Alabama
Department of Industrial Relations
Montgomery, AL
334-242-8055
http://dir.alabama.gov

Alaska
Department of Labor and Workforce
  Development
Juneau, AK
907-465-2700
www.labor.state.ak.us

Arizona
Industrial Commission
Phoenix, AZ
602-542-4411
www.ica.state.az.us

Arkansas
Department of Labor
Little Rock, AR
501-682-4500
www.labor.ar.gov/pages/default.aspx

California
Department of Industrial Relations
San Francisco, CA
415-703-5050
www.dir.ca.gov

Colorado
Department of Labor and Employment
Denver, CO
303-318-8000
www.colorado.gov/CDLE

Connecticut
Labor Department
Wethersfield, CT
860-263-6000
www.ctdol.state.ct.us

Delaware
Department of Labor
Wilmington, DE
302-761-8000
www.delawareworks.com

District of Columbia
Department of Employment Services
Washington, DC
202-724-7000
www.does.ci.washington.dc.us

Florida
Department of Economic Opportunity
Tallahassee, FL
850-245-7105
www.floridajobs.org

Departments of Labor (continued)

Georgia
Department of Labor
Atlanta, GA
404-232-7300
www.dol.state.ga.us

Hawaii
Department of Labor and Industrial
  Relations
Honolulu, HI
808-586-8842
www.hawaii.gov/labor

Idaho
Department of Labor
Boise, ID
208-332-3570
www.labor.idaho.gov

Illinois
Department of Labor
Chicago, IL
312-793-2800
www.state.il.us/agency/idol

Indiana
Department of Labor
Indianapolis, IN
317-232-2655
www.in.gov/labor

Iowa
Labor Services Division
Des Moines, IA
515-281-5387
www.iowaworkforce.org/labor

Kansas
Department of Labor
Topeka, KS
785-575-1460
www.dol.ks.gov

Kentucky
Department of Labor
Frankfort, KY
502-564-3070
www.labor.ky.gov

Louisiana
Louisiana Workforce Commission
Baton Rouge, LA
225-342-3111
www.ldol.state.la.us

Maine
Department of Labor
Augusta, ME
207-623-7900
www.state.me.us/labor

Maryland
Division of Labor and Industry
Baltimore, MD
410-767-2241
www.dllr.state.md.us/labor

Massachusetts
Labor and Workforce Development
Boston, MA
617-626-7100
www.mass.gov/lwd

Michigan
Department of Licensing and Regulatory
  Affairs
Lansing, MI
517-373-1820
www.michigan.gov/lara

Minnesota
Department of Labor and Industry
St. Paul, MN
651-284-5005
www.dli.mn.gov

Departments of Labor (continued)

Mississippi
Department of Employment Security
Jackson, MS
601-321-6000
www.mdes.ms.gov

Missouri
Department of Labor and Industrial Relations
Jefferson City, MO
573-751-4091
www.labor.mo.gov

Montana
Department of Labor and Industry
Helena, MT
406-444-2840
www.dli.mt.gov

Nebraska
Department of Labor
Lincoln, NE
402-471-9000
www.dol.nebraska.gov

Nevada
Office of the Labor Commissioner
Las Vegas, NV
702-486-2650
www.laborcommissioner.com

New Hampshire
Department of Labor
Concord, NH
603-271-3176
www.labor.state.nh.us

New Jersey
Department of Labor and Workforce
 Development
Trenton, NJ
609-659-9045
http://lwd.state.nj.us/labor

New Mexico
Department of Workforce Solutions
Albuquerque, NM
505-841-8405
www.dws.state.nm.us

New York
Department of Labor
Albany, NY
518-457-9000
www.labor.ny.gov/home

North Carolina
Department of Labor
Raleigh, NC
919-807-2796
800-625-2267
www.nclabor.com

North Dakota
Department of Labor
Bismarck, ND
701-328-2660
www.nd.gov/labor

Ohio
Division of Industrial Compliance and
 Labor
Columbus, OH
614-644-2223
www.com.ohio.gov/dico

Oklahoma
Department of Labor
Oklahoma City, OK
405-521-6100
www.ok.gov/odol

Departments of Labor (continued)

Oregon
Bureau of Labor and Industries
Portland, OR
971-637-0761
www.oregon.gov/boli

Pennsylvania
Department of Labor and Industry
Harrisburg, PA
717-787-1116
www.dli.state.pa.us

Rhode Island
Department of Labor and Training
Cranston, RI
401-462-8000
www.dlt.state.ri.us

South Carolina
Department of Labor, Licensing, and
  Regulation
Columbia, SC
803-896-4300
www.llr.state.sc.us/labor

South Dakota
Department of Labor and Regulation
Pierre, SD
605-773-3101
www.dlr.sd.gov

Tennessee
Department of Labor and Workforce
  Development
Nashville, TN
615-741-6642
www.state.tn.us/labor-wfd

Texas
Texas Workforce Commission
Austin, TX
512-463-2222

www.twc.state.tx.us

Utah
Labor Commission
Salt Lake City, UT
801-530-6800
www.laborcommission.utah.gov

Vermont
Department of Labor and Industry
Montpelier, VT
808-828-4000
www.labor.vermont.gov

Virginia
Department of Labor and Industry
Richmond, VA
804-371-2327
www.doli.virginia.gov

Washington
Department of Labor and Industries
Tumwater, WA
360-902-5800
www.lni.wa.gov

West Virginia
Division of Labor
Charleston, WV
304-558-7890
www.labor.state.wv.us

Wisconsin
Department of Workforce Development
Madison, WI
608-266-3131
www.dwd.state.wi.us

Wyoming
Department of Workforce Services
Cheyenne, WY
307-777-8650
www.wyomingworkforce.org

State Agencies That Enforce Laws Prohibiting Discrimination in Employment

Note: Phone numbers listed are for each department's headquarters. Check the website for regional office locations and numbers.

State Agencies That Enforce Laws Prohibiting Discrimination in Employment

United States
Equal Employment Opportunity
  Commission
1801 L Street, NW
Washington, DC 20507
800-669-4000
TTY: 800-669-6820
www.eeoc.gov

Alabama
EEOC District Office
Birmingham, AL
205-212-2100
800-669-4000
www.eeoc.gov/birmingham/index.cfm

Alaska
Commission for Human Rights
Anchorage, AK
907-274-4692
800-478-4692
http://humanrights.alaska.gov

Arizona
Civil Rights Division
Phoenix, AZ
602-542-5263
877-491-5742
www.azag.gov/civil_rights/index .html

Arkansas
Equal Employment Opportunity
  Commission
Little Rock, AR
501-324-5060
800-669-4000
www.eeoc.gov/littlerock/index.cfm

California
Department of Fair Employment and
  Housing
Sacramento District Office
Sacramento, CA
916-478-7200
800-884-1684
www.dfeh.ca.gov

Colorado
Civil Rights Division
Denver, CO
303-894-2997
800-262-4845
www.dora.state.co.us/Civil-Rights

Connecticut
Commission on Human Rights and
  Opportunities
Hartford, CT
860-541-3400
800-477-5737
www.ct.gov/chro/site

State Agencies That Enforce Laws Prohibiting Discrimination in Employment (continued)

Delaware
Office of Labor Law Enforcement
Division of Industrial Affairs
Wilmington, DE
302-761-8200
www.delawareworks.com/industrialaffairs/
  welcome.shtml

District of Columbia
Office of Human Rights
Washington, DC
202-727-4559
http://ohr.dc.gov

Florida
Commission on Human Relations
Tallahassee, FL
850-488-7082
http://fchr.state.fl.us

Georgia
Atlanta District Office
U.S. Equal Employment Opportunity
  Commission
Atlanta, GA
404-562-6800
800-669-4000
http://www.eeoc.gov/field/atlanta

Hawaii
Hawai'i Civil Rights Commission
Honolulu, HI
808-586-8636
www.hawaii.gov/labor/hcrc

Idaho
Idaho Commission on Human Rights
Boise, ID
208-334-2873
http://humanrights.idaho.gov

Illinois
Department of Human Rights
Chicago, IL
312-814-6200
www.state.il.us/dhr

Indiana
Civil Rights Commission
Indianapolis, IN
317-232-2600
800-628-2909
www.in.gov/icrc

Iowa
Iowa Civil Rights Commission
Des Moines, IA
515-281-4121
800-457-4416
www.state.ia.us/government/crc

Kansas
Human Rights Commission
Topeka, KS
785-296-3206
www.khrc.net

Kentucky
Human Rights Commission
Louisville, KY
502-595-4024
800-292-5566
www.kchr.ky.gov

Louisiana
Commission on Human Rights
Baton Rouge, LA
225-342-6969
http://gov.louisiana.gov/HumanRights/
  humanrightshome.htm

State Agencies That Enforce Laws Prohibiting Discrimination in Employment (continued)

Maine
Human Rights Commission
Augusta, ME
207-624-6290
www.maine.gov/mhrc

Maryland
Commission on Human Relations
Baltimore, MD
410-767-8600
www.mccr.maryland.gov

Massachusetts
Commission Against Discrimination
Boston, MA
617-994-6000
www.mass.gov/mcad

Michigan
Department of Civil Rights
Detroit, MI
313-456-3700
www.michigan.gov/mdcr

Minnesota
Department of Human Rights
St. Paul, MN
651-296-1283
800-657-3704
www.humanrights.state.mn.us

Mississippi
Department of Employment Security
Jackson, MS
601-321-6000
www.mdes.ms.gov

Missouri
Commission on Human Rights
Jefferson City, MO
573-751-3325
www.labor.mo.gov

Montana
Human Rights Bureau
Employment Relations Division
Department of Labor and Industry
Helena, MT
406-444-2884
800-542-0807
www.erd.dli.mt.gov/human-rights-bureau.html

Nebraska
Equal Opportunity Commission
Lincoln, NE
402-471-2024
800-642-6112
www.neoc.ne.gov

Nevada
Equal Rights Commission
Las Vegas, NV
702-486-7161
http://detr.state.nv.us/nerc/NERC_index.htm

New Hampshire
Commission for Human Rights
Concord, NH
603-271-2767
www.nh.gov/hrc

New Jersey
Division on Civil Rights
Trenton, NJ
609-292-4605
www.nj.gov/oag/dcr/index.html

State Agencies That Enforce Laws Prohibiting Discrimination in Employment (continued)

New Mexico
Human Rights Division
Santa Fe, NM
505-827-6838
800-566-9471
www.dws.state.nm.us/LaborRelations/
 HumanRights/Information

New York
Division of Human Rights
Bronx, NY
718-741-8400
www.dhr.ny.gov

North Carolina
Employment Discrimination Bureau
Department of Labor
Raleigh, NC
919-807-2796
800-NC-LABOR
www.nclabor.com/edb/edb.htm

North Dakota
Human Rights Division
Department of Labor
Bismarck, ND
701-328-2660
800-582-8032
www.nd.gov/labor/human-rights/index.
 html

Ohio
Civil Rights Commission
Columbus, OH
614-466-5928
888-278-7101
www.crc.ohio.gov

Oklahoma
Oklahoma Office of the Attorney General
Oklahoma City, OK
405-521-3921
www.oag.state.ok.us

Oregon
Civil Rights Division
Bureau of Labor and Industries
Portland, OR
971-673-0764
www.oregon.gov/BOLI/CRD

Pennsylvania
Human Relations Commission
Harrisburg, PA
717-787-4410
www.phrc.state.pa.us

Rhode Island
Commission for Human Rights
Providence, RI
401-222-2661
www.richr.state.ri.us/frames.html

South Carolina
Human Affairs Commission
Columbia, SC
803-737-7800
800-521-0725
www.state.sc.us/schac

South Dakota
Division of Human Rights
Pierre, SD
605-773-3681
www.dlr.sd.gov/humanrights/default.aspx

State Agencies that Enforce Laws Prohibiting Discrimination in Employment (continued)

Tennessee
Human Rights Commission
Nashville, TN
615-741-8525
800-251-3589
www.tennessee.gov/humanrights

Texas
Commission on Human Rights
Austin, TX
512-463-2642
888-452-4778
www.twc.state.tx.us/customers/jsempl/
  employee-rights-laws.html

Utah
Anti-Discrimination and Labor Division
Labor Commission
Salt Lake City, UT
801-530-6801
800-222-1238
www.laborcommission.utah.gov/divisions/
  AntidiscriminationAndLabor/index.html

Vermont
Attorney General's Office
Civil Rights Division
Montpelier, VT
802-828-3657
888-745-9195
www.atg.state.vt.us/office-organization-
  information/office-organization/public-
  protection-division/civil-rights.php

Virginia
Office of the Attorney General
Division of Human Rights
Richmond, VA
804-225-2292
www.oag.state.va.us/Programs%20and%20
  Resources/Human_Rights/index.html

Washington
Human Rights Commission
Olympia, WA
360-753-6770
800-233-3247
www.hum.wa.gov

West Virginia
Human Rights Commission
Charleston, WV
304-558-2616
888-676-5546
www.wvf.state.wv.us/wvhrc

Wisconsin
Equal Rights Division
Madison, WI
608-266-6860
http://dwd.wisconsin.gov/er

Wyoming
Department of Employment
Labor Standards
Cheyenne, WY
307-777-7261
www.wyomingworkforce.org/job-seekers-
  and-workers/labor-standards/Pages/
  default.asp

SHRM and Nolo Resources

SHRM and Nolo Resources

The Society for Human Resource Management (SHRM) and Nolo both provide a number of resources on employment law, policies, and procedures, and other issues of special interest to the HR profession. Both organizations have websites with lots of free information on HR topics, and both offer written materials on a variety of subjects. If you need help with an HR question or issue, you should be able to find the answers in our products.

SHRM Resources

Some of SHRM's resources are available to nonmembers; access to much of our comprehensive HR information is a benefit of membership. For additional information, go to the SHRM home page, www.shrm. org. Below are some of the SHRM resources related to human resource management.

Selected Titles from the Society for Human Resource Management (SHRM)

- *101 Sample Write-Ups for Documenting Employee Performance Problems: A Guide to Progressive Discipline & Termination*, by Paul Falcone
- *Business Literacy Survival Guide for HR Professionals*, by Regan W. Garey
- *The Cultural Fit Factor: Creating an Employment Brand That Attracts, Retains, and Repels the Right Employees*, by Lizz Pellet
- *The Essential Guide to Workplace Investigations: How to Handle Employee Complaints & Problems*, by Lisa Guerin
- *From Hello to Goodbye: Proactive Tips for Maintaining Positive Employee Relations*, by Christine V. Walters
- *Got a Minute? The 9 Lessons Every HR Professional Must Learn to Be Successful*, by Dale J. Dwyer and Sheri A. Caldwell
- *HR Competencies: Mastery at the Intersection of People and Business*, by Dave Ulrich, Wayne Brockbank, Dani Johnson, Kurt Sandholtz, and Jon Younger
- *Human Resource Essentials: Your Guide to Starting and Running the HR Function*, by Lin Grensing-Pophal

- *Leading with Your Heart: Diversity and Ganas for Inspired Inclusion*, by Cari M. Dominguez and Judith Sotherlund
- *Managing Diversity: A Complete Desk Reference & Planning Guide*, by Lee Gardenswartz and Anita Rowe
- *Performance Appraisal Source Book: A Collection of Practical Samples*, by Mike Deblieux
- *Solving the Compensation Puzzle: Putting Together a Complete Pay and Performance System*, by Sharon K. Koss
- *Staffing Forecasting and Planning*, by Jean M. Phillips and Stanley M. Gully
- *Stop Bullying at Work: Strategies and Tools for HR and Legal Professionals*, by Teresa A. Daniel

Additional books can be found at www.shrm.org/Publications/Books.

Magazine and Newsletters

Members receive SHRM's periodicals as part of their benefits; some publications are available to nonmembers by subscription or request.

- *HR Magazine* (monthly) features in-depth analyses of trends and events affecting human resource management. Key articles also appear on SHRM's website. Go to www.shrm.org/Publications/hrmagazine for the current issues and an archive of past issues.
- *Workplace Law Bulletin* (twice a month) provides updates on the most recent legal issues relevant to HR professionals. Go to www.shrm.org/LegalIssues.

Government Affairs

The Society for Human Resource Management is a leader in influencing workplace laws and regulations through the Government Affairs Department (www.shrm.org/advocacy). The department designed to influence legislation and regulations on all levels.

- *Federal Legislative Program.* On the federal level, SHRM has been an influential voice on key workplace issues, such as workplace flexibility, employer-provided education assistance, labor and employment issues, immigration reform, health care, and employee tax and benefit issues.

- *State Affairs Program.* The State Program tracks legislation in all 50 states and publishes the biweekly *Pending Legislation Report.* In addition, the state program provides advocacy and legislative resources on the Government Affairs website.
- *Employment Regulation Program.* SHRM closely monitors employment regulations from organizations like the Department of Labor, Department of Homeland Security, and the Equal Employment Opportunity Commission. When appropriate, SHRM delivers comments and testimony on regulations that impact the workplace.

HR Disciplines

SHRM's *HR Disciplines* (www.shrm.org/hrdisciplines) include news, features, research materials, webcasts, discussion areas, and more on a wide spectrum of HR disciplines:

- *Benefits* deals with the various forms of indirect employee compensation that employers use to attract, recognize, and retain workers.
- *Business Leadership* deals with the processes and activities used to formulate objectives, practices, and policies aimed at meeting short- and long-range organizational needs and opportunities, and focused in particular on human capital issues.
- *Compensation* deals with the various forms of direct compensation that employers use to attract, recognize, and retain workers.
- *Consulting* deals with the practice of delivering all aspects of HR management as an external provider, and with the professional and business issues associated with operating such a practice, including client development, contracts, client management, etc.
- *Diversity* deals with the differences and similarities that make individuals unique, such as individual and organizational characteristics, values, beliefs, experiences, backgrounds, preferences, and behaviors, as well as how organizations can leverage those qualities in support of business objectives.
- *Employee Relations* includes the processes of analyzing, developing, implementing, and administering the employer-employee relationship; performing continuing evaluation of it; managing employee performance; ensuring that relations with employees comply with

applicable federal, state, and local laws and regulations; and resolving workplace disputes.

- *Ethics and Sustainability* deals with the social impact of business decisions in the area of employment practices, corporate governance, and sustainability and philanthropy, as well as with the role of the HR profession in improving the quality of life of employees, their families, and the community at large.

- *Global HR* includes matters such as management of global workforces, expatriation and repatriation, HR practices and laws around the world, and those arising in specific countries and regions.

- *Labor Relations* deals with the elements of formal labor-management relations—protected activities, unfair practices, union organizing, recognition, and representation elections—as well as collective bargaining and contract administration.

- *Organizational and Employee Development* address improving organizational effectiveness and training employees to meet current and future job demands, change management, coaching, leadership development, succession planning, social networking, knowledge management, measurement systems, and outsourcing employee development.

- *Safety and Security* is about organizational efforts to prevent and/or mitigate loss, risk to or from personnel, threats to its physical assets, damage to its technology and intellectual property, and risks arising from all elements surrounding the work environment.

- *Staffing Management* deals with strategies, tactics, and processes for sourcing, recruiting, hiring, and retaining the human resources needed to support business objectives as home and abroad.

- *Technology* includes matters involving HR information systems, automated scheduling and timekeeping systems, the technology aspects of workplace security, trends in technology, effective practices, and vendor and software selection.

SHRM Research

SHRM's Research Department (www.shrm.org/research) compiles and publishes detailed analysis of critical employment- and HR-related data:

- *Customized Benchmarking Service.* With a database of more than 140 metrics from over 5,000 organizations, SHRM's customized benchmarking database offers human capital, health care, retirement, and welfare metrics within and across a variety of industry types.
- *SHRM Compensation Data Center.* SHRM, in collaboration with Towers Wyatt Data Services, provides SHRM members with accurate and customized salary information for an entire spectrum of jobs ranging from top executive to entry level positions.
- *SHRM Leading Indicators of National Employment® (LINE®).* Based on surveys of HR professionals at over 1,000 manufacturing and private service-sector organizations, this monthly report includes indicators on hiring expectations for the month ahead, recruiting difficulty, new-hire compensation, and job vacancies in exempt and nonexempt employment.
- *The SHRM Labor Market Outlook Report.* This quarterly report is based on a survey of hundreds of HR professionals across U.S. regions and industries that asks them about layoffs, hiring, and job growth.
- *SHRM Survey Products.* SHRM produces several types of products based on data collected from the SHRM members as well as outside samples (e.g., employee samples, nonmember samples, etc.).
- *Metro Economic Outlook.* These reports provide comprehensive analyses of the economies of the largest metropolitan areas in the United States and include a combination of government and SHRM-generated data, as well as insights from experts that are connected to each metro area's economy.
- *SHRM Polls.* SHRM conducts short to mid-length polls on current issues impacting the workplace, general HR, and business topics.

HR Knowledge Center

The HR Knowledge Center (www.shrm.org/TemplatesTools/AskAnHRExpert) is home to a wide variety of services and resources running the whole gamut of HR practices. SHRM members will have access to a number of sample policies, job descriptions, forms, RFPs, mission statements, and PowerPoint presentations. In addition, how-to guides are available that provide step-by-step instructional guides designed to walk an HR professional through the practical process of how to complete day-to-day HR tasks.

SHRM Multimedia

SHRM offers a variety of free and fee-based podcasts, videos, webcasts, and e-learning presentations by noted experts on a broad range of HR topics, including employment law (go to www.shrm.org/multimedia).

Nolo Resources

Nolo offers a variety of resources on HR compliance and employment law.

Books

Nolo publishes many titles for employers, managers, and human resources professionals, including:

- *Dealing With Problem Employees*, a comprehensive resource for handling tough discipline and performance issues, including detailed information on minimizing legal exposure if you have to fire an employee.
- *Create Your Own Employee Handbook*, which provides all of the information and policies you need to draft or update your company's handbook, and includes access to policies you can cut and paste to create your own handbook.
- *Smart Policies for Workplace Technologies*, which provides sample policies and information for email, camera phones, instant messaging, and more, and includes access to policies you can use in your workplace.
- *The Performance Appraisal Handbook*, which explains how to effectively evaluate employee performance without getting into legal trouble.
- *The Essential Guide to Workplace Investigations*, a step-by-step guide to investigating complaints and misconduct, including detailed information on investigating harassment, discrimination, workplace violence, and theft.
- *The Job Description Handbook*, which explains how to create, use, and update job descriptions effectively, and includes access to a PowerPoint training presentation.
- *The Manager's Legal Handbook*, an introduction to many of the legal issues managers face every day, including discrimination, wage and hour issues, firing and layoffs, employee privacy concerns, protecting trade secrets, and much more.

- *The Employer's Legal Handbook*, a comprehensive guide to employment law, written with the small business owner in mind.
- *Hiring Your First Employee*, a step-by-step guide for small business owners who have decided it's time to hire.
- *Consultant & Independent Contractor Agreements*, which provides all of the information and sample contracts you need to work well with independent contractors—and avoid having them reclassified as employees.

Nolo's Website

You can find free articles on a wide variety of employment and HR topics on Nolo's website, www.nolo.com, which includes articles on:
- hiring employees
- hiring independent contractors
- wage and hour laws
- personnel policies and procedures
- family, medical, and other types of leave
- discrimination
- workplace privacy
- firing workers, and
- obligations to workers who are leaving the company.

Also check out our forms and employment law blog (www.employment legalblawg.com).

Index

M

Major bodily functions (ADA), 41, 45, 47

Major life activities (ADA), 41, 45, 46–47

Managers (NLRA), 271, 275

Mandatory retirement
ADEA exceptions, 34, 35
See also Age discrimination

Marital status discrimination, state laws, 379–393

Maritime and longshoring safety standards (OSH Act), 298, 299

Married couples. *See* Spouses

Mass layoffs (WARN), 427, 428, 430, 431. *See also* Layoffs; Worker Adjustment and Retraining Notification Act (WARN)

Meal breaks. *See* Breaks

Meals, pay deductions for, 163

Mechanics, 167

Mediation
OSHA whistle-blower mediation program, 346
USERRA mediation services, 400, 411

Medical benefits. *See* Consolidated Omnibus Budget Reconciliation Act (COBRA); Health benefits

Medical certification (FMLA). *See* Certifications (FMLA)

Medical examinations and tests, 50
drug tests, 50, 95
genetic monitoring and tests, 239, 242–243, 246
GINA confidentiality rules and, 242–243

Medical information, 239

FCRA rules, 140

GINA acquisition of information rules, 242–246

GINA confidentiality requirements, 238, 242, 246–248

Medical leave. *See* Family and medical leave; Family and Medical Leave Act (FMLA)

Medical savings accounts (COBRA), 62

Medicare eligibility
COBRA and, 64, 67, 71–72, 73
retiree health benefits and, 312, 316–317, 318

Mental illness, state antidiscrimination laws, 379–393

Mental impairments (ADA), 44, 45, 57

Mergers or acquisitions, 330, 398

Merit or performance pay, 127, 217

Messengers, 162

Military employees, civilian, 122

Military identification cards, 261

Military servicemembers
child support orders and PRWORA reporting, 331–332
EPA and, 122, 124
military caregiver leave, 198, 202, 203, 204, 219–223, 226
qualifying exigency leave, 198, 202, 203, 204, 209–210, 213, 216, 226
state military leave laws, 413–424
temporary military leave for salaried employees, 158
See also Family and Medical Leave Act (FMLA); Uniformed Services Employment and Reemployment Rights Act (USERRA)

Military status discrimination, 368
state laws, 379–393

Selected Titles from the

31192020396972